A PRIVILEGED LIFE

Memoirs of an Activist

by Daniel N. Clark

Walla Walla, Washington

A PRIVILEGED LIFE

Part One: 1943-2001

Chapter Detail

Part One: 1943-2001

A PRIVILEGED LIFE

Prologue

Every life has stories to tell. I've become more keenly aware of that recently as a result of research and reading for the organization of a living history company at Fort Walla Walla Museum. Bringing to life characters out of a community's frontier past and telling the pioneers' stories has helped bring home to me the importance of written accounts of our own lives as we create history for those who follow us.

I have written these memoirs primarily for family and friends, and for the organizations whose history is described, though I'm glad to share these accounts with others. Together they tell the story of someone living in a small town whose values of diversity, internationalism, nonviolence, and social action have played out in a variety of fruitful projects, including international human rights, local history, the environment, music and dance, and alternative conflict resolution, among others.

Although most of this was written in the summer and fall of 2001, the final chapters were added in 2013, and an appendix provides an update since then. What follows is the report of a highly privileged life with greater than normal independence and opportunities, leading to involvement in a broad variety of projects. Thanks for looking through these writings.

Part One: 1943-2001

Genesis

Family Roots

My parents met at the University of Oregon, where they were students. My father, Reed Lafayette Clark, was the eldest son of Edmond Lafayette Clark, a merchant who owned a small department store in Lebanon, Oregon. His grandfather had been a merchant in Nebraska, where my father was born in 1908. Edmond's family background was mainly English and Scottish, except for a claimed connection to the French General Lafayette who fought on the side of the Americans during the revolutionary war, and whose name was carried by the first male born in several generations of Clarks. My father's mother, Pearl Hitchcock, was of Scottish and English stock, with a trace of Dutch. On her mother's side they were Reads in England in the twelfth century, where Sir Bartholomew Read was reportedly Lord Mayor of London and his brother John Read was Mayor of Norwich. In 1630 they came to Massachusetts and later to Connecticut, where they became Reeds.

When my mother, Estelle Johnson, was eight, her family homesteaded in northeastern Montana near Scobey, where her father, Frank Johnson, established a hardware and farm implements store. Frank's family was Scottish and English, with some Irish, and had come down from Canada to settle along the Red River between Minnesota and North Dakota. The family claims to be related to the 17th President of the United States, Andrew Johnson. The English primarily settled on the North Dakota side of the river, and Frank's father established the town of Quincy there, where he owned a blacksmith shop, store, and hotel, as well as a farm. Frank was born in Quincy in 1878. On the Minnesota side of the river were the Norwegians. Estelle's mother, Julia Nelson, was born there in 1883 after her parents emigrated from Norway. Julia's parents succeeded in giving each of their ten children a college education, and Julia graduated from Concordia College with a degree in music and fine arts.

Though the other side of the river was off-limits for each group, Frank and Julia bridged the gap, married, and began farming on the North Dakota side of the Red River Valley, where my mother was born in 1908. They gradually moved west along the railroad until they finally settled at the end of the line where the town of Scobey, Montana was born three months before their arrival. They made their fortune in Scobey, then lost most of it in the Crash of 1929.

While Frank was branching out from hardware and implements to car dealerships in several western states, Julia was bringing her children up as musicians in the Johnson Family Orchestra. Estelle learned the violin as well as elocution, her eldest sister Adelaide sang and played saxophone, her brother Norman played trumpet, her younger sister Phyllis did ballet and was a violinist, and all of them played the piano. Their family orchestra barnstormed around the countryside putting on dances and concerts in which they sang, played, danced, and gave humorous readings. In 1924 wanting more sophistication for her children, Julia organized the family's move to Eugene, Oregon where each of the children in turn enrolled in the University of Oregon's school of music.

Although both of my parents entered the University of Oregon as freshmen in 1926, my mother had to drop out for a year due to a paralytic illness, and was told she would never walk again. Refusing to accept that, she regained her health, and for decades was known for her several-mile daily walks around town until her death at 83. After my father graduated in 1930, he landed a job teaching math and science at Lebanon High School, as well as serving as head coach of its football, basketball, and baseball teams, where he was credited with building a new athletic field including lights and grandstands, and a new gymnasium.

Reed met Estelle the next year when she was hired by the Lebanon school district to supervise their music programs. Although it was the bottom of the depression and most schools were in bad financial shape and were dropping their music offerings, Lebanon was the one school in the region that was starting a new music program, so all fourteen graduates of the University of Oregon's school of music that year applied for the position. Though not at the top of the class, Estelle drove to Lebanon and met individually with every member of the school board; whatever they asked, she assured them in convincing tones that she could do it, and got the job. Reed's younger brother Hunt had dated Estelle in college, and correctly predicted the two teachers would be married within a year, though Reed scoffed at the idea of being interested in one of his younger brother's sweethearts. In 1936, their first child, Reed Lafayette Clark, Jr., was born a few strokes after midnight on January 1 and won the city's baby derby.

Reed coached his football team to their first undefeated season in Lebanon's history that fall. With a new family member to feed, though, and my mother having been forced to resign her job since married couples weren't allowed to work at the same school, he left teaching the next term and went to work for Sears Roebuck in order to increase the family's income. After starting in a training position in the warehouse at Klamath Falls, he was transferred to Seattle as manager of the regional Sears warehouse, and in 1941 was sent to Walla Walla to manage the Sears retail store there.

I arrived as a somewhat late-in-life surprise for my parents on May 24, 1943. Soon after I was born, our family moved from a small home across Alvarado Terrace from Walla Walla's Menlo Park to a large Cape Cod house on well-landscaped grounds near Prospect Point School south of town, and we lived there until I was in college.

Although successful in his father's mercantile trade, after seven years as manager of the Walla Walla store, Reed left Sears in 1947 after he called a visiting Sears executive a horse's ass, and was transferred to Chicago. Following a brief visit to the windy city, Reed and Estelle decided to stay in Walla Walla, and Reed agreed to work for a real estate and investment company owned by Don Sherwood, the community's wealthiest man. For more than thirty years he sold and managed real estate for Sherwood & Roberts, Inc., and retired as vice-president overseeing its real estate offices throughout several western states.

Reed and Estelle were pillars of the Walla Walla community. Reed served as chairman of the school board, president of the Chamber of Commerce and of his church's board of deacons, chaired the United Way campaign, served on the board of the YMCA and the Rotary Club, and also as a member of fundraising committees for Whitman College. Always an organizer, he was the founding president of the local board of realtors and formed two booster clubs for local athletics.

For her part, my mother was active in the local chapter of the American Association of University Women, played violin in the Walla Walla Symphony, sang in a variety of musical groups, and in later years was an active golfer and a prolific oil painter. Her own organizational efforts were primarily musical. As a teacher in Lebanon she introduced operettas and some other special programs in the schools. In Walla Walla she organized the first youth concerts by the symphony, managed the Congregational church choir, and provided leadership for a variety of other musical events.

In addition to their respectability and community service, Reed and Estelle were good parents and admirable people. My mother was a hard worker, made almost all her own clothes, maintained our large yards, walked and exercised daily, encouraged her children at musical and other pursuits, worked to expand our vocabulary, got the family to the Congregational church every Sunday without fail, and repeatedly taught me to "hoe out your row." By that she meant that I should finish what I started, and always do my share.

My father also worked hard, was cheerful, community-minded, an avid sportsman, loyal to whatever efforts or people he was associated with, energetic, economical, and successful at whatever he took on.

Both my parents were financially conservative, and rarely spent or allowed me to spend money on luxuries. Long distance phone calls and eating out were considered luxuries in our family, and seldom occurred. Despite being a real estate broker, my father never acquired real estate of his own other than our home and an adjoining field given him by a neighbor in trade for a small cottage on our property. I'm glad to have internalized that practice of keeping financial expenditures to a minimum, which has been beneficial throughout my life, giving me a level of personal freedom and independence few others seem to enjoy.

Besides economy, another principle appears to have been part of my makeup at an early age — the sense that what is right will ultimately prevail, and that it's safe and good to stand up for it. Whether this assumption arose from the security of my home, my parents' socio-economic status, the seemingly benign nature of the authority structures around me, my innate disposition, or a combination of these, I don't know. I do know that I've always felt confident standing up for those who appeared weak or wronged. In elementary school I remember befriending and protecting a classmate who had been held back for several years and was big as a man, but was teased and bullied until he would cry. I also regularly came to the aid of another student who had a nervous disorder and was constantly ridiculed.

My father was politically conservative, though this seemed to be mainly a function of the company he kept. At heart my father was apolitical. I can't remember him ever expressing an individual opinion about politics or for that matter about religion, life, or anything other than sports. As a student, when I tried to talk to him about politics it simply annoyed him, particularly when I pressed him for his own views or tried to pry out of him positions he had learned from his friends so I could challenge them. He wasn't interested in such things. My mother on the other hand often asked me what I thought of public questions such as ballot issues, and usually told me she agreed with me, but not to tell my father.

Early interests and education

Though my father rarely talked to me about what he was doing or thinking or what I should be doing, it was clear that both my parents were committed to public service and good citizenship. For her part, my mother encouraged me to become involved in the youth group at our church, in musical events, and in anything else going on culturally, and was proud when I won the junior citizenship award at Prospect Point Elementary School. She also reinforced my natural egalitarian feelings by calling my attention to the injustice of racial discrimination when it was in the news, or when some unfortunate incident occurred regarding one of the few non-whites in our community. Because I liked to argue and always defended the underdog, people often told me I was destined to be a lawyer.

I've always had a natural fascination for people from other backgrounds and cultures. This led me to apply to spend the summer of 1960 with a family in Rosario, Argentina as Walla Walla's first exchange student under the American Field Service program. During an orientation session in Washington, D.C. I was able to question U.S. Attorney General Bobby Kennedy, and in Argentina appeared on television for a discussion at the Pink House with Argentine President Arturo Frondizi, both of which whetted my interest in politics. Back in Walla Walla my exchange student experience was considered big news, and I was invited to give talks about it at all the service clubs and PTA groups in town, giving me early experience with public speaking.

Because of my interest in politics, international relations and law, my brother told me I should major in political science at college. My father then consulted his friends, including prominent lawyer Shine Minnick who told him that Whitman College in Walla Walla was a better place for me than Washington State University, which I was considering. If it hadn't been for the experience of going abroad as an exchange student I would probably have insisted on leaving Walla Walla for college; as it was, I was agreeable, and I've never regretted that decision, even though my family's frugality meant living at home my freshman year when I would rather have been on campus.

During my time at Whitman I spent the summer of 1963 in Europe with the People-to-People program founded by Dwight Eisenhower, and on returning helped organize a Whitman chapter. On the way home from my European summer, I was sitting in the New York City Greyhound depot when the juke box played a new song by Bob Dylan called "Blowing in the Wind," and special buses began loading for a big event in Washington, D.C. Instead of taking a bus toward Walla Walla, that afternoon I was the only white person on one of the buses heading to the capitol where I was able to join the March on Washington and be present for Rev. Martin Luther King's "I Have a Dream" speech.

During my senior year in college, I served as president of Whitman's People-to-People chapter and at the request of some international students organized Whitman's first soccer team for some games with Walla Walla College. I also wanted our team to play Eastern Oregon State College in La Grande, but the Whitman athletic department wasn't interested in a new sport they knew nothing about. In addition to soccer games, we organized the first International Night at Whitman, featuring students from abroad talking about their background and showing items from home.

In 1964, Whitman professor George Ball together with Donald Blake, the first black to teach at Walla College, jointly led a march from the Whitman campus to the county courthouse as a memorial to the three Unitarian ministers killed during civil rights protests in Selma, Alabama. That appears to have been the first march in modern-day Walla Walla and I was glad to have been part of it.

I was also active in partisan political activity at Whitman, first as a member of the Young Republicans and a participant at local Republican precinct caucuses, and later as a member of the Young Democrats. My family traditionally voted Republican; my earliest political memory is of listening to our big console radio during the Republican convention of 1952 when Eisenhower was nominated. At Whitman I was first elected secretary and later vice-president of the Young Republicans; my disaffection began when I was urged to advocate for the abolition of social security. In my junior year I ran for president of the Young Republicans on a platform of opening diplomatic relations with China, which represented a quarter of humanity but was not legally recognized by the United States. I lost the election to Walter "Skeeter" Minnick, whose father was Shine Minnick, a local party leader known as Mr. Conservative. At that point I decided my views were more consistent with the Democrats, and changed my party affiliation. Walt held out as a loyal Republican until about 1996 when he unsuccessfully ran for the U.S. Senate as a Democrat in Idaho, and was later elected to Congress as an Idaho Democrat.

On entering Whitman I was interested in a career in the diplomatic service. Robert Fluno, for many years head of the Whitman political science department, convinced me this was not a good idea. Foreign Service officers, he pointed out, are usually relegated to fairly menial tasks serving the policies and politics of whatever administration is in power, normally under the direction of an untrained political appointee awarded an ambassadorship as a party payoff. Instead, he nourished my respect for civil liberties and civil rights, and turned my attention to law.

Walla Walla to California

Though I also applied at Stanford and the University of Washington, the law school at the University of California at Berkeley was my first choice. Berkeley was where things were happening both politically and culturally. In the spring of 1965, with a B.A. in political science from Whitman "with distinction in major study" and a letter of recommendation from Whitman President Louis Perry, I visited Berkeley while Mario Savio was on trial for his activities with the Free Speech Movement. When I stopped by the admissions office to see what I could do to help move my application along, the secretary promised she would place my file at the top of the stack on the Dean's desk. A couple of weeks later I was accepted.

My father of course preferred the idea of paying in-state tuition to the University of Washington, and again consulted his friends. Happily for me, Harvard graduate Shine Minnick, who had recommended I go to Whitman, had recently hired a law graduate from the UW whom he considered inadequately trained, and he advised my dad that Berkeley was a fine law school and was my best choice. So I owed him additional thanks.

Berkeley was not only a fine place to learn the law, it was alive with cutting edge social, political, cultural, and religious thought and activities. The night before classes began I left the International House after wishing my Hindu roommate a good evening and attended a party where I met my first socialist. I remember peppering him with a variety of questions left over from a comparative economics class I had taken at Whitman concerning the technical problems of distribution and compensation in a socialist economy, which were fascinating to me but irrelevant to him. A mediator in this discussion was another law student from Los Angeles who was also fascinating to me and in three years would become my bride.

A great deal was going on in Berkeley and the San Francisco Bay Area in the Sixties, and most of it was exciting. I spent some time doorbelling for Jerry Rubin in his campaign for mayor of Berkeley, calling among other things for free bicycles throughout the city, and also working for the election of Peace and Freedom Party candidate Bob Scheer for Congress. As far as the Vietnam War, it was plain to me that Americans had no business killing Vietnamese, particularly in their homeland. This was by any definition an unjust war, and I participated in marches, vigils, and leafleting to protest it.

Religion and Nonviolence

In Berkeley I also met my first pacifist, Luke Hiken, another student at the law school. As my views matured, I had become convinced that beyond the injustice of this particular war, all compulsory military campaigns were wrong, since they demand that we become the servants of whatever politicians are in power, killing for them on command, including frequent attacks on noncombatants through the bombing of cities and villages. I told the draft board my position, and volunteered instead to be drafted for alternative service in the federal War on Poverty where I believed I could do some good.

The evolution of my religious views began my first year at Whitman, when I began to seriously question the Christian theology of my youth, principally the doctrine of eternal damnation or eternal bliss meted out to every person by a loving God at the end of lives varying greatly in length and circumstances, which made no sense to me. I was also concerned about the claim that among the world's religions only Christianity is true, that only Christians can go to heaven, and not many of them at that. These views seemed to lack cultural or historical perspective, as well as internal consistency. Although I had joined the Congregational Church while in high school, in my first two years of college I lost respect for Christianity, and knowing nothing else, for all religion.

That view changed during my junior year at Whitman, when I took a course from Dr. George Ball on world religions. With the help of Huston Smith's book "The Religions of Man" (Harper & Row, 1958) and George's highly sympathetic presentations, I was introduced to the Upanishads and Bhagavad Gita of Hinduism, the Chinese Tao Te Ching, and to various Buddhist scriptures, in addition to the various western traditions. These eastern scriptures became gateways for me to a new approach to life and religion, and have since become lifelong friends.

In Berkeley I was able to meet and was inspired by a variety of Hindu and Buddhist teachers. I also discovered the Quakers—a religious community that combines mysticism and absence of doctrine with social concern and egalitarianism—and without all of the cultural trappings of the East. In the Quakers I was surprised to find a spiritual home that combines both sides of my being—the contemplative and the active.

Barbara

I knew right away that my fellow law student Barbara Hershey was what I was looking for. Barbara was dark-haired, beautiful, intelligent, and concerned socially. Since she was also the most attractive of the fourteen women in our law school class of 300, I knew that my admiration was shared by many of my classmates. Following our initial encounter the day before school had begun, for two years I watched from afar. Finally the summer before our last year of law school she came my way.

Except when I was out of the country, I had worked every summer in the canneries and food processing plants in Walla Walla from the time I was 16. In 1967, the Summer of Love, I landed a job with the Alameda Legal Aid Society in its office in East Oakland. Barbara had also been hired, and halfway through the summer she was sent to the East Oakland office. The first thing I did when she arrived was to flee.

At that point I hadn't yet discovered the Quakers, and had just finished attending a series of talks by the Hindu teacher Chinmayananda from India. By the end of the talks I was so impressed by his message that I had resolved to drop out of school and become a monk. Despite Barbara's arrival at the Legal Aid office, I resigned my summer job and hitchhiked up Highway 101 to Neskowin Beach on the Oregon coast, my parents' traditional vacation spot, to tell them my decision and to plan the next stage of my life. I returned to the Berkeley cottage I was living in two weeks later, and before long concluded I wasn't ready to devote all my time to meditation. In addition, I realized that if I dropped out of school, it was likely I would be drafted. I therefore pleaded for my job back, and the Legal Aid Society was kind enough to rehire me. At the end of the summer, after working and having lunch together for several weeks, Barbara and I agreed to take all the same courses for the coming term, and were soon cutting classes for regular walks through the university's arboretum. On June 16, 1968, the day after our law school graduation, we were married in Tilden Park in the Berkeley Hills.

After our wedding in the Brazilian Building and a several day honeymoon in Mendocino at the cabin of Legal Aid Director Tom Fike, we spent our first couple months of marriage in our Berkeley apartment studying for the California bar exam, which happily we both passed. Rather than applying for well-paying jobs in a corporate law firm in San Francisco or somewhere else, we both wanted something different and began looking for legal aid jobs, as did a number of other Boalt Hall law graduates. The only job we were able to find was a clerk position with Merced County Legal Services, part of the War on Poverty in the San Joaquin Valley, and I was the one hired.

In Merced we rented a farm house in the middle of rice fields. While we were waiting for the results of the bar exam, the director of our legal aid office either resigned or was fired along with the only other lawyer in the office, leaving me as both law clerk and acting director. Most of our clients were deep in debt, so I became a specialist in bankruptcy law, learning firsthand how in the wealthiest country in the world lack of universal health insurance and low wages keep many people in poverty and often drive them to financial ruin. After several months the continued funding of our program was in doubt, so I took a job as a staff attorney for the newly-established Solano County Neighborhood Legal Assistance Agency in Vallejo, and we moved to the north end of the San Francisco Bay.

Since there was no available housing in Vallejo we rented a house in nearby Napa. As lawyers in the area weren't hiring, Barbara opened her own law practice in Napa, which continued until our first child, Rebecca, was born. Barbara then decided she preferred the freedom of being a mother and free agent, and closed her office. While we were expecting Rebecca, the draft board sent me a dependency deferment, which I hadn't requested, in order to avoid dealing with my claim to conscientious objection.

In Berkeley I had introduced Barbara to the Quakers at the Berkeley Friends Meeting where I began attending. When we found no similar group in Napa, we decided to try to organize a Quaker meeting of our own there. Since we didn't know anyone in Napa, we simply put a listing in the town newspaper's church directory one Friday announcing that the Napa Friends Meeting would gather in our home that Sunday at 11 a.m. Fate smiled on us when Peggy Carey, a long-time Napa resident, former attendee at the Berkeley Friends Meeting, activist, and all around good soul, by chance looked at the church directory that day for the first time in months. Peggy then called all the members of a disbanded Unitarian group she had attended. On Sunday morning, instead of no one showing up as would otherwise have happened, twenty people came up the long winding driveway to our small rental house in the middle of a 15-acre prune orchard. Over the next year this somewhat idyllic setting was regularly transformed on Sunday mornings into what some experienced Quakers referred to as a "gathered meeting", that rare spiritual coming together which is considered the highest goal and achievement of successful Quaker meetings.

When Solano County Neighborhood Legal Assistance opened a new office in the northern part of the county, Barbara and I moved to a more modern house in an abandoned apple orchard near Vacaville. My activities during that period centered on work, where, among other things, we brought the first civil rights case in the federal court for the eastern district of California, successfully challenging racial discrimination against black tenants by a major Vallejo landlord. In 1970, I became executive director of the agency, and was instrumental in expanding its space and resources to meet the needs of a large low-income community, including several members of the Black Panther Party who occasionally invaded our offices seeking to recruit our African-American staff.

The continuing growth of Bay Area bedroom communities like ours and the lengthy commute to San Francisco for urban culture and amenities convinced us to begin looking up and down the Pacific coast states for more "livable" towns. To us, that meant a small city with a college located far enough from major cities that it had developed its own culture. When we visited Walla Walla to spend Thanksgiving with my parents, Barbara immediately fell in love with the community and said we had found our town. I agreed and began interviewing with Walla Walla law firms.

Back in Walla Walla

I was told that Cam Sherwood, senior partner in one of Walla Walla's oldest law firms and brother of the man my father worked for, was looking for an associate so I arranged to see him. Cam was a good man who loved to talk to excess. When we met, besides handing me his tax returns he showed me an article about Jerry Rubin whom he called a communist and public enemy. Thinking about those free bicycles I had campaigned for, I suspected this would be the wrong office. I was also concerned when Cam assured me that he and his partner always went home by 6 p.m. and made it a practice never to work on Sundays.

Barbara and I had agreed early on that we would not let the practice of law dominate our lives, that we would live simply, and would place high value on freedom and integrity. With that in mind, I decided it would be best to try to practice with a Democrat who kept more reasonable hours. I talked next with Jack Williams, the senior partner in the only Democratic firm I knew of in town, who told me they had no space for another lawyer, but recommended I visit with Steve Ringhoffer, who he said needed help with his practice.

Steve turned out to be a good match. He was a moderate Republican from an old Walla Walla family who gave me freedom to do whatever I wanted. Steve kept gentlemen's hours, and was happy to have me do the same. He and his father Herb had both attended Harvard law school, and Herb had for many years been the most respected lawyer in Walla Walla, representing all of its banks and many of the community's major businesses. Steve's own love, though, was science. Herb had insisted he become a lawyer, and while he had agreed, he dealt with the disappointment by neglecting his practice.   As a result, many cases in what now became Ringhoffer and Clark had been languishing for years for lack of attention, which I was glad to be able to give them, as well as developing a criminal law practice of my own along with other interests.

Barbara, Rebecca and I arrived in Walla Walla on April 1, 1971 to a home we had purchased south of town on Prospect Road, a few hundred yards from my old elementary school. The next year the birth of our second child, Jeremy, rounded out our nuclear family.

Low Income Legal Services

Shortly after returning to Walla Walla, I was appointed chair of the legal aid committee of the Walla Walla County bar association and was charged with setting up a formal legal aid program for the county. Until then, if a low-income person was involved in a non-criminal matter and couldn't afford a lawyer, they could request that the president of the bar association appoint a pro bono lawyer for them—if they happened to know about this informal practice, which was rarely the case. If whoever was the current bar president was aware of this custom himself, which often they weren't, then they might try to find a local lawyer to assist the client without charge, something that happened at best only once or twice a year.

The Blue Mountain Action Council, our local War on Poverty agency, was interested in working with the bar association to set up a more active program. Within a year we had established a legal aid office in BMAC's offices in downtown Walla Walla staffed by what we were told was the first VISTA Volunteer ever to be assigned to a local bar association. Our first volunteer, Gary Greenfield, was a non-lawyer at the time who later entered law school. Though his successor, Jim Barrett, was a law graduate, he wasn't currently licensed as an attorney in Washington so I volunteered to act as a supervising attorney so he could handle legal aid cases in court.

One of Jim's legal aid clients was Kenny Mines, a young black man whose legal problems drew me into early confrontation with local authorities. Not long before I returned to Walla Walla the U.S. Supreme Court had decided the landmark cases of *Argersinger v. Hamlin* and *Tate v. Short*, for the first time applying equal protection and due process principles to municipal courts, and prohibiting the common practice of jailing convicted defendants who couldn't afford to pay a fine or who hadn't had a lawyer to defend them. These were important protections for low-income people, who often sat in jail while more prosperous defendants paid a fine and went free.

I was curious to see how these new Supreme Court decisions would be applied in our town, since the traditional sentence for minor offenses tended to be "thirty dollars or thirty days." My partner Steve had invited all the lawyers and judges in town to a welcoming party for me at his home, so I used the occasion to ask Bill Roach, the long-time municipal court judge who was a friend of my brother, what he thought of the new rulings. I was surprised to learn that he had never heard of these important cases, and went to some length to explain to him the details of these new pronouncements of the highest court in our land—specifically the rule that a jail sentence could not be constitutionally imposed on a defendant who couldn't afford a lawyer unless one was appointed for him, and that a defendant couldn't be jailed because he was unable to immediately pay a fine while someone with money went free, but had to be given time to pay or an opportunity to work the fine off through public service during normal working hours.

Several months after the party I heard from Jim that Kenny Mines had just gotten out after being jailed for several days by Bill because he couldn't pay a fine, and that no lawyer had been appointed to represent him. I mentioned this to my friend John Biggs, the deputy city attorney in charge of prosecuting cases in municipal court, who said he'd look into it. Some time later Jim told me this practice was still going on and that Kenny was in jail again after a new municipal court charge, so I asked Jim to tell Kenny to come and see me if he wanted to put a stop to that. When I asked John Biggs about this again he told me that after our conversation he had arranged a meeting that included the county prosecutor, the city attorney, Judge Roach, and others, and that after considering what to do about these Supreme Court rulings, they agreed just to ignore them.

Kenny contacted me when he got out of jail, and we filed suit in federal district court in Spokane seeking an injunction and damages from the City of Walla Walla for constitutional violations. We also named the city attorney and the judge as defendants, and alleged a conspiracy to deprive Mines and others of their civil rights.

The first response of the city attorney was to demand that I return my key to the law library our two law firms shared. He also asked the president of the bar association, at that time Cam Sherwood, to censure me for suing a fellow attorney. Cam assured me he had been in the same position when he was a young lawyer, and wouldn't think of bringing that complaint before the bar association.

The city attorney's second response was to raise the legal principle of absolute prosecutorial and judicial immunity from damages for any official in any case within their jurisdiction, no matter how malicious or intentional their violation of a defendant's constitutional rights. This type of immunity seemed to me to be outrageous, but turned out to be the law.

Although we were barred from collecting damages because of that rule, we were still entitled to an injunction ordering the defendants to comply with the law, which would be a great embarrassment to the City. To avoid this, the City of Walla Walla agreed to resolve the case by entering into a consent order under which it would be required to adopt an ordinance providing for the payment of $100 damages for each day any future defendant was proven to have been jailed in violation of these rights, and also providing for the offer of city employment at the minimum wage for any defendant unable to immediately pay a fine. As a result, Walla Walla became the only jurisdiction in the country where a defendant could recover damages for a violation of these civil rights by a judge or prosecutor.

11

This story should have ended at that point, but it didn't. Several months later Jim Barrett told me Bill Roach was continuing to give out sentences on the same basis as before—"pay the fine if you can, and if you can't, you go to jail"—though Bill had finally begun to appoint lawyers for defendants who couldn't afford them. I represented a new defendant in the first case brought under the new ordinance, who received $300 for the three days of unconstitutional imprisonment he had been sentenced to. The hearing officer was Yancey Reser, one of Cam Sherwood's new law partners, who later was a superior court judge.

That case should certainly have been enough to bring about respect for a defendant's constitutional rights in Walla Walla Municipal Court, but it wasn't. Not long after this initial award against the City, I heard a further tale of woe from a defendant in Bill's court who had just been released after serving time in jail for not being able to immediately pay a fine, despite having a court-appointed attorney. After we filed a new claim for damages under the ordinance, I learned my client had been brought back in front of Bill on a new offense.

In the new case against my client, John Biggs was again the prosecutor and the appointed counsel for the defense was a young lawyer who was also employed as an occasional prosecutor for the city through John's office and who later became county prosecutor and a superior court judge himself. The two lawyers and the defendant had apparently agreed on a guilty plea and a recommendation for a $25 fine. This type of recommendation was nearly always accepted by the judge. However when John explained the agreement to Bill, he decided to also tell him that the defendant had a pending claim for damages against the city for Bill's violation of his rights under the new ordinance. According to my client, on hearing that Bill said to him, "Well, A may have a claim against B, but B may also have certain rights against A. In this case, while you may have a right to sue this court for damages, I have a right to impose a fine of $500 and a penalty of six months in jail on you for commission of this offense. I've decided to continue this sentencing hearing for two weeks to give you time to think about whether you really want to continue with your case against the city." The defendant's counsel apparently stood silent, making no objection to this blatantly improper action by Judge Roach.

My client was a recent parolee, and was literally shaking in his boots as he sat at my desk telling me that he had no choice but to dismiss his claim against the city. I urged him not to, and told him I would protect him from additional punishment if he stuck with it, and he ultimately agreed. Yancey Reser was again appointed hearing officer over the objection of the city attorney who didn't like his ruling in our first case. The hearing before Yancey was tape recorded, and when I asked Bill if it was true that he said to my client, "A may have a claim against B, but B may also have certain rights against A," Bill denied it. "Well," I asked, "didn't you use words to that effect?" "Well, yes," he admitted, "words to that effect." Yancey then awarded us $500 damages. Though at first Bill threatened an appeal, he then thought better of it and ended up imposing on my client a $25 fine as recommended in his pending case. After that, there were no further constitutional violations of this kind in Walla Walla Municipal Court.

My service as legal aid chair for the bar association continued until 1977, when our legal aid program was taken over by Spokane Legal Services, and later by the statewide Evergreen Legal Services program. Evergreen ultimately closed the local office, but continued to provide low-income legal services in Walla Walla and other rural counties through a statewide panel of attorneys which I was a part of for many years. That program has now been supplemented by a new pro bono attorney program administered by the Blue Mountain Action Council which I also participate in, and also by a new staffed office of the Northwest Justice Project.

Community and Prison Work

Instead of joining service clubs, the focus on my community work has been on specific projects and boards where I thought my presence could be useful. One of these was the Walla Walla Mental Health Center where I served as legal counsel and president, and for which I located and helped acquire new office quarters in a gracious old mansion near downtown. Another was the Blue Mountain Humane Society for which I also served as an officer and legal counsel and helped arrange space for a new animal shelter at the Walla Walla airport.

I also agreed to serve on the board of the Walla Walla Symphony, where I introduced the apparently novel proposal that the problem of many empty seats in the concert hall be solved by giving free tickets to the poor. Though the board approved the project, Jose Rambaldi, the Argentine conductor and music director, opposed the idea, and it ultimately was abandoned. While I love symphony concerts and continue to attend regularly, I soon realized that symphony societies usually have enough community support among the well-to-do as not to need my active participation. I suspect my resignation from the board was greeted with relief by many. In later years, the symphony's role in the Walla Walla community was considerably strengthened under the long-term leadership of Israeli-born conductor and musical director Jaacov Bergman.

At the other end of the social spectrum was the prison. Soon after our arrival, Jean Krapfel, a very concerned and kind-hearted woman, came to my office to see if I could help an inmate she was visiting. Before long I began working with a group of prisoners whose dream was to establish an upholstery shop outside the main walls in the old women's prison, where they would live, work, and lead more normal lives. I helped them form the Bridge Rehabilitation Project, which we incorporated as a non-profit, charitable organization, and also assisted them in getting a federal law and justice grant for their operations.

The Bridge board, on which I served a term as president, was structured so that a majority of its members were inmates, with a minority of townspeople. The inmate participants were treated with respect, wore their own clothes, had free access to a telephone, ran an upholstery business that was respected in the community and throughout the state, and exhibited a minimum of violence towards each other and the staff. The project went well until one day a participant got tanked up on "pruno," the inmate-produced liquor, and walked over to Warden Bobby Rhay's house next door for a talk. Though Rhay had introduced many reforms at the prison, including an experiment in inmate self-government, that was too much; he decided that a relaxed operation like this didn't belong on the grounds of a maximum security prison and closed it down.

During the Seventies I was appointed by the superior court to represent a number of inmates charged with crimes inside the prison. These included a capital case involving a defendant charged in the celebrated murder of Blackie Palmer in the inmate government office, and an alleged knife assault by inmate Ken Agtuca on officer James Payne. Palmer, a black inmate, had his throat slit from ear to ear and bled to death on the floor of his office, apparently at the hands of one or more members of the Bikers Club. At that time the Bikers Club was located in the next building behind a locked door through which correctional officers could pass only with inmate permission. Although most members of the bikers, including my client, were convicted murderers, all three biker defendants charged in the Palmer case were acquitted on the testimony of two officers who swore that they saw the defendants some distance away from the scene before the time of the attack as determined by the coroner, from where they couldn't have reached the area in time to kill Palmer.

Similar time conflicts failed to convince jurors of Agtuca's innocence in the Payne assault, though they may have been influenced by pretrial publicity, since Agtuca and several other lifers climbed up several hundred feet on the new water tower at the prison while awaiting trial and refused to come down until their demands for better treatment were met. When the time for his trial arrived, I had to go out to the tower while my client lowered a rope tied to a basket in which I put a pen and a waiver of time document so that the trial could be postponed.

On my visits to clients at the prison regarding civil or criminal matters as well as inmate programs in those days, I was able to wander everywhere unescorted, as did inmates and other visitors. Unfortunately, the freedoms of the prison reform period of the Seventies brought on abuses, including a high level of inmate violence against other inmates. The penitentiary is a very different place now, divided into a series of separately gated areas, with heavy control of all movement, and any inmate participation in policy or administration has been ended.

My significant involvement with the prison also ended in the Seventies, other than a brief experiment with an Alternatives to Violence Project, and a time when there was a small Quaker group meeting there. Except for an occasional civil case involving a prisoner, my only activities at the penitentiary since then have been related to capital punishment protests at the time of five separate executions, as well as a statewide campaign to reduce the overall reliance on imprisonment, which I'll describe in more detail later.

Family Life

After living for two years on Prospect Road, we moved farther south of town to an old farmstead at the corner of Powerline and Hill Roads. Here we experimented with homesteading, putting in a large organic garden, tending a small fruit orchard, raising milk goats, chickens, and even planting an acre of organic wheat which we tried cutting and threshing by hand. We bought a tractor, dried fruit, made goat cheese, gathered our own eggs, and enjoyed the great vistas across the Walla Walla valley and toward the Blue Mountains.

Our awareness of environmental issues was rising, and in 1976 Barbara wrote a small book entitled, "Becoming an Environmentalist—or How I Learned to Stop Worrying and Love the Energy Crisis" detailing our family's efforts to live lightly on the earth. We self-published the book as Cottonwood Publishing Company, and it received high praise from Mother Earth News as well as respectful mention in regional newspapers and steady patronage by a professor at the State University of New York who assigned it to his classes for several years.

At our farm place we also cultivated the contemplative life. Soon after we moved to Walla Walla Barbara and I organized the Friends Meditation Group involving several people with Quaker backgrounds and others who were simply interested in meditation, which met on Sunday afternoons in an upstairs room at the First Congregational Church. Our Powerline Road house also became a location for contemplative gatherings. On one occasion, we hosted a talk by a visiting ascetic known as Swami Alaya. On another, we organized a Zen mini-sesshin, during which, between sitting and walking meditation, we put the participants to work in our gardens! We also converted one of our outbuildings into a meditation house where Barbara and I encouraged each other to spend all or part of a day while the other took responsibility for the children and other household tasks, a practice we would continue later at a cabin we built in the mountains.

Although the Walla Walla Valley is semi-arid, with only 12-18 inches of rain a year, it sits at the feet of the Blue Mountains whose north-facing slopes are covered with moss and ferns reminiscent of a rain forest, providing great contrast for the valley dweller. In 1976, we acquired a five-acre parcel of mountain land sixteen miles east of Walla Walla in a wooded canyon along Mill Creek and just over the line into Oregon. Here we built a 20' diameter yurt, whose 16-sided framed walls and high-pitched, free-standing roof were supported by a cable, or tension band, just under the eaves, based on principles William O. Douglas brought back from Mongolia and introduced to the west through an article in the National Geographic in the late Sixties. We also put up a more traditional latticework and canvas-enclosed version of the yurt as a meditation hut. Our idyllic spot along what we called Krishna Creek became the site of a series of weekend Zen retreats we put together under the leadership of Genjo Marinello, a Seattle Zen priest and Quaker.

In addition to the main yurt and the small yurt, we moved two buildings up from our Powerline Road place. The first was a tack house which for a short period became my law office; the second was a two-hole privy, since Oregon environmental laws wouldn't allow indoor plumbing due to the narrowness of our canyon, where it was impossible to get more than 100 feet away from our year-round creek in order to install a septic tank and drain field.

In addition to a retreat for our friends and community, the following year the cabin became our home for a time. While we were still on Powerline Road, though, other significant activities were taking place.

The Community School

When our children were preschool age, Barbara and I were among the first members of the Parent Cooperative Preschool being organized by Walla Walla Community College. Another of the co-op parents, Mike Friedman, began talking with us about problems of "teaching to the center of the class" prevalent in the public schools, and called our attention to books by John Holt and Jonathan Kozol on free schools and open classrooms, where children could be self-directed and learn at their own pace. Both of us liked the idea.

In January, 1973, the three of us called a community meeting to rally parent support for the establishment of a voluntary open classroom program in the public schools for those parents who wanted their children to experience that approach. Unfortunately, a newspaper article after the meeting stressed comments by a few parents that were very critical of the public schools, which got us off on the wrong foot with the school district.

We believed it would be easy for the district to establish one or two classrooms as an experiment, for those families interested in what was a respected educational alternative. In the face of the criticism though, the district dug its heels in and insisted that every child had to attend the same type of class, arguing that even if the open classroom approach proved to be successful, it wouldn't be fair for some children to receive a different educational experience from others. The only thing the school board would agree to was to establish a parent/staff committee to study the issue. As a result, the committee met for nearly a year before the assistant superintendent chairing the meetings admitted to us that his instructions from the superintendent were not to agree to anything. Their apparent strategy was to only go through the motions of a study-- basically to "committee us to death."

Though she had only been in town for two years, in frustration Barbara ran for a seat on the school board against the incumbent chairwoman and another candidate who was head of the high school booster club. One of Barbara's campaign ideas was to have our large milk goat pull a cart in the fair parade with a sign saying, "Has the school board got your goat?" When she arrived with our children, unfortunately the parade officials refused to allow her in the main parade citing a rule against political candidates that had never before been applied, though they did allow the entry as part of the kids' parade with no sign. When the election results were announced, Barbara had lost the primary by only eight votes.

After being shut out of the public schools, our parents group decided to form its own school. In 1974, we incorporated the Community School as a nonprofit organization for which I served as president. We arranged donated classroom space at Grace United Methodist Church, hired Cindy Gregoire, a sympathetic teacher, received official certification from the state education office in Olympia, offered a large number of scholarships, and charged the lowest tuition of any private school in the state, less in fact than the public schools lost in state matching funds for every child we enrolled.

While the school was successful in the eyes of both parents and students, after our first year hostility from the school district resulted in dissension within the church, which notified us that they would not provide us space for the coming year. Though it seemed a noble and successful experiment, since we were unable to find another location, the Community School closed its doors, and the next term its students entered the public schools, and for the most part fared better than either their parents or the school district had expected.

HAD and the Left Bank Restaurant

Barbara and I had been gradually moving toward vegetarianism since our days in Berkeley, originally for mental calm and clarity, and later for humanitarian and environmental reasons as well. Since Walla Walla had no vegetarian restaurants, in 1976 we developed a plan with our friends Trudy and Jon St. Hilaire to offer vegetarian food and musical entertainment in part of the historic Schwarz Building along Mill Creek at First and Main. Our idea was that Trudy would be the chef, Jon would handle management and entertainment, and Barbara and I would supply legal expertise and capital. A vacant shop in the building faced Mill Creek, and we wanted to make it Walla Walla's first sidewalk café and vegetarian restaurant. This fit nicely with a proposal recently announced by the citizens group Historic Architectural Development, Inc. (HAD) for a community plaza at First and Main with a fountain coming up out of Mill Creek next to our intended restaurant space.

The Schwarz building was on the National Historic Register and had been the site of the old Walla Walla City Hall, an armory, Stahl's Opera House, a dance hall, a roller rink, and a variety of ground floor shops. Unfortunately, new owners of the building had made a deal with Fidelity Mutual Savings Bank of Spokane to tear it down in order to construct a new branch bank there. The bank was proposing to put up a modern, single-use one-story glass building in the historic center of Walla Walla, clearly at odds with the rest of our 1880's multi-story red brick downtown.

When I learned this, I went to meet HAD's president Erma Jo Bergevin, who wanted to fight to save the building but was getting tired and asked me if I would take over as president of the organization. Since that appeared to be the only way to keep HAD involved, I agreed and led a delegation to meet with the president of the bank and his staff in Spokane. Our request was that they save the building, use part of it for their branch bank, and rent out the balance of the shop space to keep pedestrian traffic on the block. We gave them a San Francisco study showing how devastating banks can be to a city neighborhood when they replace multiple first and second story uses with a single, relatively low-traffic occupant. We also told them that unless they cooperated, we would oppose their application to the Federal Deposit Insurance Corporation for the required permission to establish a bank on an historic site.

In response, the bank agreed to pay an engineer $50,000 to study the economics of rehabilitating the old building. The local owners had previously announced it was unfeasible to save it, since it would cost $150,000. The bank's engineer concluded the building was impractical for its use since it would cost a million dollars to rehabilitate it for their purposes.

At that point the three owners threatened to sue us for interfering with their profitable bank deal, and the Union-Bulletin, our local newspaper, criticized us editorially for our impracticality and for not respecting private property rights.

Next we told the bank that if it wasn't economical to save the building, they should replace it with something compatible in scale and texture with the surrounding buildings, as well as providing space for multiple uses, including a restaurant. To our surprise, the bank president offered us a veto over the new design they were working on, and said that if we couldn't agree on a compatible design, they would give up the site.

Though knowing we'd be sued if we didn't agree on a final design and the bank withdrew, we accepted their offer. The bank then unveiled their second design at the Walla Walla Country Club in a meeting with the property owners, HAD, and various community leaders. This version was similar to the modernistic Olin Hall structure at Whitman College and was by the same architect, and was also wholly out of keeping with the historic center of the downtown. Though the circumstances of their unveiling were designed to avoid another rejection, we refused to approve.

The bank's third and final design is the one you can see at First and Main in Walla Walla today—a two-story, red brick building, wholly compatible with those adjoining it, and which accommodates multiple uses including space for a restaurant and wine tasting room, with a fine plaza where many of our community's public events take place. Both the bank and the owners were happy with the design, we were ecstatic, and the newspaper printed a lead editorial reversing itself and celebrating the success of our efforts on behalf of the community.

Barbara and I then turned our attention to establishing our planned café. Unfortunately, while all of this transpired Trudy had taken another job and was no longer available as chef, and the new space had also become more expensive than we had originally planned. The alternative we came up with was to form a closely held corporation with ten investors, which is the maximum permitted without formal securities registration, all of whom would have to be committed to creating a gourmet sidewalk cafe with quality entertainment.

What we proposed to investors was that we hire staff, establish the restaurant in the style we wanted, run it for a year, then sell it either to the staff or someone else rather than continuing to operate it by committee. Our plan was to recruit creative people who were interested in making this happen rather than making a profit, which restaurants rarely do. Barbara and I thought we could do this at the time for $20,000. With that many investors no one would have more than $2000 at risk, which we could expect to recoup from new job and investment credits, as well as investor patronage.

As it turned out, rather than the low-budget enterprise we had envisioned with the St. Hilaires, the investors we assembled insisted on employing an interior decorator, and hiring a well-known chef from Bend whose demands for the kitchen alone cost us $50,000. The result was the creation of the Left Bank Restaurant serving French country cuisine, which was the town's finest restaurant for about seven years, To fund the additional costs, our corporation took out a bank loan whose debt service was too much for the manager we hoped would buy us out at the end of the year. Because of that, we continued to run the restaurant by committee until Phyllis and Bob Pulfer, part of our original investors, agreed to take over the restaurant and its obligations. The Pulfers ran the Left Bank for several more years in good style before selling to a new owner who soon closed it. All the original owners recouped their investments, and the town was graced with elegant cuisine and surroundings for seven years, though not with vegetarian cuisine. Though the chef we hired was vegetarian and there were some vegetarian offerings, most of the menu contained meat products.

My activities with Historical Architecture Development, Inc. continued for awhile, including the drafting of an exterior design review ordinance for downtown buildings which was not adopted, the making of architectural awards, and a design for the restoration of a full downtown block. In 1978, when HAD was considering the purchase of the historic Kirkman House for restoration as a museum, I left the board because I believed this significant restoration project would consume all of HAD's energies and end its more general work in the community, which has since proven to be true. Ten years later, I was to serve as the founding chair of the Architecture and

Downtown Committee of Walla Walla 2020, a new organization which would take up some of the work relinquished by HAD.

The Legal Defense Association

When we moved to Walla Walla in 1971, I began to handle criminal cases for the first time, and had considerable success. The traditional system for the representation of criminal defendants unable to afford an attorney was for the judge handling the case to appoint a lawyer, and at the end of the case to determine what the lawyer would be paid. This way of doing things was not designed to encourage vigorous representation of the accused, since many attorneys hesitated to aggressively challenge a judge who was both their employer and paymaster. Spirited defense was therefore fairly rare, and on one occasion I remember Judge Albert Bradford's outrage when he felt I was advancing the cause of an accused prison inmate in too energetic a manner.

In 1975, the state bar association completed a study of the various ways of delivering indigent criminal defense in Washington, including appointment and compensation by the trial judge, a contract system under which the county signs an agreement with one or more attorneys to provide all needed representation for a flat fee, a staffed public defender's office, or the creation of an independent association of criminal defense lawyers that would handle appointments, case investigation, and compensation under a general contract with the county. The study concluded that the weakest system was one dominated by the judge and the strongest system for counties the size of Walla Walla would be the creation of an independent criminal defense association, for which they were offering a startup grant program.

Though our local bar association was extremely conservative and rarely reached agreement on any substantial change, when I became aware of the report and the grant opportunity I arranged a meeting of the young lawyers who were handling most of the court appointments at which I proposed the creation of an association of the kind being recommended. The young lawyers all agreed to the proposal, after which we asked for a meeting of the full bar. To the surprise of most, after hearing one young lawyer after another approve the project the association endorsed the change in the system without opposition.

We then incorporated the Walla Walla County-Columbia County Legal Defense Association for which I served as part-time administrative attorney. We applied for and were awarded a state grant, hired a retired deputy sheriff as our investigator, enlisted the membership of a larger number of attorneys than had previously handled such cases, and negotiated contracts with every court in Walla Walla and Columbia counties with the exception of the College Place Municipal Court.

The Association developed a unique client cost-sharing system unknown in other counties, as well as a more effective screening system for financial eligibility. This resulted in 7% of the applicants being found ineligible compared to almost 100% eligibility under the former system, while 22% were determined to be able to pay at least part of their fees where in the past no participation was required. The allowance of attorney fees by the Association was also significantly below the amount previously budgeted for appointed counsel in each court we contracted with.

To increase professionalism in our field, we also presented the first criminal law seminar ever offered in Walla Walla County, and began to develop research and form files to share expertise and increase efficiency. In addition, we arranged a meeting between defense counsel and the prosecution, and another meeting with the judges to discuss wide-ranging reforms in the handling and docketing of criminal cases that would benefit everyone involved. For the first time, we had an integrated system for the delivery of criminal defense services in the two counties and a mechanism for addressing general problems and needed improvements.

The system worked well until 1978 when I took a sabbatical from my practice, at which point the members of the association demanded higher fees from Walla Walla County and were underbid by a small group of local lawyers. The county commissioners, having little commitment to quality criminal defense, chose the cheaper alternative, though one highly criticized by the state bar as ineffective, and proceeded to contract with two or three lawyers to handle all criminal cases at a lower fixed cost. That was the end of high quality public defense in Walla Walla County, with some notable exceptions over the years.

Sabbatical

In my sixth year of law practice in Walla Walla the pace of life was good. Our office was open from 9-12 and from 1-5. Steve was a night person who usually stayed up late reading at home, and didn't come into the office until 10 in the morning, though he sometimes didn't go home until 6 p.m. or later. I normally worked 9-5, having lunch downtown and taking Wednesday afternoons off, though not to play golf as most local professionals did. Unless I was in a trial, I rarely took work home.

After Steve went through a divorce and remarried, he started going home at noon and not returning until about 2, and I began to do the same. On Wednesdays though, I would work until 1:00, which meant a 4-hour day and four 6-hour days or a 28 hour work week.

Barbara and I always lived simply, and as a result, our income was adequate and we had no need to pursue clients. Even with my reduced hours we were doing fine and we had put some money away. When in the fall of 1976 real estate values began going up in Walla Walla, we woke up one morning to the realization that, having no indebtedness, if we sold our farmstead on a 30-year contract and moved into our mountain cabin, we would be financially self-sufficient and I could retire at the age of 35.

Once we were aware of the opportunity, we couldn't pass it up. In the first place, we recognized that our Powerline Road place was more than we needed or could justify. Some time before we had moved our bedrooms down to the first floor of the house, and the second floor stood unused. Then there were the numerous outbuildings only some of which we used, and unneeded acres. Calculating the present rental value of the property, we realized it was far more than we wanted to be spending on our own household.

Even more compelling was the opportunity to pursue what was most important to us, freed of the obligation to earn money. Considering our values, we felt we would be running away from ourselves if we didn't take it.

In late December I broke the news to Steve, which was a serious disappointment to him, since he had hoped I would gradually take over the practice as he moved into retirement. We agreed on a brief transition period, and by June, 1977 I moved my office first to our Powerline Road place which we were in the process of selling, then on to our mountain place when we moved there in August. By the end of the year I was successful in wrapping up my remaining cases.

I realized that as long as I could legally practice law, it would be difficult to turn clients away, so I arranged not to renew my active license as of January 1, 1978. Although I had no idea whether or when I would practice again, I described my departure as a "sabbatical," explaining that college professors traditionally were allowed one year off out of every seven, and that this was my seventh year. Superior Court Judge John Tuttle's response was, "Sabbatical? The only sabbatical I've ever heard any lawyer taking around here was down at the end of South Second Street,"meaning at the city cemetery.

Since contemplative values were most on our minds as we considered our new life, Barbara and I withdrew from every committee and community project we were working on at the time in order to experience what it would be like to be completely free of external obligations.

Clark Canyon

Our Clark Canyon place, as we called it, had electricity and a phone line but no running water other than a pipe from our gravity-flow spring which emptied at a small stone elephant just below our cabin, from where it ran back into Krishna Creek. I was surprised that for Barbara, a Los Angeles girl concerned about bears, the carrying of all our water into the cabin and the pouring of every drop we used from a pitcher into a basin was just the Zen touch necessary to entice her away from the safety of the city. She also liked our secluded setting, back beyond other cabins in a canyon all our own. She even lamented when the Klickers, who had sold us the land, tried to be helpful by dozing out a driveway to within fifty yards of our cabin, where before there had only been a long footpath.

After putting in a cowbell and a sign at our gate reading, "Ring the bell before entering the dell," our privacy was complete enough that we were able to enjoy the pleasure of sunning in the nude.

Our round cabin was built onto the hillside with piers and a wraparound deck overlooking the creek. The inside was all open, including a half loft where we slept. Though we had our two-hole outhouse up a narrow path behind the cabin, we supplemented it with a chamber pot for use in the middle of the night. We planted a few fruit trees on the hillside, and tried to dig a garden on the small bench where our cabin sat, but found more rocks than soil in the old creek bed.

We loved the rustic life. Once school started, we were basically home-schooling our children, though we arranged to send them to school one day a week for the sociability of it. When the days began getting shorter, our children found themselves more and more isolated socially, especially since the few youngsters in the neighborhood had to ride a bus all the way past Walla Walla to Milton-Freewater, Oregon for school, and it was dark by the time they got home.

Barbara and I also discovered that we didn't feel right about driving back and forth the 16 miles to town when needs or events drew us there, which we found happened more frequently than we expected. We began to realize, too, just as I had when I had "dropped out" in Berkeley, that devoting nearly full-time to contemplative activities wasn't right for us. As this became clearer, we started looking for a house in town with an extra apartment, so we could rent out one portion to cover the costs and use the rest for a place to stay overnight when we had both morning and evening commitments there.

Our Town House

In December, 1977, we purchased a home in town which we later found had been built in 1902 by a Celtic carpenter and musician, William Henry Morrison from the Isle of Mann, who had come here speaking only Gaelic and built this house for his new American bride. Further research showed that he had also built our Powerline Road place in 1929. During the depression of the Thirties, this graceful but modest home on North Main Street had been made into a duplex with two front doors, making it possible for us to rent out the front portion and to use the rest for ourselves. Luckily, it was inexpensive enough that we were able to pay cash and still have no debts.

Not long after acquiring our town house it became apparent to us that our children were enjoying their limited time in the public schools except for the long commute, that we were also interested in community activities again, and that our real center of gravity was in town. On January 1, 1978 we moved our household into the North Main house, which is still our home today, though we've done some remodeling of it over the years.

Once back in town but still free of financial needs, there remained the question of what work or activity was inherently important to us. One day as I was walking into our front apartment which served as my study at that point, I had an inspiration. What was inherently valuable to me was peacemaking. Rather than using my training as a lawyer to serve as a kind of hit man for one party against another, why couldn't I serve as a mediator to bring about an amicable settlement of any dispute which could otherwise be litigated? The idea seemed natural, powerful, and needed, and was not being acted on anywhere as far as I knew. I sat down at a table and for half an hour wrote out a plan to establish a non-profit organization as a general alternative to the court system, which over the next year I was to carry out in every particular. Up to that moment, I had never heard of mediation being used other than in labor disputes, so I went through everything I could find at our local libraries to see if anyone else was talking about or doing this. I found nothing, and decided that it had to be tried. I also decided that the idea was radical enough that it would have to be tried out in a major urban area, not in a small town.

Denver Conciliation Services

While we were still living in the mountains, Barbara had come across an organization in the Denver area called Wholemind which offered a set of experiments in breaking through our normal dualistic perception of the world to an experience of wholeness. Since the approach and experiments appealed to both of us, and particularly to Barbara, we decided that Denver would be a good place to try experimenting with my mediation idea.

Once we arrived in Denver we were able to make arrangements for the donation of office space for the mediation project in a vacant wing of the Grant Avenue Methodist Church downtown. We also met a psychologist who agreed to serve with us on the board of a Colorado nonprofit corporation we formed called Denver Conciliation Services.

With that accomplished, we then proceeded to announce ourselves to the media as the first general mediation service in the state of Colorado, which generated feature stories in the two major newspapers, the Denver Post and the Rocky Mountain News, interviews on a number of television shows, and a guest appearance on talk radio. We explained mediation as an amicable, inexpensive, and prompt alternative to the adversarial court system. Rather than taking something away from one party to give to the other, here was a way for the parties to achieve a solution to their conflict that would satisfy the needs of all sides and possibly preserve their relationship for the future, as well as avoiding the long delays and high costs of the judicial process. As a result of this publicity, we were flooded with calls, many from people wanting to be mediators.

After further research I learned that the inspiration that had occurred to me had also occurred to others, and that the U.S. Justice Department had recently funded three neighborhood justice center pilot projects, located in Los Angeles, New York, and Atlanta, and was inviting grant applications for more. An important difference between the federally funded projects and the model I had created that day in my study was clear. My vision was of a general alternative to litigation, rather than simply a way to handle those cases lawyers didn't want because they were uneconomic or too messy, which was the primary focus of some of the federal projects. Because of that I resolved to get our program underway through donated space, volunteers, and a sliding fee scale before going to a grantor who for political or other reasons might want to limit the scope of mediation to what lawyers considered nuisance cases. That is exactly what we were able to do, handling cases ranging from domestic relations to commercial, and even some criminal cases with the cooperation of the prosecution, the defense and the victims.

A few months after we opened, Mary Margaret Golten walked into our office looking for what she called a "real job," not just volunteer work. She was a bright, energetic former probation officer from Washington D.C. whose husband had been legal counsel for the National Wildlife Federation and was a new faculty member at the University of Colorado law school at Boulder. After explaining the shoestring nature of our operations, I told Mary Marg that the way to create a real job for herself was to write a grant application for us. This proved to be a great strategy, as she was successful in obtaining a federal grant of more than $100,000 for the program with the help of the Colorado Lieutenant Governor's office, not only retaining the broad scope of our program but expanding it.

By Christmas when we returned to Walla Walla to spend the holidays with my folks, despite the success of the mediation project we decided that the Denver area wasn't where we wanted to live, and that Barbara and the kids should remain in Walla Walla while I returned to Denver for a couple of months to turn the program over to others. Besides Mary Marg, our other principal mediator was Richard Evarts, a businessman who later became the director of the Dallas office of the American Arbitration Association. In addition, Chris Moore, a well-known Quaker dispute resolution trainer from Philadelphia, had inquired about coming out to join the program, but had not yet done so.

Mary Marg was our best choice for new leadership. When I left she became executive director of Denver Conciliation Services, which soon changed its name to Center for Dispute Resolution. Since then, Chris Moore and others have joined Mary Marg as partners in CDR Associates, which is today one of the most respected mediation and training programs in the world. Several years ago, Mary Marg sent me a news article out of the Denver Post detailing the program's rise, including services offered all over the country and the world. These included workshops in the former Soviet Union for government officials trying to deal in new ways with their citizens, and dispute resolution sessions in South Africa between the African National Congress and the Inkatha Freedom Party. CDR Associates' budget that year was around $1.3 million.

In March, 1979 as I drove back to Walla Walla following the heady excitement of directing a cutting edge project in a major city, I wasn't able to see anything nearly as creative and satisfying on the road ahead, though in fact there was much more to come.

Return to Law and Activism

Before leaving Walla Walla we had rented the larger apartment in our home to a Whitman College administrator. Fortunately she had moved to a house provided by the college, so on returning from our Denver sojourn we were able to take up where we had left off without too much inconvenience. We also gave notice to the chemistry instructor renting our front apartment, which we had decided to turn into a mediation and law office. After renewing my license to practice law, I began to take selected cases, and continued to practice in the same way for the next thirty years, taking or refusing new clients and cases depending on whether they interested me and on what other projects or activities I was involved in at the time.

Neutral Ground

By April, 1979 we had incorporated Neutral Ground as a Washington nonprofit organization, and had begun the process to qualify our new mediation service with the IRS as a 501(c)(3) tax exempt organization, as we had done with the Denver program. We arranged space in the First Congregational Church in Walla Walla for mediation sessions, whose pastor Emrys Thomas, agreed to serve on the board, and we handled administrative matters from our home office.

In addition to the general mediation of disputes in Walla Walla and the nearby Tri-Cities of Kennewick, Pasco and Richland where we established a satellite office, we began mediation classes at Columbia Basin College in Pasco and at Walla Walla Community College. For one of our college classes we brought in Joel Edelman, founding director of the Los Angeles Neighborhood Justice Center, to lead a training session. Along with the three pioneering neighborhood justice centers, I was delighted to discover that the Community Boards program in San Francisco, another pioneering mediation program that had gained international attention, had been founded by my law school roommate Ray Shonholtz.

Several years later, Barbara took over from me as executive director of Neutral Ground, which is not only the oldest general mediation program in the state of Washington, but also the first legally recognized dispute resolution center in the state under a new law allowing county commissioners to recognize mediation programs in their jurisdictions which meet certain criteria, and are then entitled to a number of privileges including confidentiality, not otherwise available.

Over the years, mediation and alternative dispute resolution programs, both non-profit and for-profit, have grown relatively common. Because of other activities we've been involved in, we weren't interested in expanding Neutral Ground which we always operated on a very modest sliding fee scale essentially as a community service. Although our caseload was low, Barbara was active in mediation training, devising and coordinating a conflict resolution curriculum at the elementary level which was utilized locally in several schools. We continued to offer mediation as needed until just recently when we turned the program over to a new director and a new board.

Walla Walla Quakers

Shortly before we left for Denver the Friends Meditation Group had stopped meeting when some of the older members were no longer able to attend.

While we were in the Denver area, we attended Friends Meetings in both Denver and Boulder. When we returned to Walla Walla, Barbara and I were ready to begin again, this time with a more committed Sunday morning meeting which would be the primary religious affiliation of its members, and would be integrated into the larger Society of Friends. On Easter Sunday, 1980, about twenty people gathered in a room at Whitman College's Sherwood Center in response to a written invitation which read in part:

> We live in troubled times which challenge the vision many of us have of a good and just life.

> We see
> > increasing injustice in the distribution of the earth's resources—hunger and poverty oppress many, while a privileged few wastefully consume our limited resources and accumulate more power.

increasing reliance on violence as a solution to problems—the renewal of the draft and other war preparations, the return of capital punishment, and the abandonment of rehabilitation in favor of punitive measures in our prisons,

increasing threats to individual liberties and freedom at home and abroad—burgeoning corporate and governmental power, linked with growing pressure for more legal intrusions into individual privacy for "national security" reasons and for further massive "security measures" related to the development of nuclear power.

Against the background of these challenges, the Quakers have a tradition of commitment to peace, justice, and tolerance—a wedding of non-dogmatic, individual spirituality with effective but non-violent social action, in times of war and peace, internationally and domestically.

The Friends' simple lifestyles are an effective demonstration of the satisfaction of a non-materialistic way of living. Both their simplicity and their active concern for social justice throughout the world are born of their openness to individual spiritual guidance through their silent meetings and their reliance for inspiration on all attending their meetings, rather than on formal ministers. Quakers serve as agents of social change and as peacemakers when violence and intolerance threaten to divide people.

At that gathering the Walla Walla Friends Meeting was born, and that Fall became an official "preparative" meeting of the Religious Society of Friends under the oversight of Eastside Monthly Meeting in Bellevue. We affiliated our meeting with North Pacific Yearly Meeting, a traditional unprogrammed, non-pastoral Friends body. Though I served as its founding clerk, who is the presiding officer among Friends, I was soon succeeded by Nancy Ball, who has served with me in that capacity off and on ever since. We have continued to meet on the Whitman campus, usually in the Olin Hall faculty lounge. Our numbers will probably always be small, leading us to joke about being a "perpetual preparative meeting" rather than progressing to full monthly meeting status, but some impressive things have come out of this little group and its members over the last thirty years.

Alternatives to War and Violence

At its first meeting for business in May, 1980 the Walla Walla Friends Meeting established a peace committee in response to President Carter's proposal to reinstate draft registration. In June after the new registration law was passed by Congress, we renamed this the Committee on Alternatives to War. Moving quickly, on July 3 and 4, we held a draft counselors training workshop at the Congregational Church and a public talk by WSU professor Paul Brians on "A Pacifist's Response to International Conflict." We also offered a draft information table at Pioneer Park at the community Independence Day celebration and at the Saturday Farmers Market during the initial period of draft registration which ended August 2. In addition, we handed out leaflets at the Walla Walla post office where young men were to register for the draft, and set up an information table at the College Place post office with help from concerned Adventists at Walla Walla College.

26

Though established by the Friends Meeting, we opened the committee to others in the community who joined with us in planning a three-part Symposium on Alternatives to War to be presented that fall. To advertise the symposium, we organized an entry in the Southeastern Washington Fair Parade on Labor Day weekend under the name Americans for Peace, in which thirteen people marched with flags, banners, and sandwich boards announcing the symposium while distributing draft counseling leaflets to the onlookers. The parade organizers placed us just in front of the National Guard tank, and we were pleased when the parade announcer responded favorably, telling the crowd that he'd like to see more social concerns like ours represented in the community's annual parade. After the parade, committee members returned to the fairgrounds with their sandwich boards, where they had been present every day of the fair, usually next to the military tank. For years after that, we received annual invitations from the organizers of Walla Walla's Veterans' Day Parade inviting Americans for Peace to also march in their parade.

The first session of our Symposium entitled "Why Alternatives to War--What's Wrong with What We're Doing Now?" took place on September 17 in the auditorium in Whitman College's Olin Hall, and featured the film, "War Without Winners," as well as a discussion of the ethics, economics, and efficacy of modern warfare led by Whitman religion professor George Ball and Barbara Clark. The committee offered regular draft counseling sessions at Whitman at that time, had a campus chapter as well as weekly study sessions on current events, and also sponsored a Peacemakers Essay Contest.

Our first symposium session had a standing-room-only crowd of 150 people. The second session on October 15 was titled "New Ways of Dealing with International Disputes" featuring another talk by WSU professor Paul Brians as well as the winning proposals for new approaches to peace between the U.S. and the U.S.S.R. suggested by entrants in the school, college, and community divisions of our essay contest. On October 24, after offering nonviolence training our Whitman chapter organized the picketing of U.S. Senator Henry Jackson's lecture on campus, and handed Jackson a petition signed by 300 Whitman students calling for a variety of peace measures including the ratification of the SALT II treaty.

One of the purposes of our symposium was to awaken people to the magnitude of the threat presented by the MAD policy (Mutually Assured Destruction) and the continued practice of violent conflict resolution in the age of nuclear weapons. But that wasn't enough. We realized that people and nations can't change their destructive ways of defending themselves if there aren't viable alternatives for protecting deeply held values. The final session of the symposium held on November 12 presented the concept of massive civilian resistance as a national defense, in a program titled "Civilian Nonviolent Defense--Is it practical for the US?"

Barbara and I first learned of "civilian-based defense" or "social defense" from Paul Brians, the long-time pacifist who chairs the humanities department at Washington State University located among the wheat fields of Eastern Washington. He introduced us to the work of Gene Sharp of Harvard, the foremost authority in the field of nonviolent means of political struggle as an alternative to war. Gene had written a series of books on the subject, including his definitive three-part "Politics of Nonviolent Action" (Porter Sargent, 1973), as well as a small pamphlet titled "Making the Abolition of War a Realistic Goal" (Institute for World Order, 1980).

The essence of these fascinating studies is that all governments, including dictatorships, rely on the consent and cooperation of the people in order to rule. Where acceptance and cooperation is withdrawn, governments of all kinds fall, as did the British in India in 1947 in the face of massive nonviolent resistance led by Mohandas Gandhi, and the powerful government of the Shah of Iran, which was brought down by a nonviolent revolution in 1979. According to Sharp,

> The theory that power derives from violence, and that victory goes to the side with the greater capacity for violence, is false....If we want to reduce drastically, or remove reliance on war and other types of violent conflict it is necessary to substitute a nonviolent counterpart of war, 'war without violence,' by which people can defend liberty, their way of life, humanitarian principles, their institutions and society, at least as effectively against military attack as can military means.

The answer, he and others conclude, is to prepare and train the civilian population in advance to defend against external or internal threats through a variety of means.

At our final symposium session we announced a further four-part workshop on "The Nonviolent Defense of Walla Walla County" to be offered during Whitman College's Interim session held in January between semesters, at which we hoped to have Gene Sharp appear. When I talked with him at length by phone, I learned that although he was booked for that time, he was delighted by the depth of our study and our idea of preparing a county plan. He graciously said that we had obviously given the specific application of these principles more thought than he had, and that we were in the best position to present the workshop ourselves.

With Gene's endorsement, that's what we did. The first workshop session took place on January 10 in the Lyman Hall lounge, and was attended by nine or ten people, mostly from the community. After I gave a brief introduction on the theory and practice of civilian-based defense, the session was interrupted when Barbara came into the room and motioned me over to the side where she whispered excitedly and handed me a piece of paper. I told the class something very unusual was taking place, and though it had to be kept in strict confidence, under the circumstances I needed to share it with them. I then read the following letter bearing the embossed seal of the United States of America:

January 9, 1981

Committee on Alternatives to War
c/o Barbara Clark, Chairperson
PO Box 1222
Walla Walla, WA 99362   SPECIAL DELIVERY

Ladies and Gentlemen:

You are not to divulge the contents of this letter except as authorized below.

It is my duty to inform you of a grave crisis facing our nation and to request your assistance at this most critical moment of our history.

We at the highest levels of the United States government have for some time been following with apprehension the development by the Soviet Union of both a defensive and offensive capability far beyond our existing technology. We are now faced with the reality of that capability and have just witnessed a secret demonstration by the Soviets of their ability to completely deflect our present nuclear strike force and at the same time to penetrate our defenses with weapons capable of destroying our nation in its entirety. We are completely satisfied that the Soviets have at the present time the power to destroy our civilization without risk of substantial harm to their own society.

Following the recent demonstration, we have been advised by the Soviet Union that in their estimation the accession to power of President-elect Ronald Reagan would constitute an immediate and unacceptable threat to world peace. The Soviets have therefore informed us that at 12:01 a.m., January 18, 1981, the armed forces of the Union of Soviet Socialist Republics will commence the occupation of all United States territories, including the continental United States, and that all military and police personnel of the United States and its state and local governments will be expected to surrender their arms at that time.

In view of the overwhelming military superiority of the Soviet Union at the present, we see no alternative but to comply with their request if we are to avoid wholesale and senseless destruction of our nation.

The Soviet Union has stated that its intention is to utilize its current military superiority to create a world state free from war. In doing so, its first acts will be to occupy and disarm all military powers. This will initially be accomplished through the Soviet armed forces; however it is their intention, they tell us, to make a gradual transition to an international peace force under the control of a democratically selected world government. We do not know whether their statements reflect their true intentions, or precisely what form their occupation will take.

Although we do not know precisely when Soviet troops will arrive in Walla Walla County, we urge you to begin immediately to plan for the nonviolent defense of those institutions and activities which are essential to our culture. In order to avoid a national panic and to allow groups like yours planning time, we have decided to delay a public announcement of the Soviet occupation until 6:00 p.m., Friday, January 17. At that time, we will instruct all military and police personnel to surrender their arms as of 12:01 a.m., January 19 or upon contact with Soviet personnel, and will instruct all citizens and officials of Walla Walla County to cooperate with you fully in any defense activities you decide to implement.

In the meantime, you are to make known the contents of this letter only to those persons essential to the defense planning activities of your committee.

We trust with your help and leadership to be able to preserve the essence of our national life. Perhaps, God willing, we will even come through this test stronger as a people. As events progress, we hope to be able to coordinate in some way the defense of our national values among the various regions of our country. For now, leadership must be decentralized. Because of this, the future of the country is literally in your hands.

May God grant us strength and wisdom.

Yours faithfully,
James Earl Carter,
President and Commander-in-Chief

JEC/r
cc: National Security File

The letter bore a signature which appeared to be that of President Carter.

There were gasps and ashen faces as the letter was read. At the end, other than a little nervous laughter from one or two of the participants, there was complete silence in the room.

"Of course," I told them, "we have to realize this letter may be a hoax. But since we're already planning to devote the rest of the week to doing just the kind of defense planning the letter asks of us, we might as well get on with it." "Let me see that letter," one of the skeptics said, as he came up, took the heavy paper in his hand, examined the signature, and rubbed his thumb over the seal. "Well, it looks genuine enough," he admitted.

Thus began our task of deciding which Walla Walla institutions and activities we considered critical to our freedoms and society, and how we would go about defending them. At the end of the first day, I admonished people to remember the request for confidentiality and not to divulge the contents of the letter to anyone outside the room. Nevertheless, at our next session, twice as many people showed up.

By the end of that week we had prepared a written plan including residential, workplace, and organizational defense committees, a graduated set of responses beginning with initial protests of any activity that threatened one of our core values, followed by direct action including sit-ins, dismantling or destruction of equipment, and refusal to work by critical personnel if the threatened activity continued, then secondary resistance and boycotts, and finally total non-cooperation through a general strike. For the full plan, see Appendix C.

Just as we were giving final approval to the plan, another letter arrived addressed in the same manner. This time it read:

Dear Barbara,

I have good news for you

We have been following the activities of your group and other groups who received my letter of January 9 concerning the Russian occupation. After reading your draft report, I conferred with President-elect Ronald Reagan, and we decided to make one final joint attempt at negotiations with the Soviets.

As a result of these negotiations, I am happy to inform you that the armed forces of the Union of Soviet Socialist Republics will not be invading on Sunday. President Brezhnev has agreed that in view of your firm determination to resist any plunder of U.S. prerogatives, it would be cheaper for the Soviets to simply stay home on the condition that the United States agree to replace its current offensive strike capacity for the type of citizen defense system you propose, which we have agreed to do.

We are therefore inviting you to take charge of our nation's nonviolent direct action defense program, and are readying a suite of offices for you in the Pentagon. Please assemble a staff of the most creative members of your committee for this task.

May God grant us strength and wisdom.

Yours faithfully,

James Earl Carter,
President and Commander in Chief

P.S. The inaugural ball is black tie. JEC

The letter was simply signed "Jimmy".

"Wait a minute," demanded one of our workshop participants, "who wrote that letter?" "I did," I answered. "What do you mean, you did?" he persisted. "Let me see that," he said, again fingering our correspondence with a perplexed look. Though many of our participants certainly knew that these letters were simply a pedagogic device, the scenario they presented was plausible enough that most came away with a new respect for both the vulnerability of our technological defenses and the potential strength of a massive, well-prepared nonviolent response to aggression.

On a more personal level, when I was recently asked to give a keynote talk on nonviolence and self-defense for Walla Walla University's Peacemaking Weekend, in part I said,

> Nonviolence is action that respects the presence of the divine Source of existence in all others as well as in ourselves. Does this mean that if someone violently threatens our lives or those of our fellows we shouldn't defend ourselves?

> If nonviolence means respect for others and ourselves, it doesn't mean we must be passive to whatever comes our way. The use of physical force to disarm someone threatening us can be a nonviolent act as long as we use only the amount of force

necessary for our protection. If someone were to come into this room right now with an automatic weapon threatening to use it, I would try to do everything I could to disarm them out of respect for my own safety and for the safety of everyone else in the room. But I wouldn't dehumanize them by giving them a kick or otherwise injuring them once we're safe, or at least I hope I wouldn't.

How successful we are in living nonviolently may depend on how prepared we are for the types of confrontations we're likely to encounter. When we're threatened physically or verbally we're often caught off center, and our immediate response is to react disrespectfully ourselves. To not be drawn into violence by our would-be adversary can require thoughtfulness and creativity on our part, which can be cultivated through appropriate training. Just as soldiers and boxers train to effectively use violence, we can train ourselves in the effective use of nonviolence.

This kind of training has proved successful in both individual conflicts and for teams in both domestic and international conflicts. Our history has shown us occasions in which entire governments have fallen because of massive nonviolent civilian resistance to oppressive conditions, giving us important lessons in nonviolent alternatives to the destructive civil wars that increasingly engulf nations.

Mahatma Gandhi in India, Martin Luther King and the American civil rights movement in the United States, and the fall of oppressive regimes in the Philippines and in Iran under the Shah are examples of the ability of people to defend themselves and their dignity without engaging in the violent actions many people see as their only choice, though they regret the destructiveness and injustice that accompany them.

When we wish for and advocate for peace, what we are really asking for is respect for ourselves and others. For peace to be present, we have to live out that respect on a daily basis in our actions, our words, and our institutions.

International Development Projects

After returning from Denver in 1979, I began to contemplate the problem of the tremendous disparity of wealth between the United States and the countries where many people lack food and other basic resources, and how we might help alleviate that. The world is a big place and the problem of hunger and poverty is so large we're usually overwhelmed when we think about it, and as a result do little or nothing in response.

To break the problem down into manageable pieces and therefore make it more practical to respond, I began advocating a new kind of sister city project. Instead of matching wealthy communities as we have often done in the past, I proposed matching a rich community with a poor one as a way to stimulate concern and the sharing of capital as well as understanding.

In January, 1980, along with some other Walla Wallans I incorporated a non-profit organization called the Sister City Hunger Project, which we later changed to Community-to-Community Development Projects. The stated purpose of the organization was "to alleviate world hunger through establishment of direct sharing relationships between towns and cities where hunger is a continuing problem and towns and cities which have an ongoing surplus of resources."

In contacting a variety of international development organizations including Care, Oxfam, AFSC, Bread for the World, and others, I learned that two of the poorest nations in the world are in our hemisphere, Haiti and Honduras. Since I don't speak French but do know some Spanish, I decided to focus on community-to-community relationships between North Americans and Central Americans.

Explorations in Central America

After some preparatory work in Walla Walla, in November, 1980 I spent a month travelling in Central America to explore possible relationships with peasant cooperatives needing capital for development projects in Nicaragua and Honduras. I took along a "traveling minute" from several Quaker meetings introducing me to Central American Friends. I had also been asked by Friends World Committee for Consultation to look into a conflict between Honduran Friends and the Guatemalan-based Central America Yearly Meeting.

On the way down I stopped in Mexico City to talk with some Quakers involved with the Friends World Committee and the Mexican Friends Service Committee. After also visiting the Quaker community in Monteverde, Costa Rica, I arrived in Managua just in time to take part in some of the activities of a visiting American Friends Service Committee delegation. Through AFSC, I met Geraldine Macias, a former Maryknoll sister married to the head of the Popular Social Christian Party in Nicaragua who was also Vice Minister of Labor in the government.

Geraldine's husband Edgar introduced me to Guillermo Mejia, the vice-president of his party, who took me to visit a fishing community living in makeshift homes at Mateare on Lake Managua, about 25 miles north of the capital. Many were suffering from malaria, in addition to the effects of the contaminated water they obtained from sink holes, as well as under-nutrition due to lack of employment. They launched their boats at night while the water was calm, and then went individually to Managua each morning to sell their small catch usually at a poor price.

Guillermo had been working on the idea of relocating these families farther from the lake to a mosquito-free piece of land with good water. There was some land available and he was interested in the possibility of our helping with the purchase. About five manzanas (8.5 acres), enough for 50 small homes, was selling for around $1500 he told me. The new houses would be made of concrete block and would cost about $675 each with the people doing the work themselves. Together we talked with some of the fishermen who also wanted to organize a fishing cooperative, but couldn't get a loan from a bank. With a cooperative, they could market their fish together, saving time and money and getting a better price. Guillermo suggested that it might also be possible to develop another cooperative industry, such as furniture making, to provide work for the fishermen during the day. When I told them I thought we could help, they suggested the possibility of calling a meeting of the community the following week to discuss these possibilities. I told them I'd telephone Guillermo from Honduras to find out what they decided.

The next day I left by bus for Honduras, where I stayed in Tegucigalpa with Andres Carranza, a Honduran Friend working for CEDEN, one of the major Honduran development agencies. Andres was the lay leader of a tiny Friends Church in Tres de Mayo, one of the poorer barrios of the city. He and the members of his church adhered more to traditional Quaker values than most Central American Friends, and had an interest in social service for its own sake rather than as a means of evangelism. They wanted to add a second floor to their very humble church building to house a cooperative workshop to train and employ people in the barrio, which seemed to me to be a very good project, particularly in light of the constant stream of displaced farm workers coming into the capital and the resulting shortage of jobs.

After we visited an evangelical Friends Church in a more prosperous neighborhood of the city, Andres and I took a bus for Chiquimula, Guatemala, to attend the Central America Yearly Meeting of Friends. The American missionaries there from California offered me a room with two beds , and there was some awkwardness when I insisted that Andres take one of them rather than sleeping on the floor of the open air mission buildings with the rest of the Central Americans. I later learned that this was the first time an Indian had been permitted to spend the night in the missionaries' rooms.

When we returned to Tegucigalpa, I visited with the staff of CEDEN, and also with Tim Wheeler, a Quaker who was the Honduran Director of Heifer International. Tim took me to a monthly meeting of all international agency staff in Tegucigalpa, where I was asked to speak briefly about our project, and was able to talk individually with representatives from CARE, Save the Children Foundation, Meals for Millions, USAID, and Catholic Relief Services, all of whom expressed an interest in potential cooperation.

I had met previously with the director of IFC, a Honduran government institute for the promotion of cooperatives, which with the assistance of Heifer International was working with three groups of women who wanted to form a rabbit cooperative near Danli, close to the Nicaraguan border. Because of the possibility that we might be interested in cooperating in the proposal to the extent of providing funds for the purchase of six manzanas of land (10.2 acres) at a cost of about $2250, a couple of days after the meeting with the international agency staff, Tim and I with Mario from the IFC set out to visit the women's groups in an IFC Land Rover with Mario driving.

A few kilometers before Danli we came over a hill to find our lane blocked by another Land Rover parked crosswise with a truck coming at us in the other lane. We missed both vehicles by swerving into a ditch and turning over, breaking out our windshield. When we climbed out of the vehicle, both the parked Land Rover and the truck had disappeared. Although I was just shaken up and Mario was fine, Tim broke some bones in his nose and face, and after being checked out at a hospital took a bus back to the capital. I was determined to go on with our visit to the women's groups which were up in the mountains. When a replacement vehicle arrived though, we had traveled only half a mile over a rough dirt road before my neck and back were hurting enough that I couldn't go on and we had to return to Tegucigalpa, too.

Though we didn't know it at the time, we learned later along with the rest of the world that the U.S. was secretly arming and training Nicaraguan counter-revolutionaries in those mountains for an invasion of Nicaragua, as the USAID/CIA staff at our lunch meeting undoubtedly knew.

Over the years, whenever my chronic cervical pain resulting from the accident flares up, I call this "my CIA neck."

Going back to Nicaragua, I learned the fishermen's meeting had been postponed, but was able to meet with several other development agencies, though no specific projects were identified. Returning to Honduras, I visited a hilltop community near Choluteca called Cayanini, where there was interest in establishing a chicken cooperative as well as goat raising. It was agreed that the community would hold further meetings and would send me an itemized list of needs which we would consider funding with administrative help from CEDEN. At that point, feeling satisfied with the contacts we had made in both Nicaragua and Honduras, I flew home to Walla Walla.

Evolution of Community-to-Community Development Projects

Back in Walla Walla, I followed up on possible projects identified during the trip, including the potential fishing cooperative near Mateare, the chicken cooperative in Cayanini, and the cooperative workshop in Andres' church in Tres de Mayo, as well as some other contacts. I also began to sell Central American cooperative products through Pueblo to People, a private marketing effort run by Daniel and Marika Salcedo, whom I had met in Tegucigalpa. The products included Guatemalan palm leaf hats and Honduran sling chairs, which Barbara and I marketed at community fairs in Walla Walla and at northwest Quaker meetings for several years. These sales combined economic and political returns for Central American cooperatives, since a brochure was attached to each product explaining the political and economic conditions under which it was produced.

I returned to Central America in August, 1981, this time with Barbara and our kids. This time we began in Costa Rica where we visited the Quakers at Monteverde, then traveled by bus to Managua and from there to Tegucigalpa to follow up on my prior contacts and to explore new ones we had developed since the first trip.

In Managua we visited the Taller Diaconia, a workshop run by Geraldine Macias to train and provide employment for young artisans who worked with clay, wood and cloth, for which Community-to-Community made a grant and also arranged for marketing through a Walla Walla art gallery. In Tegucigalpa, we visited Daniel Salcedo, whom we had hosted in a visit to the Pacific Northwest in May, during which we introduced him to a group of regional consumer cooperatives who agreed to market cashews from the Choluteca region of Honduras.

We had received a grant proposal from the Nicaraguan Catholic development agency CONFER for assistance to a planned chicken cooperative which we had intended to fund following a field visit, but neither this group nor several others we were in touch with survived the early organizational stages, which demonstrated the great difficulties in putting together the basic elements of a cooperative project including leadership, common purpose, and a practical business plan.

On returning home, we brought a beautifully carved and painted wooden cross from Taller Diaconia as a gift to the First Congregational Church in Walla Walla as positive fruit of a creative but controversial offering the church's associate minister, Larry Gaffin, had taken at a Christmas Eve service two years before. On that occasion, as the collection plates were being passed Larry announced that the evening's offering would be going for a very special purpose, which he didn't identify, and that he hoped the congregation would give generously.

Because it was Christmas Eve, the church was full, and so were the collection plates. When they were brought back to the alter to be blessed, Larry said that instead of the money simply going to the church, he was going to pass the collection plates around again, and this second time anyone with a special need or project or who knew of someone with a special need can simply take out money for that. Or, he said, if they wished they could of course put more money in.

Since I had grown up in that church and had played trumpet solos there when I was a student, I had been invited that night to play the trumpet for some special music, and was seated in the front of the church up in the choir loft. When Larry announced the plates were being passed again for anyone's special projects, I remember thinking that this was a noble and daring idea which would utterly fail, because in this respectable and proper congregation none of the members would take a dime out of the plate for fear of what others might think.

Normally the collection plate wasn't passed to the choir, but feeling generous, the first time around I had motioned the usher to bring the plate over and had put some money in. Because of that, once the second passing of the plates was completed which were even more laden since no one had taken anything out, I also needed to be included, and Larry brought the plates over to me in the choir loft. On a sudden impulse, I said to him, "Do you really mean this? If so, I'll use the money for the international development project I've been thinking about." He grinned and said "Sure."

At that point I took a deep breath and with my pulse racing and every eye in the church on me I reached into the collection plates with both hands and took out everything I could hold. Not surprisingly, there was a collective gasp from the congregation. To add to the apparent scandal, when the church treasurer, Frank Bowen who was a friend of my mother, went up to the altar to count what was in the remaining plates at the end of the service, I told him I'd also be interested in using those funds for my project. He gamely agreed except for checks made out to the church, and only wanted to count everything before turning it over.

This was a wonderful example of the efficacy of "casting your bread upon the waters," since if I hadn't gone out of my way to put a small amount into the collection plate the first time around, the hundreds of dollars which returned wouldn't have been available for our development project.

As it turned out, Larry had not discussed this unconventional offering with the church's board of trustees or with the senior pastor, Emrys Thomas, who was out of town that day. On his return, Tommy telephoned and wanted me to return the money. Larry and I resisted, and it was finally settled that I would provide a description of the project and an accounting for the funds for publication in the church bulletin.

Until the moment of that "offering," I had been undecided as to whether to actually launch the project. I've told Larry he is really the father of Community-to-Community and all that later flowed from those first trips to Central America, since once I had publicly received those funds I couldn't turn back.

Though Community-to-Community did some useful educational work and made some small economic contributions in Central America, including the later development of rural water systems in Nicaragua by Scott Renfro and others to whom we turned the corporation over in 1991, a more far-reaching fruit of that work was the establishment of the Central America project of a new international peace and human rights organization.

Peace Brigades International

Mahatma Gandhi first spoke of a peace brigade, or *shanti sena*, in 1922, during Hindu-Muslim rioting in India. Since then, many people have become interested in the idea of nonviolent intervention in conflict by contingents of trained nonpartisans, as well as massive nonviolent action by partisans as an alternative to armed conflict, and some have taken concrete action on those ideas.

My personal interest began in the winter of 1980-81 when our Friends Committee on Alternatives to War presented a symposium and workshop at Whitman College in Walla Walla on civilian action as a national defense. After that I began to ponder whether those same principles might be applicable to peacekeeping and peacemaking at the international level.

I knew that Gandhi had envisioned the possibility of international peace brigades, and that since his death, nonpartisan brigades had functioned within India during periods of widespread Hindu-Muslim violence. With further research, I learned that the World Peace Brigade had been formed during the early Sixties, and had been active in assisting the Zambian independence movement. The WPB also organized the Delhi-Peking March in 1963 involving several well-known international activists and others at the time of the Indian-Chinese border conflict. Although I wasn't aware of it, in fact there had been a number of other precedents for nonviolent action at the international level, as detailed by Yeshua Moser-Puangsuwan and Thomas Weber in their excellent book, "Nonviolent Intervention Across Borders" (University of Hawaii Press, 2000).

In July, 1981, during an interest group organized by FWCC (Friends World Committee for Consultation) at North Pacific Yearly Meeting, I introduced the vision of a nonviolent army interposing itself between warring factions to encourage a ceasefire and permit peaceable consideration of issues in conflict. Following that session, I had the personal conviction that such a nonviolent army should exist, and that Quakers were a worldwide body of peacemakers who had the capacity to initiate it. To pursue that concern, I was appointed a representative to the Friends World Triennial to be held in Kenya in August, 1982.

In a conversation with George Lakey, a leader of the Movement for a New Society in Philadelphia, he suggested I contact Charles Walker, a Quaker veteran of the World Peace Brigade which had become inactive when the U.S. civil rights movement drained away much of its resources. Charlie, who also lived in the Philadelphia area, had just completed a book on this subject called "A World Peace Guard," and was excited to hear from me. He said the idea was starting to occur again to widely separated people, and wanted to know where and how I thought it might actually be applied. My response was that such a presence was needed in Central America, where there was tremendous repression and several guerrilla wars underway. Charlie also mentioned a Consultation on an International Peace Brigade which was being planned for the end of August on Grindstone Island in Canada.

Some New York Friends, led by Elizabeth Cattell, Eugene Bronstein, and Lee Stern, had also put together a group called the Ad Hoc Committee for a World Peace Army, which was making plans for an East-West march across Europe.

In August, 1981 our family left for Central America with a "traveling minute" from the Walla Walla Friends meeting to continue work I had begun on community-to-community development projects as well as these issues, which read:

> To all Friends Whom it May Concern:
>
> We commend to you our members, Daniel and Barbara Clark, and their children, Rebecca and Jeremy, as they visit among you to explore our concerns for the development of community to community relations between North Americans and Central Americans, and for the possibilities of establishing a nonviolent international peace force able to contribute to the peaceable resolution of disputes between warring nations and peoples.

On the way to Central America we visited Philadelphia where we met with Charlie and another Quaker veteran of the World Peace Brigade, George Willoughby. George was doubtful the Grindstone consultation would be held because of financial and other problems, and wouldn't be attending himself. Charlie was more positive about it, and invited me to participate. In New York we also visited Friends involved in the World Peace Army.

In Costa Rica, we discussed the peace brigade concept and the coming Triennial and Grindstone Consultation with Friends at Monteverde, who expressed support. In Honduras, we saw news reports of the aerial bombing of a Guatemalan village temporarily occupied by guerrillas, and I remember wondering why the International Red Cross didn't itself move into the village to provide a protective presence for civilians, which I saw as a potential role for a peace brigade.

At the end of our Central American travels in late August I telephoned Charlie, who told me the Grindstone Consultation would be held and urged me to attend.

Grindstone Island

The Consultation on an International Peace Brigade held at Grindstone Island in Ontario was organized by Ray McGee of the California-based Peaceworkers organization, Narayan Desai of the Sarva Seva Sangh and Radhakrishna of the Gandhi Peace Foundation in India, Piet Dijkstra with the Foundation for the Extension of Nonviolent Action in the Netherlands, and Charles

Walker of Pennsylvania. It was envisioned as a conference limited to around 20 people who were already committed to the concept of a peace brigade, and was to address the practical issues of bringing such a brigade into being.

Primarily because the expected financing had not come through, many of those invited were not able to attend. Regrets were received from Hildegard Goss-Mayr of Austria, Sulak Sivaraksa of Thailand, Brig. Gen. Michael Harbottle of the UK, Stanley Samartha of Switzerland, Paul Hare from South Africa, and Michael Nagler, Lynn Shivers, Carl Kline, and George Willoughby of the USA, as well as Radhakrishna and Piet Dijkstra. Additional invitations had been sent to people in Japan, Australia, and Sri Lanka.

The eleven participants in the consultation were: Charles Walker, Ray McGee, Narayan Desai, Jaime de J. Diaz a Catholic priest with CODECAL (Corporation for Cultural and Social Development) in Colombia and president of the World Council for Curriculum and Instruction, Murray Thomson of Project Ploughshares in Canada, Hans Sinn, a Canadian nonviolence trainer and social defense advocate, Henry Wiseman, a Canadian serving as director of Peacekeeping Programs at the International Peace Academy in New York, Gene Keyes, a Canadian scholar and writer, Mark Shepard, a U.S. peace journalist, Lee Stern, Peace Secretary of New York Yearly Meeting of Friends, and myself. By religious background, we were six Quakers, a Hindu, a Catholic priest, a Jew, a Protestant minister, and a universalist.

On the bus down from Ottawa, Henry Wiseman made clear to me that his status at the conference was only as an observer, that his director, General Indarjit Rikhye, had asked him to attend, and that he didn't expect much to come of it.

I knew Grindstone only by reputation as a conference center occupying a small island. It had been the site of an experiment in civilian-based defense written up by Theodor Olson and Gordon Christiansen in a book called "Thirty-One Hours: The Grindstone Experiment" (Canadian Friends Service Committee, 1966), in which George Willoughby participated as a protestor occupying the island and Hans Sinn, a member of the Grindstone Cooperative, as an invading soldier.

The consultation began on the evening of Monday, August 31 with introductions of the participants. Each session was chaired by a different person, and began with someone else giving an inspirational reading. The first session, chaired by Hans Sinn, began with a reading from Gandhi by Ray Magee and introductions. On Tuesday morning, with Jaime Diaz chairing, Charlie read from Martin Luther King and the session was devoted to statements of the concerns and approach of each participant. My own statement emphasized a sense of urgency, given the proliferation of mass weaponry and violent conflicts in the world, the need for a third party not hamstrung by UN vetoes, and one which could act as a partisan for a nonviolent means of struggle rather than as an advocate for specific ends. Narayan, whose father had been Gandhi's personal secretary, also stated that the situation was urgent, that the peace movement was moving too slowly, and that human survival was at stake.

At the end of the morning, I was asked to give the reading for the next session, which was to begin just after lunch. Gandhi and King had already been given and are difficult to follow. At a loss as to what to offer, a few minutes before the next session was to begin I went into the conference center library and browsed the shelves in vain. Finally I closed my eyes, blindly put my hand out and opened a book to a passage by Tolstoy that was both appropriate and inspiring. Just when we were all feeling our inadequacy for such a demanding task, Tolstoy admonished us that while many would say that we had no business launching a major enterprise for peace and justice in view of the poverty of our resources and the formidable nature of the challenge, we had no choice, that destiny demanded it.

After this reading and a report by the initiators, our afternoon session was devoted to proposals for the deployment of brigades, and a discussion of organizational alternatives. These included an ad hoc committee for each mobilization, an organization oriented toward the United Nations, or an ongoing independent organization. The deployment discussion led off with my concern for a peace brigade in Central America, particularly in Guatemala where the government had been wiping out remote villages and neighboring Mexico was rebuffing refugees. Others noted the need for teams in southern Lebanon, the planned east-west peace army march in Europe, and the situation in Northern Ireland. Later on, the conflicts between India and Pakistan, Colombia and Venezuela, Belize and Guatemala, and Ecuador and Peru were mentioned.

On Wednesday morning, Charlie reviewed the prior day's sessions and queried the group about the mission, characteristics, size, leadership style, discipline, attitude towards partisanship, and appropriate roles of the organization we were contemplating. Henry Wiseman then raised a question that was on all of our minds. Given the fact that none of us were official representatives of our organizations, did we really believe we had the authority and capacity to launch such an organization? Henry, to our surprise, proceeded to answer his question strongly in the affirmative. Yes, said the skeptic now converted, we were competent to act as a founding group for an international peace brigade, and we should do so. Everyone else agreed with him, and suddenly we had crossed the threshold.

The rest of the day featured talks by Narayan Desai regarding the Shanti Sena in India, by retired General E.L.M. Burns on his experience as the first commander of the U.N. Emergency Force in the Sinai, and by Charlie Walker on the problems and assets of international nonviolent action. After hearing the report of a committee appointed to recommend an organizational form, we decided to establish an independent, ongoing organization with broad scope.

Next came the naming process. We were all asked to submit proposed names which we thought would sit well with governments, foundations and the general public, and each was then read out and discussed. During a coffee break "Peace Brigades International" was first voiced by Narayan, then seized on by Charlie, and on reconvening accepted by everyone.

To govern the organization, an international council was agreed to on which 15 additional people would be invited to serve together with the participants as founding members. We also established a directorate consisting of Narayan Desai, Jaime Diaz, and Murray Thomson, with Charles Walker, ex officio, and an administrative team composed of Charles Walker, coordinator, Raymond Magee, treasurer, and Dan Clark as secretary, as well as several standing committees.

On the final day at Grindstone, we adopted the Founding Declaration of Peace Brigades International, which read,

> We have decided to establish an organization which will form and support international peace brigades. We find this historically and morally imperative.
>
> Peace brigades, fashioned to respond to specific needs and appeals, will undertake nonpartisan missions which may include peacemaking initiatives, peacekeeping under a discipline of nonviolence, and humanitarian service. We also intend to offer and provide services to similar efforts planned and carried out by other groups.
>
> We appeal in particular to:
> --peoples of diverse cultures, religions and social systems ready to contribute in new ways to the nonviolent resolution of conflict;
> --all those who seek to fulfill the high principles and purposes expressed in the Charter of the United Nations, and
> --all who work to preserve human life with dignity, to promote human rights, social justice and self-determination, and to create the conditions of peace.
>
> We call upon individuals and groups to enlist their services in the work of local, regional and international peace brigades. We are forming an organization with the capability to mobilize and provide trained units of volunteers. These units may be assigned to areas of high tension to avert violent outbreaks. If hostile clashes occur, a brigade may establish and monitor a cease-fire, offer mediatory services, or carry on works of reconstruction and reconciliation.
>
> Those who undertake these tasks will face risks and hardships. Others can provide support and show solidarity in a multitude of ways.
>
> We are building on a rich and extensive heritage of nonviolent action, which no longer can be ignored. This heritage tells us that peace is more than the absence of war.
>
> We are convinced that this commitment of mind, heart and dedicated will can make a significant difference in human affairs. Let us all join in the march from falsehood to truth, from darkness to light, from death to life.

First Steps

Of the three members of the administrative team, Ray Magee had reluctantly agreed to serve "pro tem" as he put it, since his primary focus was on the organization Peaceworkers, whose goal was to get the UN to offer or sponsor unarmed peacekeeping as a part of its own services.

Charles Walker, though his heart and soul were in peace brigades, worked for the Friends Suburban Project, a local organization offering community mediation and conflict resolution training, which didn't leave much time for PBI administrative work. As a result, we established the secretariat of PBI in the office at my Walla Walla home.

One of our first tasks was to begin filling out the International Council to increase our resources and legitimacy. At Grindstone we had approved a list of 18 nominees from which the administrative team was to attempt to fill the 15 additional seats. Some of these were long-time workers in the field whom Charlie knew and agreed to invite. Another was folksinger Joan Baez, whom Narayan intended to visit along with labor organizer Cesar Chavez; unfortunately he was unable to do this before returning to India.

I agreed to contact another well-known nominee, Adolfo Perez Esquivel of Argentina, the winner of the 1980 Nobel Peace Prize. This took some doing, but after several months and considerable difficulty, Adolfo ultimately agreed to join the Council, influenced in part by the recommendation of Hildegard Goss-Mayr of the International Fellowship of Reconciliation (IFOR). Hildegard had worked in Latin America with Adolfo's organization Servicio, Paz & Justicia (SERPAJ), and also agreed to serve. After a variety of communications over several months from me and other PBI Council members, Joan Baez finally accepted our invitation. Other than the addition of former U.S. Attorney General Ramsey Clark whom I met in New York the following year and who agreed to be a member of our Central America Committee, that was the extent of our celebrity recruitment. While celebrities are an important resource in the development of an organization, the real work is usually carried on by others.

Another task we all shared was to get word out about the formation of PBI by publishing articles, writing letters, and holding talks with potentially interested organizations. I agreed to make contact with Friends bodies, and in early November, 1981, I attended the annual meetings of Friends Committee on National Legislation (FCNL), Friends Coordinating Committee for Peace (FCCP), both in Washington, D.C., and the Section of the Americas meeting of Friends World Committee for Consultation (FWCC) in Indiana. I was able to obtain an official statement of support for peace brigades from each of them, as well as an agreement by FCCP to sponsor and receive charitable contributions for PBI until we received our own tax-exempt status. At the FWCC meeting I also received an invitation from Jorge Hernandez of the Mexico City Friends Meeting to talk about PBI at the General Reunion of Mexican Friends scheduled for January in Mexico City.

Besides offering possibilities for international work, a general letter we sent out announcing the formation of PBI encouraged local groups to establish community peacekeeping teams to which we would offer training assistance. In Walla Walla, our Friends Committee on Alternatives to War sponsored the organizational meeting of a Walla Walla Peace Brigade and began planning a training session on nonviolent tactics and third-party intervention skills applicable to circumstances ranging all the way from interpersonal and local community conflicts to international brigades. Lee Stern was also working to establish a local brigade in New York City to respond to Ku Klux Klan activities and other violence there through the Alternatives to Violence Project and Charlie Walker was in the process of developing a brigade in the Philadelphia area.

Central America Project Explorations

My own focus for international work continued to be on Central America. While visiting Washington, D.C. in November, 1981, I attended a conference put on by NISGUA, the National Network in Solidarity with the People of Guatemala, where I briefly met Julio Quan, a Guatemalan exile working with Friends World College. A speaker at the conference was Vinicio Cerezo, leader of the Guatemalan Christian Democratic Party. Though years later he would be elected President of Guatemala, at the time he was engaged in the very dangerous act of simply running as an opposition candidate critical of the government. I mentioned to someone at the conference that an important function of a Guatemalan peace brigade, if there had been one at that point, would be to accompany Cerezo and other threatened candidates during the campaign in order to deter attacks against them.

Another hot spot in Central America was the conflicted border between Nicaragua and Honduras, where US-sponsored counterrevolutionaries were making raids into Nicaragua, provoking counterattacks by Nicaragua and leading to Honduran claims of invasion. There were also problems on Honduras' western border where Salvadoran refugees fleeing the guerrilla war in El Salvador were being harassed by the Honduran army and pursued and sometimes forcibly repatriated by the Salvadoran army. On the same visit to Washington, D.C. I discussed the Nicaraguan/Honduran border conflict at the headquarters of the Organization of American States (OAS) with Undersecretary General Val McComie, who in response to my question suggested that the OAS might be able to provide sponsorship for PBI border teams with the consent of the governments involved.

Since Charlie didn't think we would have enough resources to field our own brigade in the near future, I proposed that we send a document I had drafted to Quaker organizations entitled, "Some Possibilities for Unarmed Peacekeeping and Peacemaking in Central America" to which I attached the endorsements we had received from Quaker organizations in November and a letter inviting a response. The paper called for an unarmed international brigade to serve in Honduras and the border areas of Nicaragua to lessen tensions, protect refugee camps, serve as an escort for threatened persons, and provide a monitoring presence at critical borders, among other possibilities. Upon approval by the PBI administrative team and favorable response from the directorate and Council members, I sent the paper and letter to various Friends bodies, including Friends World College, whose president responded that FWC was very interested, and that I should contact Julio Quan of the college.

Talking by phone with Julio, who was then living and teaching in Costa Rica as the director of the Latin American Center of Friends World College, we arranged to meet in January in Mexico City during the General Reunion of Mexican Friends. When we met there, he agreed to be the Central American member of a three-person team that would travel through Nicaragua and Honduras in May exploring possible peace brigade activities. PBI Council member Jaime Diaz of Bogota, Colombia became the South American member, and I served as the North American member.

In preparation, Jaime visited Costa Rica and Nicaragua for a few days in March. In Costa Rica he met Julio and made preliminary contacts with the Central America Office of the United Nations High Commissioner for Refugees (UNHCR), the Interamerican Institute for Human Rights, and the advisor to the President of Costa Rica for the planned U.N. University of Peace. In Nicaragua he met with the rectors of the National University and the Catholic University, as well as the National Assembly of the Clergy.

Costa Rica

The team began its trip on May 14, 1982 in San Jose, Costa Rica, with a meeting with officials of UNHCR to discuss the security needs of Salvadoran refugees in Honduras. Philip Sargisson, the head of UNHCR's Central America office, explained their plan to establish UN reception centers for refugees along the Honduran border with El Salvador to provide an international presence as security for new refugees entering Honduras, as well as for the segment of the local Honduran population that had been assisting refugees and was now threatened. Sargisson said they wanted to place one UN professional protection officer in each of the three reception centers planned for La Virtud, Guarita, and Colomoncagua, and asked if PBI could provide three volunteers to serve with each protection officer for a term of three to six months. We said we would consider it, and it was agreed we would visit the UNHCR office in Tegucigalpa, Honduras, as well as the border areas where the centers were to be established.

We also wanted to explore the possibility of establishing training facilities and a secure base of operations in Costa Rica, from which operations could be carried on throughout the region. Executive Director Hernan Montealegre of the Interamerican Institute for Human Rights, a nongovernmental body established jointly by the Interamerican Court for Human Rights of the OAS and the government of Costa Rica, expressed serious interest in our mission and in the possibility of the Institute sponsoring a training program for peacekeepers once concrete projects were identified. The Secretary-General of the Catholic Bishops Conference of Costa Rica also expressed strong interest and requested a concrete proposal for assistance upon the completion of our explorations.

In 1981, when my family and I had visited the Quaker community at Monteverde, an idyllic hamlet adjacent to a cloud forest midway between San Jose and the Nicaraguan border, the Friends there had said they would be interested in hosting a training center for future peace teams, and the team explored that possibility further during our visit there on the way to Managua.

Nicaragua

One of the most serious areas of international tension in Central America at that time was the Nicaraguan-Honduran border. The attacks into Nicaragua by the Somocistas (ex-National Guardsmen under former President Anastasio Somoza) were tolerated by the Honduran government and actively supported by the U.S. and possibly other governments who feared that the Nicaraguans were supplying the Salvadoran guerillas, and because of general hostility to the Sandinista revolution. The situation was made more complex near the Atlantic coast by the presence of Miskito Indian refugees from Nicaragua, a number of whom had become affiliated with the Somocistas after having fled a Nicaraguan relocation program to clear the border area of civilians in order to better secure the area against incursions.

More recently a problem had also developed on Nicaragua's southern border with Costa Rica, where both Somocistas and counter-revolutionary followers of leftist Eden Pastora had launched attacks from Costa Rica into Nicaragua, apparently prompting incidents of retaliatory border crossings by the Sandinistas. The team was interested in possible service of observer units on both borders with the capacity to rapidly investigate any further incursions and provide objective reporting to both countries as well as to international organizations and other interested parties.

In Managua, we talked by phone with Foreign Minister Miguel D'Escoto and met with senior Nicaraguan diplomat Leonte Herdocia, as well as others at the foreign ministry. Serious interest was expressed by the Nicaraguan government in possible service by PBI along the Honduran border, as well as in the possibilities of our assisting in the resolution of the Miskito Indian problem, in which both the Sandinistas and UNHCR saw negotiated repatriation as the best solution.

At the time of our meeting with the Nicaraguan Foreign Ministry on May 18, plans were being discussed for a joint meeting concerning these issues to be held two days later between the Honduran and Nicaraguan military commands. The Nicaraguans encouraged us to discuss our ideas with Honduran Foreign Minister Edgardo Paz Barnica who had recently presented a general peace plan for the region, including a proposal for an international presence at borders and other strategic points.

Other visits by our team in Nicaragua involved briefings on the Miskito problem by church officials, and a general discussion with the Chancellor of the National University who offered encouragement.

Honduras

Unfortunately Julio wasn't able to travel with us to Honduras due to an illness in his family. Jaime and I arrived in Tegucigalpa on May 19, where we met with Charles Bazoche at UNHCR who had been briefed about our visit by Philip Sargisson. Colomancagua was the only remaining refugee camp on the Salvadoran border at that time and was reachable only by light plane. Bazoche told us we would be flown there the next morning by the only pilot capable of landing at the treacherous strip there. The only possible conflict was our need to meet with the Honduran Foreign Minister as requested by the Nicaraguans.

On hearing of our desire to visit with the Honduran foreign minister, Bazoche, a somewhat disdainful Frenchman, flatly told us we would never get an audience with Paz Barnica due to our private status and because of the fact that when I called the foreign minister's office for an appointment I didn't refer to him as "Excellency." He expressed surprise when Paz Barnica's office promptly returned my call to tell us we could see him the next morning at 10:30, which was the same time as our planned flight to Colomoncagua. Unfortunately, we made the mistake of postponing the meeting with the foreign minister to take advantage of the flight, which as we prepared for takeoff was cancelled when the pilot discovered the plane had a cracked cylinder.

45

Our next meeting was with Colonel Turcios, coordinator of the Honduran Refugee Commission, which was composed of the Ministers of Defense, Foreign Affairs, Interior, Labor, and Health, and had to approve any agency working with refugees. Before meeting with Turcios we had been told by Noemi de Espinoza, president of the Committee for Development and Emergencies (CODE) and Francisco Meraz, director of the Catholic agency CARITAS-Honduras, that ever since the Salvadoran refugee camps had been moved away from the border to Mesa Grande the plan to establish refugee reception centers in their place had been repeatedly discussed but never approved by the Honduran government.

Turcios assured us that the reception centers were an agreed condition of the removal of the camps, and that reception center staff would have free access to the border area in order to protect refugees. He said the Refugee Commission would be meeting the following week to adopt written regulations for the centers, and that he would present PBI's desire to work with the refugees to the Commission. He also agreed to try to arrange an interview for us with Col. Bueso, the number two man in the Honduran military, who would be leading the Honduran delegation to the planned military talks with Nicaragua.

On May 21 we received a briefing from several UNHCR protection officers working in the border area and learned that the refugees were confined to the Colomoncagua camp at 4 p.m. each day and that all international personnel including doctors and staff were required to leave the camp by 5 pm. This resulted in the deaths of several babies due to lack of medical care during the night.

When we went to the Foreign Ministry for our rescheduled meeting with Paz Barnica we found he had been called to the President's office to discuss the Nicaraguan-Honduran meeting of the previous day out of which a joint commission had been established for further discussions of a proposal for joint border patrols by army units of the two countries. In his place Paz Barnica had arranged for us to see the Vice-Minister who received us cordially and assured us that he would give the Minister a full report of our conversation, that the Minister would discuss it with the President, and he would then respond to it. He also suggested we send a written statement concerning our proposals.

In our discussion we emphasized our interest in placing teams on the Nicaraguan-Honduran border as a means of implementing Point Three of Paz Barnica's proposal for the "Internationalization of Peace" which called for international supervision and vigilance at critical borders and pledged Honduras' readiness "to open its territory without reserve to whatever type of international supervision and vigilance would be in harmony with the basic proposition of finding and strengthening peace." Vice-Minister Rivas, though polite, was unresponsive.

That evening we left Tegucigalpa for San Marcos in southwestern Honduras via the Carribbean port city of San Pedro Sula with a car and driver provided by the UN. In San Marcos where a UNHCR office was located we met Padraig Czajowski, the UN protection officer for the Virtud and Guarita area, as well as other UN staff.

Padraig drove us to the new refugee camp at Mesa Grande, where we met with met two leaders who along with other refugees from the Colomancagua camp had written a letter to UNHCR in Geneva protesting their conditions and requesting transfer either to Mexico, Nicaragua, or other countries where Salvadoran refugees had previously been received. They told us of threats to their security from the Honduran army, lack of free movement of refugees between the two sections of the Mesa Grande camp, prohibitions on the sale of refugee products on the Honduran market, and problems with the availability of foodstuffs and medical care. Other refugees we spoke with had been in the camps for more than two years and were facing another move because of the planned reduction of the refugee population at Mesa Grande from 8000 to around 2500.

After returning to San Marcos, we began a grueling three-hour drive over a rocky track to the mountain town of La Virtud from which a refugee camp had been recently removed. Although the exact border was in dispute, Salvadoran troops were occupying a ridge overlooking the town and the UN house was in the main plaza across from a Honduran military post where soldiers were able to observe everyone coming and going. The town's electrical generator had ceased operation six years before, and there was no electricity or running water. There were no telephones in the town, though there was telegraph service, and the UN had a shortwave radio in the house.

Spending the night in the UN house, we heard repeated gunfire in the distance and were told that the night before there had been gunfire immediately outside the house. In our conversations with the local people we found considerable hostility toward refugees as economic competitors and as subversives in a town predominantly aligned with the military party in Honduras. The hostility extended to anyone who helped refugees, so some local people who did so needed protection from their own army. On one occasion a group of drunken Honduran soldiers apparently tried to break down the door of the UN house.

Although Padraig informed us it was all right to take photos of the town square to send to PBI, when we did we were approached by three Honduran soldiers from the garrison who motioned with their guns that we were to go with them to their barracks. As we crossed the plaza I saw a woman who did cleaning for Padraig and told her to let him know what was happening, which gave us some expectation that help would be on the way. Even so, after the iron doors of the barracks clanged shut behind us and we were out of sight of the world and at the mercy of the soldiers surrounding us, I had a taste of what it must be like for many Central Americans and for people around the world who are seized, often clandestinely, and mistreated with impunity.

In our case Padraig arrived within a few minutes to help explain the reason for our visit and that our intention was not to photograph the military post, only the general plaza. The officer in charge seemed satisfied with this explanation and ordered us released without taking our film or our names.

After La Virtud, we drove one and a half hours to Guarita where another major border camp had been removed and a refugee reception center was planned. Three hours from the border by horseback, Guarita had electricity and running water, the local people were friendlier toward refugees, and even the atmosphere around the army barracks was more relaxed.

The problem was how to patrol and to create an international presence in the large area between the town and the border in order to assure new refugees protection from both the Salvadoran and Honduran armies. With no continuing international presence, no new refugees had entered the area in the three months since the removal of the camp to Mesa Grande. By contrast, at La Virtud several families had reached the UN protection staff since the removal of the camp there, often as the result of a child coming to the UN house and taking the officer on a long journey through the brush to where the refugees were hiding. In Guarita we also saw opportunities to do constructive work in cooperation with several development agencies which could provide an increased measure of protection for local Hondurans.

After Guarita we returned to San Marcos and from there to Tegucigalpa where we were scheduled to fly the next day to Mocorron, the primary Miskito Indian refugee camp in Honduras. Because of trouble with the UN car, we arrived in Tegucigalpa too late for the scheduled plane which meant that we also missed the tropical storm Aleta that hit the Carribbean coast of Honduras and Nicaragua that day leaving 65,000 homeless.

After communicating with the PBI administrative team and directorate about these opportunities and receiving their approval to proceed, we held a final meeting with UNHCR officials in Tegucigalpa at which we proposed that PBI provide two volunteers to serve initially in Guarita, two in LaVirtud, and an additional two to be provided at the time the Colomoncagua reception center was established. PBI volunteers would serve a minimum of three months and would be provided credentials signed jointly by the UN and the Honduran government. The UN was to be responsible for their housing and board as well as their transportation and equipment.

Since we were scheduled to leave Honduras the next day for a brief visit to El Salvador after which we would be meeting with UN staff again in Costa Rica, we asked that a response to our proposal be communicated to the UNHCR office in Costa Rica later in the week.

Before leaving for El Salvador, we met in Tegucigalpa with representatives of several Honduran peace churches who were putting forth a proposal for formal recognition of conscientious objector status under the Honduran conscription law. In this meeting which included my friend Andres Carranza of the Honduran Friends Church we explored ways Honduran pacifists could broaden their base of support by reaching out to Catholic and other churches with a growing peace testimony, as well as the possibility of their contributing to the diffusion of Honduran-Nicaraguan border tensions through actions similar to the Tica-Nica Association that was working to improve relations between Costa Rica and Nicaragua.

El Salvador

On May 25, we flew to San Salvador to learn more about refugee and other problems within El Salvador itself. In previous meetings we had heard about increasing attacks on internal refugee camps as well as attacks on cooperatives occupying land under the new agrarian reform law. There were at that time 300,000 displaced persons within El Salvador, approximately 160,000 of them in internal camps. In Nicaragua where refugees were free to work and live where they pleased, we understood the government might be willing to accept additional Salvadorans.

Our first visit was to the 1400 refugees crowded into the grounds of San Jose de Montana Seminary, showing the virtual imprisonment of thousands of Salvadoran families within their own country. We learned of threats to refugees in the camp and the murder of a priest who had visited the camp twice, and were told that visits such as ours gave the residents a greater sense of security since it is more difficult for the government to harass them when they receive international attention.

We then met with Archbishop Rivera y Damas, successor to the martyred Archbishop Oscar Romero who had taken a strong stand in favor of the poor and against atrocities committed by the army. We discussed with the Archbishop the situation of Salvadoran refugees in Honduras and within El Salvador, as well as possibilities of their transfer to Nicaragua. He told us about the historical struggle within El Salvador and his new call for negotiations, assured us he would be visiting the Honduran refugee camps in the coming weeks, and wanted to consider further the possibility of PBI involvement.

Our final visit in El Salvador was with the Rector of the Catholic University (the UCA), Ignacio Ellacurea who was later to be assassinated by the armed forces, along with several of his Jesuit colleagues. We were impressed by the University's courageous publication of a number of periodicals analyzing the situation within El Salvador and denouncing ongoing injustice and terror. He described to us the assassination, arrest, and exile of students and professors, as well as the military occupation of the campus on several occasions. "But we publish," he told us, "and will continue to do so." After suggesting that he consider PBI as a potential source for teams of international observers should the viability of the university as a forum for free speech continue to be threatened, we took a flight back to Costa Rica.

Final Meetings

While we had been in Honduras, the Costa Rican government had issued a public call for international supervision of the Costa Rican-Nicaraguan border by the OAS. On our return Alvar Antion, Costa Rica's senior diplomat and its Director-General of Foreign Relations, explained to us that Costa Rica desired unarmed international observers operating on the Costa Rican side of the border in order to convince the Sandinistas that Costa Rica was no longer being used as a base for counter-revolutionary activities, and to halt the current series of border crossings by the Nicaraguans.

He told us houses were being burned and Costa Rican campesinos driven out by the Nicaraguans who wanted to create a secure zone within four to five kilometers of the border. Several teams would be required in Land Rovers together with one or two light planes and communications equipment in order to enable the teams to immediately cable international authorities and interested governments concerning any border violations.

We explained to him our prior contact with the OAS Undersecretary General, and his suggestion that the OAS might be willing to sponsor PBI border teams with the consent of the governments involved. Antion told us that Nicaraguan junta coordinator Daniel Ortega had spoken out against the Costa Rican proposal, though Costa Rica had not yet presented a formal petition to the OAS.

He suggested that we contact the OAS again, while making clear to us that the Costa Rican government was making no commitment, and that these were strictly "preliminary discussions." We told him we would continue our contacts with his counterpart, Leonte Herdocia of the Nicaraguan Foreign Ministry to see if Nicaragua would consent to a PBI observer team with or without OAS sponsorship.

As to equipment needs, Antion indicated that OAS member countries have supplied equipment in the past for such actions, but that Costa Rica had some equipment which might be utilized by the teams. While acknowledging that formal OAS security mechanisms are often cumbersome and time-consuming, he responded positively to our suggestion that the Human Rights Commission of the OAS might be an appropriate agency to sponsor such teams. He further told us, "We agree that an unarmed presence is the strongest weapon," and stressed the important impact Quakers and other pacifists had on Costa Rican thought around the turn of the century, strongly affecting the subsequent course of Costa Rican defense policies.

In our final conference at UNHCR, with deputy chief Belela Herrera since Philip Sargisson was out of the country, we reviewed our trip and the proposal we had made to the UN in Tegucigalpa. We also discussed the situation of the Salvadoran refugees in Honduras and El Salvador, and inquired into the possibilities for their transfer to Nicaragua, should Nicaragua be willing to accept additional Salvadorans.

Although she encouraged any assistance we might give to the migration of refugees still within El Salvador, she advised against any effort to assist the transfer of refugees from Honduras because of a variety of political considerations, as well as the inability of Nicaragua to accept all who might wish to come. At the same time, she reiterated the desire of the UN that the Miskitos be repatriated to Nicaragua. Having received no word from Tegucigalpa on the acceptance of our proposal for the reception centers, she said she would try to give us a response by the next day, which was to be our last in Central America at that time.

Before leaving San Jose we had further conversations with the Intergovernmental Committee for Migration (CIM), the Latin American Biblical Seminary, the United Nations University for Peace, the Interamerican Institute for Human Rights, and the Quakers from Monteverde. When our follow-up call to Leonte Herdocia of the Nicaraguan Foreign Ministry found him out of the country, Julio Quan agreed to contact him on his return to brief him on our meeting with the Honduran Foreign Ministry, to gauge Nicaragua's willingness to receive further Salvadoran refugees, and to discuss whether Nicaragua would agree to a PBI observer team on the Nicaraguan-Costa Rican border.

As we were leaving Costa Rica on May 27, Julio received a call from Belela Herrera telling us that the UNHCR had formally approved PBI's offer of volunteers for the reception center protection teams in Honduras, and that we should coordinate the provision of our volunteers through the Honduran relief and development agency CODE.

The New York Connection

In June, 1982 the world seemed to descend on New York City for the United Nations Second Special Session on Disarmament, prompting a series of PBI meetings there on a variety of issues.

Honduras

On June 17, Ray Magee and I met with Noemi de Espinoza of CODE, who informed us that the Honduran Refugee Commission had not yet approved written regulations for the reception centers or CODE's coordination of the centers. She also informed us that as a result of a meeting in Geneva of the World Council of Churches, the Canadian Council of Churches, and the National Council of Churches of the USA, Church World Service had hired Tim Wheeler, a New York Quaker and representative of Heifer International I had previously worked with, to coordinate all volunteers in Honduras. She suggested we coordinate our proposals with Tim, and also told us that the Councils of Churches planned to send their own volunteers to the refugee camps.

In talking with Tim who was also visiting New York at that time, we proposed that PBI in cooperation with Church World Service take responsibility for the provision of volunteers at Guarita and La Virtud where there were no longer refugee camps, while the Council of Churches continued to provide volunteers at the camps themselves, and that PBI provide a training program for all volunteers in the region. Tim indicated an interest in this proposal and suggested we talk with Oscar Bolioli and Antonio Ramos of the Latin American Office of the National Council of Churches in New York, who were to coordinate the volunteer program.

The next day Charlie Walker, Ray, and I met with Bolioli and Ramos. Before making our arrangements with the UN we had been told that the Councils of Churches were suspending their own provision of volunteers to the camps; we were now told that they had a continuing volunteer agreement with the UN, and they were surprised that the UN had committed itself to accepting PBI volunteers at the reception centers. They said that before agreeing to cooperate with PBI they would have to consult further with the Canadian and World Councils of Churches, and with UNHCR in Honduras.

In order to clarify our status with the UN, Julio Quan again contacted Philip Sargisson at UNHCR in Costa Rica, and on June 22 told us by telephone of Sargisson's advice that we could proceed to place volunteers directly under the UN without further action of the Refugee Commission, and that we should cable the characteristics of our proposed volunteers to him within 24 hours as he would be in Honduras for that long and could seek their immediate approval.

PBI had already been busy recruiting potential volunteers. In Canada, Hans Sinn had sent out a mailing funded by Murray Thomson's Operation Ploughshares to over 1000 people, including a variety of Canadian organizations and peace churches, asking for volunteers and money. To further assist in the effort, Hans had been working on the formation of PBI-Canada, which

51

became PBI's first country group. After confirming our two most qualified volunteers, a medical social worker and a registered nurse with experience in Central and South America and direct service with Cuban and Vietnamese refugees in the US, we sent a telex to Sargisson proposing their arrival at UNHCR in Tegucigalpa on July 12 for service at Guarita.

Since we had received no reply, on June 25 Murray Thomson arranged a meeting with his friend George Gordon-Lennox of UNHCR in New York who telephoned Sargisson in Costa Rica. Sargisson said he had received the telex, that the information on the volunteers was insufficient, and that UNHCR-New York should telex their entire resumes to Costa Rica. When pressed, Sargisson admitted that he was having difficulty getting approval of UNHCR-Honduras, and that even if the volunteers were qualified, as they clearly were, he would have to discuss them with other agencies serving in the region and would have a reply for us the next week.

On June 30 Julio tried to reach Sargisson again, found that he had left for a month's vacation, and was informed by his deputy Belela Herrera that Sargisson had found that the volunteers were not sufficiently experienced, and that he suggested we attempt to work through another agency.

These events demonstrated to us the difficulty of doing refugee work in the fractious border regions of Honduras where battles between agencies, while more civilized, were nearly as fierce as those between armies. Sadly, while this was taking place Salvadoran soldiers massacred another group of refugees in the La Virtud region.

Nicaraguan Border Disputes

Ray Magee and I also met in New York with Gen. Indar Rikhye, President of the International Peace Academy, who expressed strong interest in the potential contribution to be made by PBI on Nicaragua's borders, as well as the possibility of participation by the Peace Academy. He suggested he make inquiries of the countries involved on our behalf, and we agreed.

I later met in Washington, D.C. with Edmundo Vargas Carreno, Executive Director of the OAS Human Rights Commission, who emphasized the important role PBI might play in the Honduran-Nicaraguan border problems, while expressing pessimism regarding the possibilities along the Nicaraguan-Costa Rican border. He also expressed grave doubts about the formal involvement of the Human Rights Commission with a non-governmental organization of any kind or in border matters in general, as did OAS Undersecretary General Valerie McComie in a subsequent conversation with me, a significant change from his initial encouragement.

While Julio was in further communication with Alvar Antion of the Costa Rican foreign ministry during this period, he had heard nothing more from Leonte Herdocia at the Nicaraguan foreign ministry.

El Salvador

On June 19, Ray Magee and I attended the first meeting of a new Working Group on El Salvador. This ad hoc group had grown out of an idea for a major nonviolent action of some kind in El Salvador put forth by Paddy Lane, a Quaker who was PBI's representative in Alaska.

The focus of the meeting was on potential projects I had identified in the report of our visit there. There was also discussion of the interest of a project in El Salvador, and the group decided it was best to coordinate any future projects there with Adolfo's organization Servicio, Paz y Justicia (SERPAJ). Pat Parkman, who would later serve as chair of PBI's Central America Projects Committee, was named as convener of the Working Group.

Other Meetings

A variety of other PBI meetings and events also took place during the disarmament session. Carl Kline of the Lisle Fellowship, Radhakrishna of the Gandhi Peace Foundation who had accepted a seat on the PBI Council, Ray Magee, and I met with 20 people on their way to a peace brigades training seminar in India to be led by Narayan. In addition, Charlie, Ray and I gave talks on PBI at the Fellowship of Reconciliation Coffeehouse set up across from the UN headquarters.

Ray and I also met with George Sherry, Deputy Director of UN Peacekeeping Operations to discuss the potential use by the UN of unarmed peacekeeping contingents such as PBI. In Philadelphia, Charlie, George Willoughby and I met with Asia Bennett, executive director of the American Friends Service Committee. In Washington, D.C. I met with the director and Central America staff of the Washington Office on Latin America (WOLA). A variety of other meetings took place involving Charlie Walker, Murray Thomson, Lee Stern, Jaime Diaz, Radhakrishna, Ray Magee, Hildegard Goss-Mayr, and others. All in all it was a productive convergence.

Incorporation and First Council Meeting

During the New York meetings we discussed the necessity of incorporating PBI as a nonprofit, tax-exempt organization for fundraising and other purposes, which we felt had been authorized at Grindstone. The question was whether to incorporate a PBI-USA as a U.S. fundraising arm, with Peace Brigades International incorporated elsewhere, or to incorporate the international organization itself in the U.S. Jaime Diaz and Radhakrishna advised that there was no reason the international organization itself should not be incorporated in the USA, a country where it is easy to move funds in and out, and it was agreed that I would prepare and file Articles of Incorporation for PBI in Washington State, acting as the incorporator. PBI was officially incorporated as a Washington nonprofit corporation on July 6, 1982, listing me as its registered agent, a role I continue to play.

From August 23-27, 1982, the Second International Consultation on Peace Brigades was held in Bergen, The Netherlands, together with the first meeting of the International Council of PBI, and the initial meeting of the directorate of the newly-formed PBI corporation.

The meetings in Bergen were hosted by the Foundation for the Extension of Nonviolent Action (SVAG) and were conducted as an open meeting of the PBI International Council with non-council participants freely taking part except when it came to blocking consensus, which was the agreed basis for all decision-making. The participants came from seven countries.

The Council agreed that project organization, administration, and fundraising would generally be decentralized, and that PBI would function under the principle of maximum local autonomy consistent with consultation and integration necessary to develop and maintain an efficient international network and coordinating body for joint training and action. It was decided that the ultimate form of the international organization should not be determined yet, and that the present PBI structures would be considered "provisional".

For the present, the corporate articles were approved for filing, and draft bylaws I presented were adopted with minor amendments. In addition to the founders, the council members who had accepted invitations authorized at Grindstone were confirmed, including Piet Dijkstra of the Netherlands, Paul Hare, a veteran of the World Peace Brigade then living in Israel, War Resisters International Vice-President Devi Prasad and Radhakrishna of the Gandhi Peace Foundation in India, Sulak Sivaraksa of Thailand, and Hildegard Goss-Mayr of Austria, along with new members WRI Secretary John Hyatt of England and Ueli Wildberger of Switzerland. These members were soon to be joined on the Council by Joan Baez of the US, Adolfo Perez Esquivel of Argentina, and Gen. Michael Harbottle of Great Britain who had served as Chief of Staff of the United Nations Peacekeeping Forces on Cyprus.

The Council acknowledged that for the present its members would not be formal representatives of the specific groups they belonged to, but of an idea—peace brigades—though it was agreed that the selection criteria for council members would include geographical, organizational, cultural, and sexual balance. Toward this end the existing directorate was continued with the addition of a European woman yet to be appointed. The existing PBI Coordinator, Secretary, and Treasurer were also continued, with the understanding that Ray Magee would serve only until a new treasurer could be found as he requested. That fall Ray was replaced as treasurer by Nancy Ball, clerk of the Walla Walla Friends Meeting.

The Council members acknowledged that the development of a network of local and regional PBI groups and contacts was critical to our work, and we welcomed the founding of PBI-Canada by Hans Sinn and Murray Thomson as PBI's first country group. Between sessions the European participants met as a subgroup and announced the formation of a European section of PBI, to be concerned with conflicts between immigrant groups and local populations as well as developing contact persons in each language area, bringing together trained people in each area, developing lists of available people, and generally collecting and disseminating information on nonviolent action and PBI.

At Bergen we also established area committees for Central America, Sri Lanka, Namibia, European Intercommunity Conflicts, India-Pakistan, and the Middle East. Their task was to develop a project exploration committee to monitor each area and to develop or recommend a response to the area's needs either directly through PBI or through cooperating with or assisting other groups. In addition the Council established a training group to be convened by Narayan Desai in place of arrangements we had made at Grindstone for training and curriculum.

Finally, we discussed methods of internal communication, as well as relations with other organizations, including the importance of cooperative relationships with the International Fellowship of Reconciliation (IFOR), War Resisters International (WRI), Amnesty International, and the Shanti Sena, among others. Electronic mail, now a mainstay of PBI, was just being developed at the time and was not available to most council members, though we arranged telex capacity for the Secretariat in Walla Walla and urged members of the Council to identify local telex links. John Hyatt, Secretary of WRI, offered to send out a PBI brochure with a cover letter to the WRI mailing list, and we encouraged other council members and PBI contact people to consider a similar mailing by other international or regional groups they were in contact with as the beginning of a grass roots fundraising, networking, and recruiting campaign.

In his concluding remarks Narayan commented on the practical approach of the group to what might have appeared to some to be a utopian concern. He noted that "we have dreamed some, but it's good to dream for life instead of planning for death," and that "if we dream for life, we may start living for life." "Still," he told the gathering, "we have been mostly practical, honest to ourselves and to the need to keep close to the truth." He noted that the conference had presented many germinal ideas, greater clarity as to concepts, broader institutional participation, and the needed combination of idealism and realism. "If some of our decisions have been wishful thinking," he concluded, "may God bless us in making these dreams reality."

At the close of the meetings, several of us joined Dutch activists in a silent peace vigil in nearby Alkmaar, the headquarters of IFOR. After that I flew to London where I stayed with John Hyatt and his family, conferred with an official at Amnesty International's headquarters about potential cooperation with PBI, as met with several other groups. On the way home I stopped in New York for several more discussions, including a good meeting with Richard Chartier of FOR and a meeting of the El Salvador Working Group.

Commitment to Central America

In June at Charlie's suggestion I had been appointed Project Director of PBI's Central America Peace Teams Project, and at the Bergen meetings was appointed convener of PBI's Central America committee which included Jaime Diaz, Paul Hare, and Julio Quan.

In the fall of 1982, we concluded there were enough possibilities for significant contributions by peace brigades in Central America to justify placing a team in the field for at least three months beginning in early 1983. Our goal was to again have a three-person team composed this time of a Latin American, a North American, and a European. The team would spend the first month visiting major conflict areas and continuing the explorations with governments, churches and popular groups begun by the earlier PBI team. After the first month, a joint decision would be made with the project committee as to what work projects would be most useful for the remainder of the initial three months, following which a decision would be made as to whether to continue the team's presence further.

In November, I made another trip to the east coast of the US which resulted in a new Central America Project Committee including PBI Council members Jaime Diaz, Charles Walker, Paul Hare, Devi Prasad, Ueli Wildberger, Hans Sinn, and Hildegard Goss-Mayr, as well as George Willoughby, Julio Quan, Richard Chartier, Philadelphia area Salvador scholar and activist Patricia Parkman, Mennonite Central Committee executive secretary Herman Bontrager, and former U.S. Attorney General Ramsey Clark who had been active with the monitoring of Latin American elections.

Although we invited SERPAJ to appoint the Latin American member for our second field team, that didn't happen, and I became a member of the team along with Hazel Tulecke, a retired Quaker educator from Yellow Springs, Ohio and Ludger Deckers, a Catholic activist from Cologne, Germany.

Guatemala

Though we also planned to look again at potential refugee work along the Honduran/Salvadoran border as well as possible work within El Salvador, Guatemala seemed to present the greatest potential for substantive change at that point. I was particularly drawn by two events to look closely at the possibilities for peace brigades work there. The first was encouragement we received from Herman Bontrager of the Mennonite Central Committee (MCC). The situation in Guatemala at the time was treacherous for Guatemalans as well as anyone else doing work involving popular or cooperative activities. As a consequence nearly all the international agencies had left, including AFSC whose staff had departed under death threats. A number of knowledgeable people told us they would consider it irresponsible for PBI to place a team there under such circumstances. The Mennonite Central Committee was the exception. They were still in Guatemala, and advised us there were possibilities there that should be carefully considered.

The second event was the "apertura" or "political opening" announced by General Efrain Rios Montt shortly after a military coup brought him to power in Guatemala in late 1982. In an apparent effort to end the guerrilla war, Rios Montt had announced that on March 23, 1983, all parties of every persuasion, including socialists, would be permitted to freely engage in political activity without harm leading to the election of a constituent assembly and the drafting of a new constitution the following year. The question was whether any significant attempt would be made by Guatemalans to exercise the rights offered by the government. Another question we asked ourselves was whether or not the presence of a PBI team would be seen as a threat by any party, as irrelevant, or as a potentially significant contribution to reducing the violence and protecting the rights of those who chose to participate in the "opening."

Hazel and I began in Mexico City on January 15 with the assistance of Roberto Garay, a member of a Catholic base community, who later became a member of our project committee. We met there with representatives of the Guatemalan Human Rights Commission (in exile), then with a representative of the Guatemalan political opposition, the Mexican Friends Service Committee, the president of the Mexican Government Refugee Commission, former Guatemalan President and current Ambassador Julio Cesar Mendez Montenegro, and others. After that we went to Chiapas, the Mexican border region with Guatemala, where we interviewed Guatemalan refugees at La Sombra, Txicao and Carmen Zahn after an attack and assassination of several refugees by Guatemalan military units whose helicopters we observed searching for more refugees on the Mexican side of the border.

From Chiapas, we traveled by bus to Guatemala City where we were joined by Ludger Deckers. There we met with Msgr. Juan Gerardi, former Catholic bishop of the conflicted Quiche province who would later be assassinated, other Catholic and Protestant church officials, trade union and indigenous leaders, US embassy staff, and a representative of the Christian Democratic Party among others. Though we had written to President Rios Montt and hoped to meet with him, instead we were given a meeting with Jorge Serrano, President of the Guatemalan Council of State who would later be elected President. After our visits in Guatemala we continued on by bus to El Salvador.

El Salvador

In the capital we met separately with officials of the National University and the Catholic University, as well as the five different human rights organizations. Our discussions focused on the potential development of a nonviolent studies program at each of the universities and the potential international protection of human rights groups within El Salvador.

When we arrived for an interview with a member of the medical faculty at the National University we learned that the day before she had been kidnapped by armed men at her clinic two blocks from the U.S. embassy. The next day we raised this issue in a meeting with Col. Reynaldo Lopez Nuila, head of the National Police and chair of the government's human rights commission, suggesting that it was hard to believe this could happen in broad daylight so close to the US embassy without the police being aware of it. He insisted that the police had no knowledge of the kidnapping and offered to open his prisons to us so we could see for ourselves that she wasn't being held there.

We then asked about the activities of both the independent and church-related human rights commissions, which he criticized as being guerrilla sympathizers. We told him we were interested in the possibility of working with each of the commissions, including the governmental group, and to accompany their members into the countryside where they were currently unable to go, in order to provide them better access to information. Col. Lopez said we would be free to work with all the commissions, that people we spoke to would not suffer, and that our representatives would be identified as officially recognized to travel throughout the country for this work which would be an important contribution to the democratic process. "We want to be transparent as a crystal," he assured us.

He then pointedly asked us whether we had any representatives from communist countries. We told him we didn't, but that we had some contacts with Solidarity in Poland, and would like to do so in the future. Apparently considering us harmless enough, he told the photographer he had brought in that he didn't need to develop our photos.

Also in San Salvador we met with officials of the Lutheran Church which provided us housing, and visited a rural refugee cooperative supported by the Catholic Archdiocese that was located nearby. On the way to the cooperative we passed a Salvadoran army unit patrolling the area, and while there received word that a member of the cooperative had been seized by the patrol. Just as we were deciding whether to approach the soldiers to make inquiries about him, word came that he'd been released. Later as we were being shown the community's water supply at the foot of a deep ravine, a company of armed soldiers appeared at the top of the ridge and began running toward us. When they reached the bottom of the ravine where we were standing we were relieved to see them continue up the other side, either as part of their training maneuvers or an attempt to frighten off some foreigners. This event underlined for us the continuing risks and courage of the church as well as the refugees from combat zones in their attempts at resettlement into productive communities.

Panama Conference, Decision-Making in Costa Rica

From February 13-18 the team took part in the SERPAJ Conference on Nonviolent Action in Central America, held in Panama City and attended by 38 people from throughout Central America as well as Mexico, Colombia and Brazil. The conference focused on the theology, strategies and tactics of nonviolent action, as well as the present situation in Central America, and proposals for nonviolent action. The conference also enabled us to continue our conversations with Guatemalan church people. In addition, we became acquainted with Alvaro Diaz, an articulate and personable attorney who was head of the Humanities Department at the University of Gran Colombia in Bogota and was the SERPAJ representative in Colombia. We were all delighted when Alvaro accepted our invitation to join the PBI team for the remainder of its initial three months in Central America.

At the close of the Panama conference, in view of the significant potential presented by Guatemala, we decided to forego our planned visit to the Honduran border areas where prospects were still not good. We were ready for our planned committee meeting with Julio Quan and Pat Parkman in Costa Rica from February 18-21 where we would decide what to do next.

As to Guatemala, while the responses of the parties we talked with varied according to their position in the conflict, it was clear there was tremendous distrust of the government's good faith and its ability to provide a true political opening, particularly while a counterinsurgency program was being carried on in the countryside. At the same time it was apparent that no firm decisions had been made concerning possible political activity and most groups were adopting a "wait and see" attitude, since little could be known until March 23 when the new laws were to be promulgated and the existing state of siege lifted. What seemed clear was that any relaxation of the existing repression would see a renewed degree of popular activity on a variety of levels: exiles returning to the country, increased labor union, campesino, and student activity, opposition political party registration, and the possible establishment of an openly functioning human rights commission within Guatemala.

Beyond indications of a guarded return to increased political activity, the team's interviews almost universally concluded with the suggestion by Guatemalans that the presence of an international monitoring team would be important because of its capacity to do first hand reporting of abuses of political and human rights, that it "could save lives," and would be an inhibiting factor in the repression of groups attempting to organize and exercise their rights in the new period.

We were told in various interviews that "this is certainly the time to be present in Guatemala," that "the next six months could determine whether any real changes will come about in the current structures," that "politically speaking, this is the time to struggle, this is the moment," and that "your presence could be very, very important."

Our conclusions, which were also adopted by the project committee, were that while there was a serious and well-founded lack of confidence in the government's intentions, and that additional discussions with Guatemalans and observations of developments needed to occur before committing ourselves to a long-term presence, a PBI team should be placed in Guatemala for the first month of the "political opening" beginning March 23, and that a recommendation should be made by that team as to whether to continue the PBI presence during the entire year leading up to the planned constituent assembly election in 1994.

Beginnings in Guatemala

On March 21, after visit ing Nicaragua and Honduras, our team member Hazel Tulecke opened a PBI headquarters in Guatemala City at Julio Quan's vacant home, which we had inspected during our visit and later agreed to rent. Our plans for the arrival of the other two team members, Alvaro Diaz of Servicio and Ludger Deckers, had fallen through so we were scrambling to replace them. Alvaro had applied for a Guatemalan visa in Bogota, and when he explained in detail the purpose of his trip his visa was denied. This was a mistake we avoided in the future by having team members apply only for tourist visas until we had negotiated full legal status in the country for PBI, which often took years. In Ludger's case, his primary interest was in the kind of refugee work that Honduras might offer, and he had decided the Guatemala project was not for him.

The able replacements we recruited for Alvaro and Ludger were Alain Richard, a Franciscan priest from France we had met at the Panama conference, and Pablo Stanfield, an American linguist and Quaker from Seattle I had met at the General Reunion of Mexican Friends the year before. Although we had had no contact since our brief meeting in Mexico City, as I was frantically searching for who might best fill out our Guatemala team during this critical period, Pablo called me seemingly out of the blue seeking more details about the new peace organization I had told him about, and within a week he was in Guatemala.

With our first project team in the field, it was now critical that PBI organizational responsibility be shared by a broader group of people. At that point I was International Secretary of PBI whose secretariat was in the office of my home in Walla Walla, as well as Central America Project Director whose full project committee had not yet held a face-to-face meeting. I was receiving and responding to correspondence about PBI from individuals and organizations all over the world, writing articles, editing, producing and mailing the quarterly newsletter PBI REPORTS, recruiting and evaluating volunteer applications, consulting with committee, council, and team members, doing PBI's legal work, and dealing with a variety of other tasks.

The recruiting task alone was a demanding and very important one. The selection criteria we had adopted in Costa Rica continued to call for a team composed of a Latin American, a North American, and a European, with both sexual and religious balance. Team members were to be fluent in Spanish, should have some previous experience in a Third World country and with nonviolent action, be politically aware but without political affiliations which would prejudice the project, should have a commitment to nonviolence and to the specific project, and have an ability to work easily with others. Personal interviews were obviously desirable, yet were very difficult given the distances involved. In addition to our three person in-country team, we wanted to develop a larger brigade ready to respond to a potential call by the team for a short-term emergency presence. We also needed to develop a broad international communications network of individuals along with governmental and humanitarian agencies able to immediately respond in order to deter potential abuses of our team members or those they protect.

Philadelphia Meetings

To respond to these needs we arranged a series of meetings from April 22-25 in Philadelphia that included a general conference on Peace Brigades in Central America, as well as a meeting of PBI's Central American Project Committee to be coordinated by Pat Parkman, a knowledgeable and responsible member. Among the matters to be addressed were a decision on whether to continue the presence of the PBI team in Guatemala, and my request for the appointment of a new full-time Central America Project Director.

These meetings were attended by about 35 people and were important for the future of PBI in a variety of ways. The participants included Herman Bontrager of the Mennonite Central Committee, George Willoughby of the Movement for a New Society (MNS) at whose conference center the meetings were held, and council members Charles Walker, Hans Sinn, and Lee Stern. Julio Quan who was appointed PBI representative in Costa Rica was present, as were Roberto Garay as PBI representative in Mexico, Philip Hazelton and Jo Leigh Commandant of PBI-Canada, Betsy Fairbanks of the Resource Center for Nonviolence in Santa Cruz, and Guatemala team member Hazel Tulecke.

Hazel presented the written report and recommendations of the PBI team which had been in Guatemala since March 22 as well as her personal perspectives. During their month in the country the team members had been in contact with various sectors of Guatemalan society, their activities had resulted in a stay of execution for two religious workers condemned to death by the government's secret tribunals, and they had received an invitation to present a university forum on nonviolence following a special showing of the film "Gandhi."

After discussing the team's report, the committee made several important decisions:

1. To continue the team's presence in Guatemala, with the intention that it should remain there for a minimum of a year,
2. To expand the size of the team to five persons, stressing its international character by avoiding a preponderance from any single country or region, and seeking at least one member able to serve the entire year with others serving a minimum of three months,
3. To establish a Ready Response Brigade able to create a larger international presence in Guatemala or elsewhere in Central America during a short-term crisis, and
4. To develop an international network of organizations and individuals able to disseminate and act on reports of the team and to provide general support for the project.

The committee also received reports about and discussed the situation in El Salvador and along the Nicaraguan-Honduran border.

Regarding El Salvador, Pat Parkman reported on our exploratory team activities and the visit she made there following our committee meeting in Costa Rica, as well as our follow-up letters to the two universities and two of the human rights groups, the Human Rights Commission of El Salvador (independent) and Socorro Juridico, a lawyers' group, both of which had expressed interest in cooperating with PBI. Since no response had been received, we telephoned them during our meetings to see if they still wanted PBI help, learning from our calls to the two universities that they were still interested in PBI participating in a study of the problem of violence and its solutions within El Salvador and would be contacting us again after further meetings between the two universities on the subject. We were only able to reach one of the human rights groups, which had not received our letter, but said they would be discussing the question further.

We decided that Pat should be authorized to pursue the university project on behalf of PBI since it could also be carried on in part at other sites in Central America outside of El Salvador. As to possible work with human rights organizations, because of Julio's adamant opposition to our working within El Salvador at that time in view of what he considered to be unreasonable security risks, we decided we were not in a position to consider that work immediately, but would keep in contact with interested groups and consider further any proposals we received.

Regarding the Nicaraguan-Honduran border, a letter from European members of PBI was read expressing continuing concern about the Nicaraguan border situation and how PBI might relate to this explosive international situation. We had also been contacted by the organizer of Vigil for Peace, a group of about 20 unarmed North Americans who had taken up positions along the northern part of the border during the first week in February, while large-scale U.S.-Honduran military maneuvers were taking place near the border.

Calling for military non-intervention in Central America, the group dug in for five days along an area of the border where confrontations between Somocista counterrevolutionaries and Nicaraguan troops were common, hoping to discourage any incidents which might provoke a confrontation or trigger a major incident during this show of military strength. The primary organizer of the vigil asked PBI to consider a further response there in the future. As we gathered in Philadelphia we recognized that an occasion might present itself before long in which a PBI Ready Response Brigade could have an important role to play there, which was in fact not long in coming.

As to project administration, my request for a full-time Central America director was satisfied by the appointment of Jo Leigh Commandant as project director and the establishment of a Central America Project Office in Toronto, where a support group for PBI would be organized to assist in the project administration. Jo Leigh, proposed by George Willoughby, was a Quaker psychiatric social worker who had immigrated to Canada from Texas and was a member of MNS. She had been heavily involved in Native Peoples' rights, had traveled in Mexico and Peru, and had served as a representative to a UN conference on North and South American Indian rights in Geneva, as well as an election observer in Bolivia.

I was asked to continue to chair the project committee, and Jo Leigh and I together with Charlie Walker as PBI Coordinator were authorized to act as an executive body for the larger committee between its meetings. We were also asked to act as a personnel committee for the selection of volunteers. In addition, we agreed to add Roberto Garay and Betsy Fairbanks to the project committee.

Although PBI had adopted a general budget of $75,000, exclusive of project costs, and a $50,000 budget for the Guatemala project, we had only raised around $15,000 by that point, so no compensation could be given, and we all continued to work as volunteers.

The task of developing a broad international network was an important one for the project, and not long after the conference the first occasion for alerting that emerging network presented itself. Though the official state of siege was lifted on March 23 when the new electoral laws went into effect, the Guatemalan government's secret military tribunals had not been suspended and their continued existence was undermining its offer of a "political opening" and respect for human rights. Six people were currently under sentence of death by the tribunals in which the accused had no access to the evidence against them and no knowledge of the identities of their judges or accusers. Since this was inconsistent with the government's promise to permit open political activity of every kind with safety for the participants, we urged everyone we were in contact with to write to President Rios Montt, to contact the nearest Guatemalan embassy, and to take other steps to bring an end to the tribunals.

While we began to recruit new members for the Guatemala team to join Pablo Stanfield, who was appointed the team's coordinator, we also began planning another peace brigades conference in California where we hoped to promote the formation of local groups as part of our envisioned Ready Response Brigade. In the meantime, the situation along the Nicaraguan-Honduran border began to heat up.

Nicaraguan Border Brigade

When the initial PBI exploratory team visited Central America in 1982, the conflict along the Nicaraguan-Honduran border was one of our primary concerns. Even at that time, Nicaraguan contras were active enough in the border area to create a number of incidents between Nicaragua and Honduras, which were in turn being used by the United States as justification for increased militarization of the region. Our preliminary discussions with the Nicaraguan and Honduran foreign ministries and with the OAS regarding possible PBI observer teams had generated expressions of interest, but nothing further.

In early July, 1983, a delegation of 150 North American religious people visited Nicaragua and traveled to the town of Jalapa on the Honduran border, where they held a vigil for several hours before returning to Managua. Following this, several of the vigilers, including Paddy Lane, proposed the establishment of an ongoing nonviolent presence by U.S. Christians in Jalapa, a provincial capital which had often been attacked and was rumored to be the site selected by the Nicaraguan counterrevolutionaries for the establishment of a provisional capitol inside Nicaragua. The proposal was for Witness for Peace to begin its presence in Jalapa on October 1, 1983, to shield the town from further attack.

The response of the Nicaraguan government was positive, except that it considered October 1 too late. The Sandinistas were convinced the contras would launch a major attack in September, hoping to show the U.S. Congress concrete progress before U.S. covert funds were due to be cut off on October 1. Another factor in Nicaragua's concern was the presence of thousands of U.S. troops across the border in Honduras and on 19 ships on both of Nicaragua's coasts that were taking part in the announced US/Honduran Big Pine II maneuvers, which were feared to be a cover for either an indefinite U.S. military presence or a planned invasion of Nicaragua.

On August 16, Witness for Peace forwarded to PBI the request of the Nicaraguan government for an international presence in Jalapa prior to October 1 when the Witness for Peace team was expected to arrive. Although PBI had no Ready Response units organized at the time, we had already alerted our network about the Nicaraguan border conflict in view of the Big Pine II operations.

We envisioned PBI's Ready Response Brigade as a crisis response unit composed of contingents from various regions able on short notice to place their members in Central America for brief periods, and to provide supportive actions in their home areas. In addition to an international crisis team, each brigade was to have local members whose role would be to make contact with the media, government officials and other groups, care for team members' personal affairs, and carry out actions in support of the international team's presence. Local units would also be available for peacekeeping and peacemaking in local or regional conflicts in their home areas.

On July 30, we held a conference on International Peace Brigades at the Friends Center in San Francisco with the specific goal of establishing local units in the San Francisco area. The Peaceworkers organization handled local arrangements, Michael Nagler, President of Peaceworkers gave a moving introduction to the conference, Charlie, Ray, Jo Leigh, Alain Richard, and I each gave short talks on peace brigades in Central America, and we held workshops on a variety of topics including a Ready Response Brigade for Central America. The event was attended by about 70 people and resulted in the formation of local PBI groups in San Francisco, Salinas and Santa Cruz, as well as an interview and article by the Christian Science Monitor newspaper and other publicity.

Among the conference participants were Scott Kennedy of the Resource Center for Nonviolence in Santa Cruz, David Sweet of Witness for Peace, David Hartsough of AFSC and Jack Schultz, an innovative general contractor, mechanical engineer, aviation pilot, ship's captain, navigator, diver, and photographer from Santa Cruz. At the close of the conference, Jack was authorized to organize a Santa Cruz contingent of the Ready Response Brigade and arrangements were made for the Santa Cruz unit to be headquartered at the Resource Center for Nonviolence along with Witness for Peace.

Because preparation of a Santa Cruz Brigade was already underway and appeared to have excellent local support resources, in mid-August when we received the Nicaraguan request, we decided to invite the brigade to respond to the Nicaraguan appeal by organizing a ten-person team to be present in Jalapa the last two weeks of September. A six-person local steering committee was set up for the brigade consisting of Scott Kennedy, director of the RCNV, Betsy Fairbanks, RCNV staff and PBI Central America Committee member, Phil McManus, RCNV staff, David Sweet of Witness for Peace, and Jane Fessenden and Francis Wright. Both Jane and Francis were members of the Social Concerns Committee of the Santa Cruz Friends Meeting where Jack was a member and with whom we had consulted before authorizing him to coordinate recruitment of the brigade.

It was agreed that applicants for the brigade were to satisfy certain PBI criteria such as minimum age, familiarity with Spanish, and experience with nonviolent action, and were subject to approval by PBI as well as the local steering committee. Our mandate to the local steering committee was to coordinate the organization and preparation of the Santa Cruz Brigade prior to its deployment in consultation with PBI staff as set out in a special memorandum we prepared for the Jalapa brigade on strategies, tactics, and procedures. After deployment, project decisions were to be made by PBI Central America Project staff.

The brigade's preparation and training were planned to occur in two stages: their initial preparation in Santa Cruz utilizing local training resources, followed by international training near Mexico City with PBI Central America project staff, PBI Guatemala team members, and members of Roberto Garay's Maryknoll Christian base community which was to host the brigade during its training there.

The key elements in our political strategy for the brigade were (1) we wanted to be sure that all the parties who had a stake in the matter knew we were on the ground in Jalapa, and (2) we wanted to make a similar offer of a protective presence to Honduras, in order to make clear our nonpartisanship. In a public statement regarding the project's purposes, we declared that its primary objective was

> to establish a known, unarmed international presence in the town and immediate environs of Jalapa, Nicaragua, for the specific purpose of inhibiting and discouraging rebel or foreign military attacks against it.

> The secondary objectives of the Jalapa Brigade are (1) to focus international attention on the escalating conflict between the current Nicaraguan government and U.S. and Honduran-assisted counterrevolutionary forces attacking it, (2) to encourage the parties to the conflict to pursue political rather than military solutions, and (3) to demonstrate the use of active nonviolence as an effective means of peacekeeping and peacemaking in international conflicts.

To accomplish these objectives, as PBI Secretary I sent letters to the foreign ministers of both Honduras and Nicaragua as well as to the Contadora Group nations (Mexico, Panama, Colombia and Venezuela) who were promoting a peace plan for the region, and to the U.S. Undersecretary of State for Latin America. These letters described our intended action in Nicaragua and our offer of a similar brigade to Honduras, and were delivered in person to the U.N. missions of the Contadora Group in New York, to the U.S. State Department and the Nicaraguan Embassy in Washington, D.C., and to the Honduran Foreign Ministry in Tegucigalpa. In addition, we briefed personnel of the United Nations Secretariat on the project.

In Honduras, we also presented a formal request to the government for PBI observer teams to freely visit areas where U.S. and Honduran troops were to be stationed during the Big Pine II operations, as well as for the border areas where suspected incursions were occurring. In Tegucigalpa PBI staff personally delivered a letter to a representative of the counter-revolutionary Nicaraguan Democratic Force, the principal "contra" group. At the Honduran foreign ministry, PBI project representatives were again received courteously, but without response.

Prior to the brigade's arrival in Nicaragua, we issued a news release which went to all major international, US and Canadian news services; press conferences were held in Toronto and San Francisco, one was planned for Mexico City, and a notice went out to PBI's growing network of individuals and organizations concerned with peace and justice in Central America.

I agreed to serve as director of the Jalapa project which was to be overseen by PBI's three-person executive committee for Central America in liaison with Julio Quan in Costa Rica who was at the time the PBI Central America Representative. Charlie had prepared a training memo for the brigade's use as part of its local preparation stage. Unfortunately, because Julio was not permitted to enter Mexico, the international part of the training was moved to the more hectic atmosphere of Managua.

On September 13, 1983 a nine-person PBI brigade arrived in Managua. The following day the brigade was presented on the platform at a huge Independence Day rally before the diplomatic corps and news media by Daniel Ortega, coordinator of the Nicaraguan Junta, who called them "Friends of Humanity." Ortega subsequently mentioned the presence of the brigade again in his speech as chief of state to one of the opening sessions of the U.N. General Assembly in New York. Following an additional training session in Managua by PBI, a briefing by Nicaraguans, and a meeting with the U.S. Ambassador, on September 17 the brigade together with Jo Leigh Commandant traveled by jeep to Jalapa, a town of about 9000 people swollen by refugees and situated about four kilometers from the Honduran border.

During their stay in Jalapa, the major attack the Sandinistas feared was in fact launched from Honduras by the contras. While battles raged elsewhere in the border region, there was no attack on Jalapa. Brigade members established vigils at dawn and dusk in the town plaza and in surrounding villages, where people joined them in song, prayer and discussion. The team broadcast to an international radio network they were able to set up called "Radio Peace International" which established links to ham radio operators in many countries and focused constant attention on their presence. Other team activities included planting a peace garden, teaching Morse code in the schools, and helping harvest coffee for a local cooperative.

For the two weeks the brigade was in Jalapa not a hostile shot was fired. Together with the fact that contra attacks dramatically increased throughout the adjoining border region during the same period, this was convincing evidence to Nicaraguan officials that the brigade's presence had indeed brought peace to Jalapa. Sixto Ulloa Dona, a spokesperson for CEPAD (Evangelical Committee for Development Aid, a coalition of 34 Nicaraguan religious groups) told the team in a farewell message,

We in Nicaragua are totally in your debt. You have done something the Christians in Nicaragua have not done…The proof of your triumph lies in the fact that no attacks were made while you were in the Jalapa area. The contras are intelligent and fully understand the consequences to your peacekeeping team.

While the Jalapa brigade was a success, and demonstrated the power of an unarmed international presence to deter violence, putting together such a brigade in a short time was a difficult thing to do. This was confirmed by the fact that the ten-person Witness for Peace brigade that was to replace the Santa Cruz group on October 1 didn't arrive as planned. However, WFP for Peace was able to place four people in Jalapa in mid-October, and over time came to be a powerful presence for justice and peace in Nicaragua and other places in Latin America.

As for the Santa Cruz Brigade, all of the functions of developing a brigade had to be compressed into an approximately three-week period, including recruiting and selection of members, general preparation and orientation, deepening members' understanding and practice of nonviolence as well as nonpartisan, third-party skills, team building and development of a leadership structure, and gaining a better understanding of the socio-political conditions in the region of service. This time frame inevitably involved compromises regarding standards of leadership, recruiting, training and support, without which the brigade would not have arrived in Jalapa during this critical period of increased attacks.

In part, difficulties arose from the lack of opportunity by project staff to visit the brigade while it was being organized and trained, and from a reported lack of clarity by the steering committee as to its responsibilities in relation to the brigade. Mistakes were also made in naming the initial brigade organizer as coordinator of the field brigade—a matter which should have awaited a joint decision by the brigade, the local steering committee, and PBI project staff—as well as in moving the international training to Managua where there was insufficient time to deal with many unresolved matters within the team before it was actually placed in service.

Yet as I said in a November, 1983 article in the quarterly journal Transnational Perspectives,

> given the rise of military activities in the world, and the threat that any conflict may be "globalized", it is clear that to "fight war, not wars" in any effective way, large numbers of peace brigades must be able to be organized and deployed in a variety of situations. To accomplish this will inevitably require flexibility as to selection and preparation criteria, and the uncomfortable realization that peace brigades, while working for peace without, will not always be peaceful within.

While the Jalapa brigade was definitely imperfect, by most accounts our biggest mistake would have been not to have accepted the challenge of a Nicaraguan border brigade as we did.

Guatemala and Beyond

On August 8, 1983, a new military coup unseated Gen. Efrain Rios Montt as president of Guatemala and replaced him with the Guatemalan defense minister, Gen. Oscar Humberto Mejia Victores. A fruit of the new coup was the abolition of the secret military tribunals which PBI and other human rights organizations had severely criticized under Rios Montt. At the same time, the new regime sought closer links with the U.S. in its pursuit of a military solution to the problems of Central America, and killings by all sides in the Guatemalan countryside increased.

Mexico City Meetings, Change of Secretariat

PBI's presence in Guatemala continued despite the coup. From December 2-12, 1983, Guatemala team members joined PBI's International Council members and Central America Committee for a series of meetings at the Casa de Los Amigos in Mexico City to review our work in Central America as well as PBI's administrative structure.

During our Central America Committee meeting we were thanked by two Guatemalan brothers who had been sentenced by the secret military tribunals. Describing their capture, the torture of one of them, and their six month long ordeal in prison after being sentenced to more than ten years imprisonment for conspiracy against the government though they had not been charged with that crime and no evidence against them had been produced, they told us their release at the time the secret tribunals were abolished was the result of the international pressure PBI had helped to generate.

Following evaluations of the Guatemala project and the Nicaraguan-Honduran border project and reports on possible future work elsewhere in Central America, it was clear to everyone that despite having made important progress much remained to be done, and that many new possibilities for nonviolent action existed, including action within Costa Rica and along its border with Nicaragua.

In October, after our previous contacts, PBI formally offered its services to the Costa Rican government in its border region with Nicaragua. In response to a US proposal to place up to 1000 U.S. Army personnel in Costa Rica "to build roads in the border area," an alternative offer was then made for a US/Costa Rican peace brigade to build the roads instead, and was endorsed by former Costa Rican President Jose Figueres who had presided over the abolition of Costa Rica's army. That offer successfully derailed the US attempt at militarizing the Costa Rican border.

Discussions were also underway with Costa Ricans for the organization of seminars throughout the country on the application of the principles of civilian-based defense, with the hope of ultimately gathering ideas from the different sectors of Costa Rican society into a national civilian-based defense plan to be presented to the authorities, a concept later to be explored in Nicaragua as well.

An important item on the agenda at our International Council meeting in Mexico City was consideration of my resignation as PBI Secretary. At the time of our San Francisco meetings, I told Charlie the burden of my travels was becoming too great for my family, and that I had promised Barbara I would step down as Secretary by the end of the year. This was a necessary move for PBI in any case, since given our level of activities PBI's administrative headquarters needed to be closer to major centers of population and political power. When I mentioned my family problem to Julio some time before, he had said, "Get a new wife." Instead I decided to "get a new life."

In the "Report of the Secretary" delivered to the Council at Mexico City, I reviewed the activities of the Secretary and Secretariat over the last 15 months since our council meeting in Bergen. These included the editing and publication of four issues of PBI Reports, the last three in both English and Spanish with arrangements for translating them into French, production of a PBI brochure in English and Spanish, issuance of periodic updates between issues of the Reports all of which were sent out to our mailing list of approximately 500 people in 20 countries, development of a volunteer application form and agreement for service, obtaining U.S. tax exempt status, developing and circulating written guidelines for the formation of local units of the Ready Response Brigade in addition to coordinating and leading the second PBI Central America team, helping coordinate the Philadelphia conference and our committee meetings there resulting in the appointment of a full-time project director for Central America, planning and coordinating the San Francisco conference, serving as project director for the Jalapa Brigade, and coordinating the Mexico City conference and meetings. During that time regional PBI organizations had also been active, including a three-day meeting of the European section at Havelte, The Netherlands, a conference presented by PBI-Canada in Toronto, and the formation of PBI groups in Puerto Rico and Colombia as well as the beginnings of a group in Nigeria, and local brigades in several cities.

Although PBI had formed a finance committee, the inadequacy of its finances was still one of its most pressing problems. In considering who could best take over the duties of PBI Secretary, my candidate was George Willoughby, a respected international peace activist, Quaker, Gandhian, founding member of MNS and veteran of the World Peace Brigade, who lived near Charlie in the Philadelphia area, which would be a good place to locate the PBI Secretariat. When I put the question to George, I was very pleased when he said he would be willing to serve if requested. Charlie and the others readily agreed, and in Mexico City the International Council formally appointed George as PBI Secretary as well as chair of a new PBI Administrative Committee which included Charles Walker and several others from the Philadelphia area, for the first time giving PBI a substantial base in a single locality.

Although I resigned as chair of the Central America Projects Committee at the same time, again to be replaced by George, I agreed to continue on that committee as well on as the International Council, to serve on several other PBI committees, and to continue as legal counsel for PBI.

Since February, 1984 when the PBI Secretariat was formally transferred from Walla Walla to Philadelphia, much has happened to PBI, fifteen years of which is related in considerable detail by PBI volunteers Liam Mahony and Luis Enrique Eguren in their eloquent and moving book, "Unarmed Bodyguards—International Accompaniment for the Protection of Human Rights" (Kumarian Press, 1997), which I will summarize here.

Guatemala

In March, 1994 Nineth de Garcia contacted the PBI Guatemala team about the capture of her husband, a union leader, at a police roadblock, and his subsequent disappearance. Pablo

Stanfield responded that she should consider bringing together others with similar problems. The next month, PBI team member Edith Cole, a Quaker psychologist from California who had learned of PBI from an article I had written, visited the Committee of the Mothers of the Disappeared and Assassinated (COMADRES) in El Salvador, one of the groups we had contacted during our visit in 1983. On her way back Edith brought a tape recorded message from them to the women of Guatemala.

When asked a few days later to accompany several families requesting an audience with Archbishop Peñados about holding a mass for the disappeared, Edith played the tape to about 20 women in the Archbishop's waiting room. They were so moved by this message and the courageous actions of the Salvadoran mothers that they decided on the spot to form a similar group in Guatemala and immediately asked the Archbishop to allow them to hold meetings in his palace as Archbishop Oscar Romero had done in El Salvador. While Peñados agreed to perform the mass, he was understandably reluctant to host the meetings of the new group, perhaps fearing the same fate as the martyred Romero. As they left the palace Edith offered the women the use of the PBI house for their meetings, which was the beginning of a powerful new element in Guatemalan political life.

Hundreds of people, mostly Mayan women, began coming to the PBI house for the weekly meetings of the Grupo de Apoyo Mutuo (Mutual Support Group, or GAM), which became the only openly functioning human rights organization in Guatemala at that time. The GAM organized memorial masses. They also published newspaper ads listing disappearances and calling for official investigations. By August they were granted a meeting with President Mejia Victores. Finding his discussion with them unsatisfactory, in October the GAM organized the first mass protest in Guatemala in years, a twenty-mile march from San Lucas to Guatemala City consisting of hundreds of people accompanied by a team of peacekeepers trained by PBI.

In November, the GAM members publicly accused the security forces of responsibility for the disappearances, held a sit-in at the Guatemalan Congress building, and again met with the President, who this time agreed to establish a cabinet-level commission to investigate the disappearances. GAM also began calling for international investigations and the tying of further aid to Guatemala by other nations to human rights improvement, including specific appeals to the European Union, the US, the OAS, and the UN.

In response, GAM members started receiving death threats, began to be followed, and one member's home was searched. President Mejia accused them of being linked to "the forces of subversion." On March 31, 1984 the public relations officer of the GAM, Hector Gomez, was found dead. His body showed signs of beating and burns, had no tongue, and his hands were tied behind his back. On April 3, PBI's Alain Richard warned cofounder and secretary of GAM Maria Rosario Godoy de Cuevas not to leave her home for any reason because she was also in danger of being killed. The next day she was found dead in her car in a ravine with her brother and her two-year-old son, who had been ill. The cause of their deaths was strangulation; the child's fingernails had been pulled out.

These events created a serious crisis for the GAM, many of whose members went into exile or left the group. They were also the cause of renewed commitment by those who remained and round-the-clock escorting of the surviving leadership by PBI, which began a pioneering new form of human rights protection. In addition to accompanying the two remaining GAM directors who were now on a death list, PBI alerted the international community to the attacks and the escorting by PBI, as a result of which the US State Department sent a communiqué to the Guatemalan government indicating the U.S. did not want more killings of the families of the disappeared, and nearly every embassy in Guatemala expressed similar concerns. A committee of the U.S. Congress voted to cut nearly all direct military aid to Guatemala and to put human rights conditions on economic aid. There were no other killings of GAM leaders.

By the fall of 1985 elections were held under the new constitution which had been adopted by a constituent assembly as promised. Nonetheless, disappearances continued. On October 31 over a hundred GAM members began a five-day occupation of the National Cathedral to call for an independent commission to investigate the fate of 775 family members, the first occasion in which the cathedral had been taken over for political or humanitarian reasons in its 200-year existence. The occupation, with PBI volunteers standing by on the street day and night, was a serious blemish on Guatemala's new image of democracy, occurring as it did three days before the primary elections.

In response, General Mejia, as President, ordered PBI's volunteers expelled from the country for "manipulating" the GAM, a practice PBI had scrupulously avoided. Before leaving, Alain Richard met with Vinicio Cerezo, the apparent winner of the presidential election, and urged him to protect the GAM, which he agreed to do. PBI brought in new volunteers before those expelled had departed, so the continuous protection of the GAM by PBI was able to be maintained.

Before President Cerezo's inauguration in January, 1986, under pressure from the military, the constituent assembly passed an amnesty for all prior human rights violations, which the GAM also protested. As Mahony and Eguren write of the GAM leaders

> For many Guatemalans, these women were the country's sole symbol of courage and resistance, the only ones who refused to forget the past or deny the truth of the present. By late 1986, the GAM was renowned in the international human rights community. Its leaders began traveling around the world, speaking out against Guatemala's human rights record. Holding weekly or biweekly demonstrations in front of the National Palace, the GAM criticized the amnesty law and pressured Cerezo for a commission to investigate the disappearances....

> In the years that followed, Nineth de Garcia was one of the most frequently quoted political figures in the country... In 1987, the group received the Carter-Menil human rights award and used the proceeds to buy its own house, which became an important center of popular movement activity. In 1988, it began organizing demonstrations in highly militarized rural areas and initiated the first public exhumations of clandestine cemeteries, uncovering and identifying victims of massacres. In subsequent years, its offices were bombed several times, and many members were killed, but the GAM never gave up. In 1996, Nineth Montenegro (de Garcia) took her seat in the Guatemalan Congress, continuing the struggle for human rights in a different arena.

Once GAM had its own house, PBI's Guatemala team began to take on additional protection for an expanding labor movement and other organizations taking advantage of the new political space created by the GAM's actions, beginning with a thirteen-month PBI presence outside the Lunafil factory during its occupation by striking workers. Afterwards PBI went on to accompany individual labor leaders, and maintained a presence at dozens of strikes and key union offices.

The next major phase of the new Guatemalan activism in which PBI also had a part was an historic movement for Mayan rights in the countryside. In the spring of 1988 residents of Quiche province delivered a letter to President Cerezo protesting their required service in the oppressive "civil patrols," carried banners in the May Day parade proclaiming their refusal to serve, and demanded the removal of the military from their communities, and notified the human rights ombudsman of their refusal.

 The principal organizer of the Mayan peasants, Amilcar Mendez, then began receiving threats that he and his family would be executed unless he left the country within 60 days. The threats also mentioned "your Communist gringo friends." Mendez had been receiving assistance from PBI since 1983 including help fleeing the country to Toronto in 1986 in the face of previous threats. After the new threats PBI began accompanying Mendez twenty-four hours a day and opened a second PBI house in Santa Cruz del Quiche near Mendez' home to support the new movement.

PBI also activated its emergency response network to demand that President Cerezo protect Mendez. Over time PBI had developed a telephone tree which included thousands of people around the world, who within a few hours could send hundreds of telexes, telegrams and letters to government officials in Guatemala and their own countries urging protection for people the team knew were threatened.

On July 31, three days after the deadline expired for Mendez' departure, the Council of Ethnic Communities (CERJ) was formed by hundreds of campesinos from Quiche province in a meeting at his home. The purposes of CERJ were to provide human rights education, investigate government wrongdoing, resist service in the patrols, and work against cultural and ethnic discrimination. After three months, the CERJ claimed a membership of 6000 and had obtained unanimous resistance to service in the patrols by nearly 40 villages. Because of these developments, PBI maintained two volunteers at the PBI house in Quiche for about four years. At the same time, PBI began receiving requests for accompaniment from other groups taking part in the powerful new Mayan rights movement begun by the CERJ.

The CERJ's work and persistence brought the legitimacy of the forced civil patrols into question by authorities within Guatemala and internationally, including the Guatemalan Congress, the OAS, the UN, as well as the press and public. Like Nineth de Garcia of the GAM, Almicar Mendez acknowledged that he would not be alive without international accompaniment. As time went on, Mendez invited broader international support for the CERJ, as well as accompaniment by other organizations. In 1995, he was elected to the Guatemalan Congress, and in 1996 the Guatemalan government began dismantling the patrols.

Local activists were not the only ones to be attacked in Guatemala. In January, 1989 a former member of the GAM falsely claimed to have been a guerrilla, said he had helped found the GAM for the guerrillas, that Almilcar Mendez and a PBI volunteer were both guerrillas, and that PBI and other international organizations were cooperating with the armed opposition to discredit Guatemala. Other than having been a member of the GAM though not a founder, there was no evidence to corroborate any of his assertions. That May while PBI was accompanying Rigoberta Menchu, the Mayan author and activist who was later to receive the Nobel Peace Prize, as well as other members of the Unified Representation of the Guatemalan Opposition (RUOG), PBI received a bomb threat at its Guatemala City headquarters, although nothing was found.

On August 15, 1989 shortly after a first floor room in the GAM house was destroyed by a bomb, two hand grenades were thrown over the garden wall of the PBI house blowing out most of its windows. Fortunately no one was injured in either attack. However on December 20, 1989, PBI volunteers Meredith Larson, Rusa Jeremic, and Mitch Goldberg were attacked and wounded by two men with knives near the PBI headquarters. A month before, Sister Dianna Ortiz, a U.S. nun who was teaching school as a rural missionary, was abducted, tortured and raped by Guatemalan police under the apparent command of a North American, a crime for which former Minister of Defense General Victor Gramajo was later found guilty by a U.S. court.

These attacks caused a serious debate within PBI's project committee about whether PBI was willing to risk the increasing possibility of a volunteer's death. PBI's decision was to continue in Guatemala, but also to generate the greatest international pressure it could. As Mahony and Eguren describe it in "Unarmed Bodyguards,"

> The week following the attack, PBI published an ad defending its work in every major Guatemalan newspaper. It was signed by dozens of members of the U.S. Congress, members of parliaments from Canada and Europe, international church leaders, and other well-known international figures. At the same time, ads condemning the attack on PBI were published by dozens of other Guatemalan organizations. Several embassies made public statements, U.S. Ambassador Thomas Stroock personally telephoned the families of the volunteers who had been attacked, and he visited the PBI house several times.

> Meredith Larson returned to the U.S. for medical treatment. In January and February, she gave dozens of public presentations in the United States about PBI's experience in Guatemala. She spent weeks going from one congressional office to another telling her story and urging the legislators to sign a letter to (President) Cerezo. PBI's U.S. chapter organized its national network of supporters to barrage these same officials with constituent telephone calls. The letter sent to Cerezo was ultimately signed by 111 U.S. senators and representatives. Similar campaigns in Canada and Europe generated other high-level messages of concern.

> U.S. Representative Theodore Weiss went on to submit an amendment to the 1990 appropriations bill conditioning military aid to Guatemala on the results of investigations into a list of human rights abuses, including the attack against PBI...A few months later,

innkeeper Michael Devine, another U.S. citizen, was murdered by Guatemalan soldiers, after which overt U.S. military aid to Guatemala was suspended altogether.

The PBI team in Guatemala moved into a more secure house in April 1990 and held another reception for the diplomatic and press corps. The organization had achieved a new prominence both in and out of Guatemala…PBI now frequented government offices, and ambassadors visited the PBI house. The violent attacks against PBI stopped.

According to PBI volunteer Maria Gabriela Serra, "From the moment of the bombing, we achieved legitimacy with the authorities that we'd never had before….When you have government ministers and ambassadors coming to your house, that's sending a clear message to the death squads…"

By January, 1993, when thousands of Guatemalan refugees began their internationally negotiated return from Mexico to resettle in new committees in the countryside, they were accompanied not only by PBI but by a multitude of international organizations and individuals, and the principle of international accompaniment had come of age. Although they suffered great hardships and eventual attacks, the refugees continued to be accompanied by a succession of internationals following PBI's pioneering example.

In 1996 the guerrillas and the government signed negotiated peace accords, and calls for PBI accompaniment became fewer and less urgent. In 1999, after 16 years, PBI decided to close its Guatemala project and to focus its attention on other countries.

Other Projects

In 1987, PBI had placed a team in El Salvador at the request of Bishop Medardo Gomez of the Lutheran Church and several other Salvadoran organizations, which continued there through the end of the civil war and until 1991. Among the many groups and individuals accompanied by PBI was COMADRES, the Mothers of the Disappeared and Detained. During the climactic full-scale guerrilla offensive on San Salvador in November, 1989, the army entered the University of Central America and murdered six priests, including Rector Ignacio Ellacuria and others we had visited in 1982-83. International workers were also arrested, including PBI team members Karen Ridd from Canada and Marcela Rodriguez from Colombia, whose account of their interrogation and beating by the treasury police, and Karen's courageous and successful refusal to be released without Marcela is one of the most moving stories in PBI's history.

In 1989 in Sri Lanka, PBI opened its first project outside of Latin America. From the time of its founding PBI had been following the dual civil war there between the majority mostly Buddhist Sinhalese and the minority predominately Hindu Tamils in the north, as well as the rebellion by the largely Sinhalese Marxist People's Liberation Front known as JVP in the south, which had resulted in many murders and disappearances. In 1989, the Sri Lanka Bar Association requested PBI protection for lawyers who were being assassinated for bringing habeas corpus petitions for detained and disappeared persons. PBI went on to accompany many activists and organizations in Sri Lanka until 1998, when requests for accompaniment were diminishing and the government demanded the right to censor PBI's human rights reports before they were published if it was to continue to work there.

From 1991 to 1999, PBI operated a North America project dealing with conflicts involving indigenous peoples, primarily in Canada. After participating with the coalition Cry for Justice in Haiti in 1993, from 1995-2000 PBI placed its own team there which focused on extensive training in nonviolent conflict resolution, rather than accompaniment. This work expanded on earlier peace and human rights training provided by PBI in Guatemala and El Salvador, including conflict resolution, negotiation methods, group processes, political analysis and other topics.

In addition to Cry for Justice, PBI has carried on two other projects with partner organizations: The Balkans Peace Team from 1994-2001, and International Service for Peace (SIPAZ) in Chiapas, Mexico, beginning in 1995.

In 1994, PBI opened a continuing project in Colombia involving the largest teams in PBI's history. Since 1998, PBI has had its own team in Mexico, and since 2002 has renewed its work in neighboring Guatemala. From 1999-2010 PBI carried out an Indonesia project, and from 2006-2013 in Nepal. PBI opened new projects in Kenya and Honduras in 2013, and is preparing to renew its Indonesia project in 2014.

PBI's International Secretariat has been in London since 1992. The organization now has country groups in Australia, Belgium, Canada, France, Germany, Italy, the Netherlands, Norway, Spain, Sweden, Switzerland, the UK and the United States, as well as active members and representatives in other countries. It maintains an excellent website at www.peacebrigades.org and an annual budget in excess of $3 million.

In 2001, PBI was nominated for the Nobel Peace Prize by the American Friends Service Committee, a 1947 winner of the prize. According to the AFSC statement,

> PBI has a sustained, deep commitment to non-violence in working for peace and human rights and provides a successful model for how ordinary people with extraordinary courage can support local workers for peace in some of the most dangerous of the world's conflicts.

> PBI's extraordinary record of accomplishment is powerful proof that non-violence and peaceful approaches to human rights and social change can work when supported by the international community. In more than twenty years of work in some of the world's most violent conflicts, no one under PBI protection was killed while they were being protected, nor have any PBI volunteers been killed....

> PBI has not received as much international attention as its work warrants.... Its mission, program, and methodology are compatible with the high honor of the Nobel Peace Prize.

The greatest honor of all is having been associated with the committed and courageous activists working with and protected by PBI over the years; they continue to deserve our support.

The Latin Connection in Walla Walla

When I was growing up in Walla Walla, I didn't know any Latino kids in the elementary schools. In high school, Vince Coronado was the only Latino I was aware of and we elected him student body president. On the other hand, the fields were full of Mexican farm workers, single men who lived in labor camps, moved on after the asparagus harvest, came back for the cherries and apples, and went home to their families in Mexico for the winter. In 1959 when I began working summers in the canneries there were no Latino workers there with the exception of the sanitation crew. A handful of Texas-born Latino families had come up first as migrants and then had settled in our area. One of the families ran a restaurant but most were hired as field foremen or for year-round farm work.

At present, Latinos make up over 20% of the population in Walla Walla County and about 50% in the city of Milton-Freewater just across the border in Oregon. The work force of the canneries before most of them closed was over 90% Latino, and there are currently quite a few Latino business and professional people as well as blue-collar workers, though most are still employed in farm, food processing or landscape work. Many recent immigrants are here without documents, and their lack of legal status has opened them to some exploitation and hostility from both Anglo and Latino residents.

The Valley Cultural Awareness Committee—Origins and Activities

In January of 1982, Barbara and I assisted veteran nonviolence trainer Bruce Kokopeli of Seattle in the presentation of a wide-ranging Nonviolence Training Workshop in Walla Walla. The three-day workshop was sponsored by the Committee on Alternatives to War of the Walla Walla Friends Meeting and covered personal and group nonviolence, defensive, assertive, and third party skills. The weekend workshop was attended by twenty people from the community, all of whom decided to continue to train themselves to be able to respond creatively to conflict at whatever level it presented itself, including personal, community, and international. Following the workshop the name of our committee was changed to the Committee on Nonviolent Conflict Resolution to reflect its broadening focus.

Along with continued trainings for its own members and others, in April the Committee organized a variety of community events coinciding with the national Ground Zero Week focusing on the potential effects of nuclear attacks. These included a benefit dance, a radiation fun run beginning at Ground Zero at the Walla Walla airport which was an acknowledged nuclear target, street theater, visiting speakers, films, panel discussions, and a town meeting, as well as a second Americans for Peace entry in the fair parade on Labor Day Weekend.

After that, our Committee began to assist Catholic sisters Ann Peressini and Virginia Paul with the development of a bicultural teen center in the largely Latino Washington Park neighborhood in Walla Walla. We also began an investigation of a series of racial incidents in the orchard and fruit-packing community of Milton-Freewater just across the border into Oregon, out of which came a new community relations organization.

In September 1982 Javier Olivares who was a participant in our nonviolence workshop came to us with news of an inter-racial murder in Milton-Freewater, and showed us a petition and an anonymous flier being circulated there protesting the presence of "illegal aliens." The murder resulted from the activities of a group of young whites who were preying on undocumented immigrants by luring them into remote places where they robbed and humiliated them. In this case a young Mexican had been picked up at a bar and invited out to a rural park, where he was robbed, sodomized, and left naked with the expectation that he would be too embarrassed to report the incident. In fact he did report the matter to the police, who were familiar with his assailants but did nothing. The night of the murder he encountered one of his attackers in a city park and stabbed him to death.

The petition had preceded the murder, was signed by 540 people from the town of around 5000, and asked for the removal of alien farm workers who were undocumented. Following the murder the anonymous flier attacked migrant workers and aliens in general, lamenting public subsidy of the migrant day care center, labor camp, summer school classes, and swimming pool passes, as well as the number of aliens present in the parks and schools.

Our Committee on Nonviolent Conflict Resolution was concerned about these developments and sent a four-person investigatory team to Milton-Freewater to meet with community leaders, farm workers, and anyone else willing to talk with us about improving the situation. Barbara, Javier, and I were team members, along with Milton-Freewater area resident Richard Bixby who was a member of the Committee as well as the Friends Meeting. We met initially with the city manager, the police chief, church leaders, and folks at the migrant labor camp. On November 8, we invited a larger group of community members to a meeting at the local high school to discuss our recommendations for the formation of a bicultural human relations committee in Milton-Freewater. At that meeting the Valley Cultural Awareness Committee was born, which provided cultural relations services in Milton-Freewater and the broader valley over the next twenty years.

Following additional meetings at Milton-Freewater Orchard Homes, the local labor camp, which were attended by farm workers and businessmen from the Latino community, members of the local Chamber of Commerce and others from the Anglo community, the VCAC initiated what was to become the oldest annual Cinco de Mayo fiesta in the state of Oregon. Our event featured a soccer tournament coordinated by long-time VCAC President Santos Garcia, food booths, kids' games, and an entertainment stage which I organized for many years. In later years we added a royalty contest managed by long-time VCAC Secretary Mauri McCabe, a community parade leading to the main fiesta site organized by high school soccer coach and later VCAC President Jose Garcia and his wife, and an evening dance.

In addition to a community celebration of Latino culture, on a number of occasions VCAC activities included crisis intervention, trainings, advocacy, and community education.

Our crisis intervention work began when we invited a representative of the U.S. Department of Justice's Community Relations Division to come to Milton-Freewater to meet with us. One of the Department's resulting recommendations was the establishment of a rumor control program, which we put to important use the following year. We also brought trainer Bruce Kokopeli back to the valley in January, 1983 to lead one of several nonviolence trainings we presented for committee members and others at the Milton-Freewater labor camp. CNCR trainers Barbara Clark, Richard Bixby, and Cindy Robinson helped lead these trainings as part of VCAC preparations for putting bicultural teams on the streets if needed during any period of increased tensions.

The first service by the VCAC's Crisis Intervention Unit occurred on Saturday, August 20, 1983 after the early morning shooting death of 21 year-old farm worker Ignacio Sanchez near a Freewater tavern. Friends of the victim began arming themselves to take revenge on a Latino they suspected of being the murderer because as far as they knew no one had been arrested. The VCAC learned of their plan and also learned that an Anglo suspect may have been arrested, which the authorities hadn't disclosed.

In classic bureaucratic fashion, the Milton-Freewater police department whose chief was out of town denied that an arrest had been made and refused to provide any information about the case, initially frustrating our efforts at rumor control. We then appealed to the Oregon State Police, one of whose officers, John Gaukroger, was a member of our committee. John understood the importance of what we were doing and confirmed that an Anglo suspect in the murder was in custody though on a different charge, which we also confirmed through the county jail.

With this information the committee immediately sent a team led by Santos Garcia to find the victim's friends and let them know a suspect was in custody. Other committee members meeting at John and Blanca Gaukroger's home drafted a VCAC flier in Spanish telling of the murder, the arrest of a suspect, that the motive had been robbery, and that several other interracial incidents had occurred that weekend which made it important that people not go to the taverns that evening and that they stay home on Saturday and Sunday night. The events referred to in addition to the murder included an incident near the labor camp where two Anglos had chased a Latino who they said had thrown a rock at their car, a case of hit and run by a Latino driver, and a case of drunk driving which resulted in a Latino driver assaulting the police followed by an assault by the police on the driver, making it a very hot weekend.

Our flier invited the Latino community to come to a meeting at the labor camp recreation room that Saturday night at 9 p.m. to discuss the situation. Though the local Catholic priest had agreed to announce the meeting at a Spanish mass and reception held that evening, when we arrived at the labor camp the door to the recreation room was locked and we were met by the manager and two police officers he had summoned to prevent us from entering the camp.

Landlord-tenant rights at the camp had recently become an issue, and the intoxicated camp manager who didn't speak or read Spanish apparently feared we were trying to organize the tenants against him, and told the police to arrest us if we entered the camp. As Javier and I stood there looking at the growing numbers of camp residents gathered outside the doors of the locked recreation room, we discussed what we should do. Finally, we decided that too much was at stake to just walk away, so we walked into the camp, distributed our fliers, and held a brief open air meeting with those gathered there.

Happily, before we were finished or arrested police chief Bill Biggs arrived and took charge of the situation. Bill was one of the founding members of the VCAC and had been involved with us in preparing our crisis intervention plan, but apparently had not informed his department. At our request, Bill agreed to personally accompany us that night in monitoring the main tavern block in Freewater. To our relief there were fewer Latinos out that night than anyone could remember and there was no more trouble. The rest of that weekend also passed without incident.

For three days following the killing, the official media continued to report that no suspect was in custody. After Lee Laws was formally charged with the murder, at that point there was a second rumor circulating in the Latino community that he was being released. Law enforcement officials again refused to provide information until we applied some pressure, after which assurances were given us that Laws was not being released, and the VCAC was able to pass this on to the community as well. Laws' first trial resulted in a hung jury. At his second trial he was convicted of the manslaughter death of Ignacio Sanchez and sentenced to 20 years in prison.

In reviewing these incidents and our response, the VCAC concluded that

1. Acts of retribution aimed at an innocent person who was suspected to be the killer of Ignacio Sanchez were planned, based on suspicions bred by a lack of official information provided by law enforcement agencies,

2. The Committee's investigative and intermediary activities directly resulted in the avoidance of such mistaken acts of violence by specific individuals,

3. The Committee's written statement and oral advice to the Latino community were important in reducing the turnout at local taverns the night following the killing and in averting further incidents....

Our official report also acknowledged that the fact that the VCAC flier was wholly in Spanish and not comprehensible by local officials led to suspicion of the Committee's actions, and that the level of communication between the Committee and local law enforcement and labor camp officials left much to be desired.

In an effort to improve communication, in May, 1982 the VCAC had begun publishing VISTAS, a bilingual newssheet. With a small grant from the McKenzie River Gathering in Eugene, 1500 copies of each issue were distributed free to all of the residents of the Milton-Freewater and Walla Walla labor camps, as well as to a variety of community service agencies, businesses and individuals.

In successive issues of VISTAS, Javier and I wrote about farm worker protection laws, problems with farm labor contractors, an effort to establish a farm worker service center as an alternative to contractors, the availability of low-income legal services, immigration issues, complaints of abuses and the formation of a tenant council at the Walla Walla labor camp, tenant requests for more recreational facilities at the Walla Walla camp, and possibilities for a tenant council at the Milton-Freewater camp. There were also stories about a successful VCAC request to double the size of the basketball court at the Milton-Freewater camp, cultural events at the local colleges and in the community, a voter registration drive, VCAC assistance with equipment at the Pioneer Posse Grounds, formation of a bicultural chess club at the saddle shop run by Santos Garcia and his friend Salvador "Chava" Negrete, the organization of Radio Hispano on the Whitman College radio station during the summer of 1984 in cooperation with members of IMAGE of Walla Walla, and other matters of interest to Latinos and those working with them.

VCAC advocacy over the years included a successful campaign to bring Spanish language television to the valley as well as the appointment by the Walla Walla County Commissioners of the first Latino member to the board in charge of the totally Latino Walla Walla Labor Camp. Following that we focused on problems with the administration of the Milton-Freewater labor camp, and partnered with the City of Milton-Freewater to try to upgrade the management of the camp and seek more openness and community participation at the board level there.

In the fall of 1984, the VCAC co-sponsored a leadership training session at the Walla Walla labor camp with the tenant council, bringing in Latino leaders and professionals from the community to try to increase the leadership capacity and skills of Latino residents of both labor camps and in the general community. The Committee also sponsored visiting theater companies featuring Latino and Native American themes, and contributed costume funds for a local Mexican folkloric dance group. Funds raised through the VCAC's Cinco de Mayo scholarship fund under the leadership of Milton-Freewater city manager Jim Swayne and Watermill Foods CEO Bill Albee provided thousands of dollars of college scholarship aid to Latino and other students from Milton-Freewater schools.

The VCAC maintained a bicultural membership, sponsored annual Cinco de Mayo fiestas at Shockman Field in Milton-Freewater, and continued to be available to respond to other community needs as they arose until its dissolution in 2009 when it passed the cultural relations torch on to the Walla Walla Diversity Coalition.

Evergreen Legal Services

In 1983, Evergreen Legal Services, the statewide program providing free civil representation for low income people, contacted me regarding the Walla Walla Farm Labor Camp operated by the County Housing Authority. Since most attorneys in our area represent landlords, Evergreen had not been able to find a Walla Walla attorney willing to represent the camp tenants in their conflicts with the administration, and I agreed to do that.

In April, 1983 a complaint had been filed with the Farmers Home Administration by the Blue Mountain Action Council, our local anti-poverty organization, alleging arbitrary and improper administrative practices at the migrant farmworker camp funded by the federal government. Their primary concern was that individual migrant workers were being turned away while vacant units were being illegally reserved for certain farmers or farm labor contractors, and that units were being illegally occupied by ineligible non-agricultural workers.

After I had represented a number of individual tenants or tenant applicants, the need for some kind of tenant organization at the camp became clear to me, and I talked the idea over with Javier

Olivares, who was living there at the time. Together we proposed the formation of a tenant council for which I agreed to serve as legal counsel and which became the major player in negotiating a management plan, as well as a new lease that for the first time met federal regulations. This was also the camp's first management plan and the first time a lease was ever translated into Spanish at this then all-Latino camp of mostly monolingual Spanish-speakers. One element we insisted on in the plan was that the also monolingual (English only) manager begin taking Spanish lessons.

In 1984, Evergreen's farmworker division began to concentrate its resources on abuses of workers by farm labor contractors who controlled many of the fieldwork jobs in the Walla Walla Valley and elsewhere in Washington. The problematic system of middlemen between the people who own and operate farms and the people who work them seasonally was complicated further by the difficulty of communication when growers and migrant workers are unfamiliar with each other's language. The successful contractor has the advantage of knowing both Spanish and English as well as where the jobs and workers can be found, and may also transport workers to the field, and provide housing, food, negotiation of contract terms, field supervision, and payroll.

As in other locales, worker complaints here involved issues of misrepresentation of the amount of wages to be paid and whether the work was to be piece rate or by the hour, excessive charges for transportation and other services, failure to pay wages when due and in the proper amount, threats of deportation or violence if complaints were made, deductions for social security without forwarding them to the government, and failure to comply with worker compensation laws regarding injuries.

Among the contractor actions Evergreen filed was a federal class action suit against the largest farm labor contractor in Walla Walla County, who contracted with approximately 25 growers annually. I agreed to serve as co-counsel for the farm workers in that case, which involved claims of failure to register as a contractor; failure to keep required records; failure to disclose wage rates, employers' names, period of employment, type of work to be performed, contractor's charges, and other required information; threats, intimidation and coercion; use of improper vehicles for transportation; failure to pay wages when due and in the proper amount; improper deductions for housing and transportation, and other matters. An agreed order was entered as to part of these claims, awarding the workers damages, an injunction against further violations, and provision for a special arbitration panel to hear any future claims. That contractor was later criminally prosecuted and sent to prison for immigration fraud.

Beyond selective enforcement actions, it was my view that a farmworker agency or cooperative was needed to provide on a community basis the services now performed by private contractors, as well as other needed services for farm workers. Though such an organization was proposed and we made an attempt in 1985 to create a Farmworker Service Center of the Walla Walla Valley, lack of both confidence and cooperation among the various agencies resulted in funding problems, and the effort failed to get underway.

Immigration Law and the Interfaith Sanctuary Committee

Walla Walla area asparagus growers began bringing in Mexican farm workers under the government's bracero program in the 1940's. Before that our crops were mostly harvested by local residents and US migrants. In 1964, the last year of the federal program, which was ended because of the adverse effect it was having on domestic employment as well as a variety of abuses, about 180,000 seasonal workers from Mexico were brought into the United States.

After the bracero program ended, local growers continued to depend on Latino farm workers, many of whom came across the border illegally. In the 1980's the last non-Latino farm workers moved out of the Walla Walla labor camp and the bulk of both field and cannery work was being done by Latinos, while Anglos moved to better paying employment. Most of the farm workers were Mexicans who arrived in the early spring, stayed until November when the field and cannery work ended, and went home to Mexico for the winter where the weather was better and their extended families were waiting for their return.

Immigration Raids

The economic benefits of a large, low-cost work force were apparent to local growers and food processors who were glad for the seasonal influx and growing year-round Latino population and wanted no interference from the Immigration and Naturalization Service, which usually agreed to stay away. At times though, for political reasons or on the basis of specific complaints, the INS deported particular workers or conducted general raids on the fields and other work places.

In the spring of 1984, while Congress was considering an amnesty program for workers and residents who had been here for long periods, the INS began an apparent effort to deport as many aliens as possible before adoption of the new law. The Walla Walla Valley saw the most intense INS activity in many years with the arrests of hundreds of workers. I was acquainted with a number of these workers, many of whom had lived here for years and whose children were born here and attended Walla Walla schools.

These arrests were a severe crisis for the Latino community in the Walla Walla area since the closest immigration law attorneys were about 270 miles away in Seattle and they charged high fees. Because there was no practical legal representation available to many low income workers here, I began to take on a number of deportation and other immigration cases. I had become fairly fluent in Spanish through my work in Central America and with residents of the local labor camps. As the only Spanish-speaking attorney in the valley, I began to develop a substantial caseload which expanded further once the amnesty law was adopted with its promise of legal status to farm workers and residents who could document their long-time residence here.

The Sanctuary Movement

This period also saw a substantial influx of refugees fleeing the civil wars in Central America, particularly Guatemalans and Salvadorans. Because of US aid to the military regimes there, most of those fleeing were being cynically refused refugee status by our government, spawning the sanctuary movement among religious people in the US.

In January, 1984 I travelled to Seattle for an immigration law seminar in Seattle in order to learn how to defend these refugees whose numbers were increasing in the Walla Walla area. By April, the Walla Walla Friends Meeting had begun to discuss what response to make to the refugee situation, and in early May the Meeting began considering the possibility of a sanctuary declaration. Following several INS raids, on June 3 the Meeting adopted a Declaration of Sanctuary which read:

> The Walla Walla Friends Meeting, a Quaker church, declares its readiness to provide sanctuary in the homes of its members to political refugees from El Salvador and Guatemala who are in present danger of arrest and deportation by authorities of our government.
>
> We take this step out of human concern and religious obligation. We are told that our nation's laws prohibit us from offering aid and comfort to Central American refugees who have fled their homes in terror. We find such a prohibition to be contrary to our religious duty. We are particularly concerned because our own country's military aid has been used against the homes and families of these refugees.
>
> We take this step openly, with full appreciation of the seriousness of disobedience of the law. We feel that not to offer assistance to our brothers and sisters in need under these circumstances would be a more serious moral wrong, as well as a violation of the U.N. Protocol Relating to Refugees, to which the U.S. is a signatory.
>
> We intend to provide sanctuary to refugees who we are satisfied would be in danger if they were forcibly returned to their own country. In the event of an attempt by the authorities to deport any political refugee afforded sanctuary by our Meeting, it is our intention to use every lawful avenue available to us to resist such deportation.
>
> In the event any member or supporter of our Meeting is charged with a crime because of the offer or provision of such sanctuary, we encourage our members and supporters to sign statements of complicity and to present themselves to the authorities as co-defendants, since our act is a corporate one.
>
> We invite other churches and individuals to join with us or to support us in this offer of religious sanctuary through endorsements, pledges of personal or financial assistance, or through similar offers of sanctuary.

Our Friends Meeting sought additional support and resources through a request for the endorsement of its action by its oversight Eastside Friends Meeting in Bellevue and by our regional organization of Friends, North Pacific Yearly Meeting, both of which approved. Prior to giving general publicity to our declaration, we also wanted to organize a local interfaith sanctuary coalition.

The first meeting of the Walla Walla Interfaith Sanctuary Committee was held on July 17, co-chaired by Barbara Clark of the Walla Walla Friends Meeting and Sister Virginia Paul of St.

Patrick Catholic Church. Other members of the evolving coalition were clergy or parishioners from First Congregational, Central Christian, White Temple Baptist, Pioneer United Methodist, Grace United Methodist, Christ Lutheran, St. Paul's Episcopal, First Church of God, Walla Walla College Seventh Day Adventist, Central Presbyterian, and Christian Science churches.

In November, 1984, a five-car caravan of Guatemalan refugees on their way from Walla Walla to seek winter employment in Florida were seized by immigration authorities in Kansas. The five families and several single men had been living in the Walla Walla area for approximately two years. All 23 of those arrested were taken to Texas where they were continuing to be held. Fortunately, the members of our Walla Walla sanctuary committee were able to raise sufficient bail to secure the release of the single men, while the families finally obtained release on their own recognizance pending deportation.

Although no other Walla Walla church declared itself a sanctuary, in January 1985 the Walla Walla Interfaith Sanctuary Committee approved the following statement signed by forty of its members and which we published in our local newspaper:

> We deplore the indictment of religious workers by the United States Government for their assistance to refugees from the war and violence in El Salvador and Guatemala.
>
> We also deplore our government's failure to provide fair treatment and safe haven to these refugees, as required by principles of international law and elementary justice.
>
> We believe assistance to the refugees in our midst is a religious and moral duty. In the book of Isaiah, we are enjoined to
>
> > Hide the outcasts,
> > > Betray not the fugitive;
> > Let the outcasts…
> > > Sojourn among you;
> > Be a refuge to them
> > > From the destroyer.
>
> In the Book of Leviticus, the Lord said to Moses, "If strangers live with you in your land, do not molest them. You must count them as your own people, and love them as yourselves, for you were strangers in the land of Egypt."
>
> We also believe that assistance to refugees is a legal right under the First Amendment to the U.S. Constitution, which guarantees the free exercise of religion.
>
> We pledge our support to the refugees among us, as well as to those who may be persecuted for assisting them. We invite people of goodwill to join with us in this offer of assistance, and we invite those in need to contact us for help.

On March 5, 1985 our Interfaith Sanctuary Committee held an Ecumenical Service of Prayer and Dedication Concerning Central America at Pioneer United Methodist, led by people from a variety of churches. The Committee also carried on a number of other educational activities, including talks by speakers from Central America and local people who had visited there, films, the issuance of alerts on Congressional issues, information booths, and creation of a lending library on Central America issues.

In July, 1986 we received a request to assist Carlos, a 19-year old Salvadoran held by the INS in a for-profit detention center outside of Houston. Many of his friends had disappeared in El Salvador, and he had fled when he could no longer leave his house in the war-torn San Miguel region because of fear of being seized by the military. At the time of his arrest he was on his way to Walla Walla to join his mother, who had also fled after receiving death threats earlier in the year. Carlos' mother raised a portion of his bail, our Friends Meeting advanced the balance, and the Interfaith Sanctuary Committee sought additional contributions in order to create an ongoing bail fund.

As coordinator of the sanctuary group's legal committee, when Carlos arrived in Walla Walla, I agreed to represent him in a political asylum application as I had done for several other Salvadorans. The problem was that the only immigration judge in Seattle at the time, William Nail, had heard dozens of Guatemalan and Salvadoran asylum applications both in Seattle and in Arizona and had never granted one, no matter how clear the evidence and the law were.

Under both US and international law, a person is entitled to political asylum if they were individually targeted for repression or were a member of a targeted class in their home country, and had a good faith fear for their own safety. Carlos was a conscientious objector who had served as a volunteer with the Red Cross in neighboring Honduras. As a young single male in a province engulfed by war, he was a clear target for forced recruitment by both sides or for retribution for failure to serve. Judge Nail, however, denied his claim as he denied all others. We were aware that survival rates were very low for forcibly repatriated refugees once they stepped off the plane after being sent back home. Fortunately for Carlos and for another Salvadoran I represented, we were successful in challenging the judge's bias on appeal, the appeal panel granted them asylum, and they were not sent home.

Because of the availability of farm work in the Walla Walla area, cautious refugees were normally able to live independently and to blend into the general community. Formal protection by a sanctuary group such as ours wasn't as critical as it was in the urban areas, and neither our Interfaith Sanctuary Committee nor the Friends Meeting was ever called on to actually house a refugee, though we did occasionally provide work for Carlos and others. Ultimately with the granting by Congress of extended voluntary departure status for Salvadorans and Guatemalans, refugees from those countries were allowed to remain in the United States until the wars there were over, and the work of the Interfaith Sanctuary Committee ended without incident.

Hanford

About 50 miles from Walla Walla as the crow flies lies the Hanford Nuclear Reservation near Richland, Washington, where the Manhattan Project produced the atomic bomb which destroyed Nagasaki, Japan during World War II. In the deadly Green Run of 1944, authorities at Hanford had also intentionally released harmful radiation into the winds of Eastern Washington heading east toward Walla Walla to see what effect it would have. Despite false claims of complete safety at Hanford, we now know that there were many other accidental and intentional releases of harmful levels of radioactivity into the air, water, and soil at Hanford and the general vicinity over the years, repeatedly compromising the health of Hanford workers, area residents, and the environment.

In 1985, the federal government was continuing to make nuclear weapons materials at Hanford when a series of citizen inquiries and nonviolent protests were begun that resulted in the termination of all nuclear weapons production there.

Nagasaki Day

My active involvement began on the evening of August 8, 1985 when Jan Karon, a friend of ours from Sumpter, Oregon, called to say she was planning to commit civil disobedience at Hanford the next day as part of an action by the Seattle Nonviolent Action Group (SNAG), and wondered if I would be willing to represent her. When I said I would, she soon called back to find out if I would also be willing to represent others in the group, which I agreed to do.

On August 9, Nagasaki Day, 15 people formed a human chain across the road taking day shift workers to the Plutonium-Uranium Extraction (PUREX) facility at Hanford where in addition to the Nagasaki bomb nearly 60% of all plutonium used in U.S. nuclear weapons had been manufactured. PUREX, with the adjoining N Reactor, was also to be the primary source of plutonium for the 17,000 new nuclear weapons planned by the U.S. over the next decade and a half.

The blockaders were arrested at approximately 7 a.m. after police diverted traffic to another route. Two of the 15 were juveniles and were released shortly to their parents. Of the remaining 13, nine refused to give their names or addresses and began a fast in the jail. Since all of those fasting were from the Seattle area and did not want to have to return to the Tri-Cities after being released, we negotiated a plea agreement the same day, under which they received one day jail sentences with credit for time served.

The remaining four defendants, Scott Renfro and Rita DePuydt of Bellingham, Richard Lane of Richland, and my friend Jan Karon, elected to stand trial, and I was able to arrange their release on their own recognizance.

The trial was originally scheduled for October 14 then put off to December 9. I recruited Walla Walla attorneys Michael de Grasse and Ray Williams to represent two of the defendants, while I represented Jan, and the fourth defendant represented himself pro se in order to allow us multiple statements and the greatest exposure to the court and jury.

Although we considered the possibility of seeking a change of venue because the Tri-Cities where the trial was to be held is so heavily dependent on Hanford employment, we decided to proceed to trial in the heart of the "nuclear culture" in order to obtain the maximum educational effect from the event.

The original charge against all the defendants was the misdemeanor of disorderly conduct, defined as "intentionally disrupt(ing) vehicular...traffic without lawful authority." A second count of failure to disperse was added later against the remaining four defendants, but we were successful in getting that dismissed before the trial.

The legal theories we raised were (1) self defense, (2) defense of others, (3) defense of property, (4) necessity, (5) the right to interfere in the commission of a crime, (6) justification under international law, and (7) lack of criminal intent.

We proposed to call at least five expert witnesses, most of whom we had met in Spokane at a September conference sponsored by the Hanford Education Action League (HEAL) in cooperation with Physicians for Social Responsibility. Our planned witnesses were Dr. Ernest Sternglass of the University of Pittsburg, a physicist and epidemiologist who designed the first Westinghouse water-cooled nuclear reactor and had written explosively on the correlations between fetal death, infant mortality, and low-level nuclear releases from Hanford and other sources; chemist Allen Benson of Spokane Falls Community College who had carefully tracked radiation releases from Hanford; Dr. Hugh Strailey, a Seattle member of Physicians for Social Responsibility; Hiroshima survivor Mary Fujita of Seattle, and Prof. Francis Boyle, an expert on international law and the use of nuclear weapons.

We disqualified the presiding judge before whom the case was originally set for presumed bias, but we consented to a jury trial before the court commissioner, William Platts, who we felt would give the defendants a fair hearing. Several weeks before trial, Commissioner Platts ruled that he would not allow testimony by Professor Boyle on the principles and requirements of international law, but indicated he would give the jury appropriate instructions on those principles. He also ruled that he would allow unlimited testimony by the defendants themselves regarding the defense of necessity, and would allow that defense theory to go to the jury. As to expert witnesses, he would require that their testimony be intimately linked to the state of mind of the defendants. Although he ruled that expert testimony on nuclear holocaust was irrelevant, he was interested in testimony to be provided by Dr. Sternglass on the risk of local contamination.

Since we anticipated considerable difficulty finding unbiased jurors, we asked the court to call a larger than normal jury panel. The jury list we were given contained 119 jurors, over half of whom had a present employment connection with Hanford, either from working there themselves or through their spouses, their parents or their children. Our motion to excuse all such jurors was denied. The selection of the jury took a full day, with the court excluding several Hanford employees who admitted actual bias, while denying our challenges to other Hanford workers including two potential jurors who were presently employed at the N Reactor and whose jobs would end if PUREX were shut down.

Still, we were satisfied with the jury, which included an art dealer who favored wind over nuclear power, a school teacher whose request to take notes was granted over the prosecutor's objection, and at least two jurors who said that nuclear weapons "scared" them. We felt that even if no expert testimony were allowed, if the defendants were given relatively free rein with their own testimony we could expect either a hung jury or an acquittal.

In the opening statements of counsel and the pro se defendant, we were allowed to explain in depth the defendants' belief that they and others were personally being harmed by the radioactive emissions from PUREX and by the threat of nuclear war, and that they believed that international law and other legal principles gave them the right to act.

The first defendant to testify, Scott Renfro, went over the same ground in detail. Although the court refused to allow him to read or to introduce into evidence documents he had relied on in formulating his belief, he was allowed to read and introduce a statement he and other SNAG protestors had themselves written accusing the Boeing Corporation of international war crimes as a result of its production of weapons of mass destruction targeting civilians, which included quotations from the London Agreement of 1945 establishing the Nuremberg Tribunals as well as other statements of international law, and that referenced a citizen's right under common law to arrest a felon.

Following this testimony we offered our first expert witness, chemist Allen Benson. Over the prosecution's objection the judge then made the following rulings:

1. Expert testimony would be permitted on the issue of local and regional contamination, and the jury would be instructed on the necessity defense which allows a citizen to break a law in order to avoid a greater harm

2. Although the court didn't believe that the threat of nuclear war qualified as a necessity defense, if the jury wished to believe from the defendants' own testimony that they believed they acted out of necessity with regard to nuclear war, or that they reasonably believed an international crime was being committed, it could so find, and could acquit them on that basis.

Under an agreement with the three national network affiliates, the trial was being covered by a pooled television camera in the courtroom. In addition, newspaper and radio reporters were present, and reports of the trial were being issued by the Associated Press.

After the judge's ruling that our scientists could testify as to local and regional contamination, the prosecution consulted with US Department of Energy attorneys who were present during the trial, then immediately moved to dismiss all charges. The prosecution's motion and the judge's ordering of the dismissal created an immediate sensation in the courtroom. We quickly called a news conference in the hallway in order to present our expert witnesses to the news media, and to put forward the obvious conclusion that the prosecution and the Department of Energy were afraid of our scientific testimony because they were trying to cover up the truth about radioactive emissions from the plant.

The following night, our star witness Ernest Sternglass was given further news coverage when we arranged a lecture for him at Whitman College in which he presented the testimony he would have given at the trial. This included his epidmiological studies of infant mortality in Washington State which showed 300 infant deaths had occurred as a result of a January, 1984 accident at PUREX. Though Hanford officials had initially denied any plutonium emissions, when confronted with the results of an independent study, they admitted that their original assessment had been mistaken. With these disclosures, in the end the only thing the government was able to gain by dismissing the case against these defendants was avoidance of an adverse jury verdict.

While Sternglass was staying at our home in Walla Walla, he told us about a time during his graduate studies when he had a talk with Albert Einstein, who advised him that he was ruining his mind by continuing on at the University. Just then our son Jeremy walked into the room wearing an old sweatshirt and an authentic-looking rubber Einstein mask. Sternglass first gave a violent start, then said, "Oh!" and burst out laughing. On the way back to the Tri-Cities airport he told us that he had testified at many trials, but this one was unique and he would always remember it for two reasons. The first was the dismissal of the case at the prospect of his testifying. The second was his encounter with Einstein.

Hiroshima Day

The next year SNAG carried out another action at Hanford, this time after consulting with me in advance for help drafting the following lengthy letter that was sent on July 25, 1986 by several of the protestors, including Jan Karon, to Michael Lawrence, the manager of Department of Energy operations at Hanford, as well as to the Benton County Prosecutor and Sheriff, to the Governor and Attorney General of the State of Washington, and to the President, Vice-President, and Speaker of the House of Representatives of the United States:

> Dear Mr. Lawrence:
>
> As concerned citizens of the world and of this region, we are writing to you to call your attention to the immediate threat to the health and safety of persons, to property, and to the natural environment posed by the continued operation of the N Reactor and the PUREX (Plutonium-Uranium Extraction) plutonium facilities at the Hanford Nuclear Reservation, which you administer.
>
> As the chief executive officer in charge of those facilities, we are also writing to notify you of the illegality of the continued operation of those facilities under state, federal and international law, as set out below.
>
> With regard to the threat to persons, property and the environment from the continued operation of these facilities, you are aware of the serious radioactive contamination of the air, water and soil over the course of the past 40 years of plutonium operations at Hanford, as partially disclosed by the documents recently released by your department under pressure from citizen groups. Your own personnel concede that the vast majority of all radioactive water contaminants at Hanford come from the N Reactor, and that over 90% of the airborne radioactive contaminants from Hanford come from the PUREX plant.
>
> In addition, the similarity of the N Reactor to the Chernobyl plant in the Soviet Union, whose disastrous meltdown has done worldwide damage, has resulted in pleas by well-

informed scientists and others for the immediate shutdown of the facility, whose containment technology is inadequate and outdated, whose product, plutonium, is unnecessary and itself poses a serious threat to human and environmental health, and whose waste byproducts cannot be safely disposed of.

The N Reactor and PUREX operations are in one sense radioactive time bombs waiting to go off. In another sense, their operation is like continuing to put poison in leaky barrels. Even if they don't explode, their daily operation is placing deadly contaminants into the air, water, and soil, resulting in increased rates of disease and death, and damaging the land for future generations.

Your continued operation of these facilities, under present circumstances, constitutes criminal negligence and reckless endangerment under Washington law. Under RCW 9A.08.010,

> A person is criminally negligent or acts with criminal negligence when he fails to be aware of a substantial risk that a wrongful act may occur and his failure to be aware of such substantial risk constitutes a gross deviation from the standard of care that a reasonable man would exercise in the same situation.

RCW 9A.36.030(b), defining Third Degree Assault, makes injury to another as a result of criminal negligence by means of "anything likely to produce bodily harm" a Class C felony, punishable by up to five years in prison.

Under RCW 9A.36.050, a gross misdemeanor, a person is guilty of reckless endangerment when he recklessly engages in conduct which creates a substantial risk of death or serious physical injury to another person.

In addition, your continued operation of the N Reactor and the PUREX plant constitute Crimes against Humanity and Crimes against Peace under treaties and principles of international law to which our government is a party or otherwise bound.

The operations of the PUREX plant, as well as the N Reactor, despite its collateral electrical generation, have only one purpose—the production of plutonium for nuclear weapons. Such weapons of indiscriminate destructiveness and worldwide effect plainly violate the fundamental prohibitions of international treaties such as the Hague and Geneva Conventions, which bar injury to civilians and other noncombatants, the wanton destruction of cities and towns, damage to neutral countries, genocide, the use of poisons and analogous substances, and the use of weapons which cause unnecessary suffering and widespread, long term and severe damage to the natural environment. For this reason, the United Nations General Assembly has on two occasions recognized by resolution that the use of nuclear weapons constitutes a Crime against Peace, a War Crime, and a Crime against Humanity.

Further, the Nuremburg Principles, set out in the London Agreement of 1945 signed by the U.S., make the "planning, preparation, initiation or waging of a war of aggression in violation of international treaties, agreements or assurances" a Crime against Peace, as well as "participation in a common plan or conspiracy for the accomplishment of any of the acts mentioned (above)." These Principles, since adopted by the United Nations at the request of the United States, make individuals such as yourself individually responsible for all of the crimes described, despite the fact that you are acting under governmental orders. A copy of these Principles, which also make complicity in any of these acts a crime, is attached for your reference.

Since the plutonium produced under your direction is intended for use in weapons of mass destruction, themselves illegal, many of which are designed for first-strike use, the operation of these plants under your direction constitutes a continuing international crime, as well as the state crimes set out above. These dangerous and criminal acts directly threaten us as residents of the region, as well as threatening the persons and property of others throughout this region and the world.

We request that you immediately terminate the plutonium production operations at the N Reactor and the PUREX plant at Hanford.

If you have not done so by midnight on Tuesday, August 5, 1986, and if the authorities to whom copies of this letter are directed have not required you to do so by that date, we will be obligated to take nonviolent action to interfere with the operations of those facilities.

We will take such action under the rights and duties provided us under the common law to interfere in the commission of a crime. We will also act under the rights provided in RCW 9A.16.020 to act in self defense, in defense of others, and in defense of property when an injury is about to take place. In addition, we will act out of necessity, from our clear perception that the N Reactor and PUREX are an immediate threat of enormous proportions to all of us and to the earth, from our knowledge that other means to avert this threat have proven ineffective, and from the conviction that our actions, while nonviolent, will have a significant effect on the operation of these dangerous facilities.

In summary, we will act out of a sense of duty to ourselves, to our fellow citizens, to the Nuremburg Principles, to the earth, and to high principles which compel us to act in the face of this threat.

We hope that your favorable response will make such action unnecessary.

On Hiroshima Day, August 6, 1986, twenty-nine people blocked the road leading to the N Reactor and the PUREX plant backing up traffic for two miles for a period of 37 minutes. All were arrested, and nine pled guilty to a municipal court charge of disorderly conduct, while eighteen elected to stand trial. Mike de Grasse and I again served as defense counsel, presenting the court with a list of expert witnesses and a trial brief raising the legal defenses set out in the defendants' letter as we had the prior year. This time around the prosecution disqualified Commissioner Platts and we agreed to have it heard before Judge Eugene Pratt.

When the Richland City Attorney received our brief he called me asking for a delay in the trial date so he could take the matter before the city council to be sure they wanted him to go ahead with the charges, since he was surprised by the nature of our defense and felt that perhaps they were getting into more than they had bargained for with these defendants. We refused to agree to the delay. However, at the pre-trial hearing, before we could open our mouths the judge announced that he considered the city ordinance under which our clients were charged to be unconstitutional, since it made criminal the obstruction of traffic "without lawful authority," a phrase he said was too vague to be enforceable as demonstrated by the various types of lawful authority we raised in our brief. So once again the case against our clients was dismissed, this time on the judge's own motion.

Wrap Up

The final Hanford case I handled involved the June 18, 1986 arrest of Larry Caldwell outside a Kennewick high school building where he was sitting under a tree preparing his testimony for a public hearing being held there by the US Department of Energy. The subject of the hearing was the sufficiency of an environmental impact statement for plans to modify the PUREX plant to allow it to better process spent fuel from Hanford's Fast Flux Test Facility and the N Reactor for the manufacture of nuclear weapons. Next to where he was sitting, Larry had placed 16 wooden crosses in the lawn together with a sign which read, "Hanford Nuclear Reservation—Tombstone Technology."

When school officials told him that he would have to remove the crosses and leave, he told them he was exercising his First Amendment right of freedom of speech, and that the display was part of his public comment concerning the draft environmental impact statement. A policeman was then called and Larry, a former N Reactor operator, was arrested for criminal trespass, handcuffed, and taken to jail. This time, over the City of Kennewick's objections, Judge Pratt granted my motion to dismiss the charge on the ground that the defendant was engaged in constitutionally protected speech at the time of his arrest. Our subsequent civil claim against the school district and the city resulted in their paying Larry several thousand dollars in damages.

In 1989, after a variety of Freedom of Information Act requests by HEAL and others uncovered decades of previously undisclosed documents at Hanford proving emissions and cover-ups by private contractors and federal officials alike, together with the actions of SNAG and other protestors amid rising citizen distrust, the federal government closed both the PUREX plant and the N Reactor, ended all further weapons production at the Hanford Reservation, and began the long process of cleaning up more than four decades of nuclear and chemical contamination there.

Music and Dance

Among the greatest of joys for me—along with family and projects—are music and dance.

I began developing those pursuits when I was young through the influence of my musician mother. Although no great musician myself, in grade school I took up both the piano and the trumpet. When I thought practicing both instruments was too much, unfortunately I dropped piano. In fourth grade, I began to play trumpet in the school band, and before long was sitting in the first chair, where I also sat in junior high and high school. Our elementary school was the only one in the county with a marching band, and people used to say that in the parades the Prospect Point School Band sounded like only one trumpet from a few blocks away. Since all three schools I attended had marching bands, I had the dubious honor of marching and playing in every parade in the Walla Walla Valley for eight years, stepping over the droppings of thousands of horses in the process. My tone and timing were very good, and I was regularly asked to play Taps at the funerals of military veterans. After years of neglect, though, my lip is long gone, my trumpet days are over, and I wish I had stayed with the piano.

Dancing was also something I began in grade school, when my mother arranged for several boys and girls in my class to take a series of ballroom lessons at the YWCA. The same room we used later became a regular hangout for me during high school when I spent most Wednesday and Saturday nights dancing and playing ping pong or pool there at our local teen hangout, the Shuffle Shop.

I didn't miss a school dance in high school and college. During law school I also did a little folk dancing at the International House in Berkeley and was lucky to find another dedicated dancer in Barbara. After our kids came along, it wasn't long before all four of us were attending square dances at Stanley and Relta Tucker's Timberrib, out of which came the birth of our local folklore society.

Friends of Acoustic Music

In about 1975, the Tuckers began holding old time square dances for their family and friends in their recreation building with a fine wooden dance floor that Stanley had built at their farmstead on Winesap Road near Milton-Freewater. At first we danced to recorded music, but the Tuckers are a musical family, and in 1976 their daughter Trudy and her husband Jon St. Hilaire formed the Ryegrass String Band which began playing for the dances.

When we lost Lee Perkins, our old-time caller, Richard Bixby began calling the dances. In 1984, Richard started adding a few contra dances, a phenomenon he had seen at the Port Townsend Festival of American Fiddle Tunes which he attended that same year with Jon, Trudy, and their friend Sue Gerling.

In 1985, inspired by what they saw at Port Townsend, the four of them decided to form an organization to promote traditional music and dance forms in the Walla Walla area, and asked if I would help with the legal work. On September 13, 1985, we incorporated Walla Walla Friends of Acoustic Music as a Washington nonprofit organization whose purpose is "to promote the awareness, appreciation, and use of acoustic music as well as traditional and folk dance, through the sponsoring of concerts, dances, and other musical events." That month WWFAM held its first concert at the YWCA featuring the Ryegrass String Band and classical guitarist Malcom Johnstone, and in October put on its first square and contra dance at the Tucker Timberrib.

The next month's WWFAM concert featured Barbara Clark and five other singer-songwriters. Barbara had written her first song in 1979, and by then had composed about 20 songs in the folk tradition, most with political content, which she had been singing around the area at rallies and other events, and which I've recently put into a CD. The others featured that night were Charles

Potts, Jimmy Turner, Ron Hendricks, Kurt Lash, and Gary Burton. Some of the other early WWFM offerings included folk, jazz, and children's music concerts, clog dancing workshops, a bluegrass jamboree, jam sessions, and an open mike coffee house that continued to be a popular event for several years.

Our December 1986 dance was a going-away party for Richard Bixby who was moving to Portland, and was a watershed event in many other ways. Though Richard had introduced us to contra dancing, our numbers were still low, never more than one contra line or two to three squares. At this event we had three contra lines and a level of excitement that hasn't ended.

To replace Richard, in January, 1987 we invited veteran contra dance caller Larry B. Smith from LaGrande to put on a callers workshop for us, after which Howard Ostby and I, along with Judy Fenno Morrison and Todd Silverstein, began to share the calling at our monthly dances, with music provided by the Wednesday Night Band, an open group of WWFAM members led by Trudy on fiddle. Though Judy retired from calling after a couple of years and Todd moved to Salem about the same time, Howard and I have been regularly calling our monthly third Saturday dances ever since, sometimes with the help of other callers including the last couple of years Barbara. In 1988 we added a first Wednesday dance at the bandstand in Pioneer Park during the summer months which has gone on ever since, and in recent years has even continued for other seasons at the Whitman College ballroom. On December 31, 1987 we also began a so far unbroken tradition of WWFAM New Year's Eve contra dances.

Participation in regional camps has been an important source of new dance and music styles for our local folklore society, beginning for several of us with the Fall 1987 Lady of the Lake Dance Camp at Lake Coeur d'Alene sponsored by the Spokane Folklore Society. The featured specialty dance that year was Cajun, which caught our imagination. In 1988, Barbara and I started teaching Cajun two-step, waltz and jitterbug to the music of Frenchie and the Swamp Rats, a Cajun band composed of Jon St. Hilaire on accordion, Trudy on fiddle, Glenn Morrison on bass, Joe Corvino on guitar, and Howard Ostby on the scrub board, later to be renamed Crawfish Pie. The following year's fall camp featured swing dancing, which Barbara and I also started to teach on occasion to the tunes of Swing Shift, another band composed of Jon, Trudy and Glenn, along with Jerry and Julie Yokel.

Contra Dance Classes

Contra dancing is a wonderfully vigorous, community-building activity that soon had most of us realizing we had never had more fun in our lives. An evening of contra dancing usually involves a circle or a square or two along with several contras, which are danced in a line of partners, similar to the Virginia Reel. In these dances, which came from pagan rituals and later French Quadrilles, and English Country Dancing, couples usually dance one time through with every other couple in the set, and dancers are constantly changing partners throughout the night, making them highly sociable events. The music is by lively fiddle bands playing high energy English, Irish or American jigs and reels, along with some waltzes and polkas.

To bring this zesty experience to more people, in February 1992 Barbara and I offered a four-week series of beginning contra dance classes in the Dietrich Dome at Walla Walla Community

College, followed by a second four-week advanced segment. The response was good, and that fall we moved the classes to Edison School, and for a period to Sharpstein School, also through the Community College. In 1995, we moved the classes to the Tucker Timberrib under the sponsorship of WWFAM, where they continued through 1996. Over the years we've also presented dance classes for students and alumni at Whitman College and in other settings.

Our initial announcement for the classes included the following:

> *There is nothing so necessary to human beings as the dance…without the dance, a man would not be able to do anything….All the misfortunes of man, all the baleful reverses with which histories are filled, the blunders of politicians and the failures of great leaders, all of this is the result of not knowing how to dance.*
> --The Dancing Master in Moliere's "Le Bourgeois Gentilhomme" (1670)

The merits of dancing are widely debated. A view contrary to the above praise was expressed by the Rev. J.D. Crane in "Popular Amusements" (1869):

> *The devotedly pious, the truly pure in heart, do not dance. Dancing wastes time, wastes health, scatters serious thought, compromises…character, leads to entangling associations with frivolous minds and careless hearts. Young people who are famed as "beautiful dancers" are generally good for nothing else.*

Regarding the flirtatious aspects of the dance is the following wisdom by an unknown author:

> *A good dance should include respect and importance for partner, flirtatious possibilities, plenty of activity, and above all grace—a smooth flowing statement emphasizing the dancer's real life predicament—in short, an eight minute marriage.*

Many of us in the Walla Walla area have been "wasting time and health and scattering serious thought" to our great delight for over 10 years. Although most of us agree that dancing should above all else be fun, we would also agree that the better dancers we are, the more fun we're likely to have.

> *I would not have you a dancer; yet when you do dance, I would have you dance well."*
> --Lord Chesterfield to his son (1750)

Over years of dance classes, we have introduced many new people to the joy of dancing, which we continue to do through our open, public dances, where no partner or experience is necessary.

Dance Retreats

Friends of Acoustic Music had talked for some time about putting on its own dance camp, so in 1995 I offered to organize a Wallowa Lake Dance Retreat to be held at Wallowa Lake Lodge near Joseph, Oregon. We began the retreat on Saturday, March 25 with a musicians' jam session and dinner at the lodge, followed by an evening community dance at the Odd Fellows Hall in Enterprise featuring the Wednesday Night Band which I called along with Howard Ostby and Randy Krischbaum from Enterprise. On Sunday morning after breakfast we ended the retreat with a final dance in the lodge's lobby.

This seemed to work very well, and we returned in 1996, following the same schedule with an added Saturday afternoon couples dance workshop where Barbara and I taught the Irish polka, some special waltz moves, and the Salty Dog Rag. For the evening dance we invited the local band Off the Cuff to provide the music, along with caller Larry Smith. The only problem was the lodge's owner, who didn't want us to invite people from the community to the lodge, which is why we held the evening dance in Enterprise. In addition, it bothered him to have the lobby furniture moved around for dancing, even though we were pretty much the only ones there during the slow winter season.

As a result, we looked around northeast Oregon and southeast Washington for other sites, and finally chose Camp Meadowood Springs on Weston Mountain, near the Spout Springs ski area, where for the next three years I coordinated the Weston Mountain Dance Retreat. This was a full dance camp format beginning with dinner on Friday night and ending with lunch on Sunday, with contra dances on Friday night, Saturday night, and Sunday morning, dance workshops Saturday morning and afternoon, and a Saturday night talent show. Though the camp was organized by WWFAM, it was co-sponsored by two of our neighboring folklore societies, Blue Mountain Folklife Society in Pendleton and Northeast Oregon Folklore Society in LaGrande, and it featured all of the callers and bands in our area. Specialty workshops offered during those years included English country dance, southern squares, international folkdance, and swing dancing.

After five years I needed a break, and Gina Massoni, a new caller and member of WWFAM, agreed to organize the Weston Mountain Uptown Dance Retreat to be held at the Cloggers Hall at the Walla Walla Airport. This 2000 retreat followed the same format of dances and workshops, and featured Phil and Vivian Williams from Seattle providing the dance music and musicians' workshops. Other highlights were a salsa workshop and an impromptu visit to a winery next door.

This also worked out well, and we planned to repeat the experience in 2001. Unfortunately, we learned that the dance teacher who was renting the hall had given up her lease and the Port of Walla Walla which owns all of the airport buildings was planning to tear out the wooden dance floor and stage and put in a concrete floor in order to use the building as a warehouse. In researching the history of the building, I learned that it had been built in 1941 as the black soldiers' theater for the army airbase located there during World War II, when the military services were still segregated.

Since dance halls are hard to find, and given the history of the building, I was determined to save it from destruction. My first idea was to see whether one or more community groups or private instructors might step forward to lease the building. I started out by contacting every dance and musical group in town, including the Blues Society, the Jazz Society, a country western dance group, a square dance group, and our own folklore society, as well as some private dance teachers. I also talked with local colleges, churches, martial arts instructors, yoga teachers, and others.

Finding no one willing to take responsibility for the monthly costs of the lease, utilities and maintenance, but having generated some publicity in the local newspapers about the project, I next approached the Port with the proposal that they make the building available to the community for events on a rental basis, either by leasing it to WWFAM for $1 a year with event rentals going into building maintenance and improvements, or by the Port itself managing the building as a community service, with WWFAM raising funds to equip it to accommodate banquets, concerts and other events. The Port agreed to manage it on an interim basis and to keep the building intact, while continuing to look for a long-term tenant.

With that reprieve, WWFAM began holdings its monthly dances and other events there in late 2000, including a benefit dance to raise funds to equip the hall. In addition, the Walla Walla Race Unity Coalition donated $600 for equipment and historical displays, the Little Theatre of Walla Walla donated a piano, and an anonymous donor pledged to match anything we raised at the benefit dance. With that we were able to purchase 80 chairs and 22 tables from a local hardware store that provided them at cost. Just as the equipment arrived, we learned from the Port that the hall had been leased by the Unity Church of Walla Walla, that it would be preserved intact, and that it would get a new furnace, handicap accessibility, and general upgrading.

The only question was whether the church would continue to make the hall available for dances and other community events, which it did on and off over the years until recently giving up its lease. As an act of good faith, WWFAM has purchased the church's equipment which we hope we'll be able to continue to use at the hall and make available for use by others as well.

With the renovation going on at the airport hall in 2001, WWFAM membership chair Brenda Sims took charge of the successful Around the Town Dance Retreat that year featuring the Portland Band Feline Groovy and the use of three different halls during the weekend.

Dance Compositions

One of the pleasures of being a contra dance caller is picking the dances. In addition to the "old chestnuts" some of which have been danced for hundreds of years in England and New England, thousands of new dances have been composed in recent times, particularly since the revival of traditional music and dance forms beginning in the Sixties. While many of these dances are available in written form and others can be learned at dances, when I sit down to plan a Saturday night dance I'm often dissatisfied with what's available and will compose a dance of my own. After twenty-six years of calling I find that a majority of the dances I teach and call on any evening are my own, which I've recently put together in a book titled "Come Dancing."

The most unusual dance I've ever written came out of the 1998 Weston Mountain Dance retreat. Over lunch someone raised the question of whether it would be possible to do a contra dance with two intersecting contra lines. Skepticism was high, but a challenge is always healthy, so after lunch I sat down at the registration table and wrote out the Weston Mountain Traffic Circle, involving two intersecting contra lines at right angles with a square in the middle. Following the afternoon dance workshop I invited folks to try it, and it worked well and created a lot of excitement. We tried it again successfully during the Sunday morning dance, and someone pointed out that in Southwest Indian culture a figure with four sets of double lines coming out at ninety degree angles from a circle is called a Zia. A description of this dance was published in Country Dance and Song Society News for March/April, 1999 and resulted in quite a discussion on the internet as to whether such a thing had ever been done before. Apparently something similar had arisen once or twice before, but had not previously been published. Since then the Weston Mountain Traffic Circle, or Weston Mountain Zia, has been danced regularly around the country.

Dancing in the Community

Since contra dancing is a very informal activity, unlike club square dancing with its special clothing and complicated moves, it can be easily taught to inexperienced dancers and has become a hit at a variety of community events, including an all-campus Barn Dance at Whitman College begun by Todd Silverstein in 1987 which I then called for over fifteen years, and an annual Barn Party at Walla Walla College that Howard Ostby and I called for nearly as many.

WWFAM has also held public dances as a part of the program at the Whitman Mission National Historic Site and the Downtown Walla Walla Foundation Concert Series, and its members have presented music and dance events for a variety of other community organizations and gatherings, including Victorian Balls sponsored by the Kirkman House Museum.

Through concerts, dances, coffee houses, song circles, retreats, workshops and other events, Walla Walla Friends of Acoustic Music has in many ways "danced in the community" for nearly thirty years.

Bards of the Boards

Another joyful experience came our way through Irish dancing. The first time I saw Irish dance moves was at the Dacres Saloon in Walla Walla on St. Patrick's Day in 1990 during a performance by our local Irish band Bards of the Moor. Their music got some of us up dancing, and two women showed us the Sevens and Threes, a traditional Irish reel step. At the Northwest Folklife Festival in Seattle that Memorial Day weekend, Barbara and I learned some more moves, and by the next St. Paddy's Day we were back at the Dacres doing some performance couple dancing with the band.

The following year our good friends Sandra and Dennis Cannon joined us, and we formed a four-person dance team called the Bards of the Boards, which performed for the first time at the Friends of Acoustic Music St. Patrick's Day show at the Walla Walla Little Theatre, then at the annual Cinco de Mayo fiesta in Milton-Freewater, a Three Rivers Folklore Society coffee house in Kennewick, a 16th of September celebration at Memorial Park, and again at the 1993 WWFAM Irish celebration at the golf course. After that we gradually picked up more dancers and dances until in 1994 we were alternating performance dances by our twelve-member troupe with participation dances to the music of the Bards of the Moor for our St. Patrick's Day celebration that year in the lobby of the Marcus Whitman Hotel.

The dances our Bards of the Boards troupe performed and taught included traditional Irish longways formations such as Waves of Tory, The Bridge of Athlone, Walls of Limerick, and the Haymaker's Jig, as well as traditional set dances or Irish squares, and a few dances we composed ourselves in traditional style. On a few occasions our troupe also danced and taught Scottish country dances, whose elegant style was a bit foreign to us. For about seven years the Bards danced regularly throughout our region, including multiple performances at the Downtown Walla Walla concert series, the Multicultural Arts Festival in Pioneer Park, the Cinco de Mayo fiesta, the Concert in the Park series in Milton-Freewater, Italian Heritage Days, the Caledonia Days Scottish festival in Athena, and of course on St. Patrick's Day.

People said we were a lively group to watch, and we had a wonderful time learning some of the more challenging performance dances such as the Fairy Reel circle and the High-Cauled Cap set dance. On occasion we were also able to bring others into the fairly demanding Irish figures and steps we taught.

Even though the ceili dances we were performing were nothing like the physically demanding step dancing which has been made popular around the world by the River Dance troupe and its successors, my knees eventually rebelled against our demanding rehearsal and performance schedule, and our group disbanded, later to be replaced by our less-demanding contra dance performance group, Shadrack's Delight and our French-Canadian troupe, Frenchtown Dancers. For all its rewards, there is an age past which Irish dancing is for the young.

Community Stages

Besides dancing myself, I've enjoyed on occasion providing a place for others to perform and to be entertained. When I was a young trumpeter I remember dreaming of owning and managing a night club. As an adult, I've often found myself in charge of entertainment stages, including the stage at the Cinco de Mayo fiesta in Milton-Freewater for fourteen years, the music stage for our weekly Farmers Market for its first three years, and entertainment for our annual Multicultural Arts Festival in Pioneer Park since its founding in 1994.

At our annual multicultural festival I've taken care to recruit and present good quality entertainment by musicians and dancers in order to showcase their talents, including Mexican folkloric dance groups, vocalists and instrumentalists, Scottish bagpipers, German, Italian, Middle Eastern, Native American, Irish, Chinese, Indian, African, and Pacific Island dancers; blues, jazz, reggae, Celtic, and gospel groups, international folk dancers, break dancers, and story tellers from Jewish, African, Native American, Italian, and other traditions.

Walla Walla is a wonderful community, its musicians and dancers are creative, and new talent is coming along all the time. It's always a pleasure to bring performers and audiences together for their mutual delight and satisfaction.

Walla Walla 2020

While I was doing international work for PBI, Barbara would often challenge me to devote more energy to making our own community a better place to live. In early April of 1988, she broadened that challenge to include a number of our friends and others in the community who share our values, about 20 of whom she called together for a day-long visioning session on what we wanted our community to be like in the year 2020.

At the end of the day, our vision had four major elements: We wanted a green community that preserved and renewed its trees, landscaping, and other natural resources; we wanted a community that lives lightly on the earth by recycling and reducing its waste; we wanted a human scale community, friendly to pedestrians and bicyclists; and we wanted a community that respects its historic architecture and has a strong civic center.

The question was, would we go home, sit down in our armchairs, and just wish it would happen, or would we organize ourselves to do something about it. As a result of that meeting at the Congregational Church, we formed a dynamic organization called Walla Walla 2020. We began by organizing committees on Recycling and Waste Reduction, Downtown and Architecture, Trees and Landscaping, and Bicycles and Pedestrians.

Recycling and Waste Reduction

At the founding session of Walla Walla 2020, one element of our vision that didn't exist at all was a community recycling program. On May 31, 1988, at the opening meeting of the Walla Walla 2020 Recycling Committee chaired by Candace Rose, Barbara and I offered as a possible prototype the neighborhood recycling stations we had just installed on our own block and the adjoining block of North Main.

The recycling station we had put out in the alley behind our garage had separate, marked receptacles for newspaper, glass, aluminum, and tin or steel cans. Cardboard could be folded up behind the cans. In our alley station, which was the first we installed, we used some old regular metal garbage cans. For the alley on the next block, we placed 90-gallon plastic containers that had been used by the City of Walla Walla for regular garbage collection but were now being thrown into the landfill because they were cracked and could no longer be used with the automated garbage trucks.

The market for recyclables was good at the time, and there were two recycling buy-back centers operating in Walla Walla which paid for glass, aluminum, newspaper, and cardboard. Though those centers didn't take cans, we discovered that a can manufacturing plant in Walla Walla would, and though they wouldn't pay individuals, they would credit non-profit agencies with the value of turn-ins. The problem was how to keep these useful materials out of people's garbage cans, and get them into recycling bins and to the buy-back centers. No system of education, pickup, or drop-boxes had been set up in the county.

Alley stations made it easy for everyone to deposit their materials whenever they wanted within a few steps from their home. For pickup, we developed what we considered an ingenious system. We simply let it be known through signs and letters to the neighbors that anyone who wanted to take materials out of the recycling bins was free to do so. This anarchic system worked well. Very soon after putting aluminum cans out in our bins, we could hear the rattling coming from our alley as a youth or retired person cleaned out their treasure. If any of the cans filled up, we had made arrangements with the local Goodwill Industries store to respond to a call, and they would have their truck stop by, empty the cans, and take the items to one of the buy-back centers for their own account.

When I studied the county's Solid Waste Management Plan, which had been required by state law, I noted various provisions for encouraging recycling which had never been implemented. I suggested that Walla Walla 2020 request that a county recycling committee be appointed as provided for in the plan, that we seek the cooperation of the County in implementing a system of neighborhood recycling stations and arrangements for pickups by non-profit agencies or others who might be interested, and that 2020 begin implementing the project itself in the meantime, to which 2020's recycling committee agreed.

In June, we sent a formal letter to County Planning Director Jim Beard requesting the appointment of an official county recycling committee and proposing a comprehensive recycling program in the Walla Walla area of the kind we had been discussing. I had met with Jim previously and knew he was sympathetic to the project. In August he arranged for the ten members of 2020's recycling committee together with the directors of the three non-profit agencies we were working with, Goodwill Industries, the Salvation Army, and the Lillie Rice Center, to be formally appointed by the county commissioners as the Walla Walla County Recycling Committee. The enabling resolution also directed the Regional Planning Office "to coordinate and assist the committee through low or no cost activities, including public information and promotion, support of legislation, and adoption of recycling policies as appropriate..."

In mid-August, Jim invited me to a recycling conference in Moses Lake put on by the State Department of Ecology, where I learned about a possible grant opportunity for the program. At the organizational meeting of the new county committee on August 29, 1988 I was elected chair and the committee and staff decided to proceed with the establishment of recycling stations throughout the area as resources became available, and also to apply for a state recycling grant through Walla Walla County.

Jim was agreeable to submitting the grant application but didn't have time to write it, which I agreed to do. Our initial grant was to establish a county recycling office and hotline with a part-time coordinator and to provide materials for the installation of the neighborhood recycling stations. We also distributed five-gallon buckets with a recycling logo on them which 2020 had started collecting from local restaurants and giving out to people in our neighborhoods to keep in their homes for collecting recyclables before taking them out to the stations.

In early February, we learned that our nearly $16,000 grant application had been accepted, and we began the hiring process in which Gretchen Lowe became the first recycling coordinator in eastern Washington. Gretchen was a great choice, and went on to become the full-time recycling and waste reduction coordinator for the county, continuing in that role until 2001.

For 13 years, 2020 members have continued to make up the bulk of the membership of the county committee, and many things have been accomplished, including the establishment of 50 neighborhood recycling stations, each with a volunteer coordinator, the transition to universal curbside pickup in the city of Walla Walla in 1997 with several of the neighborhood stations moving to rural locations, the establishment of institutional recycling programs by major employers and institutions including colleges, governmental agencies, hospitals and businesses through outreach by the committee, and, in later years, our Green Seal certification program.

In addition, the committee and staff have carried on educational programs in the schools and throughout the community; advocacy of community and individual composting through meetings, classes, and demonstrations which have assisted in the realization of a privately operated community composting program; booths and recycling programs at community festivals; and other programs.

At the same time, 2020 itself undertook some additional waste-reduction efforts, such as taking a leadership role in a number of Earth Day fairs where we've sold low-flow showerheads and toilet tank inserts. Under the leadership of Deborah Winter, Kathy Howard, and Sue Weiler (the bag ladies), 2020 also developed and promoted a reusable shopping bag project in the early Nineties in cooperation with several supermarkets and progressive local bag maker Cheryl Ray. As part of the campaign which included a newspaper ad listing the names of a number of people who pledged not to accept throwaway bags at stores, Barbara wrote and sang a jingle as a public service announcement for the radio stations:

Did you bring your own bag,
Did you bring your own bag,
At the market, at the drugstore,
Did you bring your own bag?
Well we really do love you,
And we don't mean to nag,
But when you went out shopping
Did you bring your own bag?

While we certainly have further to go as a community and individually to really "live lightly on the Earth," Walla Walla 2020's efforts have clearly moved us more into the forefront of recycling and waste reduction.

Downtown and Architecture

Architectural Awards

The first public announcement of the formation of Walla Walla 2020 came on December 7, 1988 when our Downtown and Architecture Committee, which I chaired for the first several years, launched its annual architectural awards competition. The initial awards were given for outstanding projects completed in 1988 involving the renovation of historic buildings, compatible new construction in an historic area, or examples of energy efficient new construction or retrofitting in residential, downtown, or other areas.

On February 28, 1989, we held our first awards ceremony. The Grand Prize went to Bill and Jackie Pancake for their rehabilitation of the 1914 Northern Pacific Railway Depot, where we held the ceremony. We enlisted as cosponsors with us in the initial competition the Walla Walla Main Street Foundation as well as Historical Architectural Development (HAD), which had given its own awards when I served as its president from 1976-1978.

For the 1989 competition we added Pacific Power and Cascade Gas as cosponsors. Mike and Adrienne May of Pioneer Title Company and their contractor Jim Nostdal won the grand prize for the restoration of their 1876 office building on Main Street.

We introduced a new category for landscape architecture in 1990, a Painted Lady Award for decorative exterior paint in 1993, and public art in 1994. Other than the gas company all of our cosponsors continued for the next fourteen years.

From the first, our awards ceremonies have been annual celebrations of progress in restoring and revitalizing the downtown and the general community, as well as an occasion to introduce the community to Walla Walla 2020 and its projects. We also hoped that honoring older buildings would encourage their renovation in preference to sprawling new construction. Dozens of projects, owners, contractors, architects, and organizations have been honored, and in turn the recipients have expressed their appreciation for the contributions of 2020 through its consciousness-raising and projects throughout the community regarding quality of life issues. A complete list of all award recipients in this process currently appears on our website at www.ww2020.org.

Historic Plaque and Research Project

Because of our interest in historic buildings, Walla Walla 2020 began receiving requests for help in putting homes or buildings on the state or national historic registers, a very demanding process for which only a few properties meet the official criteria.

Instead of devoting a great deal of time and energy to honoring a few properties, in 1994 I proposed that 2020 help preserve Walla Walla's rich architectural and cultural history by offering an historic building plaque service whose purpose would be to encourage people throughout the community to take pride in their neighborhoods, whether wealthy or humble, by honoring their history and buildings with attractive plaques showing their history.

Since the bronze plaques commonly used for historic purposes are too expensive for the more widespread use we hoped to promote, I began looking for alternatives, and was able to arrange for a handsome, painted brass plaque produced locally by Geri and Roger Benson of the Show-Off Shoppe. We included on the plaque the date a structure was built, information on those who built or occupied it, and Walla Walla 2020 as the authenticating organization, all usually for under $50

In order to assist people in locating and documenting information to go on the plaques, I also suggested that 2020 offer an historic research service, which we have done utilizing the records of the oldest title company in town, Pioneer Title.

As a prototype for the project, I researched the history of our own home at 717 N. Main, which the county assessor's notes indicated was built in 1900, but which I discovered had actually been built in 1902 as a home for his new bride by the same Celtic musician and carpenter who had later built our Powerline Road farmstead.

While the 2020 Historic Plaque and Research Service places special emphasis on structures built before 1920, any building more than 50 years old can qualify for our basic search of Walla Walla County records, the Whitman College Archives, and Pioneer Title Company records which covers the entire history of the property from the time it was bare ground.

Our first researcher was Michael Smith, a retired school teacher and Whitman College classmate of mine, who had moved back to town and was assisting Whitman College professor Tom Edwards with his book on the early history of the college. When Mike took a fulltime job as Whitman Alumni Director in 1997, we had no regular researcher until 2000 when Mary Meeker and Kathie Weingart took up the work. I continued to function as coordinator, receiving applications, consulting with the primary researchers, reviewing and editing the final reports, proposing plaque language to the owners, and arranging for the engraving and delivery of the finished plaques, as well as doing a few basic research reports.

We have intentionally kept our fees low to make the research as accessible as possible. Our maximum is $100, all but $15 of which goes to the individual researcher, with the balance to 2020. Since many hours usually go into the research and much additional time is involved in the other tasks, the project has truly been a community service, whose reward is the pleasure of seeing a growing appreciation of local history through a distribution of plaques and research reports in a variety of neighborhoods, including the downtown.

By July 2001, the project had produced research reports or plaques for over 115 historic properties, including over 75 residences and approximately 40 commercial or institutional buildings. A list of the properties can currently be found on the internet at www.ww2020.org. Our plaques for commercial buildings are placed in cooperation with the Downtown Walla Walla Foundation. We plan to put the full reports on the properties in the archives of Whitman College's Penrose Memorial Library, where they will be accessible on an ongoing basis to others.

Downtown Walla Walla Renewal

From its beginning, Walla Walla 2020 was interested in strengthening and renewing Walla Walla's downtown, which had been damaged by sprawling development and the construction of outlying shopping malls, as well as by the demolition of a number of multi-story mixed-use downtown buildings to create parking lots or construct one story, single-use buildings.

Our goal has been to preserve the existing historic building stock, promote reuse of abandoned upper floors, and assist in activities which would make the downtown more vital and attractive as a cultural, social, and commercial center for the community.

To help call attention to the wealth of unused second floor space in the downtown, in 1992 we began the 2020 Second Story Mannequin Project, sometimes called Upstairs Downtown. This featured retired mannequins donated by J.C. Penney department store, which were initially placed in the windows of the abandoned second floor of the Bee Hive Building at Second and Main, looking out and waving at passersby. The project was Barbara's idea, I found the mannequins, and 2020 members Shirley Hagman, Jeanne McMenemy, and Barbara dressed and positioned them.

Before long the Bee Hive space was rented, and we moved the mannequins to the abandoned second floor of the Book Nook or Die Brucke Building until it was reclaimed, and from there to the closed second story Walla Walla Hotel, where local artist Abigail Bridges took responsibility for costuming the mannequins and setting them up in creative poses. The Walla Walla Hotel has now been remodeled and reopened as Walla Walla Residential Suites. All of these placements drew people's attention to the buildings as well as considerable newspaper publicity.

We also wanted to preserve and reuse the old Liberty Theater on Main Street. To avoid the demolition of the abandoned theater with its gargoyles and gothic façade, we proposed that it be leased and renovated by a coalition of community groups and the local colleges for use as a community and conference center, dance hall, and theater. Others also rallied with ideas, and the building was finally acquired by the nonprofit National Development Council and leased to the neighboring Bon Marche department store which expanded into it, preserving and restoring both the façade and some of the internal theater structure and garnering the grand prize in our 1991 Architectural Awards competition.

The Downtown Walla Walla Foundation had been formed in 1984 and has done wonderful work revitalizing the downtown. One of the elements in our original brainstorming session in 1988 was a farmers market to be located in the city hall parking lot. In 1997 the Downtown Foundation established the Saturday Walla Walla Farmers Market there, and in 1999 an extension of that market was added to downtown's Thursday Night Concert Series. The market, together with its Music at the Market series which I coordinated for the first three years, have added much to the sociability of the downtown, and is a great success for the public as well as its vendors. 2020 members Sandra Cannon, Barbara, and I made up a majority of the Foundation's Farmers Market Committee in the initial years, along with chair Larry Nelson and market manager Cathy Scott.

To add to the partial roof over the main market area, I worked on a partnership between 2020 and the Downtown Foundation for the design and construction of a fanciful roof for the market stage by local sculptor and 2020 member Wayne Chabre, and arranged for contributions from several major donors to 2020, contracting with the Downtown Foundation for the administration of the project. The completed artistic structure was turned over to the City of Walla Walla as a gift.

The watershed achievement of the Downtown Foundation in cooperation with the City of Walla Walla was the completion of the Downtown Revival Project in 1992 involving the addition of trees, new sidewalks, lighting, and other improvements; giving the city's center an appealing new look, and winning the Grand Prize in our 1992 architectural awards competition, together with the Trailhead Park, now Heritage Park, another project in which 2020, the Downtown Foundation, and the City were partners.

Over the years, Walla Walla 2020 and the Foundation have cooperated on a variety of projects and events to strengthen the downtown and the community, and a number of 2020 members have served on Downtown Foundation committees and as volunteers at downtown events.

In 2001, as a result of projects such as these and the dramatic revitalization of the city's center resulting from creative activities by a variety of interests as well as a booming new wine industry, the Downtown Walla Walla Foundation received the Great American Main Street Award, the highest national honor given to downtown associations, in recognition of a renaissance and vitality in Walla Walla not seen for decades.

Trees and Landscaping

Tausick Way Landfill and the Mill Creek Bike Path

The very first project of Walla Walla 2020 was an effort by our Trees and Landscaping Committee aimed at the reclamation of the old landfill along Mill Creek and Tausick Way and the naturalization and landscaping of the bike path running past along the creek. The City of Walla Walla had closed the landfill several years previously, but had not complied with state regulations requiring the application of adequate topsoil and planting of native grasses or other permanent cover crop to restore the site and make it compatible with the surrounding area during the approximately thirty-year period before it could be safely reused or occupied.

One of our founding members, Nancy Ball, a frequent user of the recreational trail running between the former landfill and Mill Creek, learned of a plan by the City's public works director to sterilize the ten-foot wide area between the landfill fence and the bike path, and to cover it with gravel. We also learned that the city manager was planning to lease the landfill site for wheat farming. This would have involved frequent tilling, chemical applications, and serious wind and water erosion particularly in fallow years, carrying dust into the surrounding residential neighborhoods and soil and pollutants into Mill Creek, as well as greater leaching of heavy metals without a cover crop to absorb the rainfall.

After studying the regulations, on May 19, 1988 I drafted a letter from the Walla Walla 2020 Trees and Landscaping Committee to the public works director and city manager pointing out the significance of the area to the city due to "its frontage on Mill Creek and on the Mill Creek bike path, its proximity to Walla Walla Community College, its location at a major entrance to the city, and the potentially dangerous pollution possible from the site." We called for the seeding of the entire area with native grasses, and the planting of trees and shrubs between the bike path and the landfill fence for better erosion control and to create a cooler and more appealing experience for the users of a very hot and treeless stretch of the city's most popular recreation path.

We then arranged a tour of the site with city officials and staff from the U.S. Soil Conservation Service, who recommended specific grasses and a planting schedule which would avoid the necessity of heavy herbicide application for weed control and create an easy-to-manage permanent cover crop. Though the public works director planted less appropriate grasses, we were successful in getting a permanent cover crop on the landfill, and in saving the long strip next to the bike path from sterilization. The planting and maintenance of that strip became 2020's first hands-on project.

Beginning to Renew Walla Walla's Urban Forest

Walla Walla is characterized by its many large trees. Most were planted just after the turn of the century and are approaching the end of their lifespan and need to be renewed. To encourage tree planting, 2020's Trees and Landscaping Committee began a variety of projects.

First we pointed out to the City Council that two street trees were being taken out for every one planted. We suggested the city's free street tree program be expanded to provide not only replacements for street trees removed but to provide a street tree to any property owner willing to plant and maintain it in an available space, in order to begin to fill in the gaps in our canopy. The council agreed to do this, but the program is still underfunded.

We then sponsored the first Arbor Day celebration in Walla Walla in many years. As part of Washington's Centennial Celebration, we drafted a proclamation which the mayor signed declaring April 9-15, 1989 to be Arbor Week in Walla Walla, and we also announced a community planting goal of a thousand new trees in the Walla Walla area during the year. To help accomplish this, we arranged for hundreds of conifer seedlings from the U.S. Forest Service, negotiated special discounts at area nurseries, provided information on obtaining free trees from the National Arbor Day Foundation, organized tree-planting ceremonies, a tree-planting workshop by the City Parks Department, and a volunteer tree-planting brigade of students at Whitman College's environmental interest house, as well as an Arbor Week Benefit Swing and Contra Dance sponsored by Walla Walla Friends of Acoustic Music. 2020 member Candace Rose worked out an arrangement between local hospitals and tree nurseries to include a discount coupon for a tree honoring a new infant in the regular packet provided new parents.

After the tree-planting workshop, 2020 members took some left-over seedlings out to a planting strip along the Mill Creek bike trail next to the old landfill site where we planted over a hundred trees, including some locusts donated by Bob Biles, a local organic farmer. That was the

106

beginning of a several year planting and watering project on that strip for which we hauled thousands of five-gallon buckets over the riprap from Mill Creek, which was our only water source at the time.

We divided the approximately half mile strip into nine different sections, each with an individual or family responsible for planting, watering, and weed control. This project gave us a lot of public exposure along the trail as people stopped to learn about what we were doing, to encourage us, and sometimes to help out. Though the soil wasn't good and the City had assured us that nothing would grow there, through the hard work of 2020 members, low-water trees, shrubs, flowers and grasses have been established. Our efforts were helped by the installation of a drip irrigation system through grant funds 2020 obtained to extend and improve Walla Walla's bicycle and pedestrian trails. Despite haphazard watering during the hand-watering period and later sporadic failures of the drip system, most of our plantings have flourished.

In 1989 we also began a live Christmas tree program, encouraging people throughout the area to purchase live rather than cut trees, which could be planted at private homes or donated to the parks after the holidays. We arranged with a local Kiwanis club and 2020 members to help deliver the trees and pick them up.

In the spring of 1991 in connection with a community-wide Earth Day celebration cosponsored by Walla Walla 2020, we adopted another long planting strip. In the Seventies when the state transportation department built the freeway north of DeSales High School, the steep hillside coming down from the highway guard rail to the level of the playfields at the City sports complex was originally landscaped by the state, but the irrigation system had been dismantled and the area neglected.

In talks with the city and the state, I negotiated an agreement that the state pay for the materials for a drip irrigation system to be installed by the city on the state-owned hillside between Borleske Stadium and the eastern end of the complex, that the park provide the water, and that 2020 operate the system and maintain the area. Though the soil was also poor there, over the years we've planted hundreds of conifer and some deciduous trees and enlisted the volunteer efforts of students and townspeople in planting, cleanup of highway trash, and maintenance of the irrigation system, which has often suffered from rodents and other damage.

At the same time, we have also had to work hard to protect the naturalized groves of black locusts on the east end of the site from periodic attacks by transportation department officials and crews working under inappropriate regulations. Whitman College has now acquired the complex from the city, and may also preserve and enhance the trees and vegetation on the hillside.

Taking on the Asphalt Desert

I had long been interested in greening the large expanses of concrete and asphalt in Walla Walla's Eastgate area where, beginning in the 1950's era of strip development, big box stores and drive-through businesses created an automobile culture devoid of trees and other natural features.. In our original 2020 brainstorming session, I proposed the idea of an "Eastgate Reclamation Project" which our Trees and Landscaping Committee began to work on through contacts with the management of K-Mart and the Eastgate Marketplace, whose vast parking lots were a treeless desert.

On May 18, 1991, our efforts bore fruit when we formally announced the beginning of the project with the planting of 25 shade trees along Wilbur and Melrose streets in partnership with the Eastgate Marketplace, whose manager Gail Waetje said, "The greening of the Eastgate has been a long time coming. We hope this project will sprout a desire on the part of our Eastgate neighbors to get green and growing as we have."

Part of the problem we faced was that Walla Walla's zoning code made no landscaping demands on developers. My preliminary research into practices of other cities showed that most required developers to provide green landscaping as well as enough trees to shade significant portions of parking areas, while Walla Walla's code could be satisfied by simply putting in some river rock, which often happened.

In what has probably done as much as any other single effort for the greening of Walla Walla, Larry Siegel, a deputy city attorney and Walla Walla native who had traveled extensively and shared our values, agreed to study the specific landscaping requirements in a variety of other Washington cities with the help of the Municipal Research Service, and produced a report for 2020 which we used to bring about changes to the city landscaping requirements. Since 1991, new or reconstructed parking lots in Walla Walla are required to have 5% of their area devoted to green landscaping located not more than 50 feet from every parking space, and to have trees which will ultimately shade 20% of the parking area. Additional provisions have also been adopted, including the requirement that street trees be included in all commercial development or redevelopment projects.

The results in Walla Walla parking lots and commercial areas have been dramatic. Particularly satisfying is that K-Mart, which had resisted the voluntary installation of trees and an irrigation system, did a fine job of tree-planting and landscaping when required by the new code at the time of the renovation of its store, and 2020 even gave them an award for it. Other businesses are beginning to follow suit since we now have some reasonable standards, and a softening of the asphalt landscape is underway.

Xeriscape Park

When the City of Walla Walla redesigned the intersection where Main, Rose, and Isaacs come together, it created a small, vacant lot on one corner of the block where we live which became a weed patch and eyesore. I often walked along the dirt footpath running through the lot and wondered what use might be made of it. I finally got the idea of transforming it into a pocket park, and Barbara suggested making it a xeriscape demonstration park to both beautify one of the busiest intersections in town and show people a form of landscaping that uses far less water than our normal bluegrass lawns.

In January 1990, we formed a Walla Walla 2020 Working Group on Water-Conserving Plants to begin to study and "share ideas on native and other species of trees, shrubs, flowers, turf and other ground covers which would require little or no supplemental watering in our area, and to consider the establishment of a demonstration park and other means of promoting the availability and use of such species." Members of the committee included Whitman College grounds superintendent Tim Werner, county extension agent Walt Gary, city parks director Mike Petersen, Soil Conservation Service staffer Ron Long, landscape designer Marshal Doak, and the 2020 Trees and Landscaping Committee chaired by Nancy Ball and Sandy Shelin.

On March 22, as chair of the working group I wrote to the mayor and city manager requesting permission for 2020 to establish a demonstration park on the lot, which we proposed be transferred from public works to the parks department. In April the city council agreed, and with the help of many donors we began contouring the site, bringing in top soil, putting in an efficient irrigation system, installing paths with decorative stones, benches, a rock retaining wall, several basalt boulders, signage including a map showing the names of all the plants, and a sculpture donated by local artist Bill Piper. The design, which had gone through many stages, was completed by landscapers Terry and Ann Smith, and the formal dedication ceremony for the park was held June 17, 1994.

The park has been a great success, thanks to the many people who worked to create it and in particular to Nancy Ball who took the primary responsibility for lovingly maintaining it over the years.

Water Woman and the City Water Advisory Committee

Barbara's interest in xeriscaping came from a general concern about the use and availability of water in the Walla Walla Valley. In October 1989, as president of 2020, she had written to the city council proposing the establishment of a water resource task force "to address the broad issue of water use and waste, and measures for practical conservation and preservation of water quality, for the protection of both ground water and stream flows."

At that time, the city had just announced a water crisis due to the depleting of ground water from the city's aquifers and the need to maintain an agreed minimum stream flow in Mill Creek. As an alternative to shutting down its hydroelectric plant or implementing "severe rationing," the city was proposing an exemption from minimum stream flow requirements for Mill Creek, its principle watercourse. The 2020 letter asked that any decision or action by the city affecting minimum stream flows "be deferred until it is able to receive the recommendations of (the requested) task force, since available waste reduction and conservation measures may significantly affect the demand..."

Thus began Barbara's career as "Water Woman," as she came to be known from a series of columns she wrote in 1992 and that were published again in 2001 in our daily newspaper, educating the public on water issues and discussing specific ways to conserve. In 1989, she was appointed a founding member of the City Water Resources Committee established as a result of our initiative. Water issues continue to interest Barbara and in 1997 impelled her to a successful campaign for a seat on the city council. The water committee, now renamed the Water and Waste Water Advisory Committee, continues to function as an important sounding board for water quality and availability issues in the urban area, and Barbara continues on the committee as the city council's representative.

<u>City Tree Committee</u>

In 1992, it became clear that despite the efforts of 2020 and others, we were suffering a net loss of our community's tree canopy each year. In the fall, I suggested 2020 invite two other groups to join us in a request to the city council for the appointment of an official city tree committee. One of the groups was the Blue Mountain Audubon Society, a regular 2020 ally; the other was Releaf Walla Walla, an energetic new group formed around 1990 by Mike Gillespie and several other members of the Rotary Club, which brought the resources of the business community into the replanting effort we had initiated.

At the request of the three groups, on October 14, 1992 the city council appointed an Ad Hoc Tree Committee to study and make recommendations to the council on ways of protecting and strengthening Walla Walla's urban forest. The Committee was composed of a member and alternate from each of the three initiating groups, together with a representative of the parks board, the planning commission, the electric company, a local nursery, a private arborist, the parks director, the planning director, and city council and Audubon member Tom Scribner, who served as chair.

In March 1993 the committee, on which I served as vice-chair and draftsman, submitted its recommendations. These included draft revisions to the city's street tree ordinance, a draft landmark tree ordinance, a proposal and work plan for a permanent city tree committee, draft landscaping standards and design regulations for adoption by the directors of parks and development services, a proposal for the hiring of a full-time arborist and for the assumption of street tree maintenance by the city, the implementation of a community water truck service for non-irrigated street tree sites, and the development of cooperative street tree standards with Walla Walla County for the annexable areas on the urban fringe.

It was a little too much for the council to digest all at once, but later that year they did establish a permanent Urban Forestry Commission which has become an important body in overseeing city tree practices, and has recently been successful in securing the adoption of a number of our other recommendations. Much still remains to be done to assure the full renewal of our urban forest for coming generations.

Bicycles and Pedestrians

One of the key values motivating us to found Walla Walla 2020 was the importance of restoring a human scale of life in place of the automobile culture which was all around us. Walking and bicycling are healthful activities that bring us into contact with our friends and neighbors, expose us to fresh air, use few resources, are quiet and unobtrusive, and are a joy in themselves.

The walking or biking experience is enriched when streets and other facilities are designed with pedestrians and bicyclists in mind, rather than being oriented solely toward automobiles. To further these values one of the original Walla Walla 2020 committees formed in the spring of 1988 was the Bike and Hike Committee, through which we began to analyze our community's bicycle and pedestrian facilities including bus service.

In early 1989, Barbara recommended that 2020 present a proposal to the city council for the establishment of a Bicycle Advisory Committee, later renamed the Bicycle-Pedestrian Advisory Committee. Following discussion of the 2020 study prepared and presented by Barbara, on June 21, 1989 the council created the committee, the original structure of which was modeled on a Eugene committee composed of representatives of five city departments and five citizens, and was chaired by Walla Walla 2020 member John Winter.

The Walla Walla Trail Project

In the fall of 1989, Downtown Foundation director Sheila Ferguson approached 2020 with the idea of developing a community recreation trail through the downtown. She had been talking with Congressman Tom Foley about federal funds to help with the downtown renewal project, and had been told the only possibility of funding would be for a trail project. She asked if we could plan a trail whose major trailhead would be located downtown in order to bring some federal funds there, as well as to upgrade general trail facilities in the community.

John Winter and I biked around the community surveying existing bike paths and potential routes, and devised a loop trail from Rooks Park east of Walla Walla out to the Whitman Mission to the west, that included all of the existing bike paths, the cities of Walla Walla and College Place, and all three colleges. Our proposed trail added several new dedicated links, and connected them all with on-road routes and a trailhead park at an abandoned property on the south side of Main Street along Mill Creek in downtown Walla Walla. Some concept of a Rooks Park to Whitman Mission trail had been alive since at least 1976, when Walla Walla County and the cities of Walla Walla and College Place had agreed to jointly seek funding for such a project.

On January 5, 1990, on behalf of Walla Walla 2020 I drafted a letter describing the project to Tom Foley, then speaker of the US House of Representatives. The letter was also signed by the City of Walla Walla parks director, the planning directors for both the City of College Place and Walla Walla County, the director of the Downtown Foundation, and John as chair of the "Walla Walla Area Recreational Trail Joint Task Force" which we formed in order to pursue the project.

This was my first hands-on exposure to the legislative process. Like any legislative effort, it went through an enormous number of hoops, but thanks to Tom, in November 1991 it was finally approved as a partnership involving city, state, private, and federal interests, and over $375,000 of federal funds were provided over a three-year period. The state's share was $100,000 that we obtained from a successful 1990 grant application I presented to the state Interagency Committee for Outdoor Recreation (IAC).

A problem arose with the requested local cash match for our federal grant, which was to come from the downtown renewal project, when at the last minute the City lowered its contribution to that fund, leaving us $100,000 short. Fortunately, I was able to convince four members of the council that the City should come up with the remaining $100,000 out of general city funds, and the project went through.

The community facilities we added through this project included the widening and extension of the recreation trail on the north side of the freeway through an arrangement we made with the state Department of Transportation; the building of a trail from the west end of Chestnut Street to the Fort Walla Walla Amphitheatre, opening a 38-acre undeveloped portion of Fort Walla Walla Park including an irrigation system and tree plantings; and the purchase of property and the development of a trailhead park on Main Street along Mill Creek with a shelter, restrooms, playground equipment, and mural. Though we had also hoped to build new dedicated links of the trail along Mill Creek west of downtown and along Garrison Creek west of Myra Road, we ran into resistance from property owners and that didn't happen.

The downtown trailhead park property was purchased and developed in 1992 through an arrangement with Rob Robinson, the community-minded construction manager who held a court judgment against the former property owner, and who acquired, developed, and sold the property to the City in a creative deal which made our money stretch further than would otherwise have been possible. In 1994, Rob as president of the Blue Mountain Arts Alliance also arranged for the donation of the façade of the fanciful old Odd Fellows Temple on Alder Street, then led a fundraising campaign for and oversaw the reconstruction of the facade on the east wall of the park.

Other elements of the park include playground equipment and a large mural on the west wall, for which I invited proposals from several artists, out of which came an agreement with Jim Fritz, who was very successful in memorializing the outlines of several historic downtown Walla Walla buildings which had been lost over the years. Other murals were later added to the south wall along Mill Creek by youthful artists.

In 1995, further art was added to the neighborhood when members of the Whitman sorority Kappa Alpha Theta called with an offer to cooperate with Walla Walla 2020 on another community mural. Jim Fritz again helped out, this time with the creation of a transportation mural on the Mill Creek side of the old Naimy Furniture Warehouse building across Spokane Street from the park. The materials costs and some labor were contributed by the Thetas. The resulting mural featuring historic modes of transport can be seen there today.

The final artistic contribution to the park has been the Windows on the Past project led by Rob Robinson and Jeana Garske of the Blue Mountain Arts Alliance, now ArtWalla, and Walla Walla 2020 member Jeanne McMenemy. Windows is a very high quality memorialization of Walla Walla's various ethnic groups through a series of color photographs appearing in the windows of the Odd Fellows façade.

City Bicycle-Pedestrian Advisory Committee

In 1990, I became a member of the City's Bicycle-Pedestrian Advisory Committee, and began evaluating our community bike facilities. After studying the principles of good bicycling and experiences in other cities, in July 1992 I proposed a four-part program of making all streets safe for bicycles, developing and expanding efficient and appealing bicycle routes, promoting increased bicycle use and safety, and coordinating our work with neighboring jurisdictions.

It is well recognized that bike lanes in the streets increase safety for both bicyclists and pedestrians. Since Walla Walla didn't have any, in the fall of 1992 I drafted and presented an application for federal ISTEA funds for a city striping project. With the $163,000 grant we received we were able to stripe bicycle lanes in Walla Walla on four major arterials—Howard, Alder, Tietan, and Roosevelt. It also allowed us to restripe several other major arterials to provide for wider curb lanes to better accommodate bicycles along with motor vehicles, including Isaacs, Rose, Poplar, Alder, and Plaza Way, and to install a center line in the Mill Creek Recreation Trail to improve conditions for multiple users.

One of the committee's major goals was to establish a bicycle-pedestrian master plan which would help identify and fill gaps in our walking and cycling system. One gap was the lack of any pedestrian facilities on either side of Ninth Street from Jefferson Park to its intersection with Plaza Way and the Dalles Military Road—a major entrance to the city and state highway used by students, senior citizens and others to access nearby commercial and community facilities. In October 1992, the Walla Walla 2020 Walkers Committee that Barbara had put together wrote to the city about the problem, and at my urging in the spring of 1993 our city advisory committee submitted a successful grant application to install pedestrian facilities there and to study other gaps.

Unfortunately, a car dealer on the west side of Ninth who has had a sweet deal with the state to occupy part of the right-of-way for $1/year used political pressure at the state level to block any change on his side of the road. However, as a result of the grant we do have a long-overdue pedestrian trail and safe access along the east side of Ninth. Hopefully, the committee will revisit the west side at some point and resolve this major defect in our multimodal transportation system.

Regional Bicycle-Pedestrian Advisory Committee

Since it makes sense for any bicycle-pedestrian master plan for the Walla Walla area to include the city of College Place as well as the urbanized areas of Walla Walla County around the two cities, in December 1992, I proposed the establishment of a regional bicycle-pedestrian advisory committee to develop a regional plan, and to serve as an advisory committee for any of the jurisdictions not having their own committee. In early 1993 there was approval by the three jurisdictions who signed an interlocal agreement setting up a Regional Bicycle/Pedestrian Advisory Committee consisting of an elected official, a citizen, and a staff member from each jurisdiction.

In July I was appointed the City of Walla Walla's citizen representative, and served as chair of the committee for seven years. During that time, we adopted a master bicycle-pedestrian plan for the Walla Walla urban area, sponsored educational programs, monitored plans for bicycle and pedestrian facilities in new developments, got the state to construct a path linking the end of College Avenue to the Old Milton Highway, and won a grant to build a bicycle-pedestrian trail along Rose Street from 13th to the Blue Mountain Mall, a project that was on our list at the original 2020 visioning session.

A successful grant application in a competitive environment involves good timing, writing targeted to the grant criteria, good project design, and proper presentation. Since a prior staff proposal covering this project hadn't been funded, when another opportunity arose, I wrote up a new application. I presented the project to the Department of Transportation as one that would preserve a row of heritage trees along Rose Street that were threatened by the railroad which owned the property, would upgrade a vital interurban route to important community facilities, and was endorsed by the full community and all its public bodies. This time we scored well, received our grant, and the new trail facility and its old trees are doing well.

Overall Effects

The results of our bike and hike efforts have been good, including the work by 2020's own committee as well as the city and regional committees we spawned. In addition, Barbara and her 2020 Walkers' Committee have devised and published an ingenious walking map of Walla Walla funded by various merchants, showing a series of circles the radius of which represents a twenty-minute walk, in order to help people find the best routes and judge walking times. The city Bicycle-Pedestrian Committee has also put out a bicycle map showing city routes as well as recommended rides into the countryside, along with safety tips.

We've built dedicated bicycle-pedestrian trails and planted and preserved trees along them, installed striped bicycle lanes and widened curb lanes, built and enhanced parks, created murals, organized bicycle parades, and supported transit initiatives including shelters for pedestrians and bike racks for cyclists. Under the leadership of Stanley Green and Andy Pryor, the 2020 committee has also advocated for better intermodal connections and intercity service. We've co-sponsored Energy Independence Days when we challenge employers to compete for the most employees walking, biking, bussing or carpooling to work. We even created a Walla Walla 2020 precision bicycle drill team for several community parades, which I've led through a series of contra-dance like maneuvers, including some Bikes and Buses are Beautiful entries in partnership with Valley Transit.

Overall, we've raised consciousness and captured the attention of Walla Wallans regarding the merits and place of non-motorized transportation, and created a greater appreciation of walking and cycling that is contributing to a healthier, more human-scale way of life in our community.

Economic Development and Growth Management

Although issues of sustainable development and farmland protection were raised at the time Walla Walla 2020 was founded, these were not a focus of our original committee work. That changed in 1990 with the passage of the Washington State Growth Management Act (GMA), after which economic development and growth management became high profile issues for Walla Walla 2020.

This part of our work began in October, 1990 during the campaign for Land Use Planning Initiative 547, when 2020 sponsored a public talk on growth management by Seattle attorney Jeff Eustis, one of the drafters of the initiative. Though we invited interested people to stay afterwards, the only one who did was the manager of the local Pacific Power office, whom we later learned was also President of Team Walla Walla, a newly formed economic development organization. His opposition to any limitation on development was our first introduction to the power companies' desire to maximize their own profits regardless of the effects on local communities.

Although our local governments weren't bound by most parts of the Growth Management Act unless they opted in, both the county planning director Jim Beard and the city planning director Bob Martin urged their jurisdictions to plan under the Act, and in October, 1990 they agreed to do so in order to receive additional planning monies from the state.

The 547 initiative campaign had raised our consciousness of growth issues, and in 1991 we agreed to form a Walla Walla 2020 Economic Development and Growth Management Committee to begin studying requirements for the development of a new comprehensive plan and other GMA tasks. At the same time we began to work on issues of more sustainable and democratic economic development processes with Team Walla Walla. Barbara led the economic development portion of the committee while I coordinated the growth management side.

Team Walla Walla

In every town there are those who believe population growth is economically very beneficial, often because of the short-term gain which can be realized from it. Walla Walla is a fairly rare place that combines the cultural offerings of a city with the tranquility and accessibility of a small town. It sits in a fertile valley with a mild climate bordered on the east by the Blue Mountains, on the west by the Columbia River, on the north by the Snake River, and on the south by the Oregon border. Besides diversified agriculture and some manufacturing, it's a community of institutions, with three colleges, two general hospitals plus a U.S. Veterans Administration hospital, the state penitentiary, the US Army Corps of Engineers headquarters for the Snake River dams, many retirement facilities, and a traditionally stable economy. Walla Walla is also the oldest town between the Cascades and the Rockies, with tall trees and historic homes, a substantial arts community, and a cultural life that includes four live theaters and a symphony orchestra. With an urban area population of around 45,000 and growing renown as a wine and fine dining destination, its pleasures are accessible and its quality of life is hard to equal. In these circumstances, population growth might well threaten the very things people value here.

Team Walla Walla didn't see it that way. Designated as the lead economic development agency in the county, it was incorporated in 1990 by the managers of Pacific Power, the Port of Walla Walla, and the publisher of our local newspaper. Though it was the recipient of public funds from the cities, the county, the port, and the state, this non-profit group, with a board composed only of those willing and able to pay a membership fee of $1000 a year for the privilege of determining our community's future, adopted as its only program the recruitment of outside businesses to relocate to our valley.

The problems we saw with this approach to economic development was that only a few interests were at the table and they were focused on the short term. Our view was that if we could bring

115

together representatives from all sectors of the community to focus on the long term, we would discover substantial agreement on a shared vision for the future.

We decided to start our work from the inside. In reviewing the Team Walla Walla bylaws, we discovered an "associate membership" category which only required an annual fee of $50 rather than what we considered the "fat cat" rate of $1000 a year. Associate members had no vote, but did have the right to attend board meetings. Since our partner, the Downtown Walla Walla Foundation, was also unable or unwilling to pay the full fee, we both applied for associate membership in the fall of 1991 and after some delay were accepted.

Not long after that, the leaders of Team Walla Walla presented a proposal for restructuring the organization that would provide guaranteed seats on its board for the five highest paying contributors and make associate members ineligible for election to the board. Barbara, as our representative, suggested that auctioning off seats to the highest bidders on a board charged with spending public funds didn't seem appropriate. In February, 1992 Team Walla Walla withdrew the proposed changes, and instead amended its bylaws to exclude associate members from further board meetings.

Though they hadn't been successful in recruiting a single business, Team Walla Walla was receiving over $100,000 per year in public tax dollars in order to invite outside companies to come to town, some with serious environmental or other problems. Since TWW wasn't willing to provide a venue for community discussion of economic development, 2020 decided to try that itself, and in June 1992 proposed an "economic summit" to promote community understanding of economic development options as well as to build consensus on development goals.

At the request of 2020 and the Downtown Foundation, Walla Walla Community College agreed to coordinate and host the event, which was to include the cities and county, the public schools, the prison, the three colleges, the Blue Mountain Action Council, the state Employment Security Department, the Downtown Walla Walla Foundation, Walla Walla 2020, Team Walla Walla, the Walla Walla Area Chamber of Commerce, and others. Team Walla Walla and the Chamber of Commerce declined to participate, after which the Community College considered it inappropriate to proceed without them, and the summit wasn't held.

At that point we decided to take our case directly to the community. At 2020's request I drafted a White Paper on Economic Development, which 2020 formally adopted and released to the public on December 22, 1992. The White Paper relied heavily on the economic analysis of Tom Powers, head of the economics department at the University of Montana at Missoula, as set out in his excellent book "The Economic Pursuit of Quality" (M.E.Sharpe, 1988) as well as the Economic Renewal Program of the Rocky Mountain Institute.

We sent our White Paper to all elected officials and members of planning commissions in the valley. Here's what we said in part:

A vital, thriving economy is a key element in the quality of life we all seek in the Walla Walla area. Since we all have a stake in our economic success, all sectors of the public should be involved in economic development activities and planning.

The overall purpose of our economic development efforts should be sustainable, long term prosperity. We should not undertake initiatives that deplete important natural resources such as water and topsoil for the sake of short term profits. Similarly, we don't enhance the stability of our economy by the pursuit of large, non-locally owned companies dependent on fluctuating national and international markets and willing to move whenever conditions are more favorable elsewhere.

The majority of jobs created nationwide in the last 20 years have been by small, local businesses, including farms. Small, local businesses not only create most jobs, they also have greater allegiance to the local community. In addition, their diversity contributes to a stable economy, since the inevitable failure of some small businesses does not greatly affect the economy as a whole.

If local businesses produce goods or services for the local market which were previously imported from the outside, their impact is magnified. Money which had been lost to other regions is instead circulated several times within the community. The profits of locally owned companies are also circulated in the local economy, unlike the profits of externally owned companies.

A systematic program to decrease the local dollars lost from purchasing products and services from outside the community, called "import substitution" or "plugging the leaks" in the local economy, is the most powerful economic development tool available. This can be accomplished by developing local suppliers for products and services needed by area businesses. Plugging the leaks can also be accomplished by conservation programs which reduce waste of imported energy and keep local dollars in the local economy.

By supporting the prosperity and expansion of existing businesses in the Walla Walla area, by encouraging local entrepreneurship and new local businesses, and by conserving imported and local resources, our area can gain greater self-sufficiency, increased jobs, more opportunities for young people, and ongoing economic stability.

Our first goal of economic development, therefore, should be to support the founding, survival, and expansion of local small businesses. Our second goal should be to protect and improve the quality of public resources and services. These resources serve businesses and also serve all of the citizens of the area, and are largely responsible for why people want to live here. They include our schools, colleges, transportation system, water and sewer system, police and fire services, libraries, parks and recreational facilities, as well as clean air, natural beauty, freedom from congestion and blight, security from crime, friendly neighborhoods, and the richness of our cultural activities.

The importance of these public resources to the economic well-being of the community is often overlooked. In addition to their direct relevance to productivity they are the quality of life factors businesses seek when they decide where to locate. In addition, they are factors which attract or repel others such as retirees, who are free to live where they wish and whose expenditures and investments have a large impact on our community.

While incoming residents bring new resources and can be the source of new businesses, they also require new or expanded public services. In general, the effect of a growth in population from whatever source is that public expenditures increase per capita, requiring higher taxes to pay for expensive new facilities. A growth in population also means more congestion, degraded air quality, and related urban problems. Newcomers from areas with higher costs of living and generally increased demand drive housing costs out of reach for some existing residents, and most will find the qualities which attracted them to the community degraded. In the end, in an area as wealthy in culture and amenities as ours, we believe that growth will tend to impoverish rather than enrich us.

The attempt to convince outside companies and their employees to move here rather than to one of the thousands of other communities which are courting them can worsen our population pressures. Such campaigns are also expensive to run and often involve additional expense in terms of tax, environmental, and other concessions or giveaways to the prospective outside company that degrade a community's public resources.

To renew our economy and to protect its stability and our high quality of life, we need a commitment by all elements of the community to consensus building and cooperation toward a community economic development plan. Walla Walla 2020 is committed to participating in such a process.

Late in 1992 Team Walla Walla was asked by the Regional Planning Department to participate in long-range planning and to draft economic development planning policies for adoption by the County under the Growth Management Act, but declined to do so.

In March, 1993 we wrote to Team Walla Walla, enclosing our white paper and pointing out TWW's failure to adopt a democratic structure, to engage in consensus building on community goals and options, and to engage in long-range planning. We told them that our support of future public funding for TWW would depend on its commitment to these essential principles of effective and appropriate economic development, and requested notice by May 1 of what steps, if any, it would be taking in that regard. In a response from its president, TWW indicated it would be adding support of local businesses to its formal work plan as a supplement to its primary goal of outside recruiting, but would make no other changes.

In June we communicated to each of Team Walla Walla's public funding sources our request that further public funding be withheld, and that any renewal of their contracts with TWW for economic development services be conditioned on its democratic restructuring and its participation in community dialogue and consensus building. That was the beginning of the end of Team Walla Walla.

Over the next two years, in response to continued protests by 2020 as well as our scrutiny of discrepancies in Team Walla Walla financial statements, both the City and the State conditioned their contracts on Team Walla Walla's satisfying most of our demands. In addition, the City delayed its funding until it received the results of a community economic development meeting of the kind 2020 was seeking, and the Port of Walla Walla initially reduced then ended completely its funding of Team Walla Walla. In August, 1995 the new president of TWW acknowledged (1) that its mission had failed in that no new businesses had been recruited, (2) questioned whether recruiting out-of-town businesses was appropriate as the primary goal of the organization, and (3) suggested TWW consider disbanding, which it effectively did later that year.

In its place, the Port of Walla Walla has become the lead economic development agency in the county and has established an economic development advisory council that is open to the public and in which Barbara regularly participates. To our satisfaction, the economic development plan adopted by the Port embodies the major principles of 2020's white paper, including support for local businesses, democratic structuring of economic development bodies, and an express goal of providing better jobs for existing residents rather than seeking to grow the population. While the Port's practices and policies need to be continually monitored, they are now subject to debate by

118

all interested parties, and our economic development policies are now acknowledged to be the business of the entire community.

Subdivisions

In 1993, when the City of Walla Walla proposed a new subdivision code, I began working with a 2020 intern, Whitman College environmental studies and sociology student Lucia Ramirez, on a review of model subdivision ordinances and the design of new residential developments that maximize neighbor interaction, the development of a sense of community, and non-motorized transportation. What we found most appealing were neo-traditional or "new urban" designs with grid layouts offering easy connectivity and less congestion, tree-lined streets with sidewalks separated from the curb and designed to attract rather than intimidate walkers, and service and residential centers no farther apart than the five minutes the average person will walk before thinking about getting into the car.

In addition to suggesting modifications to the city's proposed code, some of which were accepted, we monitored all actual subdivision applications and testified at hearings as to their location, access to adjoining neighborhoods, and adequacy of bicycle, pedestrian, transit, and recreation facilities.

The only subdivision we challenged in a court proceeding was a sprawling, 36-unit project proposed to be located on agricultural land a mile and a half west of Touchet which violated almost every principle of good planning. The proposed subdivision was so bad that the county's environmental review committee, which regularly reviews major projects and routinely declares that they will have no significant impact on the environment, recommended a full environmental impact statement be required, and both the County planning staff and the unanimous county planning commission recommended denying the application. Nonetheless, the county commissioners approved the subdivision, as was their unwavering custom.

The developer's farm neighbors were among those upset with him for wanting to put houses in the middle of their fields, particularly since one of them had even offered to buy the land to keep it in agriculture, but was refused. The day before the appeal deadline I was asked by 2020 to draft papers for a legal action in Superior Court, which were signed by eight farmers from the area along with Walla Walla 2020. The suit under the counsel of Tom Scribner prevailed both in Superior Court and on appeal, representing the first time we had successfully joined forces with the farming community.

According to one of our farm partners, "the commissioners just threw out all the protections for farmlands we've been working hard for, and basically said, 'you can do whatever you want with your property regardless of the effect on your neighbors.' This is a bad precedent for our area and all of Walla Walla County." Unfortunately, that wasn't to be the end of bad precedents set by the Walla Walla County Commissioners.

Another important area where we successfully avoided the building of a subdivision was a large parcel of land on the south bank of Mill Creek across from the old Tausick Way landfill. On July 7, 1994 when I was reading the Waitsburg Times, the county's legal newspaper which Walla

Walla 2020 subscribes to in order to monitor important notices, I saw a notice of sale of surplus lands by the Washington State Department of Transportation, including this 30-acre urban parcel along Mill Creek with a minimum bid price of $14,250. Recognizing this as potential park lands that could be very valuable to the city, I phoned DOT to see if they had contacted the City of Walla Walla about the sale, and was told they had sent the city a notice, but had received no response. DOT also told me that a Bellevue developer was planning to bid on the property in order to put in a housing development there, but that the land could be sold to the city for a small fraction of its value if it acted promptly.

I immediately called the city parks director as well as a city councilman; both said they knew nothing about the matter, but would get right on it. As a result, the city was able to acquire this 30-acre parcel of prime shoreline property for a token price, and has created a major recreation complex there including softball and soccer fields, a skateboard park, and other amenities adding significantly to our quality of life.

Walla Walla County

Despite opting into the Growth Management Act, it soon became clear that the county commissioners did not want to plan and would resist complying with the Act.

In order to encourage compliance with GMA goals and procedures, 2020 began meeting with County planning officials early in the process, and suggesting appropriate language for planning documents. In 1993, I objected on behalf of 2020 when the Port proposed a substantial rewrite of the county's draft planning policies under GMA. Our local newspaper suggested that Port Director Jim Kuntz and I each write a column about our respective organizations' positions in order to frame the growth debate for the community. In my column, I said in part:

> Should Walla Walla grow? To what size? Should we add 5000 people? Ten thousand? Why? Should we grow constantly, without limit?
>
> It's important to be clear that the issue isn't whether we want a strong economy with jobs for everyone who lives here. We all want that, and need to work for it. The issue is how we go about achieving that goal, and whether growth is the answer or if it simply adds another set of problems.
>
> Walla Walla is currently growing without recruiting outside companies and people. We all see this in increased traffic on the streets, the housing shortage, lack of space in the schools, and gang activity. Even at our previously stable population levels, the water in the basalt aquifer has been falling an average of 4-5 feet a year for 30 years. What will happen if we have greater growth?
>
> It's important that citizens who recognize the unique value of our community begin to play a greater role in the discussion of growth and economic development issues, since the current process assumes that the pro-growth position of certain interests is settled policy, and is reluctant to consider either long term goal setting or alternatives to pro-growth strategies.

By 1994 the County had missed many GMA deadlines, as a result of which 2020 joined with the Blue Mountain Audubon Society and other conservation interests in forming the Walla Walla Conservation Council to petition the county for the adoption of proper protections for agricultural lands and wetlands, as well as a work plan for completing GMA. The group also noted that representatives of conservation interests had been left out of the county's GMA committees, and requested their appointment. Although we had threatened an appeal if the county failed to comply, since the legislature was considering damaging amendments to GMA, we decided an appeal might add more ammunition for critics of the Act, and deferred potential legal action until later.

At that time the Conservation Council was also concerned about a Wise Use ordinance the commissioners had just adopted, a version of the Catron County-style document from New Mexico that claimed county supremacy over state and federal laws and officials, as well as the local power to arrest them in order to preserve the local "custom and culture" of extracting resources from public and private lands with impunity. The ordinance the commissioners adopted was in fact a watered-down version I had suggested to the proponents when they came to meet with Barbara and me in order to deflect any opposition.

After the official adoption of the revised version with no enforceability, Whitman professor Phil Brick and others filed suit against the county challenging their authority to adopt the ordinance. In addition, a replacement ordinance was proposed to add environmental, cultural, social, and ethnic interests of local people along with the extractive interests. Though this was presented to the commissioners by Chris Howard on behalf of a rump group of Conservation Council members calling themselves Committee to Get us Out of This Mess, the only change the commissioners were willing to make was to pass a resolution acknowledging that the ordinance they had adopted had no teeth.

With large homes going up on some of the best farmland in the valley, in October1998 Walla Walla 2020 issued a further White Paper on Walla Walla County Growth Management drafted by former Milton-Freewater city manager Jim Swayne. In January, 1999 we issued an additional White Paper on Agricultural Land Use that I drafted. These papers discuss the principles of proper planning including reduction of inefficient and unsightly sprawl and protection of productive farmland, open space, and riparian areas, with details on the loss of farmland to development, which at that time amounted to over 1 million acres a year nationally. Locally, a major cause of lost farmlands was a 10 acre minimum lot size in most agricultural zones, making it easy for non-farmers to put up homes in the fields.

After further County inaction on its Growth Management Act obligations and further demands by Walla Walla 2020 for compliance, in early 2000 several 2020 members led by Nancy Ball, Doug Morton, Richard Bradley, and Jim Swayne formed Citizens for Good Governance, which together with 1000 Friends of Washington appealed the County's violations of the Act to the Eastern Washington Growth Management Hearings Board.

The board found the County in violation and ordered it to adopt a new comprehensive plan as well as interim and permanent development regulations under the Act by specified deadlines. Though these deadlines were also violated, under pressure from the appellants and the board the County finally adopted both interim regulations and a new comprehensive plan. These actions were themselves the subject of a further CGG appeal in which the City of Walla Walla joined, since the County's plan continued to allow urban growth in rural areas, and failed to provide sufficient minimum lot sizes in agricultural lands to effectively preserve them for farm use.

In 2001, the formation of the Foothills Protection Committee by farmers and landowners concerned about non-farm intrusions into the 120-acre minimum Agricultural Exclusive Zone further raised the consciousness of the community about the importance of good planning and growth management for the protection of the high quality of life Walla Walla 2020 has been working to preserve and enhance for the last thirteen years. Progress has been made, though in this as in other areas of 2020 concern, much remains to be done.

Neighborhood Organizations

Barbara and I both like the idea of neighborhood associations, which help neighbors get to know each other better, develop pride of place, address problems or needed improvements, and aid neighborhood communication with appropriate officials.

Although we had heard about neighborhood organizations during our student days in California, after that we had always lived outside urban areas until we moved into our house on North Main Street in Walla Walla.

Located near downtown, North Main is a two-block residential street of older homes with a public housing complex for senior residents at the north end. It is crossed in the middle by another two-block residential street, and this creates a four square block neighborhood. Our south and west perimeters are major arterials, with collector streets on the north and east sides. To the south is Whitman College, to the east a well-to-do area of appealing older homes, to the north is a large park and school complex bordered by newer homes, and to the west is a mixed area of older homes with a substantial number of low-income residents.

North Main has large shade trees and is a great location for walkers, since the downtown is only four blocks away, Whitman College is across the street, and a park is just to the north leading to the open fields on the edge of town. On the other hand, it's a transitional neighborhood with a high ratio of rentals, and over the years it became clear to us that it needed a greater sense of community and care.

North Main Area Neighborhood Association

After some research into the experiences of other cities as well as Walla Walla, in July 1993 Barbara and I invited several neighbors to a meeting at our house, out of which came the North Main Area Neighborhood Association.

Our kickoff activity was a neighborhood street party in August which became our signature event. We petitioned the city to temporarily close off the street where we put up banquet tables and chairs for a potluck dinner, a ping-pong table, information tables for neighborhood committees and police department materials, a sound system, a badminton net, and in later years displays of fire department vehicles and other activities.

We invited all the neighbors to introduce themselves and their families and tell how long they'd lived in the neighborhood, heard a talk by the crime prevention officer from the police department, organized games for the kids led by our son Jeremy, had people sign up for clean up/fix up, crime watch, mutual aid, and children's committees, and sang some songs.

For the initial event, neighbor Valerie Vicari wrote a special song for the neighborhood. Barbara added one of her own the following year, naming all of our streets:

> Mosey up North Main, perambulate Penrose,
> Promenade Pacific Avenue,
> Inch along Isaacs, roam down North Rose,
> And stroll on Sumach, too.
> Now you should be feeling mighty good,
> 'Cause you're in a mighty fine neighborhood!

In later years we added a neighborhood circle dance, a water-filled balloon toss competition, badminton and ping-pong tournaments, chalk and crayon art, piñatas, a bike rodeo, a kids talent show, and other events including appearances by city council candidates.

To aid communication we produced a neighborhood map showing the address of each house, and a neighborhood directory listing the names and phone numbers of all the residents including children. We even thought about adding the names of neighborhood dogs. We've also put out an occasional newsletter, the North Main Area Neighborhood News.

Our first party coincided with National Night Out, a nationwide Crime Watch effort aimed at getting citizens to meet their neighbors and to create stronger, more crime-free neighborhoods. While we have become a part of the local crime watch program, and have recruited block captains throughout the neighborhood, our association's activities have had a much broader focus.

In October 1993, we organized the first of many neighborhood cleanup days for which we borrowed a large truck from Whitman College and a neighbor's trailer to haul several tons of trash to the landfill under an agreement we negotiated with the City allowing the pooling of our individual dump passes. The day before our first cleanup we put on a yard sale to raise money for neighborhood projects for which one neighbor, too shy to attend any events, made and donated a beautiful afghan. Over the years, our cleanup days have offered an occasion for contacting neighbors with large piles of trash and discarded furniture who are usually very pleased to have them hauled away, as are we.

Our association has also been a vehicle for planting street trees throughout the neighborhood. In November 1993, we were able to plant 10 new trees under the expanded street tree program Walla Walla 2020 had worked out with the City to help fill in gaps in our urban forest.

Although our core neighborhood covers only four blocks, on several occasions we've also taken responsibility for graffiti paint-offs at adjoining Memorial Park and in the general areas around us, including a nearby abandoned warehouse, a freeway underpass, and several residential alleys.

While not everyone is willing to socialize with their neighbors, the effect of our annual parties and other neighborhood activities has been very positive. The association provides a context for getting to know people by name who might otherwise remain anonymous, and for working on mutual needs and improvements.

The neighborhood children in particular enjoy the parties, and are usually the ones who convince us of the importance of doing another one by their regular inquiries. In 1994, at the kids' insistence we held a neighborhood caroling party in December, and for the 1999 holidays, we did even better. That was the first year the Downtown Walla Walla Foundation hosted its Kris Kringle Kazoo Contest for which the first prize was $100 in gift certificates and the honor of leading the Christmas Parade of Lights.

Our friend and neighbor Candace Rose, who had led us in a kazoo chorus at a street party, was planning to enter, so Barbara and I and our daughter Rebecca went down to the event at the Die Brucke Building at First and Main to support her. As it happened, about the only people there besides the three Clarks and Candace were Timothy Bishop, the director of the Foundation, a contest judge, and a U-B photographer. To keep the event from being a complete flop, I took out my comb and Barbara and I borrowed wax paper and plastic forks from Cyndra VanDonge's sandwich and juice bar nearby. After discarding the comb, we played an unusual rendition of We Three Kings and Deck the Halls using only wax paper in our mouths and tapping on the paper with the forks for increased effect. This was a winning combination that shared first prize according to the Union-Bulletin which published our picture and gave it to the Associated Press which sent it out to newspapers around the region.

Though Candace was awarded the gift certificate and the three of us were invited to lead the Christmas parade, I suggested that a better idea would be to organize a North Main Neighborhood Association Kazoo Band for that honor. The Schuster family on the end of our block hooked a trailer full of straw to the back of their pickup and to the delight of the kids in the neighborhood as well as some of our friends who joined us for the event, we decorated both vehicles with lights and led the Parade of Lights for eighteen blocks playing our kazoos. The next year there were many more contestants in the Kris Kringle Kazoo Contest, but nobody suggested reviving our neighborhood band.

The Walla Walla Block Watch Council

Beyond our own area, we've been interested in sharing with others the benefits we've gained from our neighborhood association. One way to do that has been through city-wide block watch meetings. These had traditionally been held once every three months with all of the block captains in the city invited to hear a lecture-style presentation arranged by the police department in a room at the mall.

In 1997, in order to stimulate more grass roots ownership and input into the program, I suggested the formation of a Block Watch Council consisting of members of all organized block watches in the area and open to residents of unorganized neighborhoods wanting to find out about organizing. On April 9, 1997 the Walla Walla Area Block Watch Council was formed by representatives from 12 Walla Walla neighborhoods, whose purposes were declared to be:

—to share strategies and experience with other neighborhoods
—to communicate neighborhood needs to public officials
—to provide resources to help neighborhoods organize
—to obtain current information from police and other agencies
—to help find ways to strengthen our neighborhoods and community.

The council's initial officers were Vicky Scanlon from the North Main Neighborhood Association, secretary, Lula Belle Washington from the West Maple Street Block Watch, vice-chair, and I served as chair.

In May we put out a newsletter called "Walla Walla Area Neighborhood News" that went out to around 150 block captains in the city announcing the formation of the council, letting people know about a page on the Walla Walla 2020 website devoted to neighborhoods, and also the availability of a packet of illustrative materials prepared by the North Main Area Neighborhood Association we had given to the city's Crime Prevention Office for sharing with other neighborhoods. The packet included our neighborhood map, directory, newsletters, sample meeting agendas, street party posters, a beautification flyer, and a one-page sheet we prepared titled "So You'd Like to Start a Neighborhood Association!" that briefly outlines why, who and how, as well as where to get help.

At each of our quarterly meetings, the council agenda included sharing from neighborhoods, sharing from police departments, and a special focus topic. To further improve the meetings, we moved them to the city council chambers where all of the participants sat around a large table as equal partners rather than facing the front as in the authority-audience format.

Focus topics have included street closures for block parties, problem houses, and emergency preparedness, community policing, traffic issues, youth problems, mediation of neighborhood conflicts, development of a good neighbor code for landlords and residents, and handling of crime complaints, with relevant officials invited to attend each meeting.

Progress has been made on street closure processes and requirements, community policing, problem houses, code enforcement, graffiti removal, and other issues. The council was also active in a successful ballot measure to provide revenue for community policing, and after the onset of that program, community policing officers regularly attended the block watch council meetings along with the code enforcement officer and crime prevention office staff, which aided the handling of persistent neighborhood problems.

The good neighbor code the council developed is an excellent model of neighborliness which I haven't seen elsewhere, and was publicized in the press, distributed to all block watch captains and members of the rental property owners association, and posted on the Walla Walla 2020 "neighborhoods" webpage.

The Block Watch Council was a useful forum for sharing neighborhood experience, increasing communication between and animating citizens and public officials, alerting the community to some important issues, and increasing the resources of neighborhoods.

Prior to the formation of the Block Watch Council, we worked directly with two other neighborhood associations to form another community-wide organization that accomplished many of these same goals through programs aimed specifically at youth.

The Community Recreation Coalition

When I was growing up in Walla Walla, we had a summer recreation program in the parks, school gyms were open in the winter on Saturdays, and we had a night spot for teenagers called Shuffle Shop open two evening a week at the YWCA. For a variety of reasons these programs were discontinued in the late Seventies and early Eighties.

When gangs became prominent in Walla Walla in the early Nineties along with graffiti and drive-by shootings, Barbara and I became members of a Youth Violence Task Force put together by several public agencies. In addition to organizing a number of graffiti paint-offs in our neighborhood and in other parts of town, I began to look beyond the symptoms of youth violence and realized the need to reestablish the kinds of basic recreational programs I enjoyed as a youth that had been lost through budget cuts, neglect, or other causes.

Summer Recreation in the Parks

In 1982, after the City of Walla Walla eliminated its summer recreation programs in the parks due to budget cuts, I had been talking with city staff about the wisdom of renewing them without much response. It finally became clear to me that the City wouldn't be taking take leadership in the matter, and that any the initiative would have to come from citizens.

Around the beginning of June, 1994, I sat down to design a minimalist recreation program beginning with a single park. It occurred to me that our son Jeremy would be in town for the summer, would be looking for work, and had enjoyed working with elementary school children as an employee of an after school program in Hawaii, and also for the YWCA's Adventure Club in Walla Walla during breaks while attending Evergreen State College in Olympia. While continuing to explore other resources, I talked with him about the idea and suggested that, if nothing else, we could start a summer recreation program at Jefferson Park in Walla Walla as a pilot project with Jeremy as recreation leader, paying pay him either with a small grant from the Walla Walla Friends Meeting or out of our own pocket. He agreed, as did the Friends, and I began looking for other resources and sponsors to build on that foundation.

In June 1994, besides the North Main Area Neighborhood Association Barbara and I had formed, there were two other neighborhood associations in Walla Walla—West End Neighbors in the poorest part of our city, under the leadership of Lynn and John Knapp, and the Memorial Park Neighborhood Association just to the west of us which had been formed by Peter and Illana

Ferris who had recently moved to town from the Seattle area. The West End Neighbors had been around for a number of years, but were at low ebb. In order to help out, Peter and I went to one of their meetings at Washington Park, then heavily infested with gangs and drug dealers, where we discussed a mutual graffiti paint-off party as well as possible cooperation on summer recreation. Peter and Lynn loved the idea of our associations co-sponsoring a summer recreation project and also trying to reinstitute year round programs, and Peter volunteered to staff a part-time program at Memorial Park himself.

On June 15, we invited various agencies and organizations to a meeting at the Jefferson Park Field House to consider our proposal to establish a Summer Recreation Program in the Parks, as well as to begin discussion of a year round City of Walla Walla recreation program. When the inevitable question of liability insurance for a non-governmental recreation program was raised, we asked if there was any existing agency that could sponsor our project for insurance purposes. After a long silence, Richard Pankl of Children's Home Society saved the day, saying that his agency "could probably do it."

Out of that meeting came a decision to form the Community Recreation Coalition, a Washington non-profit corporation whose eventual members included the three neighborhood associations, Children's Home Society, the YWCA, the City of Walla Walla Parks and Recreation Department, Walla Walla County Human Services, Walla Walla School District, Whitman College, Walla Walla College, United Way, Community Connections, the Retired Senior Volunteer Program, Boy Scouts, and several others.

Three weeks later, on July 5, 1994 we opened a free summer recreation program in Walla Walla for the first time in over a decade, not in one, but in three parks. We contracted with Children's Home Society to be our employment and insurance sponsor, and with funding we obtained from several local trusts and contributions from coalition members and the general community, we hired a coordinator and three park directors, including Jeremy, and began offering recreation programs for children 8-15 years old at Jefferson, Washington, and Memorial parks every afternoon from Monday through Friday, which continued until the week before school started.

Activities we offered included chess and other board games, arts and crafts, ping-pong, badminton, croquet, volleyball, softball, tennis, and soccer which proved to be the most popular of all. The Clarks also introduced the revival of a popular Walla Walla game called peggy I'd played as a kid, a corruption of cricket using softball bats and ball, bowling pins, two-person teams and balls and strikes to advance or retire a batter. Jeremy and I were the peggy champions that summer, the Washington Park team members won the soccer tournament, and local kids in general were winners, including several teen-age assistants provided us by the Blue Mountain Action Council's Youth Employment Program.

By August our total attendance had been 2711 children, and we were beginning to plan for the fall. Our mostly Latino soccer team from Washington Park, the Aztecas, wanted to keep playing together in the fall as part of the Walla Walla Youth Soccer Association which for a variety of reasons had very few Hispanic participants, so the CRC agreed to continue to sponsor them. With Jeremy as their coach, they went 13-1-1 for the season. We also wanted to transfer our other park activities to school gyms on Saturdays during the winter, and to begin evening activities for teenagers.

In order to plan for winter gym and evening programs and to keep the soccer program going, the CRC hired Jeremy as coordinator for the fall. In addition we asked the City of Walla Walla to consider including our programs in its 1995 budget and to assume City administration of them.

For 1995, the City of Walla Walla contributed $10,000 toward our budget, and in cooperation with our partner Children's Home Society, the CRC ran another successful summer program—this time offering free lunches in three parks, Washington, Jefferson and Pioneer. Mask-making, drama, golf, and other special programs added to the continuation of our regular activities from the year before. Our average of twenty-five youth per day per park the first summer rose to thirty per park per day the second summer for a total of over 4000 participants.

In 1996, the City of Walla Walla Parks and Recreation Department assumed full responsibility for the summer recreation program, and to our great pleasure has continued to run it successfully ever since.

The Winter Gym Program

In the fall of 1994 the CRC, which I chaired, was able to negotiate an agreement with the Walla Walla School District for use of school gyms on Saturdays during winter months as open recreation sites for school age children and their families. On November 5, we began a staffed Saturday Gym Program for ages 8-18 at Blue Ridge School in the west end and Berney School in the east end of town. We served approximately 1000 boys and girls and their family members that first winter.

The next year we began a three-gym program using Berney and Green Park elementary schools as well as the new Garrison Middle School gym which became our most active site, featuring high energy indoor soccer games as well as basketball, ping-pong, volleyball and board games. In addition to open play, we arranged an indoor soccer competition between our Walla Walla sites and a similar program in Milton-Freewater led by high school soccer coach Jose Garcia working through their Horizon Project, resulting in the enrichment of both programs. Our total attendance for the season was over 1700.

Besides paying CRC/CHS staff at each site, I served as the coordinator on a volunteer basis that first year, and also arranged for the help of student volunteers from Whitman College.

Despite demonstrating the effectiveness of the winter program for two years, with an average of twenty-five participants per day per site the first year and twenty-five the second year, it wasn't until we averaged forty-five the third year that the city council agreed to fund it. On January 1, 1997 the City Parks and Recreation Department took over the program, which it is continuing to operate successfully at several sites.

Evening Activities for Teenagers

Finding a site for a teen center and sustaining attendance are both difficult. Looking around town, the most workable spot for more evening activities for teens seemed to me to be the Eastgate Marketplace, a small mall on the east end of town. The CRC board agreed, and we began negotiations with the management and merchants' association at the Marketplace, which agreed to cosponsor our activities.

On September 24, 1994 we held our first Saturday Night at the Marketplace. We featured music and lights by a local radio station, as well as a singer-songwriter, miniature golf at an arcade which stayed open late for the event, ping-pong, chess, table games, and food discounts at a couple of restaurants there. Over 350 teenagers showed up for the event, which continued as Club Eastgate on a monthly basis with the help of a very small student dance committee until April 1995. At that point attendance had fallen off, in large part because the arcade at the marketplace went out of business, and we suspended operations for the summer and didn't restart in the fall. The old Shuffle Shop at the YWCA from the 1940's to the 1970's had succeeded in part because it was run by a very active student committee from the local high schools, which we hadn't been able to develop.

In the Spring of 1995, the CRC did a survey of student recreation needs. What the students told us in their responses was that their greatest need was for evening activities for teenagers. In January, 1997, we decided to try again. After further site analysis in terms of parking, zoning, neighbors, size, cost, and other factors, we suggested the use of one or both of the high school cafeterias in Walla Walla, and the students who came to our meetings liked the idea. What they said they wanted was a safe, dependable place to socialize on Saturday nights in a religiously neutral environment, rather than a night spot run during that period by a religious organization. We proposed to the two school districts a 12-week demonstration of how such a community facility would work, beginning on March 1 at DeSales, then moving to Wa-Hi until May, when we would return to DeSales for the final three weeks.

Each facility had a stage, rest rooms, vending machines, parking, neighbors who are used to events there, and two different rooms to allow a variety of activities. The proposal was that the schools would provide the facilities without charge, and we would provide paid staff and adult volunteers, as well as youth managers. Both schools agreed, if we paid their janitors to clean up.

We started out calling it "The Zone", but a naming contest soon made it "The Diskotek". Our season went more or less as planned, from the opening evening at DeSales, where we had 58 students and 14 chaperones, to 8 weeks at Wa-Hi, where attendance was usually higher, to the final event at DeSales on May 1. Activities included music and dancing (with a disco ball), ping-pong, foos-ball, cards, food, board games, an occasional live student band, a limbo contest, and a lot of hanging out. Again the student committee, though larger than our first attempt, remained weak, and we realized we still hadn't developed the elusive youth ownership we needed to keep the activity going.

Since live bands had been one of our bigger draws, I suggested to our youth committee that for the summer of 1997 we hold a Battle of the Bands at Crawford Park, at the bus transfer center on Main Street. Our youth leaders wanted to do it, and the Parks Department agreed to cosponsor the event if we would coordinate it, so we sent out invitations to community bands, arranged for a sound system, recruited judges, and came up with a tight stage schedule that included 15 bands in three hours playing to a large, enthusiastic crowd of all ages who watched, danced, and at times plugged their ears.

After this inaugural event for Crawford Park, the City and the CRC cosponsored two more events there that summer with dancing to sound machine music by a local disc jockey. Since then, the summer Battle of the Bands has become a regular event at Crawford Park coordinated by the City Parks & Recreation Department.

In the fall of 1997, the CRC partnered with the City for a new series of evening activities for middle and high school students centered on skating parties at the YWCA's Ice Chalet and bowling parties at one of the local alleys. In order to fund staffing and other out-of-pocket costs for these events, the CRC went to the city council in late 1997 with a successful request that the city expand the recreation component of its 1998 budget as we worked toward the goal of a year-round city recreation supervisor.

Many people have spent time and energy over the years pursuing the idea of a community youth center, a perennial subject in most communities. The Walla Walla Race Unity Coalition held a Youth Forum at city hall in November, 1997, at which a number of vocal youth called for an ongoing Youth Council, which was established and jointly staffed by several organizations and agencies over the next year, including Community Connections, the Community Network, the Race Unity Coalition, the City Parks Department, and the CRC. At the core of the Youth Council, which called for the City to itself take responsibility for a youth center, were the two Wa-Hi students who had been the leaders in the CRC's evening activities, Tai Harmon and Charlene Strozinsky. Together with City parks director Mike Petersen they visited teen centers in other cities and were named to a city task force set up in 1998 in response to the request of the Youth Council and others to study the feasibility of a youth center and to report its findings to the city parks board.

The effort was animated by the decision of the Walla Walla Community Network and its director Teri Barila to become active partners with the City in the process, and the re-involvement of John Avery, a former middle school teacher and retired National Guard officer who is a dedicated and creative youth worker and had pursued this quest for years. Since 1997 when the Army and Air Force Reserve vacated their portion of the armory, the centrally-located building with its large gymnasium and many other rooms had seemed to me the natural place to locate a City-run youth center. When I looked into its availability in 1997, the manager of the State's armories at Camp Murray told me the City could lease most of it from the state at cost only, but this wasn't pursued at that time by the city. With John Avery's connections with the Guard and his rapport with the youth, he was just the person to arrange for the building, as well as to build a youth-owned program there, which is what happened over the following three years.

In partnership with Teri Barila of the Community Network and others, John spearheaded the formation of the Community Center for Youth, whose CCY Council I incorporated as a tax exempt organization in 2000. CCY contracted with the City of Walla Walla for the cooperative administration of a dynamic and successful program run on Wednesday, Friday and Saturday nights at the armory, jointly funded by a variety of governmental bodies and other supporters. More recently the program moved to the education building at St. Patrick Catholic Church, and from there to the YMCA which has assumed responsibility for this long-time community goal.

Much has been accomplished and learned over the past several years of struggle toward a safe and dependable place for all of the community's youth to gather, and undoubtedly much more will have to be learned and relearned in this demanding and elusive pursuit.

Park Improvements

As CRC members became familiar with the city's playgrounds, we began to recognize the need to upgrade their facilities in a variety of ways, including the addition of volleyball and tetherball standards at several parks, which we arranged to have constructed and donated by a local manufacturer.

Basketball Hoops

Another missing ingredient was basketball hoops in our parking lots. We started at the large parking lot serving Memorial Park and Borleske Stadium near our home. I suggested to city parks director Mike Petersen that there was a place for two baskets there, and he agreed.

We then went around town looking for other public parking lots that could be turned into neighborhood playgrounds after hours, and found several more. Mike mentioned that Ron Wilhite, a chaplain at the penitentiary and retired businessman, was the Johnny Appleseed of basketball in the region, and would probably donate backboards, hoops, and balls if we could get the standards up. I had previously met and worked with Ron when we were both painting off graffiti around town.

Before long, we had arranged for Key Technology, a local manufacturer, to produce and donate heavy-duty standards the City installed in several parking lots in town along with Ron Wilhite's backboards, baskets, and nets, that are now used by kids in a variety of neighborhoods.

Jefferson Park

It didn't take long for us to realize that our summer recreation program at Jefferson Park was handicapped by the fact that the only bridge across Garrison Creek to the adjoining Garrison Middle School play fields was at the east end of the park, while our activities were at the west end. The same lack of access plagued other users of the park and the school grounds, so in the spring of 1995 I proposed that we build a new footbridge over the creek to connect the two facilities.

I found that building a bridge between two different jurisdictions is easier said than done, but by August we had gotten the school district and the City to resolve their liability concerns and agree to the building of the bridge. We were fortunate to enlist the help of Rob Robinson of Building Dynamics to oversee the project, engineer Joe Murar to design it, and Jon Rubin of Lumbermen's Building Supply to donate the materials. The city inspector approved our design, contractor Walt Porter agreed to lead the construction party, and CRC members supplied the labor. On August 2, 1995 we held a bridge dedication ceremony honoring all those who contributed, with donated refreshments from neighboring restaurateur Rosita Gonzales.

Another achievement of our program at Jefferson Park was the creation of an anti-gang mural on the side of the old caretaker's cottage, which was led by Federico Diaz, a member of our Aztecas soccer team, with the help of about 20 other participants in our Jefferson Park program. After painting graffiti off the various park buildings, these youth came up with a design portraying a handful of gang members with guns and drugs at their feet themselves painting over graffiti, and a sign saying, "The change started in 1995…Day by day things got better…Now we work together for the same cause." Federico has since gone on to become a key adult staffer in a successful new development program called Commitment to Community that has contributed to the strengthening of facilities in several of Walla Walla's neighborhoods.

Washington Park Soccer Fields

Our biggest CRC construction project was the building of two soccer fields. Washington Park was the only major park in town without a soccer field, and was also in a heavily Latino neighborhood with a strong interest in soccer.

The effect of our recreation program on Washington Park had already been dramatic. Police calls were reduced, and instead of a gang and drug-dominated park where responsible adults and families stayed away, the presence of our program had encouraged neighboring families to come back and to continue to use the park after we had gone home. Vandalism at the park restrooms had also decreased.

What remained unchanged was a dusty, weed-infested area bordered by Ninth Avenue and Mill Creek. This undeveloped lot was owned partially by the adjoining American Fine Foods cannery, and partially by the City. Though it was a natural spot for soccer fields, and there had been talk for some time of trying at least to plant some grass, nothing had been done.

Lynn Knapp had become the second president of CRC and was also the president of West End Neighbors. For Lynn, the lack of progress on this obvious need was a constant irritant and was also an insult to the neighborhood, which had often been short-changed in terms of city services and facilities, as low-income areas often are. Our recreation programs at Washington Park had already led to a city decision to build a second outdoor basketball facility there, and in 1995, I suggested we target the building of two soccer fields at Washington Park as a CRC project.

Lynn and the rest of our board agreed, and that fall we arranged a meeting with representatives of the City, American Fine Foods, the Mexican-American Soccer League, the Walla Walla

Youth Soccer Association, Image, West End Neighbors, and the CRC, out of which came the Washington Park Soccer Committee.

At the meeting, the American Fine Foods representative pledged to either give a nominal rent lease or full title for their portion of the property to the city for the fields, the City agreed to use its portion as soccer fields, and to maintain the fields if we would build them, and the two soccer associations agreed to donate several thousand dollars to the project. In December, Lynn as chair of the committee sent out a fundraising letter to the community, which responded generously over the next two years, contributing the balance of our project budget into an account managed by United Way, which had been an active participant in all our projects.

Many people helped with the building of the field, but those who worked hardest were Lynn and John Knapp and a number of their friends from the local Russian immigrant community. By 1997, we finally secured a deed from American Fine Foods, the money had been raised, the city had approved all the plans, the fields were graded and fenced, sand for the base of the field was hauled in, the irrigation system was installed, and all that remained was to seed the fields in the fall, wait for the grass to mature over the winter, and install the goals we had purchased in the spring.

On March 17, 1998 we held the dedication ceremony for the Washington Park Soccer Fields, honoring all of the sponsors, workers, and contributors for a project that transformed a blighted space into a fine facility for healthful neighborhood and community activities. Since then the fields have been well-used, and the city along with Commitment to Community has made other important improvements to this west end park.

Other CRC Activities

Beyond these achievements, a few other Community Recreation Coalition accomplishments are worth mentioning.

A Year-Round City Recreation Program

An essential goal of the Community Recreation Coalition has been to reestablish recreation as an authentic mission of the City of Walla Walla Parks and Recreation Department. While we began with the needed summer parks and winter gym programs and worked toward regular evening activities for teenagers, our broader purpose was to restore a year-round city recreation supervisor the city had employed from 1968-1982.

In the fall of 1998 we wrote to the city council pointing out that the city now had a summer recreation coordinator, a winter gym coordinator, and on an ad hoc basis a hand in evening activities for teenagers, and that it was time to consider a year-round recreation manager in its 1999 budget, who would provide continuity to these programs as well as giving creative attention to city-wide recreational needs.

The council was in agreement, and the city hired hire Andy Coleman as what is now its full-time city recreation manager. In addition to administering the existing programs, Andy has

133

established city-sponsored adult volleyball, basketball and soccer leagues, as well as a variety of other recreation activities, bringing us back into the ranks of responsible communities providing resources for a variety of recreation needs for families and residents of all ages.

Latino and Low-Income Participation

Another of our goals has been to make recreation programs more accessible to Latinos as well as low-income people throughout the city. The marked absence of people of color in the Walla Walla Youth Soccer Association's programs was troubling to the association as well as to us, and both groups were eager to use our Washington Park Aztecas team to begin to change that.

In registering the Aztecas for the Association's fall season in 1994, we had to face both monetary and language barriers to registration. Though the soccer association technically had a scholarship program for fees and equipment, it was rarely used, underfunded, and inaccessible. We prepared a scholarship application form for the association, which until then didn't have one, and also translated it into Spanish. CRC staff then went house to house in the Washington Park neighborhood to round up the necessary birth certificates, liability waiver forms, and a token payment towards the registration fees that we had negotiated with the association.

The CRC also made a monetary contribution to the WWYSA for the establishment of a low-income scholarship fund to help enable others throughout the city to participate.

Our activities and concerns also motivated other agencies to initiate or expand their Latino and low-income outreach programs, making more accessible a variety of services and programs to people of all income levels in the community.

Fort Walla Walla Disc Golf Course

Fort Walla Walla city park on the grounds of our old cavalry fort is the site of many community facilities, including Fort Walla Walla Museum, Fort Walla Walla Amphitheater managed by Walla Walla Community College for its summer drama and other events, a Blue Mountain Audubon Society natural area, a model airplane strip, model car track, ropes course, a BMX track, a skate park organized and built under the leadership of Ron and Paula Nolte and their sons with some help and encouragement from the CRC, and a dog park.

One of the newest facilities at the park is the Fort Walla Walla Disc Golf Course established by the Community Recreation Coalition, installed initially in the old campground.

On May 5-6, 2001 the former Fort Walla Walla campground became the eastern Washington site for the World's Greatest Disc Golf Weekend, an annual promotional competition among cities around the world that don't have a disc golf course within five miles, to see which can get the most registrants for at least 18 holes of disc golf.

Disc, or Frisbee golf, is a growing sport which for the first time that year was included in the World Games. Instead of balls struck with clubs, players throw discs or Frisbees from designated tees on established holes until they reach the target, which may be an object or, on most courses, a basket. The sport is much less expensive than ball golf, and can be enjoyed by people of any age the first time out, though it can also be challenging. Because of its low maintenance and low impact on the land, once a course is set up with permanent tees and baskets, its use is usually free to the public.

Since it seemed like a great idea that needed local support, I suggested to the Community Recreation Coalition that we become cosponsors of the weekend, whose organizer was promoter and disc golf enthusiast J.J. Wilson. I also proposed that we adopt the establishment of a free disc golf course in Walla Walla as a CRC project. Our board agreed, so I drafted a letter to the editor published in our local newspaper, prepared a poster, and sent an announcement around to various people and groups in the area.

On the eve of the tournament, I helped J.J. lay out the course, adding one hole to the 9-hole course he had designed to make a 10-hole course--unorthodox in ball golf, but very acceptable in the more innovative disc golf world. With alternate tees on each hole we had a 20-hole course with temporary borrowed baskets that accommodated over 100 registrants that weekend in Walla Walla. Two months later we learned that Walla Walla was the international first-place winner among approximately 200 courses and 15,000 disc golfers, the prize being four free baskets worth around $350 each.

The closest disc golf course to Walla Walla at that time was at Columbia Park in Kennewick, and a couple dozen members of the Tri-City Disc Golf Club had come over for our weekend competition. In talking with them afterwards, it was agreed that I would do the legal work to incorporate their club in exchange for their assisting us with the immediate installation of pipe targets and brick tee markers. They would also come back to help us install more appealing gong targets they would lend us while we were raising funds to acquire our own baskets.

The CRC was able to obtain permission from the city parks department to install temporary tees and targets at the end of the weekend to keep the course in operation. Brian Serven, Don Allen, and I then formed the CRC Disc Golf Committee, and CRC President Lynn Knapp and I went before the parks board later to seek permission to install the concrete-based gongs and some more substantial concrete tee markers donated to us by Dave Konen at Koncrete Industries.

In July after learning we had won the four baskets, we applied for a grant from a local trust for the remaining six baskets we needed as well as course signage, and we received permission from the City for a more permanent course installation.

The Fort Walla Walla Disc Golf Club has since been incorporated, and another twelve holes have been added for regular play. The exciting course along the banks of Garrison Creek near Highway 125 in Walla Walla is now listed on the Professional Disc Golf Association's (PDGA) official course directory, and a growing number of Walla Wallans are improving their proficiency at the game, as rabbits, deer, and coyotes watch from the bushes.

The Diversity Coalition

In 1992, I saw a small article in the paper about a Race Unity Day celebration in Jefferson Park and drove by but didn't see anyone there. I later learned that a handful of people had turned out to eat watermelon and play a game of volleyball. The next year I saw a similar article, and this time found a Mexican folkloric dance group, local Mariachi singer Salvador Hernandez, around 500 Latinos and a dozen or so Anglos eating watermelon and pizza in the park, and I wondered who had organized these gatherings.

The Multi-Cultural Arts Festival

In early 1994 Burl Barer of the local Baha'i group contacted Walla Walla Friends of Acoustic Music about participating in a 1994 Race Unity Day event at Pioneer Park in the center of the city, and I attended a planning meeting on behalf of FAM. For over 35 years, Race Unity Day has been observed by Baha'is and their friends in the United States and other countries on the second Sunday in June. Burl's vision was to make Race Unity Day a festival as big as the annual community Fourth of July celebration in Pioneer Park. I suggested that the way to do that would be to create a community-wide coalition to sponsor it, rather than it being simply a Baha'i event.

The Baha'is were in agreement, and the result was the formation of the Walla Walla Race Unity Coalition, later to become the Walla Walla Diversity Coalition. The Coalition was composed of the Baha'is, our Walla Walla Friends Meeting, Pioneer United Methodist Church, First Congregational Church, and Congregation Beth Israel, as well as representatives of Children's Home Society, the Blue Mountain Arts Alliance, and Walla Walla Community College. That summer the coalition presented its Multicultural Arts Festival at Pioneer Park.

Our 1994 event drew several thousand people of all backgrounds to our city's principal park to enjoy a variety of food, craft and information booths, along with entertainment featuring jazz, Mexican song and dance, German and Middle Eastern dancers, Native American drummers and dancers, and Irish music and dance. In later years, we've added Scottish bagpipes, Chinese, Italian, Indian, and Pacific Island dancers, blues, reggae, and gospel groups, international folk dancers, break dancers, and story tellers from Jewish, African, Native American, Mexican, Italian, and other traditions, as well as a chess tournament, hands-on art projects, a soccer clinic, and a popular ethnic heritage map of the world on which people put pins to show where their grandparents were born.

While it hasn't rivaled our Fourth of July celebration in size, the annual Diversity Day festival has become many people's favorite community event and has continued to draw a wonderful mix of people from a variety of ethnic and racial backgrounds as well as quality entertainment from a variety of traditions. In the city's official vision set out in its comprehensive plan, our festival is described as characteristic of the community's future.

Freedom from Discrimination Month

Following our first Multicultural Arts Festival in 1994, since Walla Walla didn't have a human relations commission I proposed that instead of limiting itself to just planning that spring event, the coalition should consider becoming a year-round organization dedicated to improving human relations in the Walla Walla area, which the group agreed to do.

Between Christmas and New Years that year Barbara and I visited an Anne Frank Exhibit that was on display at Eastern Oregon University. I was so impressed by the exhibit that I wanted more people in our area to see it, and suggested to the coalition that we bring it to Walla Walla in November, 1995. Everyone agreed, and while making plans for its rental and display, we decided to combine the exhibit with a month-long series of supporting events that we called Freedom from Discrimination Month. I also suggested that we create a broader Freedom from Discrimination Month planning committee to maximize participation in these events and exposure in the community, and agreed to chair that committee.

The list of cosponsors that first year was impressive. It included the cities of Walla Walla, Milton-Freewater and College Place whose mayors all declared September as Freedom from Discrimination Month; the Walla Walla and College Place public schools; Walla Walla College, Walla Walla Community College and Whitman College; the U.S. Army Corps of Engineers; the Walla Walla Union-Bulletin; The Baha'i Community, Congregation Beth Israel, the Walla Walla Friends Meeting, and the Walla Walla College Seventh Day Adventist Church; the Valley Cultural Awareness Committee, the YWCA, Image of Walla Walla, and Shalom Student Organization, as well as Cellular One and TCI as business partners.

Our focal point for the month was the Anne Frank Exhibit together with an Oregon State exhibit called Differences & Discrimination, both of which were installed at Walla Walla Community College for two weeks, followed by a week in Milton-Freewater at their Community Building. Additional events during the month included an opening ceremony and reception at the community college with talks by WWCC President Steve VanAusdle, Whitman College President Tom Cronin, and Walla Walla College President W.G. Nelson, as well as local survivors and liberators; another opening ceremony and reception in Milton-Freewater; a three-part film series at Whitman's Maxey Auditorium; a talk by the research director of the Simon Weisenthal Center in Los Angeles; klezmer band concerts at Whitman's Chism Hall and McLoughlin High School in Milton-Freewater; a visiting theatrical performance at both WWC and WWCC; an art exhibit at Carnegie Center and the YWCA; a holocaust survivor's talk at Whitman and Walla Walla College; and an exhibit-closing celebration of cross-cultural music.

For 1996, we moved our Freedom from Discrimination Month to October, and decided to focus on religious harmony. Our keynote speaker was Bill Wasmuth, the former Catholic priest from Coeur d'Alene, Idaho whose home had been bombed by white supremacists after he organized a local human relations task force in response to activities of the Aryan Nations, and now executive director of the Northwest Coalition Against Malicious Harassment.

During this month, which also included a talk by former Haitian President Jean-Bertrand Aristide, also a Catholic priest, we held a discussion in Cordiner Hall foyer on "How do we accommodate religious diversity in our public institutions—what has been the experience of members of the various religious groups in the Walla Walla Valley?" Special guests and participants included people from Jewish, Muslim, Buddhist, Hindu, Native American, Baha'i, Quaker, Baptist, Adventist, and Catholic traditions, among others.

Later in the month, we sponsored a Celebration of Religious Diversity at the Walla Walla High School Commons, in which people from these various religious groups and traditions were invited to display materials on their customs and practices, and to perform their music or dance. The event was a great success and is remembered by many as the most harmonious religious gathering in their experience.

At the end of the month we held a Youth Forum on Discrimination in the City Council Chambers where we presented the winners of our high school essay contest on the question, "In view of the religious diversity present in the United States, should public schools sponsor prayer at graduation ceremonies?" The forum was led by students from Whitman College who had been part of a delegation we had organized to attend a Youth Summit and Annual Conference in Spokane put on by the Northwest Coalition against Malicious Harassment.

In 1997, we focused on diversity in general and moved our opening ceremonies to the Blue Mountain Mall, where we presented a three-week exhibit on Northwest Black Pioneers. Other events included a presentation on English as a second language and a second City Hall Youth Forum on Discrimination addressing the question, "How does the Walla Walla Valley accommodate racial, ethnic, and other diversity?"

We invited school and government officials to the Forum as listeners and asked them to respond to the statements of the young people, who included dropouts, skateboarders, ethnic minorities, non-Christians, and non-athletes. The forum resulted in the formation of a local Youth Council that played a role in the eventual establishment of the Community Center for Youth in 1999.

In 1998 we installed a Syracuse University exhibit at the mall that presented biological evidence disproving racial differences and showing that there is actually just one human race. Our 1999 keynote speaker was Antonio Sanchez on "Fruits of Our Labor: The Accomplishments and Contributions of Hispanics in Washington State, 1794 to the present."

Other keynote speakers for Freedom from Discrimination Month have included well-known figures such as Morris Dees, founder of the Southern Poverty Law Center whose activities have helped put the Ku Klux Klan, the Aryan Nations, and other hate groups out of business; Latino actor, director, and activist Edward James Olmos who inspired us with his innovative approaches to education for gang members and others often left behind by our schools and social system, Rajmohan Gandhi, grandson and biographer of Mahatma Gandhi; Yolanda King, eldest child of Dr. Martin Luther King, Jr.; and Hussein Hassouna, Ambassador of the League of Arab Nations. Recent themes have included discrimination on the basis of economic status, the Asian-American experience, and gender identity and sexual orientation issues.

When we put up our Freedom from Discrimination Month banner across Second Street each October, visitors and community members often tell us they assume this is all part of a national event, which makes sense and maybe someday will be.

Other Activities

Beyond our Multicultural Arts Festival and Freedom from Discrimination Month events, for several years we had an annual entry in the Walla Walla Fair Parade, and we've served as a general sounding board for human relations problems in the community. In our parade entries, organized by Virginia Harrison, we often featured kids of all backgrounds riding Phil Monfort's ponies or carousel, with the rest of us accompanying them as clowns.

Sometimes our activities have been more serious. In the fall of 1995, a Walla Walla Community College instructor told us that a student of his from Milton-Freewater had been approached by members of a racist militia that was training in the Blue Mountains for "the coming war with the muds," by which they meant Latinos. In response, we arranged a joint meeting of the Race Unity Coalition, the Valley Cultural Awareness Committee, and local law enforcement officials that was attended by the Milton-Freewater and Walla Walla police chiefs, among others. We never learned what their investigation disclosed, but assume the militia is no longer active since we haven't heard anything more about it.

As a follow-up to our discussion on accommodating religious diversity, near the end of 1996 we wrote to the city council with respect to comments that were made during our forum regarding the invocations at council meetings offered solely by members of the Walla Walla Ministerial Association, an exclusively Christian group. The letter from our coalition's founding president, Britt Barer, said:

> We support the positive purpose behind the invocation, which as we understand it is to inspire those present in a spirit of common unity. We believe that this purpose can best be achieved at City Council meetings by inviting members of the public from a variety of traditions to present brief inspirational readings. These readings should speak to all citizens, rather than speaking to or in the name of a particular religious faith....

> In view of the many different beliefs held by the citizens of Walla Walla, and the greatly varying practices of the various faiths, we do not believe it is practical for a member of any particular faith to attempt to lead our citizens in common prayer, nor do we believe it to be the role of government to organize or sponsor prayers.

> We do, however, believe it is an appropriate role of government to inspire citizens to act for the common good, and that it is worthwhile for it to do so.

> If the Council does desire to continue to sponsor or offer inspirational messages at Council meetings, we propose that the process be open to all citizens. We further propose that an advisory committee be established to assist the Council in this process, composed of representatives of all of the religious or inspirational viewpoints represented in the Walla Walla area, including freethinkers, and that the committee review readings

for their general inspirational value for all our citizens, and otherwise assist with the process. By establishing such a process, the City Council will be demonstrating its respect for the beliefs of all of the citizens of Walla Walla.

Others had also expressed concern about the existing arrangements, and a year later the council made a decision to open its meetings with an inclusive moment of silence rather than a spoken prayer.

Another project we addressed early on that played out in a different forum was the possibility of creating an ethnic history walking tour of Walla Walla. The original idea came from our member Phil Monfort who was impressed by the healing experience of an annual Unity Walk past sites of previous oppression in Richmond, Virginia, an historic seat of slavery, and suggested we consider something similar here.

I suggested that we ask a key member of each ethnic group represented in our area to prepare a history of their members in the valley, and that we create a walk through the downtown beginning at the site of the 1855 Treaty Council proceedings, along which we would tell the story of each ethnic group at some location significant to that group. As part of the project, which I was asked to coordinate, we enlisted the help of Whitman College history student Stefanie Starkovich, who agreed to do her senior thesis on the histories of immigrant groups in the Walla Walla Valley, though ultimately covering only the Germans from Russia, Chinese, and Italians.

To help complete the project, in early 1997 we asked key members of ten ethnic groups to help with the gathering and writing of the stories of their group. The ten groups we specifically focused on were the Native American, French, Chinese, Scandinavian, Germans from Russia, Italian, Japanese, Jewish, African-American, and Mexican, to which we would add British Isles and other histories. Unfortunately, although the ten ethnic representatives agreed to help with the initial work on the project, by 1998 none had followed through, and in 1998 I began to pursue another avenue to tell the ethnic histories of our community.

Fort Walla Walla Museum

In November of 1997, Barbara was elected to the Walla Walla City Council, and appointed the council's representative on the board of the Fort Walla Walla Museum. Though we had been through its various buildings before, and our folklore society had held several contra dances in its pioneer village, neither of us had paid much attention to the museum or to general Walla Walla history until then.

The Living History Company

Because of Barbara's new responsibilities, both of us made it a point to become more familiar with the museum. We found it to be rich with culture, but under-utilized. In thinking about how to increase patronage there, we concluded that a living history company might accomplish that. Some friends of ours, Clark Colahan and Barbara Coddington, visited Colonial Williamsburg about that time and brought back brochures and other materials for us, and we proposed to museum director James Payne that we organize something similar here. James agreed, and in June of 1998 we started calling people in the theater community in Walla Walla to see what help they might give us.

Our initial concept was that on selected Saturday and Sunday afternoons during the museum's regular season we would focus on a specific day in Walla Walla's history with authentic characters in the pioneer village who would be associated with specific buildings. In addition, we might arrange for some special characters relating to the particular event being highlighted, all of whom would interact with themselves and the patrons, and might also appear individually on other occasions. My own hope was that four or five people might be interested in appearing as historic figures on a regular basis, with several others on special occasions. What concerned me most was the possibility that the quality of the acting might be very poor.

My initial research into Walla Walla's history relied primarily on the information and photos in Bob Bennett's "Walla Walla—Portrait of a Western Town, 1804-1899" (Pioneer Press Books, 1980). In early June, Barbara and I sent around a concept paper and meeting invitation to 15 people representing the drama departments at Walla Walla Community College, Whitman College, and Walla Walla College, as well as the Little Theater, the museum, the historical society, Blue Mountain Arts Alliance, Whitman Mission Historic Site, the Walla Walla public schools, the Downtown Foundation, the tourism committee of the Chamber of Commerce, the Whitman College archivist, a school librarian, and an artist.

Our First Season

Our inaugural meeting was on June 29, 1998 at the museum and resulted in the establishment of a working committee composed of Jo Anne Rasmussen, drama director at the community college, James Payne, director of the museum, school librarian Michelle Shaul, artist Abigail Bridges, and the Clarks. Our task was to plan for living history presentations at the museum's Fall Festival on September 13, and our goal was to present an early Walla Wallan in connection with each of the village's buildings.

By the first of August we had about a dozen characters. Jo Anne suggested Charles Saranto as pioneering blacksmith Fred Stine. Charles had played the lead in "The King and I" as well as Daddy Warbucks in "Annie" at WWCC's summer musical in the Fort Walla Walla amphitheater, and was the only real actor among us. Barbara had recruited retired physician Dick Simon, Sr. as pioneer physician Nelson Blalock, as well as local African-American barber Rick Brown as pioneer barber Richard Bogle, an escaped slave from Jamaica.

Michelle suggested Dan Dunn to play pioneer banker and railroad builder Dorsey Baker because he owned one of Baker's desks, and she agreed to share the role of our renowned madam Josephine "Dutch Jo" Wolfe with Abigail. For the other characters, James enlisted Maureen Rice of the museum staff in the role of Lettice Clark Reynolds, the first white woman to settle in the valley after the Whitman Massacre; I invited Whitman College bookstore manager Douglas Carlson to play Sheriff James McAuliff, along with music teacher Phyllis Bonds in the role of Sarah Miner, Walla Walla's first public school teacher, as well as Andy Beard, the AmeriCorps

141

volunteer at the Kirkman House Museum as William Kirkman. To complete the initial company, JoAnne arranged for high school thespian Rorry Little to be an anonymous prisoner in the jail; and museum volunteer Deborah Stenzel played an unnamed pioneer homemaker.

Our plan for the festival was to have all of the characters at their respective buildings throughout the afternoon, and to feature a special event at one building after another every half hour. Though I didn't intend to participate myself, it became clear at our rehearsals that we needed someone to do introductions and to direct the crowd from one building to the next, and Rick Brown suggested that I was the one to do that in the role of the mayor. As a result, I took on a new persona as Walla's first mayor, E.B. Whitman, a role I continue to play.

The week before the Fall Festival we introduced ourselves to the public for the first time during a Thursday evening concert downtown, and again on Saturday at the Farmers Market, where we also led some old time dancing.

The festival itself was a great success. Our characters for the most part gave fine presentations and interacted well with each other and with the good-sized crowds. Between presentations, Amos Fine and his fiddle band played from the train station platform, and late in the afternoon I led more old-time dancing. The museum's patrons stayed later than usual and the museum's staff was delighted with this strong first showing, as we all were.

We celebrated with a dinner for the company at La Casita Restaurant, and decided to continue with all of our major characters. We then scheduled another afternoon of living history presentations and dancing at the museum for October 31, the final day of the 1998 season. We also appeared at the Kirkman House Museum's Victorian Christmas Celebration, beginning an unbroken tradition of annual appearances by our players at that event.

The 1999 Season

In January, we met to begin planning for our 1999 season, during which one or more of our growing company appeared every Sunday at 2 pm from April through October.

We provided our players with biographic materials on their character out of W.D. Lyman's An "Illustrated History of Walla Walla County, Washington" (1901) or his later two-volume "Old Walla Walla County" (1918), Frank T. Gilbert's "Historic Sketches of Old Walla Walla, Whitman and Columbia Counties, W.T." (1882), one of Robert A. Bennett's books such as "We'll All Go Home in the Spring" (Pioneer Press Books, 1984), or from other materials in the Whitman College Archives.

We've also prepared a bibliography of local historical materials and a timeline of Walla Walla history to help members become familiar with events and circumstances of their era. The method we use in our presentations is for our characters to speak and interact with each other and the audience off the cuff, with no prepared scripts. Most of us have developed our own period costumes, often after some initial borrowing from the prop rooms of one of the local theater departments or the museum. Jo Anne Rasmussen was very helpful as our initial dramatic coach with tips on avoiding anachronistic items such as wristwatches, and helping with our deliveries.

With rare exceptions, we speak in our own words and voices without assumed accents, which lends a naturalness to our presentations, and avoids a staginess or stilted quality. Rather than being actors, we've successfully taken on alter egos which can be great fun for both presenters and patrons.

In our presentations we come as time travelers to the present era from some moment prior to our death. This enables us to have looked around a bit at the current scene, to have been able to read a bit of our history, and even to have visited our graves—undoubtedly a disturbing experience. The only thing we don't have is personal knowledge of our death, since we're still alive rather than being ghosts. With this format, we can comment on a wide variety of things past and present from our peculiar perspective as visitors from the 19th century.

We schedule both individual performances as well as and full company "town meetings" on a variety of topics. For the individual presentations, the players are free to talk about or demonstrate whatever they consider dramatic or interesting in the lives and times of their characters, and are encouraged to draw the audience into questions or comments, including how past events relate to current controversies.

Our first town meeting on June 27, 1999 focused on "Law and Order in Early Walla Walla," and featured a lively debate on the merits of the vigilante movement which engulfed the area for several years during the gold mining era of the 1860's, as well as conflicts when soldiers at the fort took over the town and defied civil authorities on several occasions. In July, we addressed the always interesting topic of "Women's Role in the West," and in August took up issues surrounding the Indian wars, including the Battle of Walla Walla and the death of Chief Peopeomoxmox. On the last day of the season we held a town meeting on "Events Surrounding the Whitman Massacre." For both of these events, we invited residents of the Umatilla Indian Reservation to take part, and were pleased to have Chief Carl Sampson, the current Peopeomoxmox, at the Fall Festival for our discussion of the Battle of Walla Walla

The 2000 Season

For our third season, we added Saturdays along with Sundays during the three summer months and adopted a common theme for each month's presentations.

During April we addressed religious diversity in early Walla Walla, including Congregational and Catholic missionaries, Adventist pioneers, and a member of the dissident Mormon community led by W.W. Davies, ending with a town meeting asking, "Can we all live together in peace?" After looking at Fires and Firemen in May, in June our town meeting focused on the "150th Anniversary of the Trial & Execution of the Five Cayuse Charged with the Whitman Massacre," and asked, "Were they guilty?"

This exploration, informed in major part by the excellent book "Juggernaut: The Whitman Massacre Trial," 1850 by Ronald B. Lansing (Ninth Circuit Historical Society, 1993), is an example of our living history company at its best. We had moving accounts by Myra Eells, one of the Protestant missionaries working with the Whitmans; Father J.B.A. Brouillet, the Catholic missionary who had settled in the valley in competition with the Whitmans and had buried their bodies; Joe Meek, the former mountain man and U.S. Marshall whose daughter died as a captive of the Cayuse following the massacre and who executed the defendants; William Craig, a former mountain man who saved other Protestant missionaries from a similar fate and was married to the daughter of a Nez Perce chief; William McBean who was in charge of the Hudson Bay Company trading post at Fort Walla Walla where some of the whites from the mission sought protection; and Antone Minthorn, chair of the board of trustees of the Confederated Tribes of the Umatilla Indian Reservation, who along with cultural interpreter Marjorie Waheneka participated in the meeting. Our collective conclusions were that some of the defendants had not participated in the killings, and that many legal and factual errors occurred in the proceedings, which most people had previously considered unquestionably just.

In July we explored relations between the fort and the community and whether or not soldiers and citizens could get along; in August we looked at our agricultural roots, wondering whether it has always been boom or bust. In September we featured discussions of women's rights, including talks by Miss Susan B. Anthony who visited Walla Walla in 1871 along with Northwest suffragist Abigail Scott Duniway. We ended the museum's 2000 season in the pioneer village with a reenactment of the 1894 wedding reception for Miss Fannie Anne Kirkman and Mr. Allen Reynolds.

Our Characters

While many of our original characters continue to be represented in the company, some of the players have changed faces or passed on to other things. After our first Fall Festival, Clark Colohan who plays a fife and penny whistle took on the role of the fife-playing James McAuliff, and Barbara began her continuing role as Maria Whitman, wife of E.B. In the 1999 season, Barbara Coddington assumed the role of the strait-laced but heroic Myra Eells as well as providing costuming advice, and in 2000, Whitman College religion professor Rogers Miles joined us as Cushing Eells. Abigail Bridges alternated with Michelle Shaul as Dutch Jo, as planned until they handed that role on to Lois Hahn who has done an excellent job the last several years. In 2001 Lois was joined by her husband Rod as stage coach entrepreneur John Abbott, a role we had long wanted to fill.

Other new characters included three mountain men: Joe Meek played by court services director Mike Bates, Robert "Doc" Newell by Randall Son, and William Craig played for a period by Whitman professor and horseman Dale Cosper, along with Craig's daughter Annie played by Sarah Corley, all of whom have moved on to other pleasures.

The company has also included pioneer settler A.B. Roberts, played by Darrel Jones, whose wife Vi continues to appear on occasion as Martha Roberts, in addition to Adventist pioneers Augusta Moorehouse, Caroline Maxon Wood, and William Nichols, played respectively at times by Cheryl Jackson, Carol Parkison, and Gordon Hare; Father Brouillet who continues to be portrayed by retired teacher Jeannot Poirot; Fr. Eugene Chirouse played by professor and lavender grower Jean-Paul Grimaud; Charles Tung portrayed by Galen Tom; William McBean by Rich Monacelli; fire chief Robert J. Wolfe for several years by fire captain Greg VanDonge; soldier Michael McCarthy by historian Bob Bennett; suffragists Susan B. Anthony, Abigail Scott Duniway, and Lucy Isaacs by Jo Anne Rasmussen, Nancy Wolfe, and Liz George; packer Lewis

McMorris for a period by Brian Serven and packer and tortilla maker Sebastian Colon by WWCC multicultural director Victor Chacon; German immigrants and brewery owners John and Catherine Stahl portrayed by the Stahls' great-grandson David Emigh and David's wife Jill; newspaperman Charles Besserer played initially by Valley Times editor Terry Dillman and more recently by the Ron Klicker, our most versatile player; Italian immigrants Frank Orselli presented by local musician David Venneri and Pasquale Saturno by his great-grandson Doug Saturno, as well as others.

A number of other characters have been played by their family members, including Dick Phillips who plays his great-grandfather William and grandfather Charles Phillips, Sonja Phillips who played her great-great-aunt Esther Phillips, Ron Klicker who plays his great-grandfather Jake Klicker and great-great-grandfather Bjorn Sorenson among other characters, Russ Bergevin who portrayed his grandfather Damase Bergevin, Kathleen McCaw Bergevin who played her great aunt Mary Jane McCaw Erwin, Shaun Martin who played her great-great-grandmother Rebecca Westfall Butler, Sam Pambrun who portrays his ancestors Pierre Chrisologue Pambrun and Andrew Dominique Pambrun, Judith Fortney who plays her ancestor Suzanne Cayouse Dauphin, and Steve Plucker who portrayed his great-great-grandfather Charles Plucker.

Coordination

Presenting approximately fifty different performances a year can be very demanding. In addition to creating themes, recruiting, orienting and scheduling players and providing them with basic research on their characters and topics, there is the writing and sending off of weekly news releases, arranging for publicity photos, seeing that the sound system is set up and functioning, and a number of other tasks, including arranging substitutes when players' plans or availability inevitably change. Happily, the museum staff has taken over part of those tasks, in addition to other volunteers.

The volunteers who have taken the most active part in keeping the living history company going over the years are Dick Phillips, who served as assistant coordinator for many years, and his wife Shirl who has sewn costumes and occasionally appeared as the shy Pauline Phillips; stalwart Charles Saranto who has taken over the assistant coordinator duties from Dick including arrangements for off-site appearances; Barbara Daniel who is always willing to step in for multiple performances as school teacher Sarah Miner; Clark Colahan and his wife Barbara Coddington; and the members of the Oregon Trail Band which have included for various periods Carol Parkison, Gordon Hare, Brian Serven, and Bob Bohlman among several others.

The support we've received from museum director James Payne and others connected with the museum for our approximately fifty-member company has been wonderful. We've created a good thing for the community as well as a source of pleasure and edification for ourselves, which I hope will continue for many more years.

A Long Term Plan

My only other involvement with the museum has been in the development in 1999 of a long-term facilities plan for the 14-building pioneer village and six-building museum complex.

For many years the museum's administration and collection work had taken place in the basement of a building for which an above-ground floor was to be added, but had never been completed. On January 28, 1999, the board of the Walla Walla Valley Historical Society which administers the museum held a special meeting to consider completing that building and to discuss other elements of a long-range physical plan. In order to provide a context for proceeding with the building project, the board appointed a long-range physical plant committee consisting of directors Terry Darby, Gerwyn Jones, Vanessa Finch, Carroll Adams and Barbara Clark, as well as museum director James Payne and architect Gerald Mossman charged with making recommendations at its February 16 meeting, and asked if I would chair the committee.

Since time was short, I prepared a list of potential goals based on the those mentioned at the board meeting which I had attended, together with goals contained in a recently completed report by a building committee at the museum, as well as other goals from a long-range plan adopted by the board in 1992, and presented them for comment at the historical society's annual meeting two days later.

The planning committee met for the first time on February 2 to consider the list of potential goals, which it adopted, including some submitted following the membership meeting. We then addressed a series of questions regarding the implementation of the goals.

On February 11 we met again to consider a draft report I had written based on our preliminary discussions, and adopted a number of recommendations as well as timelines. A key question was where to put a new entrance building. After considering four different locations, we recommended that it be a two-story structure placed south of the first exhibit building and spanning the distance from the bottom of a hill where the pioneer village sits to the top of the hill where the remainder of the museum's buildings are located. This would allow a natural sequence of visitor circulation, entry from a large and convenient parking area for buses and automobiles on the upper level, and improved access between the upper and lower levels of the museum by either an elevator or stairs.

Our other recommendations concerned the facilities to be included in the new entrance building and an expanded administrative building; the importance of a more compelling façade for the museum on Myra Road; a physical connection of the five exhibit buildings as well as improvements to some of them; and the need for a master plan for the pioneer village in order to expand it and make it more compatible for living history presentations prior to any siting of further buildings there, among other details.

As to a timetable, our priorities after the completion of the administrative building were the new entrance building and the Myra Road façade, followed by the joining of the exhibit buildings, improvements to the parking area, and changes to the pioneer village for living history purposes, all of which we recommended be completed by the Lewis and Clark Bicentennial Celebration in 2004, with the other goals to be met within ten years.

Our unanimous recommendations were delivered to the board at its February 16 meeting, and were adopted by it later in the year. The existence of an up-to-date long-range plan was instrumental in the award of a $500,000 grant by the Sherwood Trust toward the completion of the administrative building, which has now been finished to provide for additional and improved storage, exhibit preparation and work space for museum staff.

The museum has subsequently prepared a revised master plan, pursuant to which it has completed a new entrance building and is working toward implementing the additional elements of its plan which deal with the remaining museum buildings.

Friends Public Policy Work

One of the things that attracted me to the Quakers was their active engagement in a world where they saw the spirit of God everywhere and in all things. Seeing "that of God" in each person means we can't be indifferent to the plight of anyone, whether in our society or in another part of the world. This sense of the Divine has been gradually growing among Friends and others to include all of the elements of life, not only humans.

Quakers have a long history of concern with matters of public policy, including religious persecution, conditions in prisons where they were often thrown, mental institutions, slavery, war and peace, and social and economic justice.

Capital Punishment

Capital punishment became part of the law of Washington Territory in 1854, was abolished in 1913, reinstated in 1919, and rendered unconstitutional by rulings of the U.S. Supreme Court in the 1960's. The last execution to take place in Washington State under the 1919 law occurred in 1963 when I was a student at Whitman College. Oregon had just abolished the death penalty through a voter initiative, and I had written a paper on that campaign after interviewing Hugo Bedeau, the Reed College criminologist who led the effort.

Friends have long opposed the death penalty for a variety of reasons: its denial of the presence of God in the person to be executed, the fact that at the time of an execution he or she is under the total control of the authorities and not a threat to anyone, and the debilitating impact on our society of the deliberate and unnecessary killing of one of its members in our name, usually to show that killing itself is wrong.

In July, 1985, as Quakers from throughout the Pacific Northwest gathered at Whitman College for their annual meeting, these concerns led us to form a caravan of cars leading to the Washington State Penitentiary for a candlelight vigil at the time of an execution. Just before midnight, Charles Campbell received a stay of execution, though he was later executed in 1994.

On January 5, 1993 Westley Allen Dodd became the first Washingtonian executed in 30 years. As Dodd's execution date approached, Portland resident Scott Prinz contacted me for legal advice about his right to protest the execution. Scott had wanted to picket across the road from the penitentiary's main gate, but had been told by prison officials that it was illegal to do so, and that no one could stand or park a car there, as indicated by posted signs.

Since this was a state highway I researched the matter and discovered that the prison had put the highway signs up itself without legal authority. When I called the prison to inquire what rules had been adopted for the exercise of First Amendment rights on the penitentiary grounds, the person I talked with said he didn't know of any. After my follow-up letter, the prison responded by constructing a fenced area for demonstrators adjacent to its main parking lot, which was divided into three sections—for, against, and a small section between them.

Scott wanted to make a more personal statement. As the hour for Dodd's execution was near, he walked onto the main prison grounds, knelt in prayer, and was arrested for criminal trespass. He asked me to represent him on that charge, and in a similar case at the time of the later Campbell execution, which I agreed to do.

In October, 1998, the evening Jeremy Sagastegui was executed, Whitman College students Aaron Perrine, Matthew Johnson, Abigail St. Lawrence, and Brianne Testa sat peaceably with several others conducting a candlelight vigil in the designated area for those protesting the execution. A few minutes after midnight when Sagastegui was declared dead, they continued to sit quietly on the grass in the fenced protest grounds surrounded by several correctional officers, and were all arrested and either handcuffed or chained. The charge against them was unlawfully using or threatening to use force or creating a substantial risk of injury to person or property. Since they were obviously no threat to anyone, merely wanting to continue their vigil at the site of a state execution, they each plead not guilty and as their attorney I obtained the dismissal of all charges against them.

Beyond the harm to society caused by the unnecessary taking of life, there is always the possibility of human error with regard to the guilt of a defendant. In light of the growing number of those on death row across the US who have been freed recently after new DNA evidence showed they were innocent, many states are now considering either abolition or at least a moratorium on the death penalty while its use is evaluated further. A new Quaker public policy committee I've helped form in Washington State is supporting those proposals.

Organizing FCWPP

The concern of Quakers for the sanctity of all people has led to the founding of a number of Quaker organizations whose central purpose is to influence public policy. These include the Friends Committee on National Legislation (FCNL); the Quaker Office at the United Nations (QUNO); the Friends Committee on Legislation (FCL) in California; the Friends Committee on Maine Public Policy (FCMPP), and more recently the Friends Committee on Washington Public Policy (FCWPP).

In 1996, Quakers involved in supporting a Friends worship group at the Washington State Reformatory at Monroe raised the need for such a public policy committee in Washington State, particularly in the area of prison and criminal justice policy. The idea was then presented to Pacific Northwest Quarterly Meeting of Friends in Washington and Idaho, which recognized the need for such a group and encouraged its creation.

148

Walla Walla Friends received a letter from those exploring the idea later that year, and we were excited at the prospect and responded positively. At North Pacific Yearly Meeting's annual session in July of 1997, an interest group had been scheduled to discuss the idea further, but when I arrived I was told there hadn't been sufficient support to proceed, and that the group had been cancelled.

Not wanting to see a good idea fail, I urged those who had been working on it to meet over lunch, and we formulated a plan to meet again in early September in Olympia, and to bring a more detailed proposal to the Fall Quarterly Meeting on September 27. Those involved in one or both of these planning meetings were Olympia Friends Tammy Fellin, Mike Hubbart, Naki Stevens, and Bob and Nancy First; Port Townsend Friends Bob Royce and Dave and Della Walker; and Steve Wilson of University Friends in Seattle.

We were encouraged by the example of the Friends Committee on Maine Public Policy which was formed in 1992 under the leadership of retired FCNL executive director Ed Snyder, and which we used as a model for our proposal. After the Olympia gathering, I drafted a Proposal for a Friends Committee on Washington State Public Policy (FCWPP), together with a proposed minute for consideration by the Quarterly Meeting approving the creation of FCWPP as an independent body composed of representatives of all interested Washington Friends Meetings affiliated with the Quarterly Meeting, "for the purpose of informing Friends on public policy issues and providing timely opportunities for the expression of Friends' concerns to public officials and others involved in the making of public policy."

In September, these documents were approved by our organizing committee and by the Quarterly Meeting at Lazy F Ranch near Ellensburg. I had also drafted proposed articles of incorporation for FCWPP as a 501(c)(4) lobbying organization, a provisional nineteen-page policy statement based on the excellent statement developed by FCNL over the years[*], an ambitious timeline which would allow us to become operational by the start of the 1998 legislative session on January 12 rather than waiting another year, and a draft letter to be sent out to the Friends Meetings in the state. These were also approved by the organizing committee.

The result of all of this was that, as the newly appointed clerk of the organizing committee, I was able to send off a letter to Friends throughout the state the day after our Lazy F meetings announcing the formation of the new organization. Our letter also invited meetings to appoint representatives to serve on FCWPP's steering committee and to attend an initial meeting of the steering committee to be held in Olympia November 15-16. On receipt of the news, our Walla Walla Friends Meeting was the first to pledge several hundred dollars towards the organization's first year budget.

At our November meeting at Black Lake near Olympia, steering committee members signed articles of incorporation, revised proposed bylaws I had drafted, adopted a provisional policy statement, developed a list of eight potential broad-area policy priorities to be sent out to Friends bodies around the state for individual and group rankings, named both an interim executive committee and a lobbying team, set the organizational meeting of the FCWPP corporation for

---

[*] The FCNL policy statement is currently available at www.fcnl.org; the FCWPP policy statement can be found at www.fcwpp.org.

January 10 at University Meeting in Seattle, two days before the opening of the legislative session, and heard a talk from State Senator Karen Fraser on issues facing the upcoming session.

All of this had come together very quickly and easily, which suggested we were doing the right thing. Nonetheless, the following weeks were an extraordinarily difficult period dealing with a member who wanted badly to lobby for FCWPP but in whose lobbying skills Friends had no confidence.

After a series of executive committee meetings by conference call, the steering committee met in Seattle and approved working committees in each of eight general policy areas, while establishing criminal justice reform, economic justice, and peacemaking as key priorities. Our remaining policy areas were education, health, the environment, civil rights, and civil society.

During the 1998 session, a lobbying team made up entirely of Friends living in Olympia met weekly to evaluate legislative hearing schedules and calendars, and sent out alerts to our network of meeting representatives, contacts, and other interested Friends on issues across the policy spectrum. We also set up an office, created a website, established a communications network, testified at a couple of hearings, and gained experience regarding the great volume of bills introduced of potential interest to Friends. In evaluating our experience immediately after the session, we noted that none of our three priority working groups had yet met.

In preparation for the 1999 session, we replaced the lobbying team with a broader legislative committee, which circulated relevant alerts from the Washington Association of Churches, along with several of its own.

We wanted, though, to move beyond our status as a group of generalists and to develop an in-depth focus on a particular policy area. To accomplish this, we issued an invitation to each of our priority groups to meet, define its policy focus, and assess its resources for affecting public policy in its particular area, and to then make a proposal for the selection of its work as a primary policy focus for FCWPP. Unfortunately, none responded.

Following the 1999 session, it was clear that what FCWPP needed was one or more people with passion for a particular policy area who would provide the leadership necessary to move us from a reactive stance to a proactive one. At our steering committee session during the Spring Quarterly Meeting at Lazy F, I suggested we lay down our current priorities and instead invite Friends with a passion and a willingness to work on a particular policy area to step forward with a proposal for utilizing FCWPP as a vehicle for realizing their goals. I then challenged everyone there to ask themselves what the single most important policy goal was for them personally.

A Prison Reduction Campaign

When I issued that challenge, I had no idea what my personal response would be. I woke up at 4 a.m. the next morning and immediately knew that my own policy passion was to try to reduce the out-of-control growth in our prison population.

From my experience with jails and prisons as an attorney, I knew they aren't a good place for human beings. Though we need to house some of our violent criminals, prisons should be used very sparingly and in most cases for relatively short terms. Since 1980, as a nation we have done just the opposite.

The United States was incarcerating five times as many people per capita as Canada and seven times as many as most European democracies, while the number of US citizens imprisoned had tripled since 1980. The direct economic cost of housing a prisoner for a year was more than the average cost of a year's education at a public university.

Feeling strongly that Washington State should reduce its prison population, I proposed that the Friends Committee on Washington State Public Policy work with state corrections officials, the legislature, and other interested people and organizations toward achieving that, and offered to lead a FCWPP criminal justice group for that purpose.

The Study Phase

In order to move toward that goal, in May 1999 I proposed a six-part, one year work program. The plan was to begin with a period of study to develop additional expertise on the workings of the current criminal justice system, as well as the most promising alternatives. This was to be followed by consultation with other organizations, state administrators, and key legislators, the drafting of specific proposals, legislative advocacy, a public education campaign, and an evaluation of what we had accomplished.

During the study phase, in addition to reviewing recent state legislation and the current sentencing structure, I read all of the research and statistical reports published over the last several years by the Washington State Department of Corrections, the Washington State Institute for Public Policy, and the Washington State Sentencing Guidelines Commission, the three primary state agencies working in this area, as well as information available through national centers such as the Sentencing Project. What I found was alarming.

Under Washington's previous sentencing structure, people convicted of felonies in Washington State until 1984 could be granted probation subject to conditions that might include some county jail time, or they could be sent to prison. Those sentenced to prison were given the maximum time provided for the particular crime. The actual time to be served in prison was determined by the parole board, which initially set a minimum term for each prisoner, reconsidered it annually, and further reduced it up to one-third for "good time" served without serious violation of prison rules. On release, the prisoner continued on parole for the remainder of their maximum term, and could be returned to prison at any time for violations of specified conditions of parole.

The new Sentencing Reform Act of 1981 (SRA) applied to crimes committed after July 1, 1984, and was the result of approximately ten years of debate about the broad discretion given judges and parole boards under the previous "indeterminate" sentencing laws. The discretion judges had been given was criticized on the basis of the great disparity in sentences given to individuals convicted of the same crime. Parole board discretion was condemned because of the unfettered control exercised over the lives of prisoners and the resulting uncertainty created, as well as public dissatisfaction with the large difference between the formal sentence and the lesser time actually served.

The SRA established a system of "determinate" sentences, or "just desserts", which are set by the judge based on a sentencing grid established by the legislature. The act basically eliminated probation or parole, and instead required a fixed sentence to be set by the judge from a fairly narrow sentencing range determined on the basis of the crime committed and the offender's prior criminal history. Exceptional sentences above or below the standard range can be imposed only upon a showing of substantial and compelling reasons, though more judicial discretion is allowed for first time offenders.

The traditional system of early release for "good time" was also largely eliminated, partly in response to the federal requirement for "truth in sentencing" as a condition of funding state prison construction. In addition to further measures restructuring the sentencing system from primarily rehabilitative to primarily punitive, in nearly every legislative session since adoption of the SRA, the legislature has increased criminal penalties, despite stable or falling crime rates.

Citizen initiatives have also significantly increased criminal penalties. In 1993, the "Three Strikes And You're Out" initiative was passed by the voters, providing life imprisonment without possibility of parole for persistent offenders convicted of certain serious crimes. The legislature then added a "Two Strikes" provision for sex offenders, the definition of which was broadened in 1997. In 1995, the "Hard Time for Armed Crime" initiative increased penalties for armed crimes and extended sentence enhancements for deadly weapons to all crimes.

The effect of these changes on prison population in Washington State has been dramatic. The total prison population in Washington State increased from 4453 in 1980 to over 13,000 by 1999, nearly tripling. Increasing sentence lengths also more than doubled the number of imprisoned offenders who were over 50 years old. DOC medical costs in turn were more than double for each offender over 50 compared to offenders under 50. Other factors in the makeup of the offender population have also changed. In 1997, 24% were drug offenders, compared to 4% in 1987. Non-violent offenders made up a quarter of the prison population in 1987, and by 1997 were more than a third.

In 1999, Washington prisons were 50% over maximum capacity, despite having added nearly 7000 beds since 1992. Such overcrowding creates unhealthy and dangerous conditions for both inmates and staff. Although overall arrests and felony crimes reported had decreased since 1990, admissions to adult and juvenile correctional facilities had risen by over 31%. The lengths of sentences had also increased. While violent crime and property crimes both decreased significantly during that period, drug arrests and convictions increased 116 % for juveniles and 39 % for adults.

For the average household in Washington, the cost of the criminal justice system grew from $683 per household in 1990 to $885 in 1997 expressed in today's dollars. That represented an average increase of 3.8 percent per year above the general rate of inflation. The average cost per bed for all levels of correctional security in Washington state was approximately $24,000 per year in 1999. In addition, each new medium security bed cost about $100,000 to construct, not counting

152

substantial financing costs. The average cost per offender on community supervision in comparison was approximately $780 per year. Additional economic costs of imprisonment included the provision of public assistance for offender families, and the inability of most imprisoned offenders to pay restitution to crime victims.

The rising cost of corrections was impacting the amount of public funds available for other basic services and public needs. DOC's 1989-91 biennial budget was $428 million, or 6.1 per cent of the state's total general fund budget, which excluded K-12 education. DOC's percentage of the budget had increased each biennium since then and was now at $849 million, over 8 % of the state's general fund budget. In times of fiscal constraint, when more public money is spent on the criminal justice system, less was obviously available for other purposes, and basic infrastructure was suffering.

Beyond the costs to house each imprisoned offender, care for their families, and provide for the damages to victims not compensated by restitution, there was growing interest in calculating the cost of various sentencing or program options in terms of the cost of recidivism, or the future criminal activity of offenders placed in the various programs or settings, a cost analysis which should also be applied to the option of incarceration.

Imprisonment without treatment was clearly not cost-effective in protecting the public, since recidivism rates for released offenders were approximately 75%, considerably more than for offenders managed in the community.

Studies showed that public funds spent on community management of offenders, on crime prevention, and on risk reduction programs instead of on prison beds yielded more public safety, helped preserve family units, and contributed to improving our general quality of life. As corrections costs continued to consume a larger part of our public budgets each year, leaving less for roads, schools and other public infrastructure, it was evident that our society couldn't afford the economic and social costs of the current overuse of imprisonment.

Available alternatives to imprisonment of offenders included electronically-monitored home detention, monitored work and rehabilitation program attendance, random drug testing, drug treatment, community service, financial restitution, victim-offender mediation, and family group conferencing, among others, as well as preventative programs such as community policing, community recreation, education, job training, and other means to lower risk factors for violations of community safety and to restore the capacity of victims and offenders to be productive citizens.

Although I had hoped to come across a written overview of the criminal justice system in Washington state that I could pass on to the other members of our working group, I didn't find one, so I wrote a six-page overview myself. This document was ultimately sent to every legislator in the state as well as to the other key officials, and received wide praise.

Consultation and Public Education

By August, we were ready to begin the consultation phase of our work program. A key body involved in sentencing policy was the state's Sentencing Guidelines Commission, composed of the Secretary of the Department of Corrections, the administrator of the Juvenile Rehabilitation Administration, two judges, two prosecutors, two defenders, two local officials, a representative of the Sheriffs and Police Chiefs Association, a victim advocate, a representative of the state Office of Financial M anagement, and two citizen members. In August, the commission's executive director, Roger Goodman, came to Walla Walla on prison business, and I met with him to discuss our project.

In discussing the commission's legal mandate, I pointed out to Roger that the state's prisons were 50% over their maximum design capacity, and that under those circumstances state law requires that the commission "recommend to the governor and the legislature revisions and modifications to the standard sentence ranges, state sentencing policy, prosecuting standards, and other standards… which are consistent with correctional capacity." He was sympathetic with our purposes, but said that the commission was too timid and political to do that and it would never happen.

Later on, I talked by phone with one of the defense lawyers on the commission who agreed with Roger, and suggested that the only way to accomplish this would be to try to get the legislature to specifically direct the commission to address the problem.

Part of our strategy was to enlist a group of allies to work with us on these issues. In September, we invited potential allies to meet with us at Lazy F Ranch for our Fall steering committee meeting. Several organizations expressed an interest in working with us on the issue, including the Washington Association of Churches (WAC), the Catholic Archdiocese of Seattle, the Washington Catholic Conference, the Washington Association of Criminal Defense Lawyers, and the ACLU, among others. Lobbyists Sara Merten Fleming of the WAC and Kevin Glackin-Coley of the Archdiocese of Seattle were able to come to Lazy F to meet with our criminal justice working group and to speak to the FCWPP steering committee, which had agreed to lay down its previous priorities and adopt the reduction of the prison population as a new priority.

We were also fortunate that one of our working group members had invited criminologist Roger Lauen, an attender at Agate Passage Friends group on Bainbridge Island who was the former director of community corrections for the state of Colorado. Roger had just written his second book published by the American Correctional Association, and was to become an important partner in our efforts.

While consulting with allies, we also took the first step in our public education plan, which was to produce a letter on the general need to reduce prison populations to be sent by Friends to each major newspaper in the state as well as to their local legislators. Some form of this letter was published in a variety of newspapers, including the Seattle Times, the Tacoma News-Tribune, the Olympian, the Yakima Republic, the Tri-City Herald, and the Walla Walla Union-Bulletin.

This also became our basic campaign document, ultimately going to all legislators, Sentencing Guidelines Commission members, and others. We wanted to talk with newspaper editorial boards as well, and were able to meet in November with a representative of the editorial board of the Seattle Post-Intelligencer which published a favorable editorial after the opening of the legislative session.

Another element in our work plan was to consult with key legislators and legislative staff, as well as top administrators to learn their views on prison growth and seek their advice on how best to proceed. In addition to the Director of the Sentencing Guidelines Commission, we hoped to meet with the Secretary of the Department of Corrections, the Director of the Washington Institute for Public Policy, and either the Governor or his criminal justice advisor, among others. In November, Roger Lauen and I scheduled a week of meetings with state officials in Seattle and Olympia and invited our allies to join us.

Our first meeting was in Seattle with Al O'Brien, a retired policeman and the Democratic co-chair of the House Criminal Justice and Corrections Committee, for which Sara Merten Fleming of the Washington Association of Churches joined us. I explained to Al that a Sentencing Guidelines Commission member had told me a comprehensive review of state sentencing policy was needed after 16 years of piecemeal amendments to the SRA, but that the commission wouldn't do such a review without specific legislative direction. He was sympathetic, and told us to draft a bill and he would consider being its prime sponsor. He also advised us that since the membership in the House was split 49-49 between Democrats and Republicans we should also discuss this issue with his Republican co-chair Ida Ballasiotes.

Next we met with Jeanne Kohl-Welles, a progressive Democratic senator from Seattle who served as a Senate liaison to the Sentencing Guidelines Commission, and were joined by Eric Paige from the Washington Catholic Conference. Jeanne said she was also willing to sponsor a bill, and advised us to talk with Bernie Ryan, senior counsel to the Senate Democratic caucus, about helping us with the drafting process.

In Olympia Roger and I had a good meeting with the Secretary of the Department of Corrections, Joe Lehmann, the governor's criminal justice advisor, Dick VanWagenan, both the director and chief of research of the Washington Institute for Public Policy, Roxanne Lieb and Steve Aos, as well as Senate staffer Bernie Ryan, and again with Roger Goodman and his research director at the Sentencing Guidelines Commission, among others.

The Proposal

There are many ways to address prison growth issues, the most common being to oppose one at a time the incremental lengthening of sentences and the continual creation of new crimes which have been occurring in recent years, as each new proposal is introduced. After our study and consultations we decided on a more comprehensive approach to the fiscal and social problems created by the runaway growth in prison populations, and drafted a measure mandating a comprehensive review of the entire state sentencing policy.

After some debate about what the form our legislation should take, we drafted House Concurrent Resolution 4426 and Senate Concurrent Resolution 8418 mandating the comprehensive review of state sentencing policy by the Sentencing Guidelines Commission, giving consideration to cost effectiveness, fiscal impacts, prison capacities, and alternatives to confinement for nonviolent offenders, and requiring recommendations to the legislature be submitted by December 1, 2001, including an alternative sentencing grid within existing prison capacity.

First circulating the draft resolutions within FCWPP, then to our allies and the public officials we were consulting with, including Bernie Ryan and Roger Goodman with whom we worked closely, we finally submitted a revised the draft to our proposed sponsors.

Legislative Advocacy

Our actual lobbying began with the effort to secure the most favorable sponsors in each house. Our goal was to secure prime sponsorship by the chairs of the relevant policy committees to which the resolution would be referred for hearing. In December during the week when party caucuses and most of the legislative committees meet to prepare for the legislative session, Roger Lauen and I went back to Olympia.

Our first break was when Al O'Brien signed our resolution as the prime sponsor in the House and obtained the sponsorship of 15 other house members, including his Republican co-chair Ida Ballasiotes, the other three Democrats on his committee, and three other house Republicans. The three remaining Republicans on his committee declined to sign.

In the Democratically-controlled Senate, it wasn't clear which of two committees the resolution would be referred to, so we approached the chairs of both Human Services & Corrections and Judiciary, and both agreed to sponsor it. Jim Hargrove, the Human Services chair became the prime sponsor, but the resolution wound up in Judiciary. Five other senators joined as sponsors, including Judiciary chair Mike Heavey.

Because the 2000 legislature was only a 60-day supplemental session, it was important for us to get an early hearing in each house. In January I returned to Olympia as a registered lobbyist for FCWPP and began to work with the committee chairs as well as our allies.

At our first hearing before the Senate Judiciary Committee on January 21, our sponsors told us to keep it short because we already had the necessary votes, but we wanted to use the occasion for some general education since we were wary of Pam Roach, an outspoken Republican senator who was a liaison to the Sentencing Guidelines Commission and had previously stalked out of the commission's legislative committee meeting after hearing discussion about the resolution, threatening to take the issue to talk radio.

After Senator Roach's outburst, the commission scheduled a formal discussion of the resolution for its January legislative committee and commission meeting. Happily, the senator didn't show up, and after my presentation and some discussion, to everyone's surprise the commission unanimously endorsed the resolution and agreed to send representatives to testify for it at the legislative hearings. Several members of the commission took the opportunity to publicly praise our overview paper, and the new chair of the Indeterminate Sentencing Review Board asked for permission to send it out in his regular mailing to key state officials.

At the televised hearing before the Senate Judiciary Committee, I led off the testimony followed by various supporters, including King County Superior Court Judge Brian Gain on behalf of the Sentencing Guidelines Commission, Kevin Glackin-Coley representing both the Washington Catholic Conference and the Archdiocese of Seattle, Sara Merten from WAC, and a member of one of the defender associations. A representative of the Washington Association of Counties also weighed in to support the resolution, encouraging consideration of local costs and capacities. No one spoke in opposition, and Senator Roach was fairly well-behaved. At its next meeting the Judiciary Committee unanimously reported the resolution out with a do-pass recommendation

After the committee's action, the prime sponsor suggested that I meet with Senator Roach in order to avoid a fight on the floor of the full senate. We met and agreed on some additional wording which I had drafted and which was then was given to the committee's staff to be prepared as a floor amendment in the Senate, and also as an amendment to the House resolution.

Our next hearing was on January 25 before the House Criminal Justice and Corrections Committee, at which the same organizations testified, receiving only minor questioning by the Republican co-chair Ida Ballastiotes. Two days later the resolution was reported out unanimously by the committee.

The fiscal analysis prepared by the commission showed a cost of approximately $160,000 to complete the study, so our next task was the scheduling of a hearing before the fiscal committees of each house. I had been communicating since mid-summer with Valoria Loveland, the chair of the Senate Ways and Means Committee and the senator from my district, and knew she was sympathetic. The committee gave us a hearing on February 1, and the resolution was unanimously reported out the next day and referred to the Rules Committee for possible floor action.

The House Appropriations Committee, which was in charge of writing the supplemental budget for the legislature that year, took a different tack. Rather than giving the resolution a hearing and reporting it out for floor action, Republican co-chair Tom Huff preferred to simply provide funding for the study and include the wording of the resolution as a budget proviso. Although we continued to lobby for a hearing on the resolution itself, it never happened, and since there were some potential problems with the budget-only approach, we decided to continue with a two-track strategy and sought to move the Senate resolution to the floor.

Once the resolution was favorably reported out by the Senate Ways & Means Committee, we lobbied to have it reported out to the floor from Rules. Here the advantage of our decision to present the measure as a resolution rather than a bill became clear, since resolutions are not subject to deadlines for committee or floor action as bills are. In order to move a matter from the Rules Committee to the floor, each Rules Committee member is given a certain number of "pulls", and a measure first has to be selected by a member from the general list at one committee meeting then approved for floor referral at another meeting. Though this was a tedious process which took two weeks, with help from our allies including Jerry Sheehan of the ACLU, the resolution was finally sent to the Senate floor.

The final step before calendaring a measure for floor debate and a vote is consideration and approval by the majority caucus. Since there are usually more bills awaiting action than time allows, we were glad when Judiciary Committee chair Mike Heavey won caucus approval by stepping forward and insisting that our important measure be calendared.

Finally, on February 18 the resolution was debated and approved by the full Senate, though not without some drama. Although the amendment we had drafted for Senator Roach had been suggested by prime sponsor Jim Hargrove and later discussed with Judiciary chair Mike Heavey, both apparently forgot this when it was introduced by Pam Roach, and accused her of surprise tactics. Fortunately our other sponsors came to the rescue, and the amendment and the resolution itself were unanimously adopted by the Senate and referred to the House.

The last hearing on the Senate version of the resolution occurred in the House Criminal Justice and Corrections Committee, which had already approved the identical house version. On February 25, after a brief hearing, the resolution in its Senate version was again reported out and referred once more to House Appropriations which refused to hear it.

By this time, the complete wording of the resolution other than some introductory "whereas" clauses had been incorporated into both the House Republican and House Democratic budgets, which provided full funding for the first year of the study. The only discrepancy was a line referring to the previously enacted legislative intent "to emphasize confinement for the violent offender and alternatives to confinement for the nonviolent offender," which was missing in the Republican version, and also in the Senate budget.

Sometime afterwards the House issued a bipartisan budget, which again included the language and funding for the study, as well as the previously missing clause, but both the regular session and a special session called to complete the budget ended with no budget agreement. The governor then called a third session and announced he would issue a new version of his original budget which had not mentioned the study. I contacted the governor's criminal justice advisor to request that the study provisions be included in the new budget, which they were, except for the same missing clause.

Since we felt the missing clause set forth an important standard for sentencing reform but wanted the measure to maintain a low profile, we quietly pointed out the difference to the Senate Ways & Means chair as well as the governor's criminal justice advisor and encouraged them to accept the House bipartisan version with the clause in it, which is what happened.

On April 27 a negotiated budget compromise was adopted by both houses that included funding for the study and every word of our resolution, and the legislature adjourned.

Evaluation

Several factors contributed to the success of FCWPP's efforts, including the period of study we undertook, our work with allies, the consultations we engaged in with public officials prior to proposing legislation, the drafting of a practical proposal, our flexibility regarding amendments, and our persistence in shepherding the measure through the many stages of the legislative process.

At the beginning we were told not to get our hopes up, that most proposals take about five years to get through the legislature, and that the most we could expect was a hearing by a friendly committee chair. When we were through and had secured the passage of a measure in an election year with bipartisan support, no vocal opposition, and every word intact, mandating the review of all aspects of state sentencing policy, one official exclaimed, "You've performed a miracle!" The director of another agency called the effort "a model of citizen legislative advocacy which could be a case study for other organizations seeking to affect public policy."

Securing the unanimous approval of the state Senate, the criminal justice policy committees of each house, and the Sentencing Guidelines Commission itself was certainly an unexpected achievement. A key factor in this success was the initial period of study, which increased our own understanding of the criminal justice system, enabling us to speak with more authority and to produce a useful overview paper and a successful analysis of where the opportunities lay for significant change.

Consultation with allies and public officials before drafting a specific proposal was also important, as was working closely with them on proposed amendments and legislative strategy, and the sharing of specific lobbying tasks. Though we received valuable advice and help from allies and friendly officials, it was also critical that FCWPP took primary responsibility for its own measure by monitoring and directly guiding its progress through the legislative process. The information and assumptions passed on to us by others, while always in good faith, were occasionally erroneous and first-hand verification and communication was vital.

As to the public education and grass roots elements common to legislative efforts, because of the lack of vocal opposition to the resolution we intentionally minimized letter writing to newspapers and legislators during the session in order to keep a low profile. Nonetheless, our initial success in the letters-to-the-editor columns and on the editorial page is a useful preface to the undoubted need for more intensive grass-roots campaigns in the future.

Our success can be largely attributed to our having taken the initiative on an issue for which the time was right for a variety of fiscal and social reasons, and having done so in an open, collaborative way.

Over the next two years, the Sentencing Guidelines Commission devoted the bulk of its time to completing the required study and formulating its recommendations, and has involved FCWPP and other stakeholders in every step of that process. The long-term results remain to be seen, but it is clear that the recommended substitution of treatment for incarceration in the case of many nonviolent drug offenders is a major part of the answer to successfully holding the line on further prison growth. It is also clear that the future will continue to be a demanding one for FCWPP and for other advocates of a more civilized and effective way of dealing with public safety problems.

Electoral Politics

Barbara and I have always been interested in the quality of local government.

In 1993, in order to stimulate a more sustainable economy through local business development, we urged our friend Charles Potts to run for Port Commissioner and worked on his campaign. In 1995, because we thought it would be good to have a member of the city council from the impoverished west end of Walla Walla, which hadn't happened for decades, we urged West End Neighbors member Nanette Gallas to run. We worked hard for Nanette, who had a master's degree in social work and would have been the only woman and the only bilingual Spanish and English speaker on the council.

Though neither of these campaigns was successful, they taught us some lessons and prepared us for a third try.

Clark for Council

Late in 1996 two whistleblowers came to Barbara with concerns that the City's wastewater treatment plant had been repeatedly out of compliance with state law, and that city administrators were failing to take corrective action, and had failed to inform the city council of the problems. Barbara and another member of the city's Water Resources Committee, retired well-driller Pat Jungmann, began an investigation into the management of the plant by the public works department as well as the department's illegal construction of a dike along Mill Creek, and discovered serious administrative problems from the city manager level on down.

In January 1997, Pat, Barbara, and several other present or past members of the water resources committee wrote to the council regarding the administration of critical water projects and proposed a meeting, which occurred in late February and included the city manager, public works director, city water manager, and a council member.

In March, Pat and Barbara proposed a further meeting to discuss "deficiencies in the processes of decision-making and communication" including the need "to have staff members present at (city council) work sessions who are fully knowledgeable about projects under discussion," the importance of public comment on issues under discussion at work sessions which was not being allowed, the need for a verbal explanation and opportunity for discussion of each item to be decided at council meetings instead of lumping together several items on a no-discussion "consent agenda," the need for the city manager to be accessible to staff at all levels rather than just to department heads, and scrupulous protection for city whistleblowers, who in this case had been sanctioned.

160

In short, neither the city manager nor the council was taking responsibility for receiving sufficient information to assure the safe and efficient operation of the city, nor did their processes provide for adequate information and scrutiny by citizens. These points were reinforced in a fiery work session with the council in May, when I joined Barbara and several others in criticizing the hostile attitude of the mayor toward citizen comments at meetings, and argued for a more open, responsive, and responsible public process.

Though some changes did occur after that, Barbara was disappointed with the defensive attitude of the council in the face of what was clear misconduct, so in July I encouraged her to run for a seat on the city council herself.

The time seemed right, and after some hesitancy, Barbara agreed to file for a position with an unexpired two year term. Though that meant she didn't have to run against an incumbent, three other candidates filed for the same seat, including the president of the local landlords association.

Well-known conservative Pat Jungmann agreed to be Barbara's campaign treasurer, and was an important ally. As Barbara's campaign manager, I put up yard signs, arranged for ads, encouraged letters to the editor, put together a fund-raising party, designed her brochure, and organized mailings. It was an easy campaign to work on, since people called us for yard signs, to contribute, and to volunteer, instead of our having to call them.

The first letter to the editor was from Pat Jungmann and got the campaign off to a great start. After that came a steady stream of the most glowing endorsements in local memory from people across the political spectrum. When the ballots were counted for the September 16 primary election, Barbara had received 68% in a four-way race. The next highest candidate, Leo Violette, received 19%.

For the two top candidates, there were still another seven weeks until the general election, with Barbara doorbelling almost every day. We waited for negative campaigning to begin, but to Leo's credit it never did, except perhaps when the newspaper asked the two candidates about the difference between them, and Leo said that it was clear cut, explaining "I'm conservative, and she's a liberal." Since city council positions are non-partisan, people were able to look past these labels to Barbara's twenty-six years of service to the community, and gave her 72% of the vote in the general election, a landslide victory.

Since taking office, Barbara has done a conscientious job of studying the issues and opening up meetings to more substantive discussion by council members and citizens alike, prompting a number of her adversaries to praise her, and to tell us they wish they had voted for her themselves. Two years later, people were so satisfied with the council's functioning that no one ran against Barbara or any of the other three incumbents who filed for re-election. Since then, Barbara has been elected for three additional four-year terms, and in 2010-11 served as Walla Walla's mayor to the delight of many citizens.

Clark for Commissioner

County government has also been a frustration to us, and to many people concerned with open, efficient public processes. The structure of county government was established in 1889 when Washington became a state, and hasn't changed much since. The three county commissioners serve as both the legislative and executive body for county government, while independently elected administrators run most of the major county departments, including auditor, assessor, clerk, treasurer, sheriff, prosecutor, and coroner.

In addition to the inefficiency of this structure, county commissions have generally been resistant to change, lacking in openness, subject to cronyism, and scornful of planning and other urban needs. This was particularly apparent to us in our attempts to protect farmland and open space through the county growth management process.

In 2000, I was in the county commissioners' chambers to speak in favor of the adoption of interim growth management regulations to protect farmland from development until the county had completed its growth management plan, which was six years overdue. One of only two or three people in the room supporting the regulations, I was surrounded by real estate agents and developers protesting any restrictions on their rights to convert the land to residential or commercial use, no matter how far from urban services. Despite being ordered by the Growth Management Hearings Board to adopt the regulations, the commissioners sided with the developers as usual and took no action.

That year the county commissioner seat for our area was up for election and the three-term Republican incumbent indicated that he would file again. Though I had never before considered running for a position I didn't think I could win, I woke up the next morning feeling entirely different about it. I decided that under the circumstances it would be intolerable to let the incumbent run unopposed, and that regardless of the odds, if no one else would run, I would. After inviting several people to a meeting in an unsuccessful attempt to find another candidate, they urged me to run, and I agreed.

I had always thought that all county offices, like city council and school board positions, should be nonpartisan instead of having a Republican sheriff or a Democratic prosecutor or county commissioner. Political parties are useful at the state and national level to help organize large legislative bodies, but not for small local bodies. I had long suggested to prospective commissioner candidates that they consider running as independents in order to make this point. I discovered, though, that it was impossible for me to do that. Under Washington state law, in order to file for a county office as an independent rather than as a candidate for a particular party, you can't simply file a declaration of candidacy during the last week in July as others can. Before that you are required to hold a nominating convention attended by at least 25 registered voters who must sign a petition for your candidacy during the convention, notice of which has to be published in a newspaper at least ten days prior to the convention. At the time I decided to run it was already too late, so I announced and filed as a Democrat, normally a guarantee of defeat in Walla Walla County.

162

Besides unnecessary partisanship, county government is ripe for reform in other ways, particularly due to the lack of an executive. Not only is county administration partially split among seven independently elected partisan department heads, there is also no single administrator for the remaining nine departments for which the commissioners serve as both a three-person executive and as the legislative body, an inefficient structure found today in no modern organizations.

There are two basic ways of reforming the structure of county government. The first is the partial approach, by adding a county administrator hired by the commissioners to handle the executive duties they have control over. The second is the type of general reorganization allowed through the adoption of a home-rule charter, under which a modern, integrated organizational system can be established, without any partisanship, and with a larger, more representative legislative body, if desired. A hybrid combination of both approaches is also possible.

I decided to bring these issues into full relief myself by proposing to reduce the $44,500 annual salaries of our part-time county commissioners in our small county to a level adequate to cover only their legislative duties, and to use the savings to hire a full-time county administrator to more efficiently handle their executive duties at no extra cost. At the same time, I proposed that a citizens' commission be appointed to consider a home rule charter for the county, in order to allow a more general reorganization of county government, such as making county offices nonpartisan, appointing rather than electing department heads, and enlarging the legislative body to allow better representation from different parts of the county.

The effect of this announcement a few days after I filed was electric, galvanizing quite a few conservatives in support of my candidacy, and at the same time garnering immediate opposition from existing county officeholders. One of the people who was delighted with my position was Carl Schmitt, a retired banker and former superintendent of banking for the State of California, who was proud to have been the only Republican in Governor Jerry Brown's cabinet. Carl agreed to be my campaign treasurer, and played a very active role in the campaign. My proposals were also consistent with a study by a blue ribbon Chamber of Commerce task force whose 1980 report recommending this had never been made public, and which I posted on my campaign website.

While I had planned to introduce these ideas later in the campaign, when Carl heard about them he insisted that I do that early on. As a result of that plus a series of early letters to the editor supporting my candidacy, instead of a leisurely month or so with campaigning beginning as usual after Labor Day, the campaign was off and running from August 1 and didn't let up until the final ballots were in on November 7.

The county is divided into three commissioner districts; in the primary residents can only vote for candidates from their district, while in the general election everyone votes on all the remaining candidates. Although a second Republican also filed for the position, after being quoted in the press as praising my ideas he abruptly dropped out. That meant that the primary wouldn't have any legal effect. Since the incumbent Dave Carey and I would both be on the primary ballot, though, the results would be an important indication of strength, and we both wanted to do as well as possible.

While I had no illusions about my prospects for winning as a progressive Democrat in a highly conservative Republican county, I decided to run a vigorous campaign in any event with yard signs, ads, buttons, brochures, mailings, endorsement letters, a fundraising party, voter forums, and even some doorbelling, all of which can be an exhausting but also an invigorating process.

While the issue of the county commissioners refusing to adopt growth management regulations motivated me to run despite the odds, it also motivated the Board of Realtors and developers to oppose me at all costs. When the Realtors invited the candidates for private interviews by their five-person interview committee, I reminded them of my father's service as president of both the state and local realtor associations, and my own investments in local real estate. I assured them that in communities that practice good planning and respect open space and a good quality of life, land values are soaring and realtors are making a good living.

Although they had surprised everyone three years before by endorsing Barbara, and two out of the five supported my campaign, the Board of Realtors decided to put its money on my opponent, and the chair of the interview committee wrote some of the most virulent letters against me.

As major advertisers, the realtors also leaned heavily on our newspaper to endorse the incumbent, which it normally does in any event, and the editorial board had no trouble doing that despite the results of their candidates' interview, which turned into the most lively and revealing debate of the campaign. I had expected the editorial endorsement of the incumbent, but in view of the paper's past investigative reporting on local issues, I was surprised at its failure to pursue two major disclosures of county wrongdoing that I provided them.

The first disclosure came out of my interviews with each of the county department heads in order to better understand their needs, operations, and perspectives. In my meeting with the county treasurer, I learned that his office holds and has responsibility for investing both county funds as well as funds from a variety of school, fire, irrigation and other special districts amounting to over $50 million a year, with a year-round minimum balance of approximately $40 million. Approximately $11 million represents temporary cash surpluses from all funds, from which the earnings are credited to the county's general or current expense fund. I was impressed by the extent of this investment responsibility, and to get a better idea of how they were managed I asked for a list of all the investments, which the treasurer said he didn't have.

I then asked for a copy of the county investment policy, which counties are required by law to adopt through a county finance committee composed of the treasurer, the auditor, and the chair of the county commissioners, in this case my opponent. The treasurer told me there was no county investment policy and that there never had been a county finance committee, though they were all aware of the statutory requirement.

After confirming this with other county officials, I provided a briefing paper to the press on the subject with citations to relevant state laws as well as additional background documents, none of which was ever reported by our newspaper, though I made a point to mention it in letters and statements from my campaign. After a later complaint to the state auditor's office, a county finance committee is now in place.

The other wrongdoing ignored by the Union-Bulletin was a violation of the open public meetings law by the commissioners in connection with a decision to erect a controversial prefab building in the historic downtown area. This came to light following a September 20 news article by the U-B surprising the community with the announcement that a no-bid contract had been let for the purchase and siting of the a new prefab law and justice building on a portion of the county parking lot at the corner of Fifth and Alder streets.

There had been no mention in the press that the project was even under consideration, nor had it been discussed with the County Facilities Citizens' Committee appointed to advise on such matters, or with the Downtown Walla Walla Foundation. Members of those groups roundly criticized the decision as inconsistent with the principles they had been advocating for, and lamented the absence of consultation, as did the public, while the Union-Bulletin praised the project for potentially saving money.

For years I had been critical of the lack of openness and public involvement in commissioners' decisions, because of their meeting in continuous public session two days a week to deal with their combined legislative and executive responsibilities, using minimal agendas that list large blocks of time simply as "miscellaneous" and for keeping minimal minutes. In addition, they would usually defer making a decision at the time a matter came up on their printed agendas, then hold substantive discussions on the issue later in the day when the press and public had left the room, thereby defeating the public scrutiny purposes of the open meetings law, while technically complying with it.

Even more serious was the practice of not listing a matter on their agendas at all, then illegally considering it in a closed or executive session, which happened on two occasions regarding the controversial prefab building project. Since I had been following the commissioners' agendas closely and hadn't seen anything about it, when the news article came out I asked the commissioners' secretary where that matter had come up on their agendas, and was told it was in executive session earlier in the week and a prior executive session in August, both under the heading "contracts." The final action accepting the bids had also been taken in an open session not itemized on their agendas.

Because these were no-bid contracts and the only contract items lawfully permitted to be discussed in a closed session were negotiations on the performance of publicly bid contracts, I filed a complaint with the state auditor's office and on October 11, I provided documentation of the violation and the complaint to the press, which again made no response or mention of the matter.

The result of the primary election representing a third of the county's voters was Clark 44%, Carey 56%. This was actually somewhat encouraging, since it was closer than many had predicted for the primary. At the same time, an analysis of voting patterns showed us that the primary district included more precincts with Democratic strength than the rest of the county.

Also, it included a significant number of absentee ballots mailed a couple of weeks earlier, which reflected a large number of supporting letters that were continually coming in from across the spectrum supporting my proposals and praising my past community service.

There had not been much response to these letters until about the final week before the primary. While I had asked my supporters not to engage in negative campaigning, apparently my opponent hadn't returned the favor, and just before the primary, attack letters started coming in. After the primary results, which were apparently closer than expected, these picked up momentum.

At times you would have thought I was the only one running, since my supporters' letters mentioned only me and the opposing letters did the same. Most opponents suggested I was a big spender who would add bureaucracy to the county, and quite a few distorted the experience of several home rule counties or my positions on county government.

Another issue in the campaign was the lack of respect for the interests of urban residents. Besides wanting to change the inefficient structure of county government and wanting it to be more open and to consider the long-term effects of its decisions, I wanted it to serve all of the citizens of the county, both urban and rural. Traditionally, although more than 70 % of the county's residents live in incorporated areas and pay taxes to the county to support a variety of services affecting everyone, the commissioners have acted as if they represent only farmers, and unfortunately many urban residents have accepted that.

An important theme of our campaign was that county government should represent everyone, urban and rural, and that all citizens have an important stake in county government. To demonstrate that, our ad campaign featured the question "Why Clark?" with pictures and the answers of my supporters from various walks of life, including several teachers, counselors, an architect, nurse, landscaper, artist, restaurant owner, winemaker, real estate broker, innkeeper, farrier, neighborhood activist, museum coordinator, musician, student, church school leader, a couple of farmers, and a 4-H leader. This was having some effect, and soon Dave responded with his own supporter ads.

Though opening the paper every day to see what was being said about me and needed to be responded to was the hardest part of the campaign, there were also a few word of mouth rumors and red herrings to be dealt with. One was that I had refused to participate in the pledge of allegiance at a morning Rotary Club candidates' forum, which made the rounds of the town with the help of the county sheriff who was there, and a city councilman who wasn't. A member of the club who had stood beside me that day and knew this wasn't true told me he had heard it from the councilman who wasn't there, who said he heard it from the sheriff. I called the sheriff who had been standing some distance behind me at the time, who told me I refused to salute the flag. I told him I had stood respectfully and repeated the pledge along with the others, and wondered what he meant. When he said I hadn't put my hand on my heart, which he felt was obligatory, I suggested that it might be obligatory in elementary school but that standing respectfully with hands at your sides is equally acceptable in my experience and is practiced with about the same frequency. In any event, I hadn't refused to participate in the pledge as he was being quoted as saying, and I told him he was obligated to clarify the matter. I then mentioned the matter to one of the superior court judges who belonged to the other Rotary Club, and he told me he always says the pledge of allegiance with his hands at his sides and that about half the members of his club did the same.

I decided that a letter to the editor explaining this would probably do more harm than good, so I simply alerted the letters editor of our regional newspapers that they might receive letters with this false charge, which they did but refused to print.

With regard to red herrings, after interviewing my opponent and others at the courthouse, a Tri-City Herald reporter asked me if I had served in the military and wanted to know my views on defense policy. I told him that wasn't relevant to a candidate for local office, while reminding him that he had already asked my religion and I had told him I was a Quaker. His subsequent story noted that one candidate was a Korean War veteran while the other was a Quaker. At a later candidates' forum, a friend of Dave's asked the same questions and also asked if it was true that I had counseled youth to avoid the draft during the Vietnam War. I told them I hadn't done any draft counseling during the Vietnam War, but that the counseling I did in the early 80's merely explained the law rather than advocating a particular position.

While I was the candidate taking the strongest stand in favor of preserving agricultural lands, paradoxically my opponent, a farmer, favored development. Nevertheless, most of the farmers supported Dave and his signs dotted the countryside while mine prevailed in the cities.

As to letters to the editor, I received enough flattering testimonials to last a lifetime. Even though it was a presidential election year with hotly contested state and federal legislative races, letters concerning our commissioner race dominated the local editorial pages. During the last week or two of the campaign they seemed to be two to one for Clark. Between our preponderance of letters and yard signs, on election night when an area television station mistakenly broadcast early results showing Clark, 63% and Carey, 37%, some of my supporters believed it. In fact, the opposite was true, as expected.

Partisanship plays a big role even in local elections, as I found when doorbelling. A lot of people told me they liked my ideas but wanted to know whether I was a Republican or a Democrat. Elections are difficult for Democrats everywhere in eastern Washington. While Al Gore won the popular vote in Washington State and the nation over George W. Bush, in the Walla Walla County presidential race the Republican candidate prevailed over the Democratic candidate by about the same margin as in the commissioner race.

Since that election, interesting developments have arisen in the Agricultural Exclusive zone along the foothills of the Blue Mountains southeast of Walla Walla, where farmers have fought to protect their ag lands and pristine views from development by commercial wineries. When a zoning amendment to allow such development reached the county commissioners, Dave voted for the amendment, and some of the farmers have said to me they wished they had cast their votes for Clark.

Law Practice

Earnings weren't a major consideration for me when I decided to become a lawyer. What interested me more were the kinds of compelling issues of public policy and civil liberties I had studied under Bob Fluno at Whitman College. I looked forward to tipping the scales a bit in favor of the less powerful and the less fortunate, and that interest has played out to a considerable degree in my practice.

Since leaving my salaried legal aid job in California, my private law work in Walla Walla has covered the gamut of general practice. At some point or another I've handled divorce, annulment, adoption, child custody, guardianship, probate, trusts, wills, personal injury, worker compensation, unemployment compensation, social security disability, labor law, criminal law, banking law, contracts, condemnation, landlord-tenant, real estate transactions, mortgages and deeds of trust, quiet title actions, partition suits, bankruptcy, collections, corporations, partnerships, immigration, and civil rights cases, including both jury and bench trials, as well as appeals in state and federal courts.

I've had the very good fortune of never having to seek clients. Fate favored me with parents who taught me thrift, a wife who values simplicity, a law partner whom I assisted with a fairly lucrative practice, and my own clients on whose behalf I've earned a number of contingent fees considerably beyond the hourly compensation rate. All of this, together with careful investments, has allowed me to be a free agent much of the time over the years, able to work without pay on one community project or another.

Though most of my law work has been compensated for on an hourly basis, some has been "pro bono" or without fee for local legal aid programs, or at a reduced fee for statewide legal aid programs. Other work has been on a contingent fee basis, which can yield far more than the hourly rate if the attorney's skills and judgment are good, and the case succeeds. Not only have such fees helped free me to do volunteer work, occasionally they've been used to provide major contributions to organizations I support. One such fee was used by the Walla Walla Friends Meeting to create a special projects fund to help with the peace and human rights work of Peace Brigades International and other social action projects the Meeting sponsors.

While many of my clients have been low-income, over the years I've done work for people at every economic level, including the very well-to-do. I've mostly limited my work to Walla Walla and adjoining counties in order to avoid travel time and to keep life relatively simple. Sometimes this has meant declining glamorous offers such as a proposal by my Argentine "brother" Pablo Borras, a wonderful man whose family I lived with during my high school student exchange experience in Argentina. In 1987, Pablo asked me to become the US attorney for his large Argentine agribusiness enterprise in transactions with the World Bank, and to receive a share in a major forestry business he was developing in northern Argentina. Though lucrative, this would have meant a radical change in my lifestyle which I politely declined.

A Conspiracy of Silence

A lawyer's memoirs wouldn't be complete without a couple of stories about unusual cases, one of which involves Roy McCann.

In the early Seventies, Roy came to see me with a tale of woe. Life had been hard on Roy; he was up in years, had lost a leg, and was living alone on social security in an old single-wide trailer in the center of Starbuck, a small town in Columbia County near the Snake River. His only friend was his mongrel dog, who had recently given birth to a litter of pups.

A few weeks before talking with me, Roy came into Walla Walla to have his artificial leg adjusted. When he returned to Starbuck, instead of being greeted by the familiar yelps of the dog and her pups, his place was silent. Finding all of his animals gone, he searched around town and inquired of his neighbors, but everyone told him they didn't know anything about it. Roy was heartbroken and offered a $500 reward to anyone who could tell him what happened to his old friend and her pups. Days went by, and no one came forward.

Finally one afternoon the teenage daughter of a caretaker at one of the Snake River dams came to town, and when she stopped for gas at the local service station someone told her she should go see Roy McCann. She did, and when Roy asked her about his dogs, she told him exactly what had happened.

The day the dogs disappeared she had been working on the restoration of the old brick jail across the street from Roy's trailer home, when she saw Roy's next door neighbor and the town mayor, who was also a deputy sheriff, come into Roy's fenced yard carrying shotguns. Thinking they were going to shoot the dogs, she started crying and ran over to plead with them, telling them she would take the pups home herself so they wouldn't be bothering people anymore with their yelping. Despite carrying guns, they denied they were planning to shoot the animals, and said they just wanted to take them to the humane society in Walla Walla to help Roy out. They then cornered the dogs, tied them up with baling wire, and drove off with them in the back of a pickup.

When Roy handed her $500, she asked what it was for since she hadn't heard about any reward, but he insisted she take it. Roy called the humane society, but his dogs had never been brought in, and he later learned they had been taken into a nearby canyon and shot. Roy said he wanted justice.

I told him his dogs had no monetary value, but his civil rights should, and I agreed to file an action for damages in Columbia County Superior Court. When I drove up to Starbuck to investigate the case, I ran into the same silence Roy had encountered; no one would talk to me. I was able to talk by phone with the girl who had given Roy the information, who told me that two other girls had some information, so I went to their school and asked to interview them in front of the school principal. One was the daughter of the mayor, who was claiming that Roy had called his home and had left a message that he wanted his dogs taken to the humane society. His daughter denied this, as did Roy. When I got home, the mayor telephoned me and said I had

169

better not come back to Starbuck alone again if I knew what was good for me.

As I walked into the Dayton courtroom on the day of the trial, it seemed the whole town of Starbuck was there, and all hostile. In order to reach the tables in the front of the courtroom where the attorneys and their clients sit, I had to walk down an aisle next to a bench on the back wall. As I did so, a burly young fellow stuck out his foot and tried to trip me. I stopped and calmly looked at him until he reluctantly drew it back and let me proceed. Since all of the town's witnesses I had subpoenaed had refused to talk with me, I asked the judge for an order requiring them to speak with me privately before the trial began, as well as a few minutes' continuance, which he gave me. Our problem was that our only real witness was the girl who had pleaded to save the dogs, and she didn't show up, saying she was ill. That meant our only hope was that, under oath, at least one of the townspeople would tell the truth.

As we seated the jury, the courtroom was hushed except for what sounded like loud flatulence, but turned out to be the sound of the rubber cup on Roy's ill-fitting artificial leg, as I had to explain to the judge and jury. This was repeated throughout the trial, to everyone's amusement.

As I recall these events, the mayor and the neighbor denied carrying guns into Roy's yard and insisted that he had asked them to take his dogs away. My faith in the honesty and courage of people was restored, however, when the postmistress testified truthfully about the dogs, the reward, the silence, and other events.

After several hours deliberation, the jury brought in a judgment for the plaintiff, clearly indicating their belief that the mayor and Roy's neighbor had perjured themselves, and gave Roy the sum of $500 as his reward money, plus a few dollars for his mongrels. To Roy, justice had been done.

A Case of Mistaken Identity

One well-to-do client I represented was a Korean couple who purchased the Marcus Whitman Hotel and Lounge in 1990 and whom I represented for about ten years. The Whitman, completed in 1928, has twelve stories and is one of Walla Walla's landmarks. My father had been the managing agent for the building for a period in the Seventies, and I was glad to be associated with it. Despite their prominence in the community, however, in 1996 my clients Dong Kang and his wife Won Ja Kang went through a nightmarish experience that pointed up some weaknesses in our legal system.

On April 2, 1996, Dong came to my office with news that his wife had been arrested by Walla Walla police on fugitive warrants from Oklahoma and Texas, and was being held in the county jail. Dong told me Won Ja had never been in either state. Earlier in the day the Walla Walla police had showed up unannounced at their condominium at the Whitman where she was the manager, arrested her, and seized her jewelry and her credit cards. After conversations with the police, the prosecutor, and a judge, I was able to obtain her release on her own recognizance before the end of the day.

170

At a hearing in Walla Walla County Superior Court the next morning I received a copy of some paperwork from Texas, which failed to state the date of the alleged offense. I then called the Harris County prosecutor in Houston to learn the details of the charge, including the date of the alleged offense so we could prove her whereabouts at that time, I was told that the prosecutor wouldn't talk to defense counsel until the defendant was in custody in Texas. I told them that would never happen, and again demanded to know the date of the offense so my client could defend herself, but they refused.

The same evening she was arrested again, this time on a Seattle jewel theft warrant, and was taken to the King County Jail where she was held overnight. The following day a Seattle attorney was arranged for her, and again obtained her release pending further proceedings.

The Kangs had never lied to me over the years, and I believed their assurances that Won Ja had nothing to do with jewel thefts of any kind. In responding to a call from a local newspaper reporter after her first arrest, I declared that she was innocent, and also learned that Won Ja's name and photo had appeared in a national jewelers newsletter "wanted" story accusing her of jewel thefts in several states, assisted by her husband. The reporter called back after her second arrest to give me a chance to retract my firm stand that she was innocent, and almost laughed when I continued to insist that she had nothing to do with any of the charges. It was clear she had already been convicted in the court of public opinion.

When I finally obtained a copy of both out-of-state warrants from the courts, I learned that the Oklahoma warrant alleged a theft on January 10 in Oklahoma City and the Texas warrant was for a February 7 theft in Houston, while the Seattle warrant was for a theft on March 8. In addition, the Kangs were being investigated for a series of other thefts occurring from August 1995 through March 1996 in San Francisco, Washington, D.C., Portland, Texas, Kentucky, Tennessee, Oklahoma, New Mexico, Colorado, Arizona, Nebraska, Georgia, and Indiana totaling over $400,000. In several states she had been identified by eyewitnesses.

With this information, I was finally in a position to begin documenting the Kangs' whereabouts, at least on the dates of the three existing warrants. I started by having my clients bring me all their relevant records, including bank statements, credit card bills, leases and other documents covering this period, and Barbara and I started preparing a chronology. Our first break was when we discovered a bank deposit on February 7; after some negotiation, I got the bank to preserve their videotape for that day which was about to be erased. I then talked with the teller who had handled Won Ja's deposit, and arranged for her to view the somewhat poor quality videotape and to confirm in an affidavit that it in fact showed Won Ja making the deposit she had helped her with on that date.

Since February 7 was the day of the largest flood in recent Walla Walla history, I also found a fireman who had inspected the Marcus Whitman Hotel that day for possible basement flooding, and had talked with a woman he assumed was Won Ja. I arranged for the two of them to meet, and he confirmed in another affidavit that she was the one he had spoken to. Along with other affidavits and documentary evidence I assembled, here was excellent proof of her innocence, if we could get Texas to look at it.

Through an investigation of the Seattle case, we were able to learn how Won Ja had come to be accused and identified as a jewel thief all over the country as the result of an initial flawed investigation by the Seattle police. In September 1995 a composite description of an Asian woman suspected of criminal activities at three Seattle jewelry stores was circulated by the police throughout the northwest. In addition to their Walla Walla hotel and condominium, the Kangs maintained an expensive home in the Seattle area, and when Won Ja did some shopping at two jewelry stores there, although no crimes occurred at those stores, the non-Asian store personnel thought she matched the description of the suspected thief. They then followed her to the parking lot and noted the license number of her car, from which Seattle police obtained a copy of her driver's license, and subsequently sent it around the country. As a result of this mistaken cross-cultural photo identification, Won Ja was subsequently charged with felonies in Seattle, Houston, and Oklahoma City, and became a suspect in many other cities and states.

The alleged Seattle theft occurred on the date of Won Ja's birthday, when she had been the guest of honor at a birthday dinner in Walla Walla attended by several business associates, friends, and family members. In addition, the jewelry store video of the suspected thief clearly showed a different person. On May 6, the Seattle charge was dismissed on the prosecution's own motion, due to insufficient evidence.

We still had the problem of keeping her out of jail while we were proving her innocence on the out-of-state charges. She was currently subject to $150,000 bail in Washington on the Texas and Oklahoma fugitive charges, as she had been on the Seattle charge. However, I discovered that if those states were to take the next step and formally request extradition and if our governor were to issue an extradition warrant to have her arrested, she would have no right to bail until the extradition hearing. The experience of being jailed in Walla Walla and Seattle and all of the accusations in the press had been very hard on Won Ja; she was humiliated and was losing sleep, and the effect of further incarceration could well have been devastating.

Normally, the only question to be decided in an extradition hearing is whether the person before the court is in fact the person charged, not whether they are guilty or not, which is a question to be tried in the other states, in this case Texas and Oklahoma. To avoid the possibility of her being held without bail, we had to convince the governor not to issue an extradition warrant. After talking with the extradition officer, I sent him all of our evidence, which I also sent off to Texas, Oklahoma, and other states investigating the Kangs, along with a personal letter explaining my relationship with them over the years, and the evidence conclusively establishing their innocence.

Texas still refused to talk to us until June, when the Kangs were able to hire a former prosecutor there to intercede. We then sent down a video of Won Ja for the Houston authorities to compare with the jewelry store videos taken there, and arranged a phone interview for Won Ja with their investigator.

While this was going on, progress was also being made in locating the actual thief through the tracing of license plates from a car rented by a Mr. Lee in San Francisco, who admitted flying to meet a Vietnamese woman in various cities at the time of the thefts, and driving her to jewelry stores, including the sites and dates of the Houston and Oklahoma City thefts. Mr. Lee had reviewed the same photo montage shown to store personnel which included a photo of Won Ja, and he denied that any of them was the woman he chauffeured.

On June 24, we received word that Texas had formally dismissed its charges against Won Ja, and Oklahoma soon followed suit. A Vietnamese woman, Huong Tran, was arrested with Mr. Lee in another jewelry store in Omaha on July 19.

What was surprising to me was that the police had never sought to interview the Kangs before sending Won Ja's photo and the accusations against them around the country and then arresting her. If they had they done so, the Kangs could have supplied the same documentary and witness evidence we later produced, without the resulting damage to their reputations and Won Ja's health. In fact, we learned that the Seattle police had ignored the denials of some Seattle store employees that Won Ja, who was the only sophisticated woman included in the police montage, was the thief they had observed.

On August 2, 1996 the Kangs, through their Seattle attorney, filed a damage action against the City of Seattle, King County, and the lead police detective Maureen Stich for unlawful arrest, imprisonment, assault, malicious prosecution, violation of civil rights, outrage, libel, slander, invasion of privacy, and infliction of emotional distress, in response to which the City of Seattle agreed to a six-figure settlement.

The Kangs also sued for defamation, invasion of privacy, and infliction of emotional distress against the national jewelers association, a Seattle jewelry store, and two Korean language newspapers that had repeatedly reported the allegations against them as fact.

Though justice was ultimately done in the Kangs' case, what would have been the result if they had fewer resources to defend themselves? The answer is clearly that Won Ja would have spent additional time in jail here before being sent on to Texas and elsewhere to an uncertain fate. Her experience also demonstrates the need for bail for those contesting extradition warrants, just as with local charges. Finally, it's a cautionary tale about the risk we all face if our photo happens to be included in a police montage shown to a witness or crime victim.

In the Kangs' case, while they were ultimately vindicated, more people are likely to remember the original charges than the ultimate dismissal of those charges. In fact, the damage to their reputation affected their Walla Walla business, and resulted in their putting the Marcus Whitman up for sale.

The hotel had been forced to close in the Seventies, and was later partially converted to condominiums. By the time the Kangs bought it in 1990 it had been going downhill for years.

For a long time, the community had been lamenting the decline of this prominent landmark, and had been hoping it might be restored. Realtors Bruce Buchanan, a former manager of the Downtown Walla Walla Foundation, and Dennis Wagaman, one of that organization's founders, proposed a listing agreement which I encouraged Dong to sign. Bruce's idea was to gather community funds for a feasibility study to restore the hotel and transform it into a conference center. The results were mixed, with enough potential to continue exploring the concept but not enough to interest any of the outside parties he was hoping would step forward.

However, a local couple, Kyle and Lorie Mussman, did become interested. The question then was whether they could come to terms with the Kangs and a Seattle bank that owned a portion of the property, on what would be a very expensive restoration and expansion project.

In very difficult and drawn out multi-party negotiations, I advised the Kangs that this was the best prospect they would have to sell their interest, and did everything I could to keep the parties at the table. In March, 1999 a sale agreement was executed which closed that July.

The Mussmans have since exceeded everyone's expectations in their restoration, renovation, and expansion of the complex, which they successfully opened as the Marcus Whitman Hotel and Conference Center, and which is drawing large numbers of groups and individuals to our community to celebrate our historic culture and our more than one hundred new wineries.

The Blue Mountain Land Trust

For years Barbara and I had admired the work of land trusts across the country in protecting natural areas, providing community recreation facilities, assisting with historic preservation, and preserving farmlands and open space.

When Jim Swayne retired as Milton-Freewater city manager around 1996 in order to devote his time to growing penstemons and other native plants on the six-acre place he bought with his wife Susan on the Old Milton Highway, we gained a new partner in a variety of community projects who was another strong advocate of land trusts.

In June, 1999 naturalist and Touchet-area farmer Carolyn Seachris told me she was having no luck getting the Nature Conservancy or the National Audubon Society interested in protecting her 247-acre farm and wildlife preserve located along two miles of the Touchet River. Barbara and I had previously explored the potential for involving national land trusts here and knew there were none willing to serve our area, so I told Carolyn that if she wanted to donate conservation easements on her property, we'd form a much-needed local land trust in order to receive them. Jim heartily agreed and we began preparing a list of prospective board members.

Among the first to agree to serve was Whitman College President Tom Cronin, and Tom's participation helped us establish what became a blue-ribbon founding board that included Walla Walla Community College Vice-President Jim Peterson, Walla Walla College engineering and environmental studies professor Jon Cole, Walla Walla County extension agent Walt Gary, retired banker Carl Schmitt, farmers Fred Kimball and Mark Wagoner, Audubon leader Shirley Muse, Umatilla Indian Reservation biologist Carl Scheeler, retired Whitman treasurer Pete Reid, and local attorney Tom Scribner.

At our organizational meeting on July 6, we were joined by Dale Bonar of the Land Trust Alliance, Chris De Forest, director of the Inland Northwest Land Trust in Spokane, and Archie

George, a founder of the Palouse Land Trust in Colfax, who recounted the wonderful things land trusts as local conservation organizations had done in communities across the country.

We then signed articles of incorporation I had drafted for the Blue Mountain Land Trust as a Washington non-profit organization dedicated to helping conserve properties throughout the Blue Mountain region of southeastern Washington and northeastern Oregon. Our corporation papers were filed with the Washington Secretary of State on July 14, 1999, and on August 4 we adopted bylaws, appointed officers, authorized an application to the IRS for 501(c)(3) tax exempt status and were in business.

Our first conservation easements were on a 50-acre tract of farm and riparian lands east of Walla Walla between Mill and Titus creeks owned by Carl and Sonia Schmitt. The land had been destined for development but will now be maintained intact perpetually, preserving both its agrarian and habitat values. Since then the trust has acquired easements on more than five hundred additional acres along various Walla Walla area streams and their adjoining uplands with a variety of environmental values.

While Jim and I have passed on responsibility to others, as the Walla Walla area continues to experience development pressure which is intensifying with the growing interest in its world-class wineries and vineyards, the conservation capacities of the Blue Mountain Land Trust will be important tools to help preserve its beauty, natural values, and productive farmland for the future.

Lessons

In 1999, a student at Whitman College asked me to speak at a workshop he was organizing on social action and civil disobedience. To prepare for it, I put together a page on some principles of social action I had learned from thirty-five years of activism, along with another containing some thoughts on civil disobedience as a result of my experience representing protestors at the Hanford Nuclear Reservation and at the Washington State Penitentiary. I've included those pages in an appendix to these memoirs.

People have often said to me, how do you find the time to do so many things without getting exhausted or burnt out? Though looking through these accounts may create an impression of frenetic activity, that has rarely been the case. For the most part my days have been calm, with plenty of exercise and time to contemplate. Partly this is because Barbara and I have been careful to maintain our independence and fortunate enough to have control over our own time. That has been possible due to the relative simplicity of our lifestyle which has limited our economic needs.

For me, quiet times are a key to effective action. Usually I take a long contemplative walk every morning, which is a time of openness that can also occur at other points during the day, for example when I step out into the garden or go upstairs to what we call the "quiet room."

It's important to act on the needs we feel, though how we act depends on the quality of our vision. In my case, the most successful actions have come when I'm able to visualize the project

I'm considering actually coming to be. If I can't see it, it probably isn't right and won't happen. If I do see it, it usually begins to take on reality. For me, this creative process—beginning with nothing, seeing an idea appear, watching that idea become reality over a period of days, months, or years, then looking back to the day when it was nothing but an idea—is one of life's great fascinations.

Gandhi, whom I consider my hero, called himself a "practical dreamer." There are many dreamers who aren't practical, and many practical people without much vision, but the combination isn't so common.

When vision does come, if it's accompanied by a sense of appropriateness and practicality, then it's only a matter of time before an opportunity will arise to realize it in some way. At that point, timing is critical. Nothing is such a good idea in my experience that it's appropriate everywhere and for all time. Nurturing an idea until the time is right, as well as recognizing when that time has arrived, are other keys to success. If there's no impediment to action, the best time for me to act on an idea is now; if I feel internal resistance, then it's better to wait.

Once the time for action arrives, an initiator has the advantage. Whatever their level of activity, most people are in a condition of relative repose, and when someone presents a positive vision, it can have great power. I've also found that whatever the initial barriers may be, to a significant degree persistent people are able to achieve what they envision.

Good ideas can of course come not just from our own quietness. Although sometimes ideas for projects have seemed to come full blown out of nowhere, just as often a new initiative has come from the suggestions or examples of others.

In the end, it seems to me that our only adversary is ignorance, sometimes our own, sometimes other people's. People are essentially the same, and what is best in them is reachable if we can find the right approach. Whatever we do certainly needs to be done with humility since there's much we don't know, and also with good humor to remind us that, after all, nothing has to happen.

Part Two: 2001-2013

Any life is always a work in progress. Having written the above accounts when I injured my back in 2001 and was forced to curtail many activities, I'm glad to add many interesting new projects that have taken place since then, in roughly the order in which they happened.

The Iraq War

In March of 2003, Barbara and I engaged in an extraordinary international peace initiative in an attempt to avoid the impending war.

On Thursday morning, March 6, in discussing the dramatic call by Helen Caldecott, founder and president of International Physicians for Social Responsibility, for the Pope to go to Bagdad as a protective presence against the planned American attack, we concluded that he would probably not be willing to respond alone, but might do so as part of a broader international religious summit and conference. We wanted to suggest such a summit to an organization capable of acting on it, and decided that the American Friends Service Committee (AFSC), as a winner of the Nobel Peace Prize, would be the most natural organization to start with.

Since the US was considering an attack in the relatively short period of time before seasonal winds and extreme heat were expected to make fighting conditions too hazardous, the timing of such a conference would be critical. If the unacceptable loss presented by the presence of world religious figures on the ground in Iraq were able to deter an attack for several weeks, it was possible that the world would gain several more months to find a peaceful solution to the crisis, including further exploration of legal and diplomatic efforts.

In order to pursue this with AFSC, I tried to reach their General Secretary, Mary Ellen McNish, but was directed to Peter Lems, who was in charge of their Iraq program. Peter liked the idea very much and requested a written proposal that he could circulate among key AFSC staff.

The letter proposal I sent to AFSC on March 6, 2003 read as follows:

Dear Friends:

As I explained to Peter this morning, my wife and I are Friends in Walla Walla, Washington, and are deeply involved in work to avoid the approaching war in Iraq, along with our meeting.

Inspired by the call by Helen Caldecott to Pope John Paul to go to Iraq as a protective presence, we propose that a broader religious summit and religious conference be organized in Iraq during this critical period when the risk of war commencing is seasonally at its height.

The proposed summit would include invitations to the Pope, the Archbishop of Canterbury, the Ecumenical Patriarch of the Orthodox Catholic Church, the Dalai Lama, the Presidents of the Union of American Hebrew Congregations and the United Synagogue of Conservative Judaism, as well as, Muslim, Hindu, Quaker, and other religious leaders. The conference would involve a somewhat broader group, including key staff and advisors, and would cover a somewhat longer period.

The purpose of the conference would be to explore solutions to the current crisis, as well as the broader role and requirements of law and morality in the world community.

It could be scheduled to begin at a time mutually determined by the Iraqi officials who would have to both consent to its taking place and provide appropriate facilities, and by the inviting organization, in consultation with the principle invitees.

It is proposed that AFSC, as a Nobel Peace Laureate and active advocate for peace and mutual understanding, be the inviting organization, in cooperation with any partners it would wish to associate, such as for example the World Council of Churches.

It is our understanding that you have had some prior discussions of such a concept, but had not identified the staff resources to develop it.

We would be glad to volunteer our services in pursuing this on behalf of AFSC, in cooperation with whatever staff members or partners you would name. As to our background, Barbara and I are both 1968 graduates of UC Berkeley law school, after receiving our B.A.s in political science at Reed College and Whitman College, respectively. Barbara is the director of Neutral Ground Mediation Service, and is a member of the Walla Walla City Council. I am an attorney in private practice, and was a founder and first International Secretary of Peace Brigades International, which as you know was nominated by AFSC for last year's Nobel Peace Prize, and I continue to serve as legal counsel for PBI. We are both founding members of the Walla Walla Friends Meeting.

The proposed summit could accomplish its protective purpose of avoiding an attack during its presence if one or more of the most prominent invitees were to attend. The conference might accomplish the same purpose if several of the prominent invitees were to give it their blessing and to send representatives. We believe the invitees would be more likely to travel to and be present in Iraq as part of a conference than to do so individually.

We would be happy to develop further details and to discuss the proposal further with you at your convenience.

As I indicated to Peter, although AFSC seems to us to be the most natural sponsor for the proposed events, were it not to seem appropriate to AFSC, we would want to seek another sponsor, and would appreciate knowing that as soon as possible.

Thank you for the good work of the Committee over the decades. We look forward to your response and to the possibility of working with you on this initiative.

Following circulation of this letter by Peter to key AFSC officials, on Saturday, March 8 we received a phone call from Peter with authorization to pursue preliminary consultations with the proposed invitees on behalf of AFSC. With that authorization, we sent letters to fax numbers and email addresses we obtained for the following religious leaders, inviting their consideration of the proposed summit and conference:

> Pope John Paul II, the Vatican
> The Dalai Lama, Tibet
> Archbishop Desmond Tutu, South Africa
> Archbishop Rowan Williams, The United Kingdom
> Thich Nhat Hanh, Viet Nam

Former President Jimmy Carter, US
Rajmohan Gandhi, India
Ecumenical Patriarch Bartholomew, Turkey
Imam, the Aga Kahn IV, Islam
Patriarch Alexii II, Russia
John McCullough, Church World Service, US
Robert Edgar, National Council of Churches, US
Bishop Wilton Gregory, Council of Catholic Bishops, US
Rabbi Michael Lerner, US.

Our intention was to extend additional invitations to Swami Agnivesh, and to other major religious leaders, as well as to follow up on the initial invitations with personal contacts through people who had close relationships with the invitees. The letter we sent to Pope John Paul II read:

March 9, 2003

Your Holiness John Paul II:

In response to the current crisis and impending war, the American Friends Service Committee is proposing a Religious Summit and Conference of World Religious Leaders to take place in Iraq during the period March 17-31, 2003.

In addition to yourself, proposed invitees to the summit include the Archbishop of Canterbury Rowan Williams, the Dalai Lama, Thich Naht Hanh, Archbishop Desmond Tutu, Bartholomew the Ecumenical Patriarch of the Orthodox Catholic Church, Hindu, Muslim, Jewish and other major religious leaders, and former US President Jimmy Carter as moderator. The conference would involve a somewhat broader group, including key staff and advisors, would cover a longer period, and might include a follow up session for the elaboration of the work of the summit and conference.

The purpose of both the summit and conference is to explore solutions to the current crisis, as well as the broader role and requirements of law, religion, and morality in the world community.

I believe you are acquainted with the American Friends Service Committee (AFSC), which was the recipient of the Nobel Peace Prize in 1947, the first time the prize was awarded to an organization rather than to an individual.

Your presence and participation in the proposed summit would undeniably draw the attention of the world's people and governments to the moral necessity for peace, and would dramatically strengthen the search underway in the United Nations for ways to defer and to remove the justification for war.

Your calls for peace have inspired the world, and your endorsement of the conference and your sending one or more representatives to participate in the conference proceedings would also be an important contribution to efforts towards the peaceful resolution of this conflict, and would further demonstrate the will and moral strength of the world community to establish lasting principles and processes for peace.

It is apparent that time is short for the effective implementation of these plans. We would appreciate the opportunity to confer with your staff at the earliest possible time regarding the proposed conference and summit, in order to be able to communicate your views and possible participation to other invitees, and to assist us in appropriate planning.

We would appreciate the name and telephone number of a staff member with whom we could discuss these proposals further. I will be available by telephone at any hour for this purpose.

We look forward to your response and counsel with respect to all aspects of the proposed events, including invitations, format, and scheduling.

With great personal respect,

For the AMERICAN FRIENDS SERVICE COMMITTEE

Daniel N. Clark

A similar letter went to other invitees.

President Carter responded through Don Moseley of Jubilee Partners, saying he had considered the proposal, which for about ten years Don had been making to him in one form or another, and regretfully declined, as he was working hard and utilizing all of his time with other aspects of this problem and other matters. Don told me he doubted that Carter would feel comfortable in Iraq, not because of security concerns, but because in a situation dominated by Saddam Hussein he would not have the level of personal control he needs to work effectively. Bishop Tutu and Rajmohan Gandhi also respectfully declined due to personal circumstances, and Rabbi Michael Lerner imposed impractical conditions on his acceptance.

We received a positive response from Bob Edgar, General Secretary of the National Council of Churches, and from a representative of the Russian Patriarch regarding potential attendance by a Russian delegation including Bishop Theofan and a Mr. Silantiev who had been planning to go to Iraq on a peace mission from March 17-19, and might also be able to take part in the conference. They asked to see the program and a list of people agreeing to participate before making a final decision.

Copies of these invitations went to AFSC's Peter Lems, along with requests for feedback and advice. In his email of Sunday, March 9, commenting on the letter to Pope John Paul II which we had also forwarded to Detroit Bishop Tom Gumbleton to seek his assistance in getting it to the pontiff, Peter wrote, "I like the names of the people on your letter, and was going to suggest contacting Bishop Gumbelton…I am so impressed with what you have already been able to accomplish."

Unfortunately, after we had worked day and night on this effort since March 6, on Tuesday morning March 11, I received a call from Mary Lord of AFSC's Peacebuilding Unit and Mary Ellen McNish, AFSC General Secretary telling me they had not authorized the initiative on behalf of AFSC, and that due to other commitments, AFSC did not have the resources to devote to it, and would be unable to sponsor such a conference. They also said that developments at the UN made the suggested beginning date for the conference no longer appropriate, and that delaying it would allow more time for planning and consultations with invitees to the proposed events.

In order to provide continued sponsorship, the Committee on Nonviolent Conflict Resolution of our local Friends Meeting agreed to be the interim sponsor while seeking other partners, and we informed all of the invitees that a new date and new sponsorship were being explored for the conference.

The response by some parties in the short time we explored the proposal was encouraging, and we believed there were many more potential partners either with experience on the ground in Iraq or with the organization of conferences and high-level contacts with religious leaders, who might be willing to share staffing duties. In addition, inside Iraq the Minister of Religious Affairs and others were calling for such a presence.

While our effort provided world religious figures with a context for intervention in order to avoid a major war, as events transpired the proposed summit and conference didn't take place, and the US invaded Iraq as threatened, engulfing the world in prolonged conflict that has resulted in hundreds of thousands of deaths and many more casualties.

Walla Walla History

In 2003, I began work on several new efforts focusing on historic relations between European immigrants and Indian tribes in the Walla Walla area, including the establishment of Walla Walla Historic Memorials to fund and commission the first statue of a Native American in our valley, as well as the formation of Walla Walla Treaty Council Days to honor the sesquicentennial of the Walla Walla Treaty Council of 1855. This in turn led to interest in the Second Walla Walla Treaty Council and Stevens Skirmish of 1856, along with proposals for an interpretive overlook at Wallula described below, and the development of the Frenchtown Historic Site west of Walla Walla, which deserves its own chapter.

Yellowbird Returns

Walla Walla has a fascinating history, which I first started researching in 1992 because I was interested in creating a statue honoring the area's Native Americans. Many places in our valley bear Indian names, including Walla Walla itself which refers to the many waters coursing through the area. But there were no monuments to Indians as there were for members of other groups, including Christopher Columbus, Marcus Whitman, a Spanish American War veteran, and a local fireman, an omission I wanted to correct.

The questions I was asking myself were whom to feature as the subject, whom to select as the artist, and how to deal with issues of cost and location. As to a subject, I wondered if there was a specific historical figure it would be appropriate to honor, or if a more generic symbol of the local tribes would be better.

Among the Cayuse and Walla Walla whose homelands included the Walla Walla Valley, the clear choice for an historic figure seemed to be Walla Walla Chief Peopeomoxmox (Yellowbird), a respected and outspoken leader at the Walla Walla Treaty Council of 1855, who was killed by the Oregon Mounted Volunteers militia later that year during the Battle of Walla Walla after he had approached them under a white flag of truce. Both his life and death offer an interesting parallel to Marcus Whitman's, since both sought peaceful relations with the other's people, and both were ultimately murdered by them. In exploring this with local historians and people I knew on the Umatilla Indian Reservation, which includes the Cayuse and Walla Walla tribes, some wanted to see a Cayuse leader featured while most felt that Peopeomoxmox was the best choice.

A natural choice for the artist appeared to be David Manuel, who was born and raised in Walla Walla, had his own museum and foundry in the Wallowa Valley, and had just been named by the State of Oregon as their official Oregon Trail Sesquicentennial sculptor because of his well-known bronzes of Native Americans and other western figures.

I contacted Dave and his wife Lee in the summer of 1992, and explained the proposal to them. Dave was interested in learning more about Peopeomoxmox, and thought it might be possible to rework the clay from a life-size statue of Chief Joseph he would be working on next in order to save some time and expense, and also suggested selling miniatures of the Peopeomoxmox figure to help fund a full-size bronze statue.

Dave and Lee were busy with a variety of other projects, and our discussions went on for several years. In early 1995, I reached an agreement with Dave and the Paula Ray Gallery in Walla Walla that Paula Ray would sell the miniatures for half of their regular commission, with the net proceeds going half to Dave and half to the costs of the Peopeomoxmox monument. Unfortunately, Paula Ray owners Phil and Jolene Smith closed the gallery and moved to Texas for health reasons soon after that.

In 1997, I learned that Jim Irwin of Walla Walla had also been working on the idea of a Peopeomoxmox statue. Jim is a local businessman and art dealer whose involvement with local veterans groups resulted in the creation of a statue of General Jonathan Wainwright placed in the center of the Fort Walla Walla parade grounds, now the US Veterans Medical Center. Jim wanted Roger McGee, the Walla Walla artist who did the Wainwright statue, to also do one of Peopeomoxmox to be placed in a prominent location somewhere in the city.

I was excited by this, and offered to help. As a result we incorporated Walla Walla Historic Memorials in 2003 as a non-profit, tax-exempt organization to raise funds and to contract with Roger. Our goal was to complete the project and be able to unveil the statue on June 10, 2005, the 150th anniversary of the culmination of the Walla Walla Treaty Council and the signing of the treaties establishing the Umatilla, Yakima, and Nez Perce Indian reservations.

Three portraits of Peopeomoxmox had been made during his lifetime, two of which were still available. Utilizing these together with his own inspiration, Roger created a miniature to show current Walla Walla Chief Carl Sampson and his family for comment and corrections. Carl, a direct descendant of Chief Peopeomoxmox, was very pleased with the miniature and gave it his blessing. With the family's approval, we began raising funds to have the piece enlarged by artist Nano Lopez, to prepare it for casting. In addition to a grant from the Sherwood Trust and other fundraising efforts, we organized a cultural celebration, auction, and dinner at the Walla Walla fairgrounds, which was a big success. Carl's son, Donald Sampson, was the CEO of the Confederated Tribes of the Umatilla Reservation at that time, and served as the master of ceremonies, while other Sampson family members took charge of the dinner.

For placement of the statue which is called Yellowbird Returns, we identified several prominent intersections, but finally reached an agreement between the City of Walla Walla and the US Army Corps of Engineers to put it at a plaza over Mill Creek on the grounds of the Corps' Walla Walla headquarters and across the street from both the Marcus Whitman Hotel and Conference Center and city hall, with the City becoming the owner of the statue and responsible for its maintenance.

On the base of the statue we affixed four bronze plaques which I drafted honoring Peopeomoxmox, the local Tribes, the Walla Walla Treaty Council, and our donors. The text of the plaque honoring the Tribes reads:

> The Walla Walla Valley is the homeland of the Cayuse and Walla Walla Tribes. The Walla Wallas, whose villages were in the lower valley near the Columbia, were described by Lewis & Clark as "the most hospitable, honest, and sincere people that we have met with on our voyage." Near their fishery site at Wallula the Northwest Fur Company built the first trading post in the inland region, Fort Nez Perce, which later became the Hudson Bay Company's Fort Walla Walla.

> The Cayuse Indians were known as expert horsemen and breeders of strong ponies, as well as for their ferocity in battle. Gov. Isaac Stevens wrote at the Walla Walla Treaty Council, "The haughty carriage of these (Cayuse) chiefs and their manly character have, for the first time in my Indian experience, realized the description of the writers of fiction."

The plaque honoring the treaty council states:

> Just east of this site from May 29 to June 11, 1855, a great treaty council was held between Governor Isaac Stevens of Washington Territory, Superintendent of Indian Affairs Joel Palmer of Oregon Territory, and many of the upper Columbia and Snake River Indian tribes. Several thousand Indians were present. It is said that in its general importance and difficulty the Walla Walla Council has never been equaled by any council held with the Indian tribes of the United States. The Council resulted in three treaties establishing the Yakama, Nez Perce, and Umatilla Indian Reservations, and the ceding of all remaining tribal lands to the United States. The treaties continue in effect to

this day, providing important protections for the Tribes, as well as for immigrants and their descendants.

In addition to our formal unveiling ceremony involving the Tribes, the Corps, city officials and other dignitaries for which I served as MC, additional sesquicentennial observances included a powwow and ceremonies at the VA Medical Center sponsored by another nonprofit we organized, Walla Walla Treaty Council Days, involving representatives of all regional tribes. We also presented a series of living history performances at Fort Walla Walla Museum that included appearances by Washington Territorial Governor Isaac Stevens played admirably by Ron Klicker, and Oregon Superintendent of Indian Affairs Joel Palmer, a Quaker whom I portrayed.

The Second WW Treaty Council and Stevens Skirmish

Though the Walla Walla Treaty Council of 1855 has become fairly well known, very few people know that in 1856, Governor Stevens held a Second Treaty Council in Walla Walla in an attempt to end the Indian war that had broken out over land invasions by whites in advance of the treaties being ratified. After calling all the inland tribes together again, Stevens failed to convince them to surrender either their lands or their arms, and he and his party were attacked as they attempted to return to The Dalles. The initial attack led to fighting in the upper Mill Creek area throughout the afternoon and night of September 19, 1856, and into the following day. This dramatic series of events, whose locations had never been determined, involved the only instance of combat with Indians by Stevens, who later died as a general in the US Army during the Civil War.

As the sesquicentennial of these 1856 events approached, I was determined to discover where they had taken place, and to organize some activities to study and commemorate them. I began by studying all the historical accounts with the help of historian Steve Plucker, a Touchet area farmer whose great grandfather had served in the US Army during the Yakima War. Once I had pieced together the descriptions of the various camps as well as the area where Stevens and his party of thirty-eight wagons had first been attacked, and then where they had circled their wagons during the 12-hour siege, I began to walk all of the ground in the area to see if I could find any places that met the various descriptions.

Though the Walla Walla Treaty Council of 1855 took place just east of where Mill Creek crosses the Nez Perce Trail along Walla Walla's Main Street, the 1856 council was said to have begun about two miles above that. In addition, Gov. Stevens had reported, "We are on a little tributary of Mill Creek about one mile from it." Going two miles as indicated above the old treaty grounds, there are only two tributaries of Mill Creek in the vicinity—Garrison Creek, which is about a half mile away, and Yellowhawk Creek, which is a mile away. Based on the historical accounts I concluded that the Second Treaty Council probably began along the left bank of Yellowhawk Creek just above where it crosses School Avenue on land now owned by the Leonetti Cellar winery.

In the midst of the 1856 council, Stevens became convinced he was in danger, and moved his camp farther up Mill Creek "about 7-8 miles" to Lt. Col. Edward Steptoe's U.S. Army camp of several hundred soldiers. Whitman College historian W.D. Lyman placed this camp on the

184

Gilkerson property which begins east of Five Mile Road and extends up the Mill Creek canyon to Seven Mile Road. When the reconvened council ultimately failed, on September 19, 1856 Stevens left for The Dalles with his party of thirty-eight wagons pulled by eighty oxen, fifty teamsters and quartermaster's men, sixty-nine Washington Volunteers, over fifty friendly Nez Perce, and more than two hundred head of loose livestock.

In his October 22 report to the Secretary of War Stevens stated, "Following me as I set out about eleven o'clock on the way to the Dalles, they attacked me within three miles of Steptoe's camp at about one o'clock in the afternoon…I moved on under fire one mile to water, when forming a corral of the wagons and holding the adjacent hills and the brush on the stream by pickets, I made my arrangements to defend my position and fight the Indians. Our position in a low, open basin, 500 or 600 yards across, was good, and with the aid of our corral, we could defend ourselves against a vastly superior force…"

Another account by one of the participants states, "small parties of Indians began to pass us on the left and soon commenced firing on our rear…But we drove on, the volunteers, and occasionally a teamster returning the fire until we had reached a small spring branch, where we corralled our wagons, including our stock. A place where three small valleys met, and as many elevations of about 30 feet, standing close in the form of a triangle…By the time we were camped, we were surrounded and fired upon from all sides. The three points having first been secured to keep the enemy from annoying the train, a charge was made upon the Indians in our rear to the left."

Another account stated, "After proceeding… two and a half miles, and coming into the valley of a small branch of Mill Creek, the whole body of Indians came on the full run for the rear of the train, and opened a fire on the rear guard which was returned in good order…The Train moved on slowly one mile further, when the wagons were formed into a corral, and the loose animals run in for security. Pickets were then placed on the highest hills, so as to prevent the Indians from firing into the corral and stampeding the animals."

Serious fighting then took place throughout the afternoon, including two charges by the Volunteers with loss of life on both sides, and continued until 2 a.m. on September 20 when the Stevens party was rescued by Steptoe's troops and escorted back to the federal camp. On the way back to the camp, and later that morning, additional fighting was reported.

After I walked and viewed all of the terrain within a reasonable distance of the Mill Creek canyon beginning at Seven Mile Road and going downstream, I found a place about two and a half miles below the likely council site where "the valley of a small branch of Mill Creek" enters the canyon. Within a mile of that point, easily accessible by wagons, is a low, open basin about 500-600 yards across, with a small spring branch, where three small valleys meet, standing in the form of a triangle, with adjacent low ridges of nearly 30 feet elevation, a ridge to the south about 500 yards away where one of the charges was described, and another stream about a mile away to the south where the friendly Nez Perce were said to have made their camp. There are very few other points in the vicinity where wagons were capable of leaving the deep Mill Creek canyon; this site, at the end of the concrete spillway leading from the Mill Creek diversion dam to

Bennington Lake, is the only one in the area that appears to meet the descriptions of the participants in these events.

To confirm the location, I organized a workshop that was held on February 11, 2006 at Walla Walla Community College under the sponsorship of Walla Walla 2020. The purpose of the workshop was to compare historical accounts, to visit likely sites, and to discuss potential commemorative activities during the sesquicentennial of these events. Participants were historians, archaeologists, tribal representatives, and interested local residents, including the farmer and an owner of a portion of the site, most of which is owned by the US Army Corps of Engineers as part of its Bennington Lake flood control project.

To assist the workshop participants, I prepared a summary and map of fifteen points of skirmish activity noted by the participants, with suggested locations for each. Some additional corroboration was provided by the first survey of the area, completed in 1860 with a resulting 1861 survey map, which show a road from the vicinity where the council apparently ended leading to the valley of the small branch of Mill Creek I had found, as well as a road passing through the apparent skirmish site and leading southwest into the valley of Russell Creek not very far from the location of the initial 1856 council site. Our workshop participants walked the area from the Mill Creek canyon to the place where the sustained fighting appears to have occurred, and there was general agreement that this was the location.

To potentially provide further evidence of the skirmish site, I then recruited archaeologist Darby Stapp and a team of volunteer metal detector operators, and we swept the private lands from the Mill Creek canyon to the Corps of Engineer property where the corral was established, which had been farmed for nearly 150 years with considerable alteration of the ground level. Though we weren't able to find anything from that period, we hope someday to do additional archeological work on Corps property in the area of the corral, for which we'll need special permits.

To commemorate the 150th anniversary of these events on September 9, 2006, I recruited Walla Walla Chief Carl Sampson as well as the head of the Whitman College American Indian Association as co-chairs of the Sesquicentennial Commemoration of the Second Walla Walla Treaty Council. As part of the commemoration, interested participants were invited to walk or ride horses from the Leon Filan farm at 853 Five Mile Road, where the ceremonies began, all the way to the probable skirmish site. The event included the sharing of food by participants, a presentation of flags by all parties, the sharing of tribal and immigrant perspectives on the Second Council and resulting skirmish, and the two-mile trek over the route of the Stevens party to the skirmish site, where final observances were held.

The participants in the project included Sam Pambrun, whose great grandfather Andrew Dominique Pambrun was Stevens' secretary, guide, and interpreter for the Second Council, and wrote a colorful account of both the proceedings and the skirmish in his autobiography, "Sixty Years on the Frontier in the Pacific Northwest." In addition, Walla Walla Chief Carl Sampson is related to Homli, who served as head chief of the Walla Wallas after the killing of Peopeomoxmox in 1855, and who was present at both the council and the skirmish. Leon Filan, who provided the site for the commemoration adjacent to his corn maze, remembers a square log building on the property with no windows and a series of small round holes on every wall about rifle height that may well have been part of the Fort built by Steptoe. Filan's family moved to Five-Mile Road in the 1940's. Other farmers and landowners in the vicinity also cooperated with the commemoration by permitting the historic trek through their lands between the Filan place and the Bennington Lake area.

Corps of Engineers rangers have been interested in the project and its historical significance for their lands, and have been working with me since 2006 on commemorative signage to be installed at the site to interpret these events.

The accounts of the actual participants in these historical events, together with a map and description of the skirmish locations are online at the Walla Walla 2020 website, www.ww2020.net/historic-sites, and also at www.wallawallatreatycouncils.blogspot.com which includes a Readers Theater script I've put together on the Walla Walla Treaty Council of 1855 using excerpts from the official transcript of that council.

The Frenchtown Historic Site

The Frenchtown Historical Foundation was founded in the summer of 1993 to pursue the idea of acquiring some of the ground where the old Saint Rose of Lima Mission Church and Frenchtown cemetery were located about eight miles west of Walla Walla.

Fur traders and trappers from the Hudson's Bay Company trading post at Wallula began settling in the area with their Indian wives and Metis or mixed children in about 1824. What became known as Frenchtown was a dispersed collection of about fifty log cabins scattered among Indian camps along a stretch of the Walla Walla River as well as its tributaries Mill Creek, Pine Creek, Dry Creek, and Mud Creek that began at present-day Lowden and extended east almost to today's Walla Walla. When American missionaries Marcus and Narcissa Whitman established their mission in the Walla Walla Valley in 1836, there were probably around a dozen French-Canadian families already occupying farms in the area.

A Catholic mission and cemetery, Saint Rose of the Cayouse, was established near the confluence of the Walla Walla River and Yellowhawk Creek in 1853, and the mission house was burned during the Yakama-Walla Walla Indian War of 1855. In 1863, a chapel was built near there, then moved down the Walla Walla where a new cemetery was established along the river. Around 1870, a log schoolhouse was added, and in 1876 the cemetery was moved to a nearby hill and the Saint Rose of Lima Mission Church was built in the lower part of what is now the Frenchtown Historic Site.

When the Frenchtown Historical Foundation was established, I attended a Rendezvous and salmon bake organized by Frank Munns and other members of the Bergevin family of French-Canadian immigrants whose ancestors had settled in Frenchtown during the early 1860's, with the help of tribal members from the Umatilla Indian Reservation The primary purpose of the Rendezvous was to remember and celebrate the friendly relations that existed between Frenchtown residents and members of area tribes. There was also a plan to move an old church onto the former mission site, and to protect and restore the abandoned cemetery. However, no agreement was reached with the landowners, and nothing came of the effort at that point.

In the summer of 2005, when the Washington State Department of Transportation began holding community meetings regarding plans for four-laning U.S. Highway 12 from the mouth of the Snake River to Walla Walla, I noted that the Frenchtown Cemetery was listed as a key heritage site to be protected along the route. As coordinator of the living history company at Fort Walla Walla Museum, I had been researching and telling the story of the 1855 Battle of Walla Walla, centered in that area, and had also been talking with members of the farm family that owned the cemetery site about creating public access to it for descendants and other interested people. In 2003 I had discussed with the board of the Blue Mountain Land Trust the possibility of their acquiring an easement and taking on responsibility for public access to the cemetery, without success.

By 2005, I had already been in touch with DOT regarding the possibility of creating a Wallula interpretive overlook as called for in an existing Snake River Bridge to Walla Walla Heritage Corridor Management Plan, and had become acquainted with some of their staff. At a public meeting, I mentioned my interest in Frenchtown to one of their environmental specialists, and he encouraged me to set up a meeting between the DOT and interested parties to discuss the cemetery and how DOT might help protect it.

Hoping that DOT might be able to acquire the cemetery, since it was located next to their planned highway expansion, I arranged a meeting in September, 2005 and invited members of the Bergevin family, leaders from the Umatilla reservation, and members of local history organizations along with environmentalists and tourism advocates.

At the meeting, DOT staff invited us to send them a letter confirming the informal requests I had made regarding their acquisition of the site as potential environmental impact mitigation. They also suggested we consider applying for a National Scenic Byways grant for which DOT might be willing to contribute a portion of the required matching funds.

Afterwards, we discussed the need to form a coalition of parties interested in protecting and interpreting the site. The potential partners I saw were the descendants of French-Canadian settlers, the Confederated Tribes of the Umatilla Indian Reservation (CTUIR), wildlife groups, environmental organizations, Tourism Walla Walla, and local historical groups.

In October, I arranged a gathering at the Claro Bergevin ranch which was the site of the French-Canadian cabin where the Oregon militia established Fort Bennett during the Battle of Walla Walla. At that meeting we shared visions for potential preservation and use of the Frenchtown site. These included (1) possible cemetery acquisition, (2) an interpretive turnout and overlook from the new four-lane highway planned just north of the cemetery, (3) acquisition and use of the field between the cemetery and the existing highway as a natural area and for access to the cemetery and overlook, and (4) acquisition and use of the farm field between the existing highway and the Walla Walla River as a habitat and wildlife preserve, and for interpretation of the St. Rose church site as well as the battle, including a view to the west towards the Larocque cabin where Chief Peopeomoxmox was killed.

Those who attended were the current Peopeomoxmox, Chief Carl Sampson and his wife Arleta; Gerald Reed, a member of the Cultural Resources Committee of the CTUIR and co-chair of the Cultural Resources Committee of the Affiliated Tribes of Northwest Indians; CTUIR wildlife and cultural resource staffers; members of the Bergevin family and other descendants of the early Frenchtown settlers, and other interested locals.

The four-day Battle of Walla Walla took place from December 7-10, 1855 over the entire area between the Larocque Cabin on the Bergevin place to the area around the Tellier Cabin a mile east on what is now Detour Road, and also on the rolling hills to the north where the new highway was planned. In my introductory comments to the group, I concluded:

> As we consider the future of this site rich in history for Native Americans, for the French and French-Canadians, for Catholics, and for people from all backgrounds interested in our history and cultures, I can see at least two distinct possibilities.

> The first possibility, or we might say probability, is that these historic fields will become filled with housing. The farm family that owns them does not wish to continue to farm them once they are cut off from the rest of their farm by the new highway, and they wish to sell them. Large homes will be the most likely result.

> The second possibility I see is that these historic grounds will be preserved and protected, as a cemetery site, for historic interpretation, as a natural area and wildlife habitat, for fishing access along the river, and for other compatible purposes.

Once everyone had spoken, all present pledged to pursue the preservation, acquisition, and interpretation of the Frenchtown property, and agreed to meet again to refine our vision and continue our efforts.

In preparation for the next meeting, I put up a website, frenchtownpartners.org, and reinstated the Frenchtown Historical Foundation's corporate status which had been dissolved due to inactivity. I agreed to serve as vice-president, and Russ Bergevin, a great enthusiast for Frenchtown, senior member of the large Bergevin family, and wonderful storyteller whom I had recruited for the living history company, became the new president of the Frenchtown Historical Foundation.

At our November 19 meeting at the Valley Chapel community center, we were joined by Sam Pambrun, whose family history in the valley goes back to his great-great-grandfather Pierre Pambrun, who was the chief trader at the Hudson's Bay Company trading post at Fort Walla Walla when Marcus and Narcissa Whitman arrived in 1836. Sam along with Russ Bergevin and Russ's cousin Claro were strong advocates for our acquiring and preserving as much of the Frenchtown site as possible. Since the DOT wasn't in a position to acquire the property itself, we sent the following letter to the landowners:

> As you are aware, Frenchtown Partners is a coalition of interested parties dedicated to preserving and interpreting the site of the St. Rose Mission and Cemetery established in 1876 on the grounds of the historic 1855 Battle of Walla Walla. Those participating

189

include members of the Confederated Tribes of the Umatilla Indian Reservation, pioneer French-Canadian families, local historians, and other area residents, as well as several non-profit organizations and interested agencies.

Our goals include the creation of a turnout and interpretive overlook from the planned highway north of the cemetery, acquisition and preservation of the cemetery itself, and establishment of a permanent access path to the cemetery and interpretive overlook from the existing highway.

Beyond these fundamental goals, we are interested in possibilities for acquisition and preservation of all or a portion of the land between the cemetery and the existing highway, as well as land south of the existing highway to the river, which is also part of the battleground and where the historic St. Rose Mission was located.

We know that you are considering development plans for the land north of the existing highway, and we would like to meet with you to discuss how the community interests we represent might be accommodated in those plans.

Best wishes,

Daniel N. Clark, Coordinator	Carl Sampson	Russ Bergevin, President
Frenchtown Partners	Chief of the Walla Wallas	Frenchtown Historical Foundation

In addition, we sent a letter to the Board of Trustees at the Umatilla Indian Reservation inviting tribal members to join us for a ceremony on Saturday, December 10, 2005 in observance of the 150th Anniversary of the historic battle. We also invited representatives of DOT and a variety of local, state, and federal officials, along with the general community.

On a very cold day, over 75 people attended the open air observance at the battlefield site, and over 100 people attended the reception and program that followed at the old Frenchtown Hall in Lowden. Our ceremonies included singing, drumming, and words from leaders of the Umatilla Reservation, greetings from Governor Christine Gregoire and U.S. Senator Maria Cantwell, talks by State Representative Bill Grant, County Commissioner Dave Carey, Whitman College President George Bridges, Sam Pambrun and several Bergevin family members including Russ, Claro, and Denise Bergevin O'Bryan.

In communicating with the landowners, though we had no money or any specific hope of raising enough for an actual land purchase, we proceeded on the theory that it was good to tell people what you want and see where that might lead. In this case, it led in a very favorable direction.

The first response we received was an offer to sell us the land at the going rate of $7500 an acre, less deductions for the sellers' retention of water and development rights.

We weren't in a position to proceed on that basis, but before long we were surprised to receive a much better offer. The landowners were in the process of developing a golf course and upscale housing complex on the north side of the new highway as well as several lots on the south site adjoining the cemetery. To facilitate their plans, they believed it would be to their advantage if the route of the new highway east of the cemetery were to be moved a bit to the south. A few days before our commemoration, they told us they would appreciate our assistance in getting this done, and if the highway were built as they proposed, they would be willing to give us title to the cemetery and approximately 23 adjoining acres, together with an option to purchase the remaining thirty acres of their property between the old highway and the river.

This was obviously a pleasing offer, but before we accepted it we needed to be sure we could do so in good conscience. After satisfying ourselves that the revised route wouldn't affect the cemetery in any way, our next question was whether it was reasonable and fair from the perspective of the neighboring property owners. In looking at all the affected properties, we concluded that it was, and that there was no reason why we shouldn't exercise our best efforts to help the landowners implement it through communications with DOT and the neighbors.

After a series of meetings in which all parties including the neighbors reached agreement, to our great satisfaction the route was changed, and the owners told us they would provide us with a deed to the 23 acres as soon as highway construction was completed.

Following these successful dealings, in March, 2006 the owners made a further proposal. If there were no appeals of required county permitting for their planned housing and golf course development across the new highway, they would deed us their remaining thirty acres of land between the old highway and the Walla Walla River, subject to their retained right to build a couple of homes on six of those acres in the northeast corner of the parcel.

Their primary motivation in making this offer appeared to be the avoidance of the type of legal challenges that a similar high end golf course and housing project was experiencing from Walla Walla 2020 and another group I was working with. That project, just east of the airport, had become the most divisive development in recent Walla Walla history, due to its impact on our community's water supply as well as other important values, and it was ultimately abandoned.

The proposed Frenchtown area golf course and development drew water from a different portion of the aquifer, would actually use less water than the current alfalfa crops grown there, and had been grandfathered in as an approved use under current zoning. Because of this, we had no intention of trying to block their development across the four-lane highway and behind a high berm, and were glad to agree to the new proposal. Since then, all of their county permitting applications have been approved without appeals, the development rights to the reserved six acres were transferred to another property, and the Frenchtown Foundation has received a deed to the entire thirty acres between the upper site and the river, which we have recently transferred to our partners, the Confederated Umatilla Tribes, whom we believe are in the best position to administer and restore this important riparian habitat property.

In addition to acquiring the Frenchtown site to preserve it as open space and protect it from development, our goals have been to open it for public access and interpretation. To achieve those goals, in 2006 we applied for and received a $35,000 American Battlefield Protection Program grant from the National Park Service. The battlefield grant funded an archaeological survey and a National Historic Register nomination prepared for us by Eastern Washington University archaeologist Stan Gough and historian Stephen Emmerson. The work of Gough and Emmerson resulted in the discovery of musket balls and other artifacts from the 1855 battle, as well as the listing of the Frenchtown site on the Washington Heritage Register, though the application for the National Register hasn't been approved.

We also received a $50,000 National Scenic Byways grant from the Federal Highway Administration in 2008 for the preparation of a Frenchtown master plan, for which we contracted with a Seattle engineering and consulting firm and Richland architect Jim Stenkamp. In October, 2008 the completed plan was adopted by the Frenchtown board, and with some revisions has guided our work since then.

We have planted the entire site with native grasses, and on the upper 27 acres have built trails, put in an entrance road and parking area, and installed interpretive signage and a large shelter. The first phase of our work was completed in time for the formal opening of the site and cemetery rededication on December 11, 2010, the 155th anniversary of the Battle of Walla Walla. On July 9, 2011, we held a Grand Opening on the two hundredth anniversary of the beginning of the fur trade in the inland region by David Thompson of the Canadian Northwest Company. Thompson came down the Columbia River on July 9, 1811 and planted a British flag at the mouth of the Snake River, claiming the area for Britain and telling the Walla Walla Indians of his company's plans to establish the first fur trading post in the region at the mouth of the Walla Walla River, which they did in 1818.

We have also initiated annual celebrations of St. Jean Baptiste Day in the Walla Walla Valley—the French-Canadian equivalent of St. Patrick's Day—with performances and participatory dancing led by the new Frenchtown Dance Troupe Barbara and I have organized to introduce traditional French-Canadian and Metis dances, including circles, squares, reels, and waltzes.

In September, 2013 we commemorated the 160th anniversary of the Saint Rose of the Cayouse Mission along Yellowhawk Creek, where, following a ceremony at Basel Cellars Winery and at the home of Bob and Cindy Gregoire on the Old Milton Highway, we have erected an interpretive sign on the Gregoire property honoring the history of that first Catholic mission in the valley.

Our latest project at the Frenchtown Historic Site is the relocation and restoration of a cabin of French-Canadian design that appears to have been built in 1837 which would make it the oldest existing cabin in Washington State.

Beyond that, pursuant to our partnership agreement with the Tribes for the cooperative management of both the upper and lower portions of the Frenchtown site, we envision eventually reconstructing the foundation of the old church in the area towards the river, where we will provide additional interpretation of the history of the mission and the parts of the battle that took place on those historic grounds.

Prisoner Transition & Reentry Efforts

The sentencing review legislation I worked on through the Friends Committee on Washington Public Policy from 1999-2000 resulted in a recommendation in 2001 by the state's Sentencing Guidelines Commission for a significant reduction in our excessively long sentences for major drug offenses, and the use of the money saved in prison costs to fund expanded drug and alcohol treatment programs both inside the prisons and in the community.

After the adoption of these recommendations by the state legislature in 2002, while I continued to oppose new proposals for increased sentences that are regularly introduced by politicians wanting to make political capital out of being "tough on crime," I began to focus more on the problem of reducing recidivism, which is new offenses by those being released. After an often lengthy period of warehousing in prisons with little or no treatment available and few if any vocational or educational programs, prisoners have traditionally been released with $40 and a bus ticket in their pocket, and no practical resources for becoming successful members of society.

Transition & Reentry Reform Coalition

To improve the success rate of released prisoners, and therefore increase community safety and reduce unnecessary incarceration costs, in 2004 I organized and chaired the Transition & Reentry Reform Coalition, a statewide group whose purpose was to study the reduction of recidivism and to implement needed change in Washington State.

Membership in the coalition was open to all non-governmental organizations and individuals supportive of its mission and willing to share in its work. We also invited governmental agencies to appoint liaisons to the coalition, and several did.

The coalition's work focused on reform of administrative policies and programs, legislative proposals, community programs, and public education. Its goals were:

1. To increase successful reentry and reintegration of released persons into society.
2. To increase the success of rehabilitative programs in correctional facilities.
3. To increase the use of community-based alternatives to formal charging and incarceration.
4. To utilize prisons and jails only within current correctional capacities, and to avoid further expansion.
5. To promote a public health model rather than a punitive model for dealing with social problems.

While the coalition became a major player in the criminal justice community in Washington State for several years, and a number of successful reforms were implemented, the political realities of the way criminal justice policy is determined are that prosecutors, law enforcement agencies, and conservative politicians dominate the field and use increased sentencing as a political football to dissuade legislators from making significant changes even though they are beginning to understand the importance of doing so in terms of public safety, community well-being, and efficient use of public resources.

Because of this, I have recently been focusing my own criminal justice work on a local non-profit I helped form at the request of several staff members at the Washington State Penitentiary along with some local prison volunteers.

The Star Project

The Successful Transition & Reentry Project (STAR) was initiated in the spring of 2004 in Walla Walla. The key organizers were staff at the Washington State Penitentiary along with community volunteers who had worked with inmates and were interested in corrections reform.

STAR's purposes are to provide transition services to inmates at the penitentiary being released throughout the state, as well as comprehensive reentry services to former inmates recently released to Walla Walla and neighboring counties from any prison, and also to their families.

STAR's successes have been recognized by the Secretary of the Department of Corrections, prison administrators, community corrections staff, former inmates and their families, and others working to reduce recidivism and increase community safety.

According to statistics provided by the Washington State Department of Corrections, the recidivism rate of STAR clients is less than half the rate of other former offenders.

Current STAR programs, projects, and activities include:

- Intensive client based case management
- Transition advice at Washington State Penitentiary
- Emergency and transitional housing
- Weekly client/family support groups and dinner
- Moral Reconation Therapy (MRT)
- Mentors program
- Job search resources and advice
- Continuing education support
- Financial management guidance
- Referrals to social service agencies
- Community service opportunities and supervision.

Our weekly dinners and support group meetings are an important part of the program, and are open to all clients and their family members, along with volunteers and board members.

As STAR's volunteer legal counsel as well as an officer and board member, I recently filed a successful application in a King County class action suit against AT&T for improper phone charges to prisoners' families, resulting in a fund of several million dollars from which STAR will receive $1,035,000. This will allow STAR to expand its services to additional clients over the next five years, to our great satisfaction since raising funds for services to former felons has always been a challenge.

Walla Walla 2020—Illahee and More

Pennbrook & the Port of Walla Walla

Walla Walla 2020's concern about sprawling development had become very well-known in our community. As a result, in late 2003 I received a call from City of Walla Walla planning director Bob Horn wondering what we would think of a proposal for a new golf course and upscale housing project to be located on 358 acres of prime farmland across the highway from the Walla Walla airport leading towards the Blue Mountains. The proponent was Pennbrook Homes, a developer from Bend, Oregon, one of the fastest growing areas in the country, which was expressing interest in annexing the property into the city.

Knowing that the last thing most people in Walla Walla want is creeping development toward the mountains, I told him that I couldn't speak for 2020 which hadn't considered this project, but I thought the organization might consider going along with this if the developers agreed to buy conservation easements on the adjoining land to the east in order to prevent the further creep toward the mountains that they probably had in mind themselves.

Instead of pursuing annexation with the city for its proposed Illahee development, Pennbrook decided to strike a better deal with the Port of Walla Walla and Walla Walla County through changes to Walla Walla's existing planning and water conservation principles.

In 2004, Pennbrook sought amendments to our county and urban area comprehensive plans and planning policies, in partnership with the Port of Walla Walla. Walla Walla 2020 and its ally Citizens for Good Governance opposed these changes, which were specifically crafted for the Illahee project. In addition to objecting that the proposed changes violated the county's established procedural deadlines and other rules, here's how my letter on behalf of 2020 summarized our position:

> Regarding the merits of the proposed policy amendments and map amendments relating to the Pennbrook development, lands with productive soils and viability for agriculture should be protected from housing and commercial development which forever remove it from productivity. This land has extremely high productivity, and based on soils, rainfall, and production history is some of the most fertile and productive in Walla Walla county, even without irrigation. Sacrificing it to high-end commercial development with increased water use at a time of diminishing supplies, plus the inexorable pressure on prime farmland adjoining the site, violates multiple policies of our comprehensive plan

and will contribute to inefficient and unsightly sprawl. Any need for growth should be accommodated through higher-density development within walking distance of urban services rather than expansion of the urban area into prime farmland. Such development creates problems for transportation, as well as for efficient delivery of other services.

Over our objections, the county commissioners approved the proposed changes to the zoning code, comprehensive plan, and planning policies specially designed for the Illahee project, and these actions were upheld on an appeal by Citizens for Good Governance.

The Port's role in this project was to sell water to Pennbrook from wells that extended into Walla Walla's diminishing basalt aquifer, which would become a source of new revenue for the Port. In order to provide the water needed for Illahee's golf course and luxury homes, the Port's plan was to acquire two additional deep wells on farmland adjoining the airport. To accomplish this, the Port applied for grants from the Federal Aviation Administration which it said were necessary for runway protection, failing to disclose the actual purpose of the planned land acquisitions as well as its contract with Pennbrook, which had agreed to supply the required matching funds for the grants.

Though Walla Walla 2020 opposed the loss of this prime farmland capable of producing two crops a year without irrigation, as well as inefficient sprawl toward our valued mountains, along with the improper placement of a housing development under an airport runway, the water deal between the Port and Pennbrook was the most threatening prospect.

Walla Walla's deep aquifer had been declining for years, with more water being pumped each year for agriculture, housing, industry, and other purposes than was being replenished. Because of that, Walla Walla had been designated by the state as a Critical Water Supply Service Area, and a Coordinated Water System Plan had been adopted for all local water supply systems. The plan required that all water systems use water from Mill Creek during the high flow seasons under the City of Walla Walla's surface water right, and that further pumping from the deep aquifer be limited to times when surface waters were unavailable. In addition, the City had begun a successful project of recharging the deep aquifer through the injection of surface water into its deep wells adjacent to the Walla Walla airport during periods of high stream flow.

Instead of complying with the Coordinated Water System Plan, the Port planned to pump and sell water to Pennbrook from the same aquifer block the city was using for its recharge program, thereby potentially defeating its efforts to replenish the aquifer.

On May 18, 2006, we gave the FAA notice of our concerns, and initiated a series of public records requests to the Port and the FAA in order to document their actions. After many hours poring over Port and FAA records, including emails, letters, reports, grant applications, and other documents, I prepared a lengthy chronology of Port actions regarding Illahee, to which I attached nearly 400 pages of incriminating documents which we then sent to the FAA with a formal complaint alleging intentional misrepresentation and concealment by the Port. The chronology can be found in the appendix to these memoirs and is worth reading.

In our complaint of August 21, 2006, we stated:

The public records from the FAA and the Port of Walla Walla provide clear evidence of a course of intentional misrepresentation, omission, and concealment with respect to both grant applications and grant agreements.

The chronology we have prepared is attached, together with a full analysis of the misrepresentations and omissions in each grant application.

The information shows that at the same time the Port represented to the FAA that these grants were needed for runway protection, it was telling the developers and local interests that it intended to use these purchases to provide water for the planned residential development. In addition, the developers agreed to pay and have paid the Port $422,175 toward the purchase price of the property, which was not disclosed to the FAA.

In view of this misrepresentation and concealment, as well as the apparent collusion of FAA staff, we are requesting a thorough review of both grant proceedings by appropriate authorities, and that appropriate steps be taken to protect the interest of the United States and its taxpayers, prior to the payout of any further federal funds.

We were gratified by the FAA's response. On October 27, 2006, the Federal Aviation Administration issued seventy-one pages of findings resulting from its investigation. Here are the key conclusions:

1. The Port of Walla Walla "misrepresented or concealed" the objective, benefits, and parties involved in its application for federal funds to purchase the 521 acre Olson farm and deep aquifer well. Misrepresentation was defined by the FAA as "material misrepresentation of presently existing or past fact, made with knowledge of its falsity and with intention that another party rely thereon, resulting in reliance by that party to his detriment." Concealment was defined by the FAA as "the withholding of information which one in honesty and good faith is bound to reveal."

2. A major objective of the Olson acquisition "was the need for Pennbrook to obtain water for its development and the Port's desire to provide water as a revenue source."

"Four months prior to discussing the Olson property purchase with the FAA, the Port entered into numerous conversations with Pennbrook regarding the supply of water. During this time the Port received an initial assessment that the Port's current water supply was not sufficient to support Pennbrook. Prior to submitting its grant application, (the) Port entered into negotiations with Pennbrook to accept $422,175 for the purchase of the Olson farm in consideration of supplying water."

"…The Port presented to the FAA numerous justifications for the purchase including RPZ, MANPADS, 50:1 transitional zone, and uneconomic remnants. On four occasions during the application period there was an opportunity to provide the FAA with an accurate representation of the Port's interest in supplying water…"

"The Port never informed the FAA of its pending agreement with Pennbrook to accept payment with the condition of supplying water. Instead, the Port continued to mislead the FAA that the primary use of the water was for the industrial park."

3. "FAA officials failed to comply with FAA rules requiring disposal of land that is unneeded for airport protection purposes on both the Olson and the 263 acre Frazier farm acquisition grants....the Port of Walla Walla is out of compliance with the grant provision requiring such disposal...Failure to come into compliance could result in withholding of further FAA funds and a further investigation of the Port."

4. FAA officials were also found to have failed to comply with the FAA's environmental review requirements for land acquisition for both the Olson and Frazier grants. While the Olson grant has been paid out and closed, an FAA environmental review of the Frazier grant is to be conducted, and the Port of Walla Walla will be obligated to mitigate any significant impacts identified as a grant condition.

5. The Port of Walla Walla was also found to have intentionally concealed public objections to the Olson grant and failed to provide disclosure as required by FAA rules, and FAA officials failed to respond to citizen objections as required by FAA guidelines. FAA officials are to be required to respond to all citizen complaints regarding both grants.

Since the misrepresentation and concealment described amounted to criminal fraud punishable as a felony, following receipt of the findings the Port hired a Washington, D.C. lawyer to appeal them to the FAA's top administrator. While not retracting the findings of misrepresentation, the FAA then softened them by a further statement that no criminal fraud was determined to have occurred.

In addition to our complaint to the FAA, we also filed protests with the state Department of Ecology and the state Department of Health regarding water plans by the Port and Pennbrook for which the Port was misrepresenting the extent of existing water rights for its various wells, and seeking to qualify as a municipal water provider in violation of all applicable plans, policies, and regulations.

Walla Walla 2020 and Citizens for Good Governance further protested the failure of Walla Walla County to require an environmental impact statement for what was the largest development ever proposed for the Walla Walla Valley, as well as being located dangerously close to airport runways and to two hazardous chlorine storage areas.

After a county hearing examiner and the county commissioners rejected our protests, Walla Walla 2020 filed a superior court appeal naming the county and Pennbrook as respondents. This litigation resulted in a settlement requiring the developer to annex the property into the city of Walla Walla and to obtain all water from the city's supply system. Additional favorable terms were included in the settlement but not disclosed.

Owing to these delays and the subsequent downturn of the economy, the developer ultimately abandoned its plans. As a result, the land continues to be a wheat field producing a fine yield of

125 bushels a year with natural rainfall, our aquifer has been protected, and for the moment sprawling development towards the beautiful Blue Mountains has been stopped.

The Mill Creek Bike Path

The most satisfying thing to us about Walla Walla 2020 has been the many proactive community projects it has undertaken, which for the most part have had broad community support. It's been wonderful to be the initiator of a variety of positive actions rather than being cast in the more negative role of having to defend against potential harm. Still, in any effective campaign for a good quality of life, the two come paired, and there are times as with Illahee where an initiative taken by others could be seriously harmful if not resisted, and legal action among other strategies needs to be contemplated.

Part of our vision for appropriate bicycle-pedestrian facilities in our community has been the extension of the Mill Creek levee trail from Rooks Park east of the city where it is paved and highly valued, to the area through downtown Walla Walla and from there west to Gose Street.

The current Mill Creek flood control levees and channel extending from Rooks Park to Gose Street were completed around 1948. Although the county appropriated $30,000 to purchase rights of way for the flood control district, no deeds were ever recorded. As a result, some of the creekside property titles still go to the center of the creek, while others go only to the north or south fence line of the Mill Creek Flood Control District, or expressly acknowledge the rights of the flood control district in some other way.

In 1989, at the request of the Downtown Walla Walla Foundation, 2020 had reviewed all of the existing trails and plans in the area and had devised a loop trail between Rooks Park east of town and the Whitman Mission the west, with a trailhead in downtown Walla Walla and connectors to College Place.

A critical portion of the northern trail follows the north side of Highway 12 west to Washington Park, then continues on the north levee of Mill Creek from Ninth Avenue to Gose Street. Though not paved, this portion of the levee has been used by pedestrians, bicyclists, horsemen, and others for over sixty years.

In order to link this portion of the trail with the trailhead in downtown Walla Walla, 2020 had gotten the US Army Corps of Engineers to include a bicycle-pedestrian path along the Mill Creek at its new downtown headquarters.

In monitoring development plans for the old cannery site along Mill Creek from Seventh to Ninth, we discovered that the City was not implementing the Shorelines Management Act along Mill Creek through the city, though legally required to do so. As a result of 2020 contacts with the state Department of Ecology, the city is now in compliance, and the community has a new tool and leverage in working with creekside developers in order to assure appropriate public recreation access along its principal waterway. This helped 2020 secure another block of bicycle pedestrian trail when new apartments were being built a block below the Corps , and has also

199

been useful in assuring the inclusion of a trail along Mill Creek in the planned development of the old cannery site to the west.

Walla Walla County had long recognized and facilitated the traditional public use of the levee between Thirteenth and Gose by the installation of bicycle-pedestrian gates at Thirteenth, Irene and Gose, as well as by the replacement in the early 1990's of the previous coarse surface gravel with finer gravel for easier walking and biking by the public.

After 2020's involvement in the enforcement of Shoreline Management rules, the public use of that portion of the levee was also recognized and aided by the City of Walla Walla at the time of the construction of a new hotel and other commercial buildings on the north bank of Mill Creek creek along Pine Street. At 2020's urging, at that time the City conditioned its shoreline permits on the provision of improved access to the north levee for bicyclists and pedestrians.

In 2007, when the cities of Walla Walla and College Place and Walla Walla County agreed on a major construction project to extend Myra Road across Mill Creek, their initial plans were also consistent with this use, including a long bridge that would have continued to allow passage along the levees by the public. Because of that, neither 2020 nor anyone else made any objections, and the county gave environmental approval and a shorelines permit for the south side of the bridge which is in its jurisdiction.

As the north side of the creek is in the city of Walla Walla, a city shorelines permit was also required. Unfortunately, a few days before the city planning commission hearing on the permit, in order to cut costs, the design was changed by the County to lower the bridge to a height that would obstruct passage by bikes and pedestrians along both levees, without notice to the public or consultation with bike-pedestrian groups or users regarding the change.

When Walla Walla 2020 learned of this, we asked that a new environmental statement be prepared because of the significant impact this change would have. The city's planning commission hearing was attended by interested users, and the commission recommended that the shoreline permit be conditioned on safe passage by bicyclists and pedestrians. The matter then went to the city council on Jan. 24 where it was sent back to the planning commission for a rehearing and any additional environmental review found to be necessary after proper notice to the public.

The county commissioners' response was to authorize the posting of No Trespassing signs and the closing off of access points to the levees, apparently thinking this would avoid the need to accommodate further public use of the levees.

Walla Walla 2020 and others then met with the County public works director to discuss ways to accommodate the needed cost saving as well as continued walker and bicycle use of the levees. As a result, an at-grade pedestrian-bicycle crossing was incorporated into the project design. However, the closure of the levees by the county commissioners remained.

Walla Walla 2020 then notified the County that the closure of the levees constituted a significant environmental impact, and violated the Shorelines Management Act as well as the City's

Shoreline Master Plan. We also noted that under the Act, interested parties have twenty-one days from the filing of the permit with the Department of Ecology to appeal to the Shorelines Hearing Board.

We were aware of the tight funding timetable for the project, and told the county that they had an opportunity prior to the filing of any appeal to remove the current obstacles to further public use of the levees, and return the situation to the status quo.

We were subject to considerable criticism by adjacent landowners and others for potentially derailing state funding of the bridge project and interfering with private property rights, but we knew that if we didn't act to preserve the public's rights to use the levees, they could be lost permanently, so we took the heat. The result was that the levees were opened again, no appeal was filed, and the bridge was built with additional at-grade crossings of the new road for bicycles and pedestrians, together with some ability to actually cross under the bridge itself. From Walla Walla 2020's standpoint, reasonable accommodations had been made for the needs of all of the parties, and the result was a success.

Mullan Road Historic Site

An important event in Walla Walla history was the building of the Mullan Road to link the steamship dock at old Fort Walla Walla on the Columbia River and the new fort in the city of Walla Walla with the steamship dock at Fort Benton, Montana on the Missouri River.

The construction by Lieutenant John Mullan and his crew of 100 soldiers and 100 civilians began in June of 1859 in Walla Walla and returned to Walla Walla from Fort Benton in October, 1860. After repairs and rerouting beginning in 1861, in August of 1862 the 655 mile road including an already existing portion from Wallula to Walla Walla was finally completed. The project provided a route for pioneer families, miners, and supplies between the two major rivers, and created the first engineered highway in the northwest.

In 1866, a memorial to the US Congress by the Montana territorial legislature pleaded for the road to be improved and reminded Congress of "the necessity for a great national highway connecting the Missouri and Columbia rivers by a good and substantial wagon road," noting that "What was a wilderness now contains a large and rapidly increasing population, producing millions of bushels of grain and millions of dollars per annum in gold and silver. The opening of this road is of the greatest, most vital importance to the people of Washington, Idaho, and that portion of Montana lying west of the Rocky Mountains."

The memorial goes on, "From Jan. 1, to Nov. 15, 1866, 1500 head of horses have been purchased by individual miners at Walla Walla; 5000 head of cattle were driven from Walla Walla to Montana; 6000 mules have left the Columbia River and Walla Walla loaded with freight for Montana; 52 light wagons with families have left Walla Walla for Montana; 31 wagons with immigrants have come through from the States via the Mullan Road, a portion of whom settled in Walla Walla valley… not less than 20,000 persons have passed over the Mullan road to and from Montana during the past season; $1,000,000 in treasure has passed down through Walla Walla and Wallula during the same period."

In the Walla Walla area, the route of the Mullan Road began at the Fort Walla Walla military garrison, now the site of the US Veterans Administration Medical Center, and proceeded north in the vicinity of what is now 13th Avenue through the current grounds of the Washington State Penitentiary to Dry Creek, and from there on across the Touchet and Snake rivers north to the Spokane River, before turning east to the Missouri.

In 1923, a formal ceremony was held to place a Mullan Road marker on the grounds of the penitentiary, presented by the governor of Washington State and accepted by the president of the Walla Walla Pioneer Association. In 1994, because of visitor restrictions on the grounds of the penitentiary the marker was moved to Fort Walla Walla Park.

One of the last projects of long-time journalist and historian Vance Orchard before his death in March, 2006 was the circulation of a proposal that 13th Avenue, the historic route of the Mullan Road, be renamed Mullan Avenue in order to provide fitting recognition of this historic accomplishment which meant so much to the early development of the Walla Walla area.

In order to honor both Vance and the Mullan Road, that month Walla Walla 2020 presented a letter to the Walla Walla city council signed by the heads of a variety of local historical and tourism organizations along with the superintendent of the penitentiary. The letter proposed that 13th Avenue, which runs from the original grounds of Fort Walla Walla to the city limits at the penitentiary, be renamed Mullan Avenue, "in order to properly designate this historic route, in keeping with Walla Walla's development as a center of history and tourism, and as a tribute to John Mullan, Vance Orchard, and the many others who worked on and traveled this road."

No action was taken on the petition at the time, but in connection with the 150th anniversary in 2009 of both the founding of the town of Walla Walla and the start of construction on the Mullan Road, I brought the issue up again, as well as for the 2012 sesquicentennial of the completion of the road and the granting of the city's municipal charter by the territorial legislature in 1862.

I had suggested to the Downtown Foundation, Tourism Walla Walla, and the City of Walla Walla in 2008 that a committee be organized to celebrate the 2009 sesquicentennial. That effort resulted in the commissioning and placement of a bronze monument at Second and Main depicting the first nine wood buildings that were erected in the town in 1859. Beyond that, the committee hoped to see a three-year series of commemorative events culminating in 2012 on the 150th anniversary of the establishment of city government under the municipal charter granted in 1862.

By that time 13th Street was being reconstructed with federal and state funds, including the building of a stormwater swale on a small piece of city land at the corner of 13th & Abadie, which an old map showed to have been an original corner of the Fort Walla Walla military reservation. In addition to proposing that 13th be double-signed as Historic Mullan Road as part of the Walla Walla sesquicentennial celebrations, our Walla Walla 2020 Historic Research Project proposed that the story of the Mullan Road be told in a series of interpretive signs to be installed around the swale, which would become a Mullan Road Historic Site.

To try to accomplish this I brought together a committee of city officials along with some interested citizens to look at the site and the potential signage I drafted, as well as some landscaping concepts. The city manager then suggested that Chris Freshley, the Portland landscape architect working with the City on the 13th Street project, would be a good resource for the design of the site. Chris prepared some conceptual plans that were ultimately approved by the committee and the city council.

While working on this, I learned that the organizers of a Mullan Road conference held each year somewhere in the northwest had been interested in coming to Walla Walla in 2012, but didn't think there was interest here. In order to add to our focus on the Mullan Road, I contacted the conference chair, Eastern Washington University historian Bill Youngs, and invited the organizers to bring the conference to Walla Walla. Bill said they had been planning to hold it in Cheney in 2012, but would be glad to work with our committee and Walla Walla 2020 to move it to Walla Walla.

What evolved from that was a fine partnership and a highly successful 2012 Mullan Road Conference from April 13-15 at Walla Walla's VA Medical Center on the grounds of the historic Fort Walla Walla, including a bus tour of the route of the Mullan Road from Walla Walla to Prescott based on early surveys we had found and overlaid onto Google Earth. The conference culminated with the rededication of the Mullan Road monument which the City had moved to our planned Mullan Road Historic Site, in connection with which we displayed examples of our proposed interpretive signage to conference attendees and the public at a reception at the nearby Foundry Vineyards.

The final year of our sesquicentennial celebrations began with a living history presentation to the Walla Walla city council on the date of the granting of the original charter, featuring Walla Walla's first mayor E.B. Whitman who was elected in April of that year, along with other living history company members portraying Walla Walla residents of 1862. Other events planned by an expanded Walla Walla Sesquicentennial Committee included the placement of permanent "Historic Mullan Road" street signs along 13th Street, the creation and hanging of banners and posters throughout the downtown and the community; the issuance of a commemorative coin with a drawing on one side of the original military fort around which the town was built and a portrait of John Mullan on the other; tours of the historic downtown prepared and led by Mayor Whitman along with several other characters from the 1860's; a sesquicentennial sculpture competition; and a Victorian Ball at the Walla Walla Armory.

In 2013, I served as the dance master for Walla Walla's second Victorian Ball presented by the Kirkman House Museum, and plans were still in process to complete the Mullan Road Historic Site.

According to Idaho State Historian Keith Petersen who is writing a book on Mullan and has reviewed our plans and proposed signage, "Your interpretive facility is going to be the finest interpretation of the Mullan Road anywhere. Congratulations on an outstanding project." Let's hope this prophecy is fulfilled.

Historic Cemeteries

Another initiative of Walla Walla 2020 in 2012 has focused on honoring historic cemeteries, including the little known County Poor Farm Cemetery and McCool Catholic Cemetery.

The County Poor Farm

I was always curious about a large tract of land labeled "Poor Farm" I saw on old maps while volunteering for the Walla Walla 2020 Historic Research & Plaque Project. In searching for it on the ground I discovered a large grassy plot in College Place with two or three tombstones leaning against a couple of old locust trees in the midst of the Country Estates mobile home park.

After further investigation with the help of Mary Meeker, our lead 2020 researcher, we identified the plot as the historic cemetery for the county's 200-acre Poor Farm established in 1891 where indigents were sent to live and work. The Poor Farm was closed when the Social Security system was created as part of Franklin Roosevelt's New Deal in the 1930's, which relieved counties of sole responsibility for the poor.

When there were deaths at the farm, the indigent residents were buried in what became known as the Poor Farm Cemetery. Most graves were marked just with small concrete cylinders bearing only a number. Family and friends could find the name and grave location of persons buried there by consulting records at the county courthouse, which had been lost for many years. They have recently been found after a new search at the courthouse which I requested.

Several upright gravestones had also been placed on graves by family or friends. After the cemetery had fallen into disuse, these stones were removed, the concrete cylinders were covered with dirt, and grass was planted over them in 1973. Playground equipment was also installed over the graves at one point, then later removed, though the footings remain. Title to the cemetery was transferred by Walla Walla County to the City of College Place in 1965.

Walla Walla 2020 has prepared signage honoring the cemetery and its nearly seven hundred inhabitants, as well as the Poor Farm itself, whose large home and barn are still standing nearby. We're hopeful the City of College Place will approve its placement in order to respectfully commemorate and mark this historic institution and its grounds.

The McCool Catholic Cemetery

I had heard about the digging up of bodies behind Walla Walla's Plaza Shopping Center about ten years ago when the area was being considered for further development.

When Pine Crest Village and Village Way were developed in the 1970's, multiple burials were encountered during construction of streets and residences in the area of an historic Catholic cemetery, and were reported to law enforcement authorities, though no action was taken to halt development or to otherwise protect the burials. By the time further construction was contemplated in 2002, our state legislature had adopted the Abandoned and Historic Cemeteries Act (RCW Chapter 68.60). Because the Act prohibits the destruction of historic graves, before proceeding with new construction two archaeological studies were conducted.

The first study encountered the burial of a Native American sitting in an upright position with no coffin, dating back more than 150 years, and indicating that this burial ground may have pre-dated European settlement. The second archaeological study found additional burials with coffins both inside and outside of the recorded boundaries of the historic cemetery. As a result, the boundaries of the original cemetery have been expanded to incorporate the ground where those additional burials have been found, pursuant to the protective provisions of the Act.

According to authors Harriet & Adrian Munnick in their book "Catholic Church Records of the Pacific Northwest," the first Catholic chapel in Walla Walla was built in 1859 at Third & Birch. In 1864 it was replaced by a frame church building at Sixth & Alder where the current St. Patrick's Church stands, and the first Catholic cemetery was located behind it to the south. The first burial recorded in that cemetery appears from church records to have been on October 9, 1859. Ten years later, because of overcrowding at St. Patrick's cemetery, on September 30, 1869 the Bishop of Nisqually obtained a deed from Robert and Margaret McCool for a 450' x 152' plot of land lying just south of the current Highway 125 to Milton-Freewater and west of the Plaza Shopping Center complex.

In October 1891, after ten years of overcrowding at the McCool cemetery, a ten acre plot south of the Mountain View city cemetery was purchased by the Catholic Church as a new cemetery. It was expected at the time that many of those having family or friends at McCool would move them to the new cemetery.

The Catholic Bishop of Spokane sold the McCool cemetery grounds to developers on October 31, 1969. More recently, the pastor of St. Patrick church gave the current owner of the McCool property a letter dated January 11, 2002 verifying that the cemetery "has been abandoned, and that all of the bodies formerly interred there were exhumed and reinterred at Mountain View Cemetery of Walla Walla." Unfortunately, that was not the case.

An article in the Walla Walla Union Journal from October 26, 1891 announcing plans for a new Catholic cemetery at Mountain View makes clear that McCool was the cemetery for Walla Walla's St. Patrick parish from 1869-1891. The article states, "The need for a new cemetery for the Catholic Church has been long felt, and the congregation on a number of occasions have endeavored to secure grounds in the vicinity of the old cemetery, but have always been unable to do so. The old burial ground, on the McCool farm, below the city, has been in use for nearly a quarter of a century and for the past ten years has been overcrowded." The overcrowding at McCool was confirmed by the second archaeological study there, which discovered that several graves contained newer coffins placed on top of older coffins.

Regarding the fate of the original cemetery near the church, the Munnicks write, "A pioneer woman who lived at the rear of the church when a child, recalled that as far back as 1903 she could peep through a high board fence and see stones with inscriptions still standing there, but remembered none of the names. Many of the graves, but not all, had been removed to the Catholic section of Mountain View Cemetery that opened in 1891. No trace of the others remains."

In church burial records for Walla Walla from 1869, when McCool was purchased, to 1891 when the new cemetery at Mountain View was established, most of the entries, including many French and some Indian names, are silent as to burial location and are assumed to have taken place at McCool.

In order to determine the names of those likely still at McCool, I reviewed the original burial records at St. Patrick Church, as well as re-interment records at the Catholic Cemetery at Mountain View which replaced it. Of the more than 400 Catholic burials shown in Walla Walla church records for this period, fewer than 120 are shown to have been reinterred at the Catholic cemetery at Mountain View, though another 30 there are listed as unknowns and might have come from McCool. That leaves approximately 250 burials presumed still to be at McCool.

In inspecting the McCool cemetery, I discovered that the east half is on the grounds of the new Affinity retirement facility which has respectfully overlaid it with an irrigation system, planted grass, and installed a rock trail and some benches. I've indicated to Affinity that the only thing lacking is appropriate signage to identify the cemetery, its history, and those still buried there, whose tombstones have long since been removed.

The west half of the cemetery is owned by the estate of the original developer, and is currently covered in weeds, with no markings of its boundaries. I've talked with the administrator of the estate, who hopes to transfer the burials there to the Mountain View Cemetery and to sell the ground for home sites.

In October, 2012, I was asked to lead a class at Walla Walla Community College on a tour of historic cemeteries, including Frenchtown, the Poor Farm, and McCool. As with the Poor Farm, Walla Walla 2020 is ready to assist with the design and cost of appropriate signage honoring this historic cemetery and those buried there.

Coal Plant Working Group

In early 2007, a consortium of multinational companies led by Edison Energy in cooperation with Mitsubishi Heavy Industries proposed to construct a coal-fueled power plant at the western end of Walla Walla County, and to attempt to sequester part of the carbon dioxide that would be generated by the plant into the deep basalt rock formations underlying the Columbia Basin of eastern Washington, southwestern Idaho, and northern Oregon.

Out of concern for the health of our community and the planet, I suggested that Walla Walla 2020 form an ad hoc committee to study this proposal, which soon developed into an independent body called the Coal Plant Working Group. At the same time, Walla Walla 2020 continued to play an active role regarding the issue, including correspondence with various governmental agencies, gathering public records and information, and organizing a scientific panel to review plans for a related sequestration study by Battelle/Pacific Northwest Laboratories, headquartered in Richland.

Whitman College geologist Bob Carson, one of our members, described the issue this way in a column for the Walla Walla Union-Bulletin:

> Wallula Energy Resource Company proposes to build a coal-fired plant to produce electricity in Walla Walla County. The plant is new technology, integrated gasification combined cycle (IGCC), and the intent is to pump 65% of the carbon dioxide (CO_2) that is generated deep into the basaltic lava flows beneath Wallula.
>
> The phrase "clean coal" is an oxymoron. Coal is a killer, from locally where it is mined to the entire earth, as a result of its combustion products. Coal mining is a hazardous occupation; many miners die quickly from rock failure, explosions, poison gas, and slowly from black-lung disease, among other related causes. The Wallula coal will come by train more than 900 miles from eastern Wyoming, where open-pit mines ravage the landscape.
>
> Coal plants release toxic mercury, and more radioactivity than nuclear power plants. Burning coal (which contains sulfur compounds) with air (which is 78% nitrogen) generates sulfur and nitrogen oxides which combine with water in the atmosphere to make acid rain that kills plants and fish, and leaches nutrients and toxic heavy metals from the soil.
>
> Carbon dioxide (CO_2) is causing global climate change. Not only is the earth warming, but there is also a tendency for wet places to get wetter, for dry places to get drier, and, because a warmer atmosphere and ocean have more energy, for more extreme weather events. Approximately half of the CO_2 emitted is taken up by our oceans, which then become more acidic. The warmer climate affects most species, from polar bears to malaria-bearing mosquitoes.
>
> A grave problem with global warming is the melting of glaciers. Washington State has lost one third of its glacial ice since 1950. We will probably be able to compensate because of other water supplies, but the Andes and Himalayas will likely lose 80% of their glacier volume within three decades. In winter, mountains store water both in snow and glaciers. Melting snow provides a spring/early summer water supply, whereas melting glaciers is often the chief water supply in late summer/fall. The economies of hundreds of millions of people dependent on glacial-melt water will be hard hit. Coastal wetlands, which are nurseries for fish, are being drowned and eroded by higher sea levels. Flooding and wave erosion from tropical storms go farther inland.
>
> Though the design of the IGCC plant proposed at Wallula is less polluting than a conventional coal plant, toxic elements in the coal will still go up the stack and into the Walla Walla Valley. What will be the effects of the pollutants on our residents, vineyards, and water, as they blow into our valley? Would the injected CO_2 pollute our

207

precious groundwater? Would it leak, resulting in the significant killing of plants or animals? Might the injection trigger an earthquake?

Just say no to our Port Commission, our County Commissioners, and the Washington State Energy Facility Site Evaluation Council, which will ultimately decide this question. Just say no to coal.

In July, 2007 Wallula Energy Resource Company, a wholly-owned subsidiary of Edison Mission Energy, in cooperation with a Wallula Resource Recovery LLC (WRR) which included a company called United Power, signed a letter of intent with the Port of Walla Walla to purchase Port land at Wallula to locate a 600-700 megawatt integrated gasification combined cycle (IGCC) coal-fueled power plant there.

In September of that year, the federal Department of Energy awarded a grant to a regional energy group called the Big Sky Partnership to fund a planned basalt sequestration test and to move it from the Hanford Nuclear Reservation near Richland to the Port's land at Wallula. United Power agreed to provide the required 20% non-federal cost-share for the Wallula site in the amount of $1.5 million, since a successful sequestration test was critical to the siting of its coal plant.

In October, the developers of the coal plant filed a request with the Washington State Energy Facility Site Evaluation Council for a potential site study, the first step in the state licensing process for their Wallula plant, which they call the Wallula Energy Resource Center Project, a 700 MW coal-fueled IGCC power plant.

In addition to signing a letter of intent for the sale of part of its Wallula property for the proposed coal plant, the Port of Walla Walla asked the Walla Walla County Commissioners to re-designate additional land at Wallula as a heavy industry zone in order to facilitate further power plant siting there.

The December 3, 2007 hearing on the Port's rezoning request by the county commissioners was a first test of the strength of our protests. Quite a few Whitman College students joined community members in testifying against the possibility of one or more coal plants at Wallula. In the past, testimony by college students at hearings by local government had been ignored, particularly by county commissioners who routinely approve all development applications, but also by more open-minded city officials. This time was different. To our surprise, following the hearing the commissioners voted to refuse the Port's request, and to prohibit the location of further power plants at Wallula.

This was a very encouraging result, but didn't affect the land planned for the Wallula Energy Resource Center plant, so our next focus was on the Port commissioners themselves. Noting that the letter of intent with the developers had an early expiration date, Walla Walla 2020 challenged the Port's commitment of the land on environmental grounds, noting that the Port had not adopted environmental policies as required by state law, and had not done any environmental analysis regarding its proposed action.

After further input by a statewide student group we were coordinating with, as well as the Coal Plant Working Group and Walla Walla 2020, in early March, 2008 the Port commissioners announced that they would not allow the sequestration test to continue on Port land unless many questions were answered regarding risks and liabilities, and agreed that environmental compliance was required.

At that point, because of the Port's reluctance, United Power contacted the state Department of Natural Resources to seek permission for the sequestration test by Battelle to be performed on adjoining land owned by DNR at Wallula .

Near the end of March, the developers' request for a state siting study for the coal plant was withdrawn, citing a delay in testing by Battelle which it said was crucial for their licensing application. The developer's spokesperson said they would re-file their request following successful testing.

In April, our Coal Plant Working Group launched a petition drive against both the testing and the planned coal plant at Wallula, obtaining over 1200 signatures that we presented to the Port commission, the Walla Walla county commissioners, and DNR.

In May, Walla Walla 2020 wrote to DNR noting the considerable public controversy surrounding the proposed test and coal plant, and requesting strict environmental compliance by DNR with regard to siting of the test on DNR land. The statewide group Students for Cleaner Energy also presented a photo petition to DNR featuring approximately 800 students, college personnel, and other citizens across Washington State opposed to the proposed plant and test, including people from Walla Walla, Olympia, Centralia, Auburn, Tacoma, and Seattle.

In early June, DNR notified Battelle of its refusal to allow the test on DNR land, citing a substantial public outcry and DNR concerns about a lengthy legal battle.

While Battelle arranged for a significantly reduced sequestration test at the nearby Boise Cascade paper mill at Wallula, the death knell for the proposed coal plant came when the financial backers of the plant withdrew, ending this threat to the Walla Walla Valley, at least for the time being.

Sustainable Walla Walla

A conference on Global Change, Local Challenge was hosted by our three local colleges in November, 2007 in response to growing evidence of global climate change and the peaking of fossil fuel-based energy production. The conference was the culmination of many months of work by a committee convened by Barbara that included scientists from each of the three colleges.

While some people such as Barbara had been aware of these problems for quite awhile, for others including me, the conference was a wake-up call about a serious challenge to a fundamental element of modern society, which is cheap energy based on the use of nonrenewable and climate-changing fossil fuels, as highlighted by keynote speaker Richard Heinberg.

In order to gauge the reality of the threat to nearly every aspect of our current life as described by Heinberg, I organized a ten-week Walla Walla 2020 study group on Global Changes and Local Responses focusing on the books Power Down by Heinberg, and Overshoot by William Catton. In addition, we read and discussed the Low-Carbon Diet—A 30 Day Program to Lose 5000 Pounds by David Gershon, as well as the Transition Primer on how to organize a community for sustainability.

At the end of our ten weeks of study, we surveyed the twenty or so participants and nearly all were in agreement with the following conclusions:

  1. Humans have overshot earth's carrying capacity
  2. Humanity should reduce its population numbers
  3. Humanity is facing an unprecedented crisis and must plan appropriate responses, since
  4. Worldwide oil production is nearing its peak
  5. Natural gas production is near peaking
  6. Significant disruptions of current systems are likely to occur
  7. Significant global warming is occurring
  8. We need to significantly reduce our carbon footprint
  9. Walla Walla should begin planning to become a transition town or lifeboat community.
  10. We should form a group called Sustainable Walla Walla to educate the community about these facts and initiate planning.

The goal of Sustainable Walla Walla (SuWW) was to provide community education on sustainability issues leading to the preparation of a community-wide sustainability plan. To accomplish that, we sponsored a well-attended community forum called "The Road Ahead;" circulated a petition to the Walla Walla City Council signed by over 1100 people calling for the establishment of a city sustainability committee; sponsored a Victory Garden tour; promoted re-skilling classes in traditional survival arts; offered a 12-week show on Whitman College's KWCW radio called FutureWalla which Barbara and I hosted; presented a weekly Community Conversation Cafe on sustainability issues, also hosted by the Clarks; and issued a number of weekly Sustainability Bulletins listing relevant events and providing useful quotes.

SuWW members were also instrumental in the formation of the Religious Leaders Sustainability Group, later changed to the Walla Walla Valley Faith Communities for Sustainability, which I chair, whose purpose is to pursue education and action on sustainability issues among local religious congregations. One of the ongoing projects of Faith Communities is an annual Alternative Gifts campaign to reduce throwaways and unnecessary consumption.

On August 27, 2008, the Walla Walla City Council agreed to establish an Ad Hoc Sustainability Committee to make recommendations to the council regarding the possibility of a permanent committee. Following the Ad Hoc committee's report, on February 10, 2010 the council adopted an ordinance providing for a permanent sustainability committee to do scenario planning for the community, and to advise city government on sustainability issues.

In order to supplement and integrate the work of the new City committee in our region, SuWW's own role in future sustainability planning and actions will be to continue to provide advocacy, education, coordination, and networking on sustainability issues for the Walla Walla area.

Sustainable Walla Walla meetings are held approximately quarterly to bring together local colleges, government agencies, businesses, and interested individuals to share plans and projects, and to continue to do community education. The group's projects have included a website which I edit, Green Commute competitions during Earth Week, periodic sustainability columns, and the publishing of weekly sustainability tips in our local newspaper.

Community Gardening

A great way to help build self-sufficiency, resilience, and stronger neighborhoods is to establish a community garden. Besides growing fruits and vegetables, a community garden grows community. At least that's what we discovered at the Rees and Sumach Community Garden sponsored by our North Main Area Neighborhood Association.

I've never been a very systematic gardener, but I've always enjoyed growing vegetables and fruits, whether on rural or urban plots. Since moving to town, in addition to having a small garden on our own land, I've been on the lookout for vacant lots that might serve as a shared garden.

Encouraged by the focus on community food security by Sustainable Walla Walla and Faith Communities for Sustainability, in late 2008 I began exploring the possibility of using a nearby vacant lot owned by Whitman College as a community garden.

With the support of Bob Biles who heads the Whitman grounds crew and had responsibility for that lot, I proposed the garden be sponsored by our North Main Area Neighborhood Association, as well as by Walla Walla 2020, which maintains an insurance policy on its Xeriscape Park in our neighborhood that might be extended to cover the garden. Both groups approved, and I approached Whitman College treasurer Peter Harvey with a proposal to lease the land from the college at a nominal rent of $1 per year for a community garden, to which the college, as a good neighbor, agreed.

Next we organized a garden committee which included Bob Biles as our garden master, and began planning during 2009 for the launch of the new garden in 2010. Since that time, here's what we've accomplished:

---Negotiated and signed a lease for the garden site with Whitman College
---Obtained formal sponsorship by the North Main Area Neighborhood Association
---Obtained insurance through a partnership with Walla Walla 2020
---Received outreach assistance from Commitment to Community
---Obtained parking area fill from the City of Walla Walla
---Established twelve initial working groups for garden organization
---Appointed a garden coordinator and a garden master

---Received an initial grant from the Walla Walla Friends Meeting
---Adopted a work plan and time table for opening the garden
---Adopted garden rules
---Adopted a garden layout
---Began to enrich the soil
---Installed a garden sign
---Began the application process for individual plots
---Rototilled the full garden site several times, working in compost materials
---Adopted a budget and resource plan
-- Assigned plots
---Organized & offered gardening classes
---Installed a fence
---Installed an irrigation system & pathways
---Built a tool shed
---Planted 30 individual plots and five common areas
---Received several additional grants and private donations
---Donated hundreds of pounds of produce to local food banks each year
---Beautified our neighborhood
---Had a great time meeting our neighbors, increasing our gardening skills, and harvesting and
   sharing our produce.
---Installed a beautiful sculptured archway into the garden
---Installed a green house.

As garden coordinator until just recently, when I happily passed those duties on to others, I've found this project to be one of the most satisfying undertakings of my life, providing daily pleasure as Barbara and I go by and often through the garden on our morning walk and return regularly to work on our own plot in the garden or on some tasks in the common areas.

There are many community gardens in the Pacific Northwest and elsewhere that we can all learn from, including our own. I heartily recommend the experience.

Saving Valley Transit

Barbara and I have been involved in many political campaigns over our more than 45 years of marriage, including our own, but the successful campaign to save our local bus system from devastating cuts was one of the most satisfying of all.

In August 2008, our Walla Walla 2020 transportation committee discussed the chronic underfunding of our local transit system, and sent a formal letter to the board of Valley Transit urging an increase in the local sales tax for transit, and pledging our support for a ballot measure to accomplish that, stating in part:

> Regarding long-term transit planning for the Walla Walla area, we agree with the statement in Washington law that the maintenance and operation of an adequate public transportation system is an absolute necessity and is essential to the economic, industrial

and cultural growth, development and prosperity of a municipality and of the state and nation, and to protect the health and welfare of the residents of such municipalities and the public in general….

We are concerned that available funding may not be sufficient in the long-term to provide for increases in operating costs necessary to meet the expanded demand for transit services due to growth in our community, rising individual transportation costs, long-term challenges to our economy, and efforts to reduce greenhouse gas emissions….

We know that local funding for current Valley Transit services comes from the Public Transit Benefit Area through a 0.3% sales tax (out of the allowable 0.6%). As the board reviews future service needs and costs, including increasing frequency of service and expansion of routes to serve public transit needs of existing neighborhoods and new developments, we encourage you to consider increasing the local sales tax rate as an option to assure VT's ability to maintain existing services as well as to provide needed upgrades. We understand that this would require a ballot issue within the PTBA, which we would be willing to actively support at an appropriate time.

Since the transit board is made up of elected officials, we knew it would be reluctant to propose a tax increase unless it was unavoidable. However, we wanted to put the idea on the table to be revisited when an occasion arose, which didn't take long. In August, 2009 Valley Transit was in the midst of a financial crisis, and the board had decided to begin making serious cuts in services.

On learning this, our 2020 transportation committee arranged a meeting with the transit manager to discuss the idea of putting a tax increase on the ballot and postponing any cuts until after the vote. He wanted to know who else besides the 2020 transportation committee would support such a measure, and was not optimistic that his board would give it a try, since the board had already taken this up, considered it impossible, and had ruled it out.

I then enlisted the support of the Walla Walla Valley Faith Communities for Sustainability group that I chair, which agreed to present a proposal for a ballot campaign to the transit board, and then called a community-wide meeting to rally support and put together a campaign committee. Though the board believed there would be no support for an election campaign among either riders or the general public, at hearings the district held on how to make its planned cuts we generated a large turnout, and also gathered over 2000 signatures on a petition calling for a vote and asking the district to put off any cuts until the ballot results were in. With this unexpected urging, as well as pledges of about $20,000 toward the campaign including a major donation from their employees' union, the board agreed to put the measure on the February 2010 ballot, and to hold off on any service cuts until the election results were in, just as we had requested.

The co-chairs of the Campaign for Valley Transit were city council member, chair of the Valley Transit board, and at that time Mayor Barbara Clark, along with Jack Barga, a retired physician and respected member of the social action committee of the local Catholic churches. I was the campaign manager, our friend Norm Osterman handled voter canvassing, and the local transit union steward Mark Brotherton and his wife Georgie were in charge of the donated campaign headquarters I arranged on Main Street thanks to community-minded landlords Rick and Debbie Johnson. For our advertising, we hired campaign consultant John Wyble from Seattle, recommended to us by the statewide group Transportation Options, who were very interested in the campaign because of its importance to other transit systems facing similar problems.

Our local newspaper, the Union-Bulletin, had editorialized against both putting the issue on the ballot and delaying service cuts until after the election, so it was important to get early endorsements from community leaders and area businesses. I started with the presidents of our three local colleges as a good base to build on. Walla Walla Community College president Steve VanAusdle weighed in first with a very strong letter to the transit board stressing the importance of the transit system to their students and staff, as well as to the economic and cultural well-being of the whole community. Whitman College president George Bridges also sent an excellent endorsement letter, as did Walla Walla University president John McVay, who did some personal doorbelling in neighboring College Place where transit is very important. With this base, we were able to obtain endorsements from leaders of twenty other nonprofit organizations and agencies in the community.

Our next target was local businesses, since we wanted to avoid opposition by the Chamber of Commerce and the business community in general, which are often hostile to tax increases. We began with the businesses whose owners are particularly community-minded, and building on their support, wound up with endorsements in all sectors of our local economy, including hospitals, medical and dental clinics, banks, grocery stores, restaurants, realty companies, hair dressers, book stores, art studios, the construction industry, general retailers, and others. From a business sector that rarely takes public stands on political issues, we received over 110 public endorsements—a rare accomplishment.

Our publicity campaign consisted of letters to the editor, print ads, yard signs, the original song "Thank Goodness for the Bus" written and sung by Barbara to accompany a YouTube slide show put together by Norm featuring local riders, a campaign brochure, mailers to voters, a website I put together, and a Facebook page.

To top it off, Norm recruited a fine group of volunteers for doorbelling and telephoning, and we made a special effort to register and mobilize students and Latino voters, working from our very visible headquarters on Main Street where our campaign committee met weekly. Georgie and Mark kept the headquarters staffed, including a great group of transit employees and members of the community, who also stood on street corners holding signs the final week of the election campaign in which ballots were cast by mail.

When we began, there was a lot of talk in the community about transit buses running empty, serving only a small segment of the population who should be paying the costs themselves, and being irrelevant to most people. By the end of the campaign we were convinced that we had educated the community about how critical public transportation is for everyone, in part by answering their questions in our campaign materials in this way:

> **Why are transit services important to our community?** Public transportation helps people get to work and school, shop at area businesses, get needed services, and participate as active citizens. It gives energy to our whole community by giving everyone

the freedom and mobility to accomplish what is important to them. Good transit service is critical to our quality of life and economic vitality.

How efficient is our transit system? Valley Transit provides approximately 800,000 rides a year. Carrying 2600 a day, an average of 27 passengers per hour per bus, it is among the top transit systems in the state as far as passengers per bus per hour, and lowest operating cost per hour.

What's the problem? After 19 years of operation, Valley Transit lost half its regular funding with the elimination of the Motor Vehicle Excise Tax in 2000. An expected source of dependable federal funding has now been eliminated and local sales tax revenue has been falling. Without additional revenues, service will need to be cut 50% by the end of the current biennium, which would eliminate most or all fixed routes.

Can fare increases solve the problem? To help generate additional revenues, the Valley Transit board has tripled fares from 25 cents to 75 cents. Even with this increase, fare revenues bring in less than 10% of annual expenditures, and need to be supplemented by other sources. Transit systems in Washington State are supported mostly by sales tax revenues. Valley Transit currently receives 0.3%, while most transit systems in the state receive 0.6%. Increasing Valley Transit's rate to the state average for transit systems in the February 9 election will provide reliable, local revenue that will allow it to continue all existing services.

Shortly after 8 pm on February 9, 2010 the election results were in. The Valley Transit measure passed 76.3% to 23.7%--an astounding victory for any tax increase in our conservative community, but particularly for one during a recession—by a greater margin than for any ballot issue in memory, thanks to all those who supported the campaign. Working together, we made the Walla Walla-College Place area a stronger community for everyone.

What's Next...?

In my 70th year, though I don't see an end of projects or opportunities, I do see the need to pass many of them on to younger people, together with whatever lessons I've learned over the years in both active pursuits and quieter ones. In the meantime, I expect to continue to be an active participant in our community and world.

APPENDEX A: AN UPDATE, 2013-2016

A variety of new projects have come along since 2013, including the Walla Walla 2020 Historic Sites and Markers Project; the Noetic Council and the Unitive Self Study Group, along with community college classes and two books on the nature of the self; the Walla Walla Alliance for the Homeless; several dance events and classes, and a dance book; and more.

The Walla Walla 2020 Historic Sites & Markers Project

In 2012, our Walla Walla 2020 Historic Research & Plaque Project, which I coordinate, began looking beyond individual research requests to sites that were important to the broader community, but whose history was often unknown.

In addition to the 2012 planning for a Mullan Road Historic Site at 13th and Abadie discussed in Part Two that we hope to be able to dedicate on the 155th anniversary of the completion of the road in 2017, since 2013 we have installed and dedicated more than a dozen interpretive signs at sites that are of significance and interest to both residents and visitors. These are discussed below and include the Walla Walla County Poor Farm and Poor Farm Cemetery in College Place, the Historic McCool Catholic Cemetery on Village Way, the site of the early Village of Halfway on West Poplar, the site of the William Davies Community on Scenic Loop Road with its story of the Walla Walla Jesus, the Edgewater Park Dance Pavilion just across Mill Creek from Heritage Park on Main Street, the historic Baker School site on East Sumach, the Halfway House on the Mullan Road at Prescott, Walla Walla's Germantown in the southwest part of the city, Walla Walla's final Chinatown in the area surrounding Rose & Fourth, the site of the Walla Walla Treaty Council of 1855 in the vicinity of Carnegie Center, and the new Wallula Historic Site established by Walla Walla 2020 at the entrance to Wallula Gap. We have also installed an interpretive sign on the Mill Creek Trail leading to Bennington Lake where a skirmish took place in 1856 between Governor Isaac Stevens party and warriors from various Indian tribes following the failure of the Second Walla Walla Treaty Council, which we'll be dedicating on the 160th anniversary of that event this year.

The Walla Walla County Poor Farm

The Walla Walla County Poor Farm was established in 1891, and at one point included 200 acres extending from present 12th Street in College Place south to Taumarson Road, and from just east of Myra Road to College Avenue. The farm was owned and run by Walla Walla County as a place where indigent residents could live and work.

Poor Farm residents lived in the large house at the corner of what is now SE Scenic View and Robin Drive, where Walla Walla 2020 has placed an interpretive sign. The house, which is still standing, has ten bedrooms and a large attached kitchen. There were various outbuildings on the grounds, and a separate hospital and a tuberculosis sanitarium were connected to the house by covered walkways. Many of the residents of the farm were ultimately buried in the Poor Farm cemetery at the corner of Mockingbird and Sandpiper in College Place, where Walla Walla 2020 has also installed interpretive signage. The Poor Farm barn, constructed with wooden pegs in place of nails, is still standing on private property on Robin Drive just north of Scenic View.

A tuberculosis hospital building located behind the farm house has been moved to the corner of Scenic View and Larch where it is in use as a private home. The story of the Poor Farm and the tuberculosis hospital located there is partially told in a novel titled "The Diary" by Francis Potts, whose mother was employed and whose father was a patient there.

The Poor Farm was closed sometime after the federal Social Security system was created and counties were no longer solely responsible for indigent welfare. The last burial and the closure of the farm took place in about 1954. The land, except for the cemetery, was then sold by the county and became a dairy farm for many years, before the establishment of a mobile or manufactured home community there. While the Poor Farm barn is used for storage as part of the mobile home park, the vacant Poor Farm house is in separate ownership.

The Poor Farm Cemetery was also established about 1891. Deceased Poor Farm residents along with unclaimed remains from the Walla Walla County Coroner's office were buried there in the cemetery in rows running north to south. Most graves were marked with small concrete cylinders bearing only a number. Upright markers were later placed on several of the graves by friends or family members. The names and location of people buried in the cemetery could be found by consulting records maintained at the county courthouse, which until recently were thought to have been lost.

After the Poor Farm closed and as the adjoining land was being developed as a mobile or manufactured home park, all large grave markers were removed, the small concrete cylinders were covered with soil, grass was planted over them, and playground equipment, footings for which are still visible, was installed on top of the graves. The outline of the graves is also visible online from aerial photographs. Ownership of the cemetery was transferred by Walla Walla County to the City of College Place in 1965. This and other historic cemeteries are protected from further disturbance by the Washington Historic Cemeteries and Graves Act, adopted in 1990.

A partial list of burials is shown on a sign at the cemetery placed by Walla Walla 2020. A full list of the approximately 700 people buried in the cemetery is shown in the county records, copies of which are available on the Walla Walla 2020 website at www.ww2020.net. The last recorded burials in the Poor Farm cemetery took place in the early 1940s.

The McCool Catholic Cemetery

Because of overcrowding at the city's first Catholic cemetery established near the corner of 6th and Alder in 1859, a plot of land known as the McCool Cemetery was dedicated by Rev. Father Mans in 1867 and acquired from Robert McCool in 1869, measuring 450' x 152'. After overcrowding there as well, in October 1891 a new Catholic Cemetery was purchased adjoining the Mountain View municipal cemetery on Second Avenue, and the Church requested descendants of those buried in the old cemetery to move all remains to the new cemetery.

On October 31, 1969, on the assumption that all burials there had been removed to the new cemetery, the Catholic Bishop of Spokane sold the McCool Cemetery ground to developers. However, official records show fewer than half of the several hundred Catholic burials at McCool to be reinterred at Mt. View.

In the 1970s, during construction of the Pine Crest Village and Village Way development, human remains were encountered in the street and on residential lots. From 2002-05, professional archaeological excavations documented the presence of additional burials both inside and outside the boundaries of the deeded cemetery. In accordance with Washington State law (RCW Chapter 68.60, and RCW 68.40.40), once five or more sets of human remains are discovered on a property, the property is considered a dedicated cemetery and is protected from disturbance. As required by law, the boundaries of the originally deeded cemetery have therefore been expanded to incorporate the area where additional burials have been found. All of the site is now protected from further disturbance by Washington's Historic Cemeteries and Graves Act, unless and until all remaining graves are removed as provided for in RCW 68.24.090.

Partial church records show 159 persons buried at McCool during the period October 1869 to July 1872, and January 1884 to October 1891 who are not listed as reinterred at Mountain View Cemetery. Burial records from 1872-1883 were not available and are not included. A list of the 159 persons not shown as reinterred is available on the Walla Walla 2020 website, www.ww2020.net, along with excerpts from archaeological investigations of the site in 2002 and 2004, signage placed at the site by Walla Walla 2020, and a printable Historic McCool Cemetery brochure.

The land comprising the Historic McCool Cemetery is currently in four ownerships. The large eastern portion of the cemetery is owned by Traditions at Walla Walla, LLC, a Spokane-based firm which operates the adjacent Affinity retirement facility. An unmarked path leads up to the cemetery from that facility, along which Walla Walla 2020 has placed a sign identifying the cemetery with the cooperation of an adjoining neighbor. Most of the western portion of the cemetery is owned by Pinecrest Village, Inc, which developed the adjacent condominiums and streets. Other than one private residence, the balance of the cemetery consists of a portion of the street and adjacent public right of way owned by the City of Walla Walla.

Before the land was sold by the Catholic Diocese of Spokane in 1969, all of the gravestones had been removed from the cemetery over the nearly one-half century of abandonment. In 2015, Walla Walla 2020 obtained permission from the City of Walla Walla to place a detailed roadside sign on the city's portion of the historic cemetery along Village Way that lists those apparently still buried there, and describes the cemetery's history.

The Village of Halfway

In the fall of 1858, Harry Howard together with a Mr. Parkeson built a log saloon in the vicinity of the current fire department headquarters at what is now 12th and Poplar in Walla Walla where Walla Walla 2020 has erected an interpretive sign, which is halfway between the new Fort Walla Walla on the hill to the west, and the old Fort Walla Walla where Mill Creek crosses the Nez Perce Trail at First and Main.

This saloon became known as the Halfway House. Others soon built around it thinking that a town would be founded there. These entrepreneurs laid off a plaza for the village of Halfway and built facing it. The additional businesses located at Halfway were Michael Kenny, a saloon, William Terry, the Bank Exchange saloon, Mahan and Harcum, a store, James Buckley and Thomas Riley, a saloon, and a bakery operated by a Mr. Meyo.

In a competition that developed between the village of Halfway and a number of other merchants who had built near the old cantonment on Mill Creek, in the end everyone realized that packers were bound to go to Mill Creek to camp and while there tended to trade at the nearest store or saloon. As a result, those on the creek had the advantage, and the merchants at Halfway moved their establishments to Mill Creek, where the town of Walla Walla was founded in November, 1859.

The first building erected on Mill Creek after Fort Walla Walla itself was a log structure constructed in the summer of 1857 by William McWhirk on the north side of Main Street where Second now crosses it. The next building was a store of poles and mud erected by Charles Belman in the spring of 1858 on the north side of Main between the creek and Second Street. The third building was made of slabs set endways in the ground and covered with shakes on the south side of Main at what is now Third, put up by Lewis McMorris for Neil McGlinchey in April 1858.

The first actual house constructed in Walla Walla with boards, a floor, and glass windows was built on what is now the northwest corner of Third and Main in 1859 after several of the commercial buildings were put up. Others soon followed, and on November 17, 1859 the town of Walla Walla was created by Walla Walla County Commissioners.

William Davies and the Walla Walla Jesus

William W. Davies (1833– 1906) was the leader of a Latter Day Saint schismatic group called the Kingdom of Heaven located in the foothills of the Blue Mountains overlooking Walla Walla from 1867 to 1881.

Davies was born in Wales to a Methodist family. In 1847, he converted to Mormonism and in 1854–55 he emigrated to Utah Territory as a Mormon pioneer to join the gathering of the members of The Church of Jesus Christ of Latter-day Saints.

After the Mountain Meadows massacre of 1857, Davies became disillusioned with the leadership of the LDS Church and became a follower of the schismatic leader Joseph Morris who was challenging the authority of Mormon leader Brigham Young. Following the 1862 Morrisite War in which Morris was killed by authorities, Davies moved with a number of Morrisites to Deer Lodge County, Montana. While in Montana, Davies told of a series of revelations which instructed him to establish the "Kingdom of Heaven on Earth" near Walla Walla.

Davies and forty of his followers moved here in 1866 and eventually established a communal society on 400 acres near the top of Scenic Loop Road at its intersection with the road now known as Mormon Grade. Davies held legal title to all property in the Kingdom of Heaven.

Davies taught his followers that he was the archangel Michael, who had previously lived lives as the biblical Adam, Abraham, and David. When his son Arthur was born on February 11, 1868, Davies declared that the infant was the reincarnated Jesus Christ, and the child came to be called "the Walla Walla Jesus."

After the announcement, the size of Davies' followers doubled; most of the new converts came from San Francisco, California and Portland, Oregon. When Davies' son, David, was born in 1869, he declared him to be God the Father, and it is said that he also declared himself to be the Holy Spirit, completing the divine Trinity.

The Davies community's main compound was located just southeast of the current corner of Scenic Loop Road and Mormon Grade in the foothills of the Blue Mountains east of Walla Walla. In the compound was the Davies brick residence, as well as a temple or central building for meetings, a school, and a variety of more humble homes. The main barn for farming operations was just north of what is now Scenic Loop Road. All of these buildings were long ago removed, and the site of the former community is currently open farm ground.

Regarding the community's beliefs and practices, on January 24, 1866, Davies claimed to have had a vision in which he saw a great white throne in heaven, and learned that God and his Son had chosen him, Davies, to reveal their will to mankind, and to inaugurate "the kingdom of heaven on earth." When his fifth son, Joseph Bowman Davies, was born on June 17, 1866, Davies announced him to be the reincarnation of John the Baptist, forerunner of the Messiah.

In the spring of the next year, 1867, Davies travelled from Deer Lodge, Montana, along the Mullan Road to Walla Walla, where he declared "this is the place," and purchased 80 acres of land where he established the Kingdom of Heaven on Earth. Men and boys of the Davies community wore their hair long as a symbol of strength. Davies claimed the ability to cure disease and prevent death, to lay down his life, and to resurrect himself.

The community sent missionaries abroad and to several areas within the United States, including Portland, San Francisco, and even back to Utah. It does not appear any effort was made to encourage local people to join, and apparently none did. All members were required to surrender their property to the community, and shared in the work, including on occasion Davies who was a brick mason. Others had to work outside the community to raise funds for it.

It is said that Davies expelled several followers from the community for immorality, and then claimed their wives for his own use, and also that he set up several women, including the school teacher, in private houses where he would visit them after dark, resulting in several births.

Although Davies claimed the power to raise the dead, the Kingdom of Heaven began to collapse in 1879 when Davies' wife Sarah died of diphtheria, and in 1880, when both Arthur and David, members of the Trinity, died of the same disease. Some of Davies' followers then sued him in Walla Walla County Superior Court for the return of property given to the community, and for fair compensation for their donated work, and won a judgment. As a result, the land on which the community was located was sold at public auction by order of the court, which essentially brought the Kingdom to a close, though some never lost faith.

At the time of its break-up, there were 43 members of the Davies group. Davies then moved to a camp he owned on Mill Creek, where he briefly attempted to revive his following, but eventually gave up and moved to San Francisco with his new wife. Davies returned to Walla Walla shortly before his death in 1906, and is buried at the Lyons Cemetery north of Mill Creek Road. Many of the long-time residents of the Mill Creek area are related to members of the Davies community.

The Walla Walla 2020 interpretive sign is at the corner of Scenic Loop Road and Mormon Grade.

The Edgewater Park Dance Pavilion

From about 1926 to about 1945, the Edgewater Park dance pavilion was located just across Mill Creek from the current Heritage Park where our Walla Walla 2020 interpretive sign is located. It was considered one of the finest outdoor dance facilities in the country, featuring both local and touring bands.

Edgewater offered open dancing, dance contests, dance exhibitions, jitney dancing, as well as boxing and wrestling matches and other events. Jitney dancing was the practice of paying for each dance in advance. Admission to a Jitney dance was free, but once inside the pavilion, dancers were escorted to a roped off area where they purchased tickets for a few cents per dance. There were usually 16 dances per hour, and between numbers, rope boys cleared the dance floor and collected the money for the next number.

One of the first orchestras to play at Edgewater was led by Jackie Coogan, an early child star of the movies, with Betty Grable, later a prominent actress, as soloist. The Edgewater itself was featured in a film called "Movie Balls" whose chief photographer said it was "one of the most attractive outdoor settings for filming dance scenes I have ever seen. There may be larger and more expensively equipped pavilions along the coast, but none have a better natural setting than this."

Edgewater Park was on land owned by the Schwarz family, and was developed with the idea that an outdoor dance pavilion would be a worthwhile addition to the city's recreation resources. During the winter and when there was inclement weather, the dancing was moved to the Arcadia Ballroom at First & Main. The Arcadia was a dependable and attractive place to go when it was rainy or cold. But when the weather was good, the Edgewater with its 8,000 square foot dance pavilion and cool breezes off the water was the place to be for dancers throughout southeast Washington and northeast Oregon. Willows lined the creek, there were benches along the railing, a bandstand on the east end, and strings of lights lit up the night.

Baker School.

The first public school building in the Inland Empire was a one-story wooden building erected on East Sumach Street in Walla Walla in 1866, where Walla Walla 2020 has installed an interpretive sign.

Prior to 1862 there had been no public school organization in Walla Walla, though a county superintendent of schools had been appointed by the Washington Territorial Legislature in 1859. In 1862 Walla Walla School District #1 was organized, a room was rented, and a teacher appointed. Progress lagged until the fall of 1864, when there was a school-age population of 203, only ninety-three of whom were enrolled. At that time a tax was levied for the erection of a wooden, one-story, two-room school building at a cost of $2000.

In August 1865, the School District paid $200 for the full block between Sumach, Spokane, Cherry & Palouse streets as a school site, which basically constituted a donation of the land by the sellers, A.J. Cain and his wife, who used the money to pay off a mortgage on the land held by Dorsey S. Baker. Classes, for which students were charged a small fee, began on this site in March 1866 in what was the first public school building in the eastern part of Washington Territory. Attendance was quite irregular, especially in the fall and spring. Those who lived a long distance rode horses, while many walked several miles to school.

In 1882, the voters of the School District approved a much more ambitious building plan, levying a tax of $17,000 to erect a larger and more substantial building. The levy didn't raise enough money, though, and additional public donations were required to enable the school to be built of brick. As a result of this, the building was named for Dorsey S. Baker, a major donor. In 1889, when the School District offered secondary classes for the first time, Walla Walla's first high school students were housed at Baker School. For the following year, high school students were transferred to Paine School, now known as Lincoln School, which had been erected in 1888, where a third floor was completed for high school purposes.

The Walla Walla School District's first high school class graduated in 1893. By 1900 the total number of graduates was eighty. In 1917 Walla Walla High School had 821 day students; another 127 studied at night.

Baker School underwent remodeling in 1931, during which the tall tower was removed and the front entrance was lowered to ground level. Baker continued to serve elementary school students until 1955, when the school was closed and sold at public auction. In 1957 the building was razed.

Halfway House at Prescott

Beginning in 1869, Benjamin and Malinda Flathers provided a forage station and accommodations for travelers along the Mullan Road near Prescott. The Flathers' station near the Mullan Road's Touchet River crossing was called Halfway House because of its location approximately halfway between the Fort in the town of Walla Walla and the road's Snake River crossing at Lyons Ferry.

Ben Flathers operated a pack train along the California coast from 1854-61 before moving his operation to The Dalles, from which he packed to the Montana mines through Walla Walla. There he met Malinda Harris, whose husband and sons had died. In 1869 they were married, and then leased and purchased land along the Touchet River from Henry Hart Spaulding, the son of the missionary.

Here they established their Halfway House just south of the present intersection of Highway 124 and 125, and west of where the town of Prescott was to be established in 1882 as a railroad station on the Oregon Rail & Navigation Company (OR&N) line.

Julia Flathers (1869-1960) was the eldest of six Flathers children all born in the Halfway House station operated by their parents for over two decades at the Touchet River crossing of the Mullan Road just west of present day Prescott. Julia's siblings were John Taylor Flathers (1870-1925), Emery Elias Flathers (1872-1949), Ivia E. Flathers (1873-1892), Baby Flathers (1875-1875), and Charles Franklin Flathers (1893-1974). The Flathers children were all educated in a one-room school maintained by their father on their ranch along the Touchet. Many Flathers descendants are stilling living in the area and throughout the Northwest.

Germantown

Walla Walla's Germantown was settled by Germans from Russia. During the mid 1700's, Catherine the Great of Russia granted German immigrants concessions to settle in Russia in the Volga River region. Later colonies were established in the Ukraine and Black Sea area. Germany was beset by wars, poverty and hunger, and many Germans saw this as a opportunity, hoping these settlements would bring them a better life. The Russian government gave them land for villages and farming. They were allowed to govern their own settlements and maintain their own religions and language, and were not required to serve in the military.

In 1874, the military service concession was rescinded, and their young men were required to serve in the Russian army. During the same period, the U.S. sent recruiters to Germany and Russia offering many of the same concessions the Germans had enjoyed in Russia. In 1890, Germans from Russia were the second largest immigrant group to come to the Northwest. Religious freedom was a strong motivation to emigrate; many were Lutheran and these immigrants brought their faith with them to the U.S.

From 1882-1920, many of these families settled in the southwest part of Walla Walla. The largest neighborhood was west of Third Avenue and south of Chestnut Street, which became known as Germantown to others in Walla Walla, but was called Russaecke (Russische Ecke—Russian Corner) by the approximately 300 German families who resided in Walla Walla. Garrison Creek which runs there was known as the "Little Volga". Most of the descendants of the first immigrants attended Garrison School, where Walla Walla 2020 has placed an interpretive sign just south of the creek.

The German immigrants from the Volga region of Russia came primarily from the "Bergseite" (hillside) area of Lutheran villages, including Frank, Walter, Kolb, Norka, Hussenbach, and Kautz, all located southwest of the governmental city of Saratov on the Volga River, and from Jagodnaja Poljana, north of Saratov.

The primary area of Russaecke was bordered by Third Avenue on the east, Chase Avenue on the west, Chestnut Street on the north, and Willard Street on the south. Outside of this neighborhood lived many more Germans from Russia, particularly in the southwest Walla Walla homes from Second all the way to the railroad tracks at Thirteenth Avenue, including Chestnut, Willow, Emma, Sprague, Military, Birch, Poplar, and Alder. Links to maps of several of these neighborhoods including city directory information from 1937 can be found in the Additional Resources box to the right.

These immigrants built homes, corner grocery stores and churches. Their children attended local schools, and were also required to attend a Sabbath school on Saturdays in their churches. German-language churches in Walla Walla included the Second German Congregational Church, first established in 1882 and reorganized in 1896 at 7th & Willow as Zion Lutheran Congregational Church, as well as the first German Methodist church in the Northwest, established here in 1883. In 1888 the first Lutheran services were held in Walla Walla, out of which came Emmanuel Lutheran Church, also at 7th & Willow. In 1896 a split occurred in the congregation and several families withdrew to form Christ Lutheran Church on Maple Street, later relocated to a new building South Second. In the early twentieth century there were said to be seven German churches in Walla Walla. English did not fully displace German in these churches until World War II.

The Germans from Russia and their descendants became staunch members of the Walla Walla community. Most of them quickly learned English, especially the men who worked at jobs on the railroad, street maintenance, carpentry, shoemaking, cutting sugar beets, picking hops, and other farm work. The women maintained their own homes, while some worked as housekeepers and laundresses for the "English" ladies. Some members of the community were fortunate enough to eventually open their own businesses. These included Johann Conrad Frank who in 1928 opened the Conrad Frank Construction Company and trained each of his sons to carry on his tradition of fine carpentry. That same year, John David Frank established a grocery store and meat market on Fourth Avenue in competition with a grocery on Maple Street opened earlier by the Hill family in about 1915.

The Walla Walla Treaty Council of 1855

In 1855, a treaty council was held in the Walla Walla Valley between Governor Isaac Stevens of Washington Territory, Superintendent of Indian Affairs Joel Palmer of Oregon Territory, and many of the upper Columbia and Snake River Indian tribes.

The council opened on May 29, 1855 on the north bank of Mill Creek in what is now the city of Walla Walla, and concluded 13 days later on June 11. Several thousand Indians were present, as well as Stevens' and Palmer's supporting staff, a detachment of soldiers, and a number of whites living in the area.

It has been said of this event, "In its general importance and difficulty [it] has never been equaled by any council held with the Indian tribes of the United States." The council resulted in the signing of three treaties, establishing the Yakama, Nez Perce, and Umatilla Indian Reservations, and the ceding of all remaining tribal lands to the United States.

The location of the exact grounds of the Treaty Council of 1855 has been a topic of considerable controversy over the years. What is clear from the reports of Gov. Isaac Stevens and his staff is that it was on the north bank of Mill Creek. Most all students of the question agree in addition that it was somewhere east of the current intersection of First and Main in the city of Walla Walla, though precisely where has not been determined.

Two local monuments refer to the Treaty Council grounds. The oldest is the treaty council stone behind Carnegie Center at Palouse & Alder, where Walla Walla 2020 has placed an additional interpretive sign. The original marker there reads, "Near this site May 29 to June 11, 1855 was held the Great Indian Council by Governor Isaac Ingalls Stevens with chiefs of the Nez Perce, Yakima, Cayuse and Walla Walla Indian Tribes of Washington, Oregon and Idaho. Placed 1925 by Narcissa Prentiss Chapter D.A.R., Walla Walla."

The second monument is the treaty rock at the entrance to the Whitman College amphitheater placed there five years later, which has two inscriptions. The first is by the class of 1930 which donated the rock, and reads in part, "Here were camped from May 24 to June 12, 1855, two thousand Indians of the Nez Perce Tribe, with their famous chief, Hol-Lol-Sote-Tote, Lawyer, attending the Great Council called by Governor Stevens."

The second inscription on the Whitman treaty rock was added in 1955, and reads, "To commemorate the 100th anniversary of the signing by their forefathers of the treaties with the United States of America near this place on June 9 and 11, 1855, this plaque is presented by the people of the Yakima, Nez Perce, Cayuse, Walla Walla, and Umatilla Indian Tribes. He-Pa-Nak-Ne-Koo Kun-Koo Nu-Nim Pe-Wa-Ynpt. June 11, 1955."

While the camps of the various participants were spread out over a large area, it appears likely that the main council deliberations took place in the vicinity of the earlier monument behind Carnegie Center. In support of this view, Whitman College historian W.D. Lyman, in his "History of Old Walla Walla County" (1918), writes:"There seems some difference of opinion as to the exact location of the conference. It has generally been thought that Stevens' camp was at what is now known as Council Grove Addition, near the residence of ex-Senator Ankeny."

The name Council Grove was given to the area just southeast of the intersection of Park & Alder Streets in the vicinity of Carnegie Center. Crescent Street, where Senator Ankeny lived, begins at Alder Street just east of that intersection, and from there curves into Birch Street. Although the current channel of Mill Creek is north of this location, according to Professor Lyman, "It appears from the testimony of old-timers that Mill Creek has changed its course at intervals in these years, and that as a result the exact identification [of the Council grounds] is difficult."

It is possible that in 1855 Mill Creek followed the curve of Crescent Street or was at least parallel to it and then continued down or parallel to Birch, as it did during the flood of 1931, before the construction of the current concrete channel. That would have put this site on the north bank of Mill Creek at the time, consistent with early accounts of its location.

Additional confirmation of this theory is found in the 1876 birds-eye view map of Walla Walla showing large trees lining the south bank of Mill Creek as it approaches Alder before continuing northwest on the bank of the creek in its current channel, as well as continuing southwest to a large grove and open space along Crescent Street, suggesting that the creek previously took this path.

Regarding the Whitman location, Lyman wrote in 1918, "William McBean, a son of the Hudson's Bay Company agent at Fort Walla Walla during the Cayuse war, who was himself in Stevens' force as a young boy, told the author nearly thirty years ago that he believed the chief point of the conference was almost exactly on the present site of Whitman College…. It seems plain…that the Indians were camped at various places along two spring branches, College Creek and Tannery Creek."

Lyman also mentions the view that the council was "near the residence of Mrs. Clara Quinn." W.W. 2020 research has identified that residence as being at the corner of Colville and Rose, just northeast of the intersection of First & Main, where Fort Walla Walla was established in 1856. The fort is also said by some to have been on the treaty council grounds.

The Treaty Council at Walla Walla ended on June 11, 1855. After three years of ensuing Indian wars, the treaties were ratified by Congress on March 8, 1859 and went into effect in April 1859.

Walla Walla's Chinatown

The first Chinese came to Walla Walla and the Pacific Northwest as part of the Idaho gold rush of the 1860's. Walla Walla was a major "jumping-off" place for men on their way to the mines, and was also a haven for those who came down from the mines for the winter.

Most of the Chinese were from the Toishan district in the province of Guangdong in Southern China, an area with an impoverished population near a seaport where foreign trade had been established. The local textile industry there had been devastated by the importation of cotton textiles from Great Britain. Many small farmers had been forced off the land, and military conflicts had resulted in upheavals in which emigration often seemed the only alternative.

After the Idaho mining boom died down, the miners moved to work on the railroads or other pursuits. Construction on the Walla Walla and Columbia River Railroad got underway in 1871 with several groups of Chinese grading the line. Upon completion of the WW&CRR, many Chinese laborers settled in Walla Walla resulting in a large increase in the Chinese population here.

During the 1880's, Walla Walla experienced another wave of immigration from China, Those who settled in Walla Walla at that time were generally small businessmen, domestic workers, and truck farmers. Chinese enterprises included laundries, dry goods stores, restaurants, and medicine shops. In 1882, for example, Walla Walla had nine Chinese laundries; in 1907, Chinese businesses included ten specializing in Chinese merchandise, two druggists, one grocer, six laundries, one medicine manufacturer, and three restaurants.

In addition, there were twenty-five Chinese truck gardens, each employing between eight and nine Chinese. Because they could not legally own land in the United States, the number of Chinese farmers in Walla Walla began to dwindle after 1920, when large numbers of Italian immigrants moved into the valley and began buying land to farm themselves, which the Chinese could only rent.

There have been conflicting reports of the size of the Chinese population in Walla Walla. One source described it as one in seven in 1880, a second as between 600-800 in the 1880's, and another "as many as 5,000" during the same period. In 1907, it is reported to have been 1250, although only 403 Chinese were registered by the U.S. census in 1900, which dropped to 197 by the official 1910 census. In any event, the Chinese population of Walla Walla has generally been regarded as the largest of any city in Washington State east of the Cascades.

As their population grew steadily from the mid-1860's until its peak in the 1880's, the Chinese in Walla Walla tended to migrate to a centralized neighborhood. The first Chinatown in Walla Walla was centered around the Oriental Hotel built in 1867, including the area along Alder and adjoining streets from approximately Colville to Third.

The first Chinese resident was Hen Lee, who opened a laundry in1861 in a log building previously used by Dorsey Baker as a store behind what later became Baker Boyer Bank on Second Avenue. A variety of other Chinese businesses and residences were located nearby, including a store on the northwest corner of First & Alder, a laundry on the northeast corner of Colville & Alder, two cabins housing a barber shop and living quarters south of Alder on the east side of Colville, as well as some two-story buildings on the north side of Alder, between Second and Third with shops below and living quarters above.

The fire of 1887 destroyed this area as well as much of the rest of the downtown. Most of the Chinese population eventually moved to a variety of locations along Rose and adjoining streets between Second and Sixth.

In 1911, prominent members of the Chinese community built the Pacific Enterprise Building at the corner of Fifth & Rose, where it is reported that ninety percent of the Chinese population of Walla Walla lived the early part of the 20th century. The structure became known locally as "the Chinese Building," and housed a variety of commercial businesses on the street level including laundries and Chinese medicine shops, as well as numerous apartments on the upper level. The Pacific Enterprise Corporation functioned as a form of quasi-government that set rules and regulations, resolved differences between Chinese, cared for the needy and infirm, and acted as liaison with the outside community.

In 1947, the Pacific Enterprise Building was purchased by a local non-Chinese businessman, who closed the residential portion, forcing approximately ninety Chinese inhabitants to find housing among the general population. On February 9, 1947, the Walla Walla Union-Bulletin reported, "...By the end of the year, Chinatown, as modern people know it will be no more. Buildings in the colony on Rose and Fifth and Sixth have been sold, and the exodus of occupants to China will begin February 15. Before the year is ended about 50 will have left."

The majority of the Chinese in Walla Walla in 1947 had come to the United States as young men in search of adventure and wealth and hadn't intended to stay, so they hadn't set down roots or married. When the Chinese Building was sold, even though they had aged here, very few felt they had any alternative but to return to China. However, a small community of younger Chinese who had formed families has remained here, and has integrated into our general population. With the razing of the Chinese Building in 1962, the contents of the building were donated to the Museum of Man at Whitman College, though relatively little was left to remind Walla Wallans of the once-thriving Chinese community.

Walla Walla's final Chinatown was located along Rose and adjoining streets, between Third & Sixth. Prior to the construction of the Walla Walla City Hall in 1908 and the adjoining fire station, the Chinese businesses located there included Charles Ong, Chinese Restaurant, Quing Mow Luong & Co, Chinese Merchandise, Hong Chong Wo Co, Chinese Merchandise, Kwong Wah Sang & Co, Chinese Merchandise, Kee Sang Tong, Chinese Merchandise. In addition, Kwong Chung Sing Co., owner Charles Tung, was located on the northwest corner of the City Hall block at Fourth & Rose. The two story Bing Kong Bow Leoung Chinese Lodge Building is was on the southwest corner of the City Hall block. On the northwest corner of the next block at Fifth & Rose was the Pacific Enterprise Building. Also, several Chinese residences were on the south side of the next block as well as on the north side of Rose.

Walla Walla 2020's interpretive sign for the final Chinatown has been placed on the northeast corner of the intersection of 4th & Rose.

The Wallula Historic Site

Wallula has many fascinating stories to tell. These include the early geologic history of the region displaying the effects of the Missoula Floods 15,000-18,000 years ago, and its role as a traditional village and gathering site for Native Americans. It was also a Lewis & Clark camp site, and the site of the first fur trading post in the region. In the 1860s Wallula became a major steamship port which brought thousands of miners to the Idaho gold fields, as well as agricultural products to market. In the 1870s, it was the terminus of the Walla Walla and Columbia River Railroad, the Northwest's first rail line of any length; in the 1880s it became a link in transcontinental rail lines.

Three successive towns called Wallula were built there, the first in 1860 on the ruins of Old Fort Walla Walla, the second along the new transcontinental line in the 1880s, and the third in 1953 when backwaters of the new McNary Dam flooded the area and the town was moved to higher ground.

From 15,000-18,000 years ago what many geologists believe were the Earth's largest floods raced through Wallula Gap. Some of these floods were as many as twenty times as large as the combined discharge of all the world's current rivers. The Gap was only large enough to accommodate about half the discharge from ice-dammed Glacial Lake Missoula, which caused the water to surge at speeds of up to 60 miles per hour through the opening at Wallula. These floodwaters created channeled scablands, surged up the Walla Walla, Yakima and other valleys, roared through the Columbia River Gorge and inundated the Willamette Valley on their way to the ocean.

Glacial Lake Missoula, comparable in size to Lake Erie, was formed during the glaciations of the Pleistocene ice age, which began about two million years ago, when a tongue of ice flowed south from British Columbia's Cordilleran ice sheet and blocked the Clark Fork of the Columbia River. When a series of approximately 2000-foot-thick ice dams broke, Lake Missoula emptied in massive floods, each lasting a few days. In these Missoula Floods, icebergs rode the waves, depositing at Wallula a variety of exotic rocks. The Two Sisters monument there is an example of some of the flood-created scablands at Wallula.

Wallula was a permanent village site for Wallulapum (Walla Walla) Indians as well as a place of intertribal encampments of Walla Wallas, Cayuses, and Nez Perces numbering several thousands in late summer. Here they traded, celebrated, discussed political concerns, renewed friendships, courted, raced horses, and gambled. Those who lived in the Wallula area between about 11,000 and 8,000 years ago lived in temporary shelters in small mobile groups, foraging a wide variety of plant and animal resources, including fish, river mussels, deer, elk, antelope, birds, rabbits, and hares. Later, the people became more sedentary and small villages appeared, including longhouses. Around 1720 the horse reached the Wallula area, greatly increasing mobility and the range of trade and resource gathering. However, the underlying culture continued to rely on a seasonal round centered on salmon fishing, root gathering, and deer and elk hunting.

The Corps of Discovery camped just south of Wallula on October 15, 1805 on their way to the Pacific Ocean. On their return in April of 1806, they camped for two nights at the Walla Walla village on the north side of the river, where Chief Yellepit gave Captain Clark a white horse, and Clark gave Yellepit his sword. The explorers then swam their horses and ferried their baggage across the river in two canoes provided by the Walla Wallas, after which the party camped for the night just north of the mouth of the Walla Walla River. In his journal, Lewis described the Walla Wallas as "the most hospitable, honest, and sincere people that we have met with in our voyage….This village consists of 15 large mat lodges. A little before sunset the Chymnahpos (Yakamas) arrived. They joined the Wallahwollahs and waited very patiently to see our party dance. The fiddle was played and the men amused themselves with dancing about an hour. We then requested the Indians to dance which they very cheerfully complied with."

In 1818, the North West Company built Fort Nez Percés at the mouth of the Walla Walla River. In 1821 this was rebuilt by the Hudson's Bay Company as its Fort Walla Walla trading post, a center for outfitting and supplying the inland empire fur brigades, as well as for trade with local tribes. Fort Nez Perces was heavily fortified, and became known as the Gibraltar of the Columbia. Beaver pelts from the vast inland region were shipped through Wallula to Vancouver, and from there were loaded onto ships for England. The authority of the Hudson's Bay Company was respected by local tribes, and many of their mostly French-Canadian Métis employees settled in the Walla Walla Valley in an area that became known as Frenchtown, often marrying local Indian wives.

In territorial days, Wallula served as a major steamship port for the inland areas of Washington, Oregon, and Idaho. The first steamboat, the Colonel Wright, arrived at Wallula in April 1859 carrying military supplies for the new US Army Fort Walla Walla at the new town of Walla Walla to the east. After that, regular steamship service could be relied upon for carrying cattle, sheep and wheat to coastal markets and for bringing settlers to the interior. Miners also used the route to travel to British Columbia, Idaho, and Montana. The steamboats on the Columbia River were eventually replaced by the major railroads which they arrived at Wallula in the 1880s.

In 1871, construction of the first Pacific Northwest railroad of any length began at Wallula. The Walla Walla and Columbia River Railroad was completed in 1875 connecting the town of Walla Walla with the steamship dock at Wallula. The only prior tracks in the region were the short portage lines at the Cascades and between the Dalles and Celilo Falls. In 1880, the Oregon Railroad and Navigation Company began a line from Wallula to Portland, which by 1883 was linked at Wallula to the Northern Pacific's transcontinental railroad. In 1888, five railroads brought as many as 15 to 30 trains a day to Wallula.

Despite a town having been established around the ruins of Old Fort Walla Walla where the steamship dock and the WW&CR railroad depots were located, the OR&N built its track and depot a mile inland because its freight business no longer relied on river traffic. A new town of Wallula was then built around these tracks to capitalize on the railroad and its workers and customers, after which the first town was abandoned. Though Wallula aspired to be "The Railroad Center of the Northwest," in 1884 the NP built the new town of Pasco, and in 1887 the Union Pacific bought the OR&N and extended its line to Umatilla, where most of the trainmen relocated in 1889. When Lake Wallula inundated the Wallula depot facilities in 1953, the tracks were moved east to their present location, and the town of Wallula was again relocated, this time to a hill to the northeast.

The first town of Wallula was established in 1860 by James Vansyckle, primarily as a depot for the gold rush into the eastern mountains of Washington Territory. It also served travelers on the Mullan Road linking Fort Benton on the Missouri River with Fort Walla Walla on the Columbia. The original town thrived during the gold rush,but declined by the late 1860s. In the 1880s the railroads created a temporary boom for the second town built a mile east along the new mainline. With the construction of McNary Dam and the 1953 inundation of both town sites by Lake Wallula, the location of most of Wallula's human history is now under water. The third town of Wallula looks down from a low hill to the northeast.

There has long been recognition of the need to create an interpretive site to honor Wallula's significant history. After several unsuccessful attempts along US 12, the Walla Walla 2020 citizens group obtained permission from the Washington State Department of Transportation for an interpretive site at the eastern entrance to the Wallula Gap at a turnout on US 730 just downstream from Milepost 5, where we have installed interpretive signage telling all seven of Wallula's stories. This site is the closest point of land to many of the events that took place at the mouth of the Walla Walla River in the 1800's and early 1900's, which is now underwater from the backwaters of McNary Dam. The site also provides access to the open space on the bluffs overlooking the Columbia River and along the river bank itself, which is a popular fishing spot.

Much of the information provided is from the book *Where the Great River Bends* edited by Robert J. Carson, with chapters by Michael E. Denny, Catherine E. Dickson, Lawrence L. Dodd, and G. Thomas Edwards. Thanks to the Wildhorse Foundation and the UP Foundation for funding the site.

More details on these and other sites and markers honored by Walla Walla 2020 are at www.ww2020.net/historic-sites.

The Walla Walla Alliance for the Homeless

One wet morning in May of 2015, as I was exercising at the track near our home, I noticed two police cars parked at our closed city swimming pool, so I walked over to find out what was going on. What I found was about half a dozen homeless people who had spent the night under the roof over the pool's entrance area in order to get some shelter. Since the baseball team that uses the building in the summer had complained, the police were moving these people and their belongings out into the driving rain to their dismay on this cold, spring day.

Walla Walla's homeless population had been increasing for more than ten years, and I knew there weren't currently enough facilities to house everyone and to accommodate their basic needs, particularly those who had very few resources. A friend of mine was serving on the Housing and Poverty Response Committee of the Walla Walla County Human Services Advisory Board, and had been looking for a site for a homeless day center which had been in the county's Ten Year Plan to Reduce Homeless for more than a decade without success. Plus, people had been coming before Barbara and the other city council members asking the city to do something about the problem, though little action seemed to be taken.

After asking the police to at least take one of the homeless people and his belongings to a park where there was a shelter for the day, I decided there had to be a place somewhere in the community to accommodate their needs, and I began driving around to look for one myself.

What I found was a piece of property that had been purchased in 2005 by a local family for use as a clubhouse, campground, and community garden for an organization serving the mentally ill in Walla Walla. Beginning in the early 1900s, the property had been the site of residences, after which it was used for many years as an automobile repair shop. When the association for the mentally ill decided to locate elsewhere, the family then rented the property to an iron fencing business until it was put on the market for sale in 2015.

The property at 708 W. Pine turned out to be uniquely suited as a site for a potential facility to provide temporary housing and services for homeless people awaiting permanent housing. It was properly zoned for that purpose, unusually buffered from conflicting uses by a highway, a railroad track, and a below-grade street on one side, was on a bus route and within walking distance of downtown and other services, and was available for purchase at a reasonable price.

Since the property was actively on the market and there were several interested commercial buyers, to allow time to consult with community agencies and leaders in order to further assess the need, the suitability of the property, and available resources, Barbara and I reached an agreement with the owners to hold the property off the market until July 1, 2015.

From May 28-June 22, 2015, we gave the following individuals or agencies, among others, tours of the property and asked for their advice: Nabiel Schawa, City Manager, Elizabeth Chamberlain, Development Services Director, Riley Jones, Building Official, Rick Boyd, Building Inspector, Tim Thompson, Fire Department; Harvey Crowder, County Community Health, Debbie Dumont, Human Services Manager; Noah Leavitt, Council on Homelessness; Eloise Phillips, Kay Maxfield, Diane Davis, Tam Lennox, Norm Osterman, Walla Walla County Human Services Advisory Board; Ben Norens, Central Washington Comprehensive Mental Health, & staff; Renee Rooker and Kelsie Beckmeyer, WW Housing Authority; Jason Wicklund, Christian Aid Center and staff; Ted Kohler, John Anthony, and Brooke Bouchey, Blue Mountain Action Council; Christie Lieuellen, United Way; Liz McDevitt, Helpline; Tim Meliah, Catholic Charities; Dave Beebe, Veterans Center; Ron Opsal, VA Medical Center; Nancy Jacobsen, Commitment to Community; Jerry Cummins, Mayor & Housing Authority board member; city council members Jim Barrow, Dick Morgan, and Allen Pomraning, and city council member and BMAC employee Mary Lou Jenkins; Glenna Awbrey, STAR Project; Steve Moss, former BMAC director & State Housing Commission member; Chuck Fulton, retired police chief, Sherwood Trust; Punkey Adams, First Congregational Church, Sherwood Trust; David Fogarty, retired planner. We also met with and offered tours to the Housing Authority board and asked to meet with the Walla Walla Council on Homelessness and the Interfaith Coalition on Poverty, along with other officials who declined the invitation during that period.

A clear majority of those who toured the site and offered advice expressed the view that there was a demonstrated need for additional shelter and services for the growing homeless population in order to assist them in moving toward permanent housing, that the site presented a rare opportunity, and that it was extraordinarily suitable for the purpose. The primary exceptions to this were the administrators of several leading agencies, principally the Walla Walla County Department of Community Health who told us that all of their funding would be going to permanent housing, and the Walla Walla Housing Authority, who said they didn't want the project in their neighborhood, though agency line staff who dealt with the homeless on a daily basis were personally supportive.

Since then, we have worked to keep discussions from "either-or" debates on permanent v. temporary housing strategy in favor of "both-and" discussions of how many steps out of homelessness are needed. While celebrating efforts to provide more permanent housing, we are convinced that the numbers of residents without permanent housing will continue to grow, and that interim steps toward long-term solutions are needed, especially because public housing and voucher programs show no sign of significant growth. In addition, once the proposed project Park is up and running, we will likely work toward other projects focused on permanent low-income housing.

On June 23-24, 2015 Walla Walla County hosted community-wide meetings in order to renew its federally-required Ten Year Plan to Reduce Homeless by 50%. During the County's first Ten-Year planning period, instead of a decrease, homelessness in the county steadily increased, and no progress had been made in meeting the need identified in the plan for a homeless day center. In response to publicity regarding our proposed development, several hundred residents attended the meetings, including homeless people, many speaking in favor of the proposed development. Because of this widespread interest, instead of a 10-year plan to reduce homelessness, the county has adopted a new plan to end all homelessness in Walla Walla County within five years, and to end chronic homeless by the end of 2016, though no provisions for temporary shelter or day center services are included.

Because it was clear that no existing agencies would sponsor our project, we called a public meeting on July 6 that was attended by more than 100 people, both housed and homeless, and those present voted to form a new community nonprofit organization called the Walla Walla Alliance for the Homeless. The organization has a membership fee of $25 or more for those who can afford it, or whatever is practical for those who can't. A steering committee along with a board of directors has been formed to work on policies, procedures, and implementation, and retired United Methodist pastor Chuck Hindman agreed to serve as chair. The group has incorporated as a Washington non-profit organization, and has been granted charitable tax exempt status by the IRS, so contributions to it are tax-deductible.

At the request of the new Alliance, individual supporters formed a limited liability company called the Pine Street WW, LLC. On August 5, 2015, the LLC, for which I serve as managing agent, purchased what is now called Madison Park in honor of Bill and Diane Madison for the same $135,000 price the Madisons had paid for it in 2005. The LLC has in turn leased the property to the Alliance for five years at a rental of $1/yr, with a right to renew for another five years at the same rental, and the right to purchase the property at the same price paid by the Madisons and the Alliance.

In September, following neighbor opposition and city council denial of our request that the city adopt a provision authorized by the legislature providing for the waiver of strict compliance with city codes for existing buildings used by nonprofits for indigent housing when they are in fact safe and sanitary, the Alliance arranged several meetings with leaders of the neighborhood association surrounding Madison Park. This resulted in the drafting of a proposed cooperative agreement between the neighborhood association and the Alliance, under which Alliance with the help of the neighbors would seek to provide day services for the homeless in the downtown area, in order to limit services at Madison Park to those actually residing there and thereby reduce the concern about increased foot traffic through the neighborhood. Unfortunately, the neighborhood association refused to sign the agreement, and insisted that no homeless persons be housed at the site.

On December 1, 2015, the Alliance filed an application with the City of Walla Walla for authorization to develop Madison Park as a micro-housing shelter facility and campground for homeless persons. After city review and public comments, on March 29, the Alliance filed a revised development application, which was referred to the city hearing examiner for hearing on July 7. In addition, a written interpretation by the development services director that campgrounds are only for "recreation and amusement" and that a homeless shelter is therefore not a campground under the city code was appealed by the Alliance to the hearing examiner. On August 1, the examiner issued his decision approving the shelter facility with a variety of conditions, and affirming the denial of the campground use. Both the Alliance and some neighbor opponents appealed the hearing examiner's decision to Superior Court, which affirmed the hearing examiner's decision.

Because the Alliance is committed to the well-being of every member of our community, it seeks to develop a facility that will be safe and attractive for its temporary residents, for the general neighborhood, and for the broader community. To address the attractiveness of its design, the plan for shelter at Madison Park relies primarily on tiny homes, the latest design concept for affordable, environmentally-sound living. Current plans, subject to building permitting, are for fourteen 8' x 12' cottage structures on concrete slabs that satisfy the requirements of the International Building Code. Plans call for the existing building on the site to be remodeled to serve as the Madison Park Commons, providing three restrooms, showers, kitchen, laundry, office space, a multi-purpose room, and a room for residents to meet with social service providers.

The Alliance has also proceeded to arrange for the provision of a variety of day services for the homeless away from the Madison Park site, including mailboxes located behind the Christian Aid Center, weekly showers and cell-phone charging at Pioneer Methodist Church, free monthly laundry service at an Eastgate laundromat in coordination with a similar program once a month at the Southgate laundromat, and public toilets provided by the City in the downtown area, open 24/7 at the request of the Alliance.

In addition, the Alliance has become the major sponsor of a city-authorized campground at Memorial Park adjacent to the municipal golf course. The campground is located at the foot of the hill leading to the Veterans Memorial Municipal Golf Course off of Rees Avenue and Highway 12 at the site of the successful Gentlemen of the Road (GOTR) music tour campground facility. The current camp was authorized and established on August 16, 2016 on city park property at the request of the Walla Walla Alliance for the Homeless, to provide a safe, legal place for homeless citizens of Walla Walla to reside while seeking permanent housing.

At a workshop on November 7, 2016, the Walla Walla city council authorized the campground to continue at least until mid-February, 2017, in order to provide stability for homeless residents during the winter of 2016-17, while the council considered the best long-term arrangements for homeless camping in Walla Walla. At a further council workshop on January 9, 2017, city staff recommended that the campground stay at its present location until at least the first week of April, after which staff recommended that it move to a city park site on Poplar Street adjoining the VA Medical Center, with the understanding that a homeless campground is expected to be needed in Walla Walla for at least 2-5 more years.

At the January 25 city council meeting, by a 5-1 vote the council decided that the permanent location of the city's homeless campground would be the present camp location or the larger triangular open space across the road from the current camp where the campground began last August. The city's next step will be to appoint a city homeless committee to make recommendations to the council on the physical structure and operational guidelines for the permanent facility.

Come Dancing

Dance events continue to play a major part in our lives. In addition to our own dancing whenever a band is playing, the occasional performance dance groups we've put together, the regular contra dances at which Barbara and I both call, the periodic contra dance classes we've offered, the WallaDance weekend contra retreats I've organized along with several tango classes, Barbara and I have recently offered classes to teach people basic couple dance steps that will help them feel comfortable getting out of their chairs and onto their feet whenever and whatever the band is playing. These include the one-step, two-step, swing step, fox-trot, Texas two-step, waltz, and polka, which have been greeted with considerable enthusiasm by the dozens of people attending them.

To provide an additional venue for couple dancing, when Walla Walla 2020 dedicated the interpretive sign at Heritage Park in 2015 to commemorate the historic Edgewater Park Dance Pavilion, instead of just recounting the history of that site as we usually do, I organized a big band dance for the occasion featuring both a 17-piece and an 18-piece big band from the community, and surrounded the outdoor dance area with strings of lights reminiscent of the historic dance pavilion of the 1920s-1940s. The response from the many dancers and musicians participating was enthusiastic, so we repeated the event in 2016, and plan on making it an annual event.

Since contra dancing is still my favorite, I published "Come Dancing—A Collection of Contras, Circles, Squares, & More" in 2014 to celebrate our contra dance culture by compiling the sixty or so contra-style dances I've composed, along with some notes about our dance events, which I've distributed to other callers and is available through online booksellers.

Self-Knowledge

Along with the active side of life, as I say in the book "Notes to my Self," which I also published in 2014, "When we are young, our attention is naturally focused on the fascinations of changing forms. As we grow older, there is a shift to what endures."

As I explained to some extent in Part One, I have long been interested in the unitive or spiritual side of life. In the last several years that interest has matured, and has generated two small books, as well as a couple of classes at our local community college, and the founding of a local group called The Noetic Council which has become the sponsor of the Study Group on the Unitive Self, for which I serve as facilitator.

Just as "A Privileged Life" provides an account of my more active side, "Notes to the Self" contains an account, though much briefer, of the spiritual or esoteric side of my life that I normally share only with other mystics. In addition, though, I have written an even smaller book titled "You are the Self," which covers some of the same ground in a form suitable as an introduction for non-mystics, both of which are available from on-line booksellers, and at times in our local book shops. Key principles from "Notes to the Self" are available online at www.unitiveself.blogspot.com, along with a link to the Noetic Council website and information about the public Study Group on the Unitive Self.

As an invitation to the study group in 2015, I sent the following article to our local newspaper:

Mystics Invited to Come Out of the Closet

Those who have experienced and have come to recognize life in all its diverse forms to be One Being, without a second, are commonly known as mystics. Because their numbers are small and their experience is contrary to our normal sense of the world as divided into separate things, over the centuries mystics have been reluctant to identify and explain themselves, and have often been the target of religious persecution.

While in the east mysticism has been more central to religions such as Hinduism, Buddhism, and Taoism and their scriptures, in the west Christian mystics have often been considered heretics, as have the Sufis and other mystics within Islam.

Aldous Huxley's 1947 book, "The Perennial Philosophy," brings together statements by mystics from most of the world's religious traditions that describe their direct experience of and identity with the Divine, increasing our understanding of mysticism considerably. A link to an online copy of this anthology is available on the website www.unitiveself.blogspot.com.

In spite of several well-known mystical sayings by Jesus in the New Testament, including "the Kingdom of God is within you," and "What you do to the least of these you do to me," as well as Old Testament sayings such as, "I Am What Am" and "Be still and Know that I am God," not until more recent times has there been openness in the west to the presence of a single Being within all life.

In our current age of relative openness as well as our increasing acceptance of the unitary nature of the physical universe as demonstrated by modern cosmology and quantum physics, the writings of Eckhart Tolle, a German-born mystic now living in Canada, have become #1 best sellers, even chosen as a book-of-the month by Oprah Winfrey.

Tolle's teachings in "The Power of Now" and "The New Earth," along with those of many other mystics, offer an experience of life that remedies the intense internal and external conflicts that alienate us from others and from our own identity. In a world of increasing divisions and need for reconciliation, the realization of a deeper unity within and beyond our apparent diversity is an important potential for everyone that is also of current interest to many.

Those who have had either an intuition or a direct experience of this reality, or are simply open to this possibility, may be interested in a public Study Group on the Unitive Self that has begun meeting on Thursday evenings at 7 pm. The group meets at Wynmrh House, 233 S. Park in Walla Walla across from the YMCA gymnasium, and is sponsored by the recently formed Noetic Council, www.noeticcouncil.blogspot.com.

The goal of this group, which is open to everyone, is to increase public understanding and recognition of the one Self, and to deepen its direct experience. As there are infinite facets to the Self, the group will meet weekly to consider selected topics, with each new topic announced publicly to encourage those with a particular interest to attend. Topics will be led by different members and chosen by the full group. In addition, there will be shelf space available for sharing books and other materials that may be useful to participants, as well as time available before and after meetings to look through or borrow those of interest. The meetings will also include a period of meditation, which is an almost universal practice of those seeking to become more aware of the Self.

When mystics are asked to explain how they experience or seek to experience reality, in most circumstances they have difficulty being understood. As one member of the Noetic Council active in a local church put it, "My Christianity is different from most. While the goal of others is to have a relationship with God, my goal is identity with God."

It is useful for all of us to have relationships with those who are capable of understanding and accepting us. If you are a mystic or are interested in mysticism but have been reluctant to talk about it, you are invited at this point to come out of the closet, and to share your experience and interest with others. It will be a benefit to all of us if you do.

Appendix B: Some Principles of Social Action

The following are several principles of social action gleaned over many years of organizing and activism, which might be useful to others.

1.   *When you see a need or an injustice, should you act or not act?* Always act. It's good for the soul. When you have the courage and take the trouble to act on what you feel is right, you send a message to yourself that the world is essentially a good place where right action is possible. To not act tells your soul its values are impractical and inconsistent with the way of the world, and it shrinks. Expand your soul.

2.   *Will action have any effect?* Action always has an effect. Have confidence that acting on what is perceived to be right has the capacity to make a difference in the world, either in the immediate present or in the distant future, in a small or large way. Right action not only heals you, it heals the world.

3.   *What action should you take?* Design your action in such a way that it will be successful on some level no matter what happens. Identify several possible goals or desired outcomes, one of which is clearly achievable and which alone will justify the action. Then build your action flexibly on that foundation, allowing larger goals to be achieved from it if circumstances prove favorable. Be practical, building around realistic but expandable goals, rather than investing all your resources on a remote possibility.

4.   *But I'm only one person!* Call several people with common interests together to legitimize and strengthen your actions. Give yourselves a name. Don't worry about numbers. Be open to as many as may want to join with you, but five or six people acting under an appealing name can do wonders.

5.   *I don't like a lot of meetings.* Be flexible. Try meeting only when there are things to be done. Hold "regular" meetings infrequently. Meetings are an art form, and should be well planned to build interest, energy, and community rather than being a drain.

6.   *I don't like conflict and divisiveness.* Approach your apparent adversaries as friends. Be honest and cordial with them. Let them know you care about what you are working for and about them. Explain your concerns and goals in terms they can embrace. Any outcome which is just will have to include their needs as well as others. Once they know you care about them, they will be more likely to try to find a way to accommodate your concerns. Help them find a way to a higher ground you can all share.

7.   *How do I keep from getting burnt out?* Keep it fun. Enjoy the moment. In the end, nothing has to happen. Your role is simply to act as effectively as you can on what you perceive to be right. The rest will take care of itself.

Daniel Clark, 1-15-99

Appendix C: Activism and Civil Disobedience

Civil disobedience has a long and noble history, although in most circumstances it should be used very sparingly, and always after thoughtful analysis. The following are some questions to be considered before undertaking it.

1.   *Can you be a more powerful and effective advocate of your position if you are in full possession of your civil rights and liberties?* When you commit civil disobedience, you put your freedom and your assets at the mercy of the authorities. This is often only for a short period, but that's not always predictable. During that period, you are removed from the arena of activism "on the street". Where can you do the most good?

2.   *If arrested, do you want to stand trial, or simply plead guilty to the charged offense?* An intention to stand trial calls for the careful design of your action to come within some theory of right, if possible. It also requires more resources, such as possible bail bonds, and the ability and willingness to return to the venue for trial as well as possible pretrial hearings and conferences with legal counsel.

3.   *Are you prepared to spend some time in jail?* Even if you're willing to post bail or to plead guilty to some offense, you may well spend a day or more in jail waiting for the possibility to do so. You need to know what this means, and to arrange some kind of support network both inside and outside the jail, if possible.

4.   *Are you willing to pay a fine and serve a probationary period?* It is not uncommon for protesters to be fined and to be given a lengthy probationary period. It can be hard to voluntarily pay a fine for doing something you consider right. Probationary periods can also include requirements that civil disobedients are unwilling to accept, such as a prohibition against returning to the place of arrest while on probation. Those who are unwilling to accept these conditions may wind up serving more time in jail.

5.   *Do you already have a criminal record or will you be harmed by creating one?* While most employers and institutions may be tolerant of a conviction for an act of civil disobedience, not all are, and a criminal record may be harmful to you unless it can be expunged. Those with a prior criminal record may not be able to negotiate the same plea bargain as first offenders, and their penalties may be higher.

6.   *Do you have an effective public relations network to make the most of your conscientious arrest?* The suffering and expense you will be going through in the criminal process and your removal from outside activity will not be worth it if no one knows about it, or if the general public is put off by their understanding of your action. Effective civil disobedience usually requires an active and effective publicity campaign.

7.   *Civil disobedience is definitely not for everyone.* Before crossing the line, be sure civil disobedience is the right thing for you and your cause at this particular time and place.

Daniel Clark   1-15-99

239

Appendix D: Report of a Workshop on Civilian-Based Defense

<u>The Need for a Program of Civilian Resistance</u>. It is clear that weapons technology is changing so quickly that we cannot continue to safely rely on weapons superiority for the defense of our way of life. If our values and autonomy are to survive, we need to develop a non-military civilian defense program which would allow us to resist any and all who would impose change upon us which would be destructive of our values and freedoms.

<u>Goals of Civilian Defense</u>. The essential goal of a civilian defense program would be to preserve local autonomy over all aspects of our domestic life. While we realize that military activities with clear international significance are legitimately a matter of international concern, there is no justification for international interference in such matters as education, the administration of justice, speech, religion, our economic structure, or other matters of traditionally local concern. Changes in these areas should therefore be a matter of local prerogative and initiative, and any effort to exercise authority over these areas by a foreign power should be resisted as an illegitimate denial of fundamental rights.

<u>Organization and Leadership</u>. In order for the entire population to participate in defense activities, each voting precinct would be organized into residential blocks of 10-15 households, each of which would have an elected block leader. Block leaders would elect precinct leaders, who would form the residential defense committee.

Similarly, workplaces would be organized into units of up to 20 workers, who would select unit leaders. Each group of workplaces would form a subcommittee of a general workplace defense committee. Subcommittees would include schools, medical facilities, justice system, manufacturing, farming, and others, all of which would be represented on the workplace defense committee.

Finally, a voluntary organizations committee would be composed of representatives of churches, lodges, recreational, and other cultural groups whose interests might be threatened. Representatives of the Residential, Workplace, and Voluntary Organizations Defense Committees would make up the Central Defense committee, which would coordinate all defense activities. Each unit leader and committee would designate two persons to assume their duties should they become unavailable and normal means of re-appointment be disrupted. Provision would be made for the secretion of leaders in the mountains or other undisclosed places to maintain contact and continuity should their safety be threatened.

Duplication equipment of various types—printing presses, mimeographs, photocopy machines— would be deposited in secure places for use in the event normal printing services were unavailable. Radio equipment would also be maintained, and appropriate codes developed for use when necessary.

<u>Tactics</u>. Once a defense network is established encompassing residential neighborhoods, workplaces, and voluntary organizations, permitting efficient communication of any threats to our values and autonomy, and instructions for resisting such threats, a scaled sequence of resistance can be implemented according to decisions by resistance leaders as to the importance and timing of specific resistance to a given threat. The resistance sequence would include:

a. Initial notice of protest of the threatening activity (through a delegation, petitions, picketing, rallies, posters, and other public criticism) and demands for cessation.
b. Direct action against the threatening activity (acts which directly disrupt or prevent the continuation of the threatened activity such as sit-ins, equipment destruction or dismantling, refusal to work by necessary personnel, refusal to provide necessary supplies to the activity).
c. Selective secondary resistance (selected acts supportive of the resistance but not directly related to it such as secondary boycotts, or non-cooperation in limited sectors.
d. Total non-cooperation and disruption of all enemy activities until the threat ceases—the general strike.

<u>Timing and Implementation</u>: Essential to the success of any defense system is advance planning and training. We should begin now to implement the recommended defense committee networks in our residential neighborhoods, workplaces, and voluntary organizations, and to hold meetings in these units to orient all citizens to the dynamics of civilian defense and of the types of resistance each person would be capable of, if our society were threatened. A well-organized and prepared populace would have a sense of confidence in its ability to defend its own values and would constitute a deterrent to any power which might assume acquiescence among our populace if we were unable or unwilling to resist militarily. The government should take responsibility for such a civilian defense program, and should the government fail to do so, citizens should prepare themselves for the non-military defense of their values.

The workshop was presented as part of the Interim Session at Whitman College in Walla Walla, Washington the week of January 10-17, 1981 by the Committee on Alternatives to War.

APPENDIX E: CHRONOLOGY, PORT OF WALLA WALLA-ILLAHEE PROJECT

09-01-98*   Moore Farm put up for sale
> The Moore Farm, 521 acres adjoining the Walla Walla Regional Airport on the northeast, is put up for sale, including one of the few deep water wells in the Walla Walla-College Place area The listing documents show the farm's 10-year history of dry-land cropping.

10-01-98*   Olson buys Moore Farm for $765,000
> Keith Olson, an engineer, hydrologist, and manager of a local engineering office, buys the Moore Farm "for investment purposes," pays $765,000, and leases it to a local farmer. Olson installs new pump and begins to increase water use over prior levels.

09-01-03*   Port sets 2009 as target for purchase of 60 acres of Moore Farm
> In its aviation capital projects report for 2003, the Port of Walla prioritizes projects at the Walla Walla Regional Airport for the following six years. Acquisition of 60.6 acres in the Runway 20 approach area, including about 4 acres on the Moore/Olson farm, is its last priority, targeted for 2009.

10-01-03*   Pennbrook site proposal submitted to city
> Pennbrook Homes, a Bend, Oregon developer, proposes to develop a large site adjoining the Walla Walla airport as a resort and housing project; the landowner and developer contact city officials regarding permits and provision of city water and sewer to the site, and the city gives notice of the proposal to other agencies.

12-26-03   Port expresses concern about Pennbrook
> Port of Walla Walla executive Jim Kuntz writes to the city expressing concerns about potential conflicts between residential development at the Pennbrook site and present and future industrial and aeronautic activities at the airport.

03-01-04*   Port and Pennbrook discuss water supply, Port advises against annexation
> Pennbrook and the Port executive discuss the Port supplying water for Pennbrook by pumping from the Port's existing well, and possibly through purchase of an additional water right from the distant Ash Hollow area. Kuntz advises Pennbrook against annexing the site to the city.

03-01-04*   Pennbrook approaches county, advises of Port discussions
> Pennbrook approaches county development director regarding county approvals, and advises of water supply discussions with Port.

03-31-04   Port, Pennbrook consult Anderson-Perry for evaluation of water supply, Olson responds
> On 3-24-04, Port and Pennbrook officials contact Olson, manager of Anderson-Perry, engineers, for an evaluation of the Port's capacity to supply water for the Pennbrook development. On 3-31-04, Olson sends a preliminary response to the Port, and on 4-29-04 provides a scope of work.

05-01-04*   Olson proposes sale of farm and well to Port
> Olson proposes to Port officials a possible sale of his farm property and well to the Port for $2,587,100, as a source of water for the Pennbrook development, and instructs his farm tenant to pump water beyond the normal irrigation season.

05-26-04   Port signs agreement with Pennbrook to pay for consultant services
> On 5-26-04, Port executive Jim Kuntz signed an agreement with Pennbrook providing for hiring of legal and engineering consultants at Pennbrook's expense to handle design, permitting, water

rights, and other legal and engineering requirements for the Port's provision of water and sewer utilities to Pennbrook. On 6-9-04, the Port commissioners approve the agreement, which is renewed on 5-25-05.

06-14-04 Port formally contracts with Anderson-Perry for utilities study, notifies local governments
On 6-14-04, Port executive signed a contract with Anderson-Perry to perform the Pennbrook feasibility study. He also notifies the city and county of the study.

06-28-04* City expresses concerns, requests that study include city water supply for project
On 6-28-04, city manager Duane Cole writes to the Port, requesting that the Pennbrook utility study also include options for water supply by the city, and expresses concerns that groundwater withdrawal by the Port for Pennbrook would undermine the city's nearby aquifer recharge program, and that the Port and Pennbrook would be benefiting from that program as well as from the city's emergency intertie without contributing to their costs. The study is not expanded.

07-01-04* Anderson-Perry draft says Olson well is needed to supply Pennbrook
Anderson-Perry issues a draft of its Water and Sewer Utilities Assessment, dated July, 2004. The draft, under discussion for several months, concludes that a new water source and an additional reservoir will be needed for the Port to supply water to Pennbrook, and focuses on the Olson property and well as the primary means to accomplish this. Unnamed secondary water sources are also studied.

07-01-04* Port tells FAA that Olson property needed for runway protection & industrial purposes
On 6-22-06, Port executive meets with Federal Aviation Administration official and discusses the need to purchase the Olson property to protect Runway 02, already protected by an aviation easement obtained in 1959. On 6-30-04, Kuntz writes to the Walla Walla city manager regarding the Olson farm, saying, "If we purchase the property a substantial water right will come with it. This is an active high production well. It will likely supply all the water needs of Pennbrook and may help the airport industrial park accommodate future growth." On 7-23-06, Kuntz writes to the FAA that the 40 acre zoning for the property presents the risk of incompatible residential development, that hand-held missiles could be fired from the property, and that its well is needed for Port industrial purposes. The Port's interest in providing water for residential development is not disclosed to the FAA, nor does the Port propose the alternative of securing any needed runway protection through additional easements.

08-01-04* Port seeks to eliminate planning policies against housing in vicinity of airport
To facilitate the Pennbrook development, the Port drafts, submits, and begins lobbying for proposed changes to Walla Walla County's comprehensive plan policies to eliminate prohibitions against housing encroachment in the vicinity of the airport, and to permit the Port to be the water supplier for nearby residential development.

08-01-04* FAA tells Port most of Olson property ineligible for funding, asks about water rights
The FAA evaluates the Port's request for funding to acquire the Olson farm, and notes the Port's national security justification is "weak," as is its argument that 40 acre zoning is incompatible with the airport. On 8-3-04, in a conference call between FAA and Port officials, the FAA informs the Port that, at most, 180 acres (35%) of the Olson property is eligible for funding. In an 8-18-04 letter response, the Port requests that FAA cover 87% of the property, with the Port paying for the balance "with its own resources." On 8-24-04, FAA requests additional justification for the Port's request, including details on the projected revenue benefit to the Port from the water right.

10-01-04* Port obtains $1,764,000 appraisal on Olson farm, Olson wants $2,313,800, mostly for water

The Port orders an appraisal of the Olson property. The appraisal is completed on 10-21-04, and shows a market value of $1,764,000. Olson's asking price is now $2,313,800, attributing 62% to the water right and well, as shown in an Illahee cost analysis prepared by the Port and in negotiation documents prepared by the Port and Olson, which recognize that a significant portion of the water right has been relinquished through non-use.

01-01-05* Pennbrook and Port pressure city to allow use of Olson well for Pennbrook

In early January, 2005, Pennbrook and Anderson-Perry officials meet with City of Walla Walla staff; city water manager Robert Gordon expresses concern about use of the Olson well for Pennbrook because of potential conflicts with the city's aquifer recharge program for its public water supply system. On 1-7-05, Gordon tells Anderson-Perry he wants future Olson well usage to be no more than current usage and asks for data on current usage of the well. Anderson-Perry diverts the question, saying that would be considered at the time of conversion from farm use, and that the Port executive and its lawyer would be working on that. The Port executive then advises Pennbrook to go around Gordon to the city manager to obtain agreement on Olson well and other requirements for the Port to supply water to Pennbrook, and also recommends that the Port's lawyer draft a letter from Pennbrook to the city for Pennbrook to approve and sign. Pennbrook notes it is clear the city wants to supply water for the project, and asks the Port executive to talk to the city manager, who Pennbrook says "needs to call off his dogs."

02-01-05* Port changes Olson property to #1 priority, FAA tells Port some of Olson property has to be sold

In his letter of 2-1-05, Port executive tells the FAA that acquisition of the Olson property for protection of runway 20 is now the Port's #1 capital priority for 2005, and that "the Port's willingness to contribute not less than $306,054 to acquire this property is an indication of our interest in protecting the airport's main runway from incompatible land uses." In responding to the FAA question about revenue benefits to the Port from the water right, Kuntz fails to disclose the Port's intention to provide water for the Pennbrook residential development, and acknowledges the probable relinquishment of 20-25% of the right from non-use. In a response dated 2-10-05, the FAA gives the Port permission to proceed with a review appraisal with the understanding that a portion of the Olson property would have to be resold by the Port to satisfy FAA guidelines.

3-25-05 Pennbrook formally offers to pay part of Olson price for Port operation of water system

On 3-25-05, Pennbrook officials write to the Port formally offering to contribute $422,175 toward the Port's share of the expected Olson acquisition costs. Pennbrook prefers that the Port manage the water system for the Illahee development, but is willing to go along with the Port's desire that the system be privately operated by Illahee with wholesale water from the Port, which the Port is to provide at 30% of city rates.

04-01-05* FAA learns about Pennbrook, questions Port regarding inconsistent statements

The FAA is alerted by a citizen to the connection between the Olson property and Pennbrook, which the FAA refers to as "a non-compatible use" in a 4-22-05 email to the Port executive, adding "it was our earlier understanding from you that the water rights would be used to develop the on-airport industrial park." In a 4-22-05 written response, Kuntz denies that Pennbrook is a non-compatible land use (despite its violation of the airport's existing master plan), and asks FAA help with the airport's financial problems.

05-10-05 Port tells FAA it wants to keep all of Olson property, stresses value of water

In a letter to the FAA dated 5-10-05, the Port executive seeks to keep all of the Olson property. Kuntz stresses the value of the water right, and the Port's intention to change it to municipal use, saying, "The municipal water right will be used for airport industrial park purposes. As mentioned in my April 22 email, the airport as a utility provider may also supply water to developments near the airport as a way to generate additional revenue for the airport."

05-11-05 Port confirms water agreement with Pennbrook including contribution to Olson purchase

On 5-11-05, the Port writes to Pennbrook setting out the terms of their "non-binding agreement" for Pennbrook's payment of $422,175 towards the purchase of the Olson property, with Pennbrook to receive a portion of the property or water if the Illahee project can't proceed, and to be required to operate its own private water supply system with wholesale water from the Port.

05-11-05 FAA official coaches Port on appraisal tactics, relents on excess land and water concerns

In an email on 5-11-05 responding to the Port's pleas for help with the financial condition of the airport, Jeff Winter, the FAA manager for Walla Walla, coaches Port executive on how to obtain a higher appraisal in order to justify FAA funding of the seller's price. Winter withdraws his requirement that the ineligible portion of the land be sold off, though he had previously stated "we are not allowed to use AIP funds to acquire land to just create a source of revenue for the airport." He also withdraws his concern regarding the Port providing water to new residential development nearby.

06-20-05 Citizens object to planning changes proposed by Pennbrook and Port

On 6-20-05, the city and county planning commissions hold a joint hearing on planning policy changes proposed by the Port and Pennbrook specifically to facilitate the Illahee project. Various citizens object to the proposed actions and to the Pennbrook project itself. On July 6, the Walla Walla city council also debates the project, and the local newspaper editorializes about it. Port officials are present at both meetings.

06-24-05* Port agrees to buy Olson property at $1,950,000 subject to FAA & Pennbrook funding

On 6-25-05, the Port notifies the FAA of its agreement to purchase the Olson property for $1,950,000, contingent on an FAA grant. On 6-28-05, the FAA's Winter responds that the FAA will cover the cost of 87% of the property as the Port is requesting. On 7-11-05, a purchase and sale agreement is executed, contingent not only on FAA funding, but on a $422,175 payment from Pennbrook, and termination of the existing farm lease.

07-12-05 Port files grant application for Olson property concealing Pennbrook plans and opposition

On 7-12-05, the Port executive files a grant application with the FAA for funds to purchase the Olson property. The application contains intentional omissions and misrepresentations.

07-14-05 FAA awards Port $1,457,946 grant for Olson acquisition

On 7-14-05, the FAA awards a grant to the Port for the Olson acquisition in the amount of $1,457,946 "in consideration of the Sponsor's adoption and ratification of the representations and assurances contained in (the) Project Application." The grant is accepted and the grant agreement executed by the Port executive on 7-27-05. Grant condition No. 7 states that, "The Sponsor shall take all steps, including litigation if necessary, to recover Federal funds spent fraudulently, wastefully, or in violation of Federal antitrust statutes, or misused in any other manner in any project upon which Federal funds have been expended." Assurance No. 31(b) provides, "For land purchased under a grant for airport development purposes...(the Sponsor) will, when the land is no longer needed for airport purposes, dispose of such land at fair market value or make available to the Secretary an amount equal to the United States' proportionate share of the fair market value of the land." No special condition requiring divestment of the unneeded portion of the property is included, despite prior reference to the requirement.

09-09-05 Port proposes FAA grant for purchase of Frazier Farm

On 9-9-05, the Port tells the FAA that the owners of the Frazier farm and deep well next to Olson have approached the Port about buying their property. On 9-12-05, the FAA suggests that farm land excess to runway protection be sold to finance the purchase of qualifying runway protection land.

09-13-05 Port and Pennbrook execute formal agreement for Olson payment

On 9-13-05, the Port and Pennbrook sign a formal agreement for payment by Pennbrook of $422,175 toward the Olson price, satisfying an express contingency in the purchase and sale agreement for the Olson closing.

09-20-05 Port and FAA discuss Olson closing and citizen protests regarding Olson and Pennbrook

On 9-20-05, Port executive Jim Kuntz writes to Jeff Winter of FAA about the planned closing of the Olson purchase on 9-30-05, as well as the request by Walla Walla resident Bud Pringle for all Port files related to Olson and Pennbrook. Winter responds on 9-21-05 that Pringle had contacted him about Pennbrook in March, and that resident Carl Schmitt recently requested FAA documents related to the Olson grant. Special condition No. 9 in the grant agreement gives the FAA power to unilaterally amend the grant provision. Despite these citizen concerns and information about the project's relation to Pennbrook, Winter takes no steps to eliminate the inclusion of excess land prior to the closing of the purchase.

10-01-05* Port closes on Olson, plans to increase water consumption from Olson well

The Olson closing is set for 9-30-05, and the Port begins implementing plans to increase water consumption from the Olson well by planting alfalfa and installing a new circle irrigation system in order to maximize its water rights claim for the Pennbrook project.

11-01-05* Anderson-Perry report details plans to use Olson well for Pennbrook, Port seeks approvals

Consistent with prior drafts, in November 2005 Anderson-Perry issues its final assessment on Port utility service to Pennbrook. The assessment states: "The Port and Pennbrook will use this assessment to proceed with necessary system upgrades and contractual arrangements…The Port of WW desires to maintain available capacity for future industrial uses. However, excess capacity will be made available to Pennbrook on an interim basis. To meet the Port of WW's goal of maintaining existing water capacity for future Port uses, water system improvements must ultimately satisfy 100% of Pennbrook's need…The Port's existing reservoir cannot provide sufficient pressure to the Pennbrook property…The Port of WW has purchased the Moore (Olson) well..The new well will be needed for redundancy before full build-out of the Pennbrook facilities…. Phase 1 improvements are needed for potable water service to Pennbrook…Phase 2 improvements are necessary when Pennbrook will need more than 400 gpm…Phase 2 improvements will generally include rehabilitation at the Moore (Olson) well, a water transmission from the Moore Well to the new ground reservoir, and associated facilities. …Pennbrook will operate a private water distribution system on the Pennbrook site." Consistent with the report, the Port seeks city and county approval to proceed.

01-01-06* County approves changes for Pennbrook, critics appeal, Port intervenes

On 10-24-05, the county commissioners approve the various changes in local planning and zoning documents requested by Pennbrook and the Port to facilitate the development; the next day critics announce a likely appeal, which they file on 12-23-05. An additional action is filed by the appellants on 12-28-05; on 1-12-06 the Port announces its intention to intervene in the appeal.

02-01-06* Newspaper focuses on Pennbrook and Port water supply controversy
On 1-8-06, 1-15-06, 1-29-06, 1-30-06, and 2-5-06 opinions critical of the Pennbrook/Port project are published in the Walla Walla Union-Bulletin, and on 2-10-06, a lead article focuses on the Port's negotiations with Pennbrook regarding details of its agreement to supply water for the development, followed by a further letter on 2-12-06. From 2-19-06 through 2-24-06, the paper publishes a total of 23 articles on the controversy surrounding the Port's water plans for Pennbrook, including expressions of concern by farm neighbors, environmentalists, water experts, officials, and other citizens.

03-14-06   Petitions opposing Pennbrook given to County and Port
On 3-14-06, petitions opposing Pennbrook signed by over 500 citizens are presented to county commissioners and the Port executive during a meeting with Pennbrook officials. By 4-23-05, petitions totaling over 800 signatures have been delivered to the Port, the county, and the city.

03-20-06 Port obtains option to purchase Frazier farm for $1,151,480
On 3-20-06, the Port signs an option agreement with Lester Frazier to purchase his 261.7 acre farm and deep aquifer well adjoining the Olson property for $1,151,480.

03-21-06 Port officials list Frazier and Olson wells as water resources for Pennbrook
On 3-21-06, Port executive Jim Kuntz and his assistant present a PowerPoint presentation and handout to a class demonstrating the relationship of the Frazier and Olson wells to the Pennbrook project. This relationship is confirmed in a slide show and handout by the Port for a property tour on 6-9-06, listing the Olson acquisition and the Olson and Frazier wells under the heading "Illahee Project," and also in a letter signed by Kuntz on 4-10-06.

05-01-06 Port files grant application for Frazier property, concealing development plans & objections
On 5-1-06, the Port executive files a grant application with the FAA seeking funds to purchase the Frazier farm. The application contains a variety of omissions and misrepresentations.

05-03-06   FAA tells Port that Frazier property is already protected by airport easement, and that most of it is unneeded for runway protection
On 5-3-06, the FAA requests justification by the Port for the use of federal funds for purchase of the entire Frazier farm, stating that the land is already protected by an aviation easement, and that 53% of it is beyond the allowed area for runway protection.

05-03-06   FAA receives inquiry on Frazier grant, rejects objections from farm neighbor
On 5-3-06, FAA official Jeff Winter receives a request for information on the Frazier grant from a neighboring farm family, followed by detailed protests on the absence of hearings and environmental review, farmer displacements, water supply motives v. runway protection, price inflation, and the planting of alfalfa and excessive pumping by the Port to the detriment of neighboring wells. In his 5-11-06 response, Winter insists that the purpose of both Olson and Frazier purchases is runway protection, and denies any environmental impact despite admissions by Port executive Kuntz that the Port planted alfalfa for maximum water consumption, and may use the Olson well for Pennbrook.

05-08-06 FAA says Frazier grant to be conditional on selling unneeded portions, Port protests

On 5-8-06, the FAA tells the Port the Frazier grant will likely be conditioned on a requirement that both the Frazier and Olson land which is excess to runway protection criteria will need to be sold by the Port, and the proceeds used to fund another eligible project. Port executive sends angry response. On 5-9-06, the FAA's Winter discusses the portions of the Olson and Frazier land that are unneeded for airport purposes, and cites FAA requirements for sale of unneeded property. Kuntz's response on 5-15-06 further resists resale.

05-18-06 Citizen group requests outside review of FAA grant actions, receives no response

On 5-18-06, the Walla Walla 2020 citizens group contacts the FAA about the Port's relationship to the Pennbrook development and requests an outside review of the acquisition and retention proposals by the Port for the Olson and Frazier properties before any further FAA action, as well as copies of all FAA records regarding these properties. On 5-31-06, Regional FAA Administrator Douglas Murphy responds to the request for public records, and promises a separate response to the outside review request. No FAA response on the review request is ever received.

06-14-06 Citizens group cautions Port on water rights abuse, relinquishment issues

On 6-14-06, members of the Walla Walla 2020 citizens group discuss with Port executive evidence that the Olson and Frazier water rights have been partially relinquished, and that the Port was planning to unlawfully pump water for alfalfa in excess of the remaining water rights in order to increase its water supply capacity for Pennbrook. Kuntz confirms his intention to pump at the maximum rate, but denies a necessary relationship between these wells and Pennbrook. This denial is repeated in a letter from the Port's attorney to Walla Walla 2020 on 6-26-06.

07-14-06 FAA awards grant for Frazier purchase without requiring resale of excess lands

On 7-14-06, the FAA awards the Port a grant of $1,118,095 for the purchase of the entire 262 acre Frazier property, with no resale requirements for the portion of the property that it has determined is unneeded for runway protection. The grant is accepted by the Port on 6-30-06.

08-03-06* Citizens group notifies FAA of apparent concealment

On 8-3-06, the Walla Walla 2020 citizens group notifies the FAA it has evidence of concealment with regard to the grants, which it wants to present to FAA prior to closing and further payment of federal funds. The group also seeks information on environmental compliance, and makes further public record requests to the Port, FAA, and other agencies.

The above chronology was filed with the Federal Aviation Administration on August 21, 2006 as part of a complaint by Walla Walla 2020 alleging intentional misrepresentation by the Port of Walla Walla with respect to the Port's federal grant applications relating to Pennbrook's Illahee Project. On October 26, 2006 the FAA issued 71 pages of findings concluding that the Port had intentionally misrepresented or concealed the objective, benefits, and parties involved in its application for federal funds, and that FAA officials had failed to comply with FAA rules in making these grants.

*The date indicated in any above entry marked with an asterisk is approximate.

August 1, 2016 Update

Author

Daniel Clark has also written "Notes to the Self," 2014, "You are the Self," 2014, "Come Dancing: A Collection of Contras, Circles, Squares, & More," 2014, and "Don't Bend Walla Walla," 2014, has co-authored "Words: Dan & Barbara's Deathless Prose, and a Few Poems," 2014, and has co-edited "A Prospect Point Reunion Book," 2014 and edited "A Garrison School Reunion Book," 2015. He can be contacted by writing to PO Box 1222, Walla Walla, Washington, USA, 99362, or to clarkdn@charter.net.

12917

Made in the USA
San Bernardino, CA
14 October 2017